The International Story

An Anthology with Guidelines
for Reading and Writing about Fiction

The International Story

An Anthology with Guidelines for Reading and Writing about Fiction

RUTH SPACK
Tufts University

ST. MARTIN'S PRESS
New York

To my father, who treasured books

Editor: Naomi Silverman
Manager, publishing services: Emily Berleth
Project management: Denise Quirk
Art Director: Sheree Goodman
Text design: Leon Bolognese & Assoc., Inc.
Cover design: Herb Mills
Cover art: Wen-ti Tsen, Mural for the Multicultural Center,
   Quinsigamond Community College, Worcester, MA, 1991

Library of Congress Catalog Card Number: 92-62786
Copyright © 1994 by St. Martin's Press, Inc.
Manufactured in the United States of America.
87654
fedcba

For information, write:
St. Martin's Press, Inc.
175 Fifth Avenue
New York, NY 10010

ISBN: 0-312-09008-0

ACKNOWLEDGMENTS

Acknowledgments and copyrights are continued at the back of the book on pages 368–69, which constitute an extension of the copyright page.

It is a violation of the law to reproduce these selections by any means whatsoever without the written permission of the copyright holder.

Achebe, Chinua. "Dead Men's Path," from *Girls at War and Other Stories* by Chinua Achebe. Copyright © 1972, 1973 by Chinua Achebe. Used by permission of Doubleday, a division of Bantam Doubleday Dell Publishing Group, Inc., and by Harold Ober Associates Incorporated.

Aesop. "The Ant and the Grasshopper." Reprinted with permission of Macmillan Publishing Company from "The Ant and the Grasshopper" from *The Fables of Aesop* by Joseph Jacobs (editor and translator). Copyright © 1950 by Macmillan Publishing Company.

Anderson, Sherwood. "The Egg." Reprinted by permission of Harold Ober Associates Incorporated. Copyright 1921 by B. W. Huebsch, Inc. Copyright renewed 1948 by Eleanor Copenhaven Anderson.

"blind." Copyright © 1985 by Houghton Mifflin. Reprinted by permission from the *American Heritage Dictionary*, Second College Edition.

Böll, Heinrich. "Like a Bad Dream." Reprinted by permission of Joan Daves Agency. Copyright 1966 from *18 Stories*. English translation copyright © by Leila Vennewitz.

PREFACE

The *International Story: An Anthology with Guidelines for Reading and Writing about Fiction* features a generous selection of thought-provoking classic and contemporary short stories from many different countries. Unique to this text is the integration of literary works with detailed guidelines for reading and writing and for crafting an interpretive essay. With its exciting international scope, the text has considerable appeal to a diverse group of readers.

The International Story addresses the academic needs of students who can benefit linguistically, culturally, and intellectually from exposure to literature. Students can begin with personal responses to the readings, including their lack of understanding, and move toward reflection and analysis, using interpretive tools explained and demonstrated in the text. As they gain confidence in their powers of interpretation, students are challenged to think critically about what they read and to develop analytical and argumentative skills that enable them to present and support their ideas.

Bringing different histories, cultural backgrounds, beliefs, biases, and experiences to the stories, students can compare their responses and thereby widen their perspectives. A deeper understanding of the stories can be achieved in the classroom as ideas are shared and meanings are unraveled.

THE LEVEL

The International Story is designed for literature-based composition courses and for advanced ESL programs that focus on the connections between reading and writing. Supporting linguistic and cultural material makes it possible for students of any background to appreciate the international literary works.

THE STRUCTURE

The International Story has four major sections: Part One: Reading Fiction; Part Two: Anthology of Short Stories; Part Three: Writing an Essay; and Glossary.

Part One: Reading Fiction

Part One provides strategies for reading short fiction. Throughout Part One, the reading/writing strategies of several students at work are demonstrated; and students are given the opportunity to engage in similar processes.

Chapter 1 focuses on students' initial reactions to what they read. The chapter presents strategies such as previewing, using contextual clues to guess at meaning, annotating, keeping a reading log, making double-entry notes, keeping a literary journal, and participating in class discussions. Students are encouraged to explore their own reactions and to recognize that there are many possible responses to a given text.

Chapter 2 focuses on analysis and interpretation. The chapter includes clear, accessible explanations of literary terms. Critical strategies help students (1) analyze the elements of a story (plot, setting, character, point of view, imagery, symbolism, tone, irony, speech, structure) and (2) interpret a story's meanings or significance. Activities invite students both to create and to analyze scenes and characters. Through these activities, they can see how language can be used both to compose and to comprehend a story.

Part Two: Anthology of Short Stories

Part Two consists of two chapters: Chapter 3, The Stories, and Chapter 4, Discussion Activities. Because the stories and discussion activities are in separate chapters, students are able to come to the end of a story and examine their thoughts about it without having to attend to someone else's agenda.

Chapter 3 comprises twenty-two complete stories from seventeen countries. The stories offer a wide range of choices in terms of length, style, period, gender, culture, point of view, and theme, yet lend themselves well to comparison. Footnotes are kept to a minimum so that students can read fluently and interact freely with the stories.

The stories are presented chronologically, according to the dates they were written or originally published. Spanning over one hundred years (1884–1989), they provide a sense of social history as they move from the nineteenth through the twentieth century. (A separate table of contents presents an alternative arrangement by geographic area).

Several of the stories were published in the United States and reflect the diversity of American culture. The stories published in other countries reflect traditions and concerns of and within many cultures, although, of course, no one story can be representative of a whole culture. Taken together, the stories allow for a rich multicultural and cross-cultural experience in the classroom. Each of the stories has universal as well as cultural meanings. Story after story raises issues about choices and challenges that all readers grapple with and attempt to resolve.

Chapter 4 provides discussion activities designed to stimulate students' reactions to the stories without being overly directive. Suggestions lead readers to make their own discoveries and to ask their own questions. The activities include reflective, analytical, and creative writing. All of the activities foster an awareness of what is involved in the shaping of a text.

Part Three: Writing an Essay

Part Three prepares students to fulfill an essay assignment to analyze and interpret a work of fiction. The four chapters include succinct guidelines to show students what they can do to achieve their writing objectives.

Each chapter tries to make students aware of what an academic audience might expect and how to go about fulfilling those expectations. Examples of student writers at work demonstrate some composing processes. At the same time, the text emphasizes flexibility: students are reminded again and again that different strategies work for different writers.

Chapter 5 provides guidelines for crafting an interpretive essay. To fulfill the essay assignment, students are guided to practice strategies such as defining the audience, taking notes, brainstorming, focusing, organizing, drafting, evaluating, revising, and completing an essay.

Chapter 6 provides guidelines for selecting evidence for critical analysis of a story. Students learn ways to analyze key words and phrases, ask questions about elements of fiction and abstract ideas in a story, and develop the vocabulary they need in their own writing. The chapter also includes suggestions for topics that students can focus on in their essays.

Chapter 7 provides guidelines for selecting, incorporating, and punctuating quotations and for citing and documenting sources.

Chapter 8 provides guidelines for proofreading and editing an essay, observing some unique conventions of writing about literature, and producing a final manuscript.

Glossary

The alphabetically arranged **Glossary** defines words and idioms taken from the stories. Multiple definitions allow for different interpretations of the passage in which the word occurs.

ACKNOWLEDGMENTS

For a number of years, students in the courses I teach at Tufts University worked with a variety of drafts of *The International Story*, which they knew only as a work in progress. I learned much from their responses, which shaped my writing as well my perspectives on literature across cultures.

Several reviewers read and responded to my work with great care and insight. I am pleased to have the opportunity to acknowledge the contributions of Diana Berkowitz, Nassau Community College; David Eskey, University of Southern California; Virginia Heringer, Pasadena City College; Linda Wallace Jones, St. Louis University; John Mathenia, University of Tennessee, Martin; Melinda Reichelt, Purdue University; and Jonathan Seely, University of Arizona.

Over the years, I have exchanged ideas with many colleagues about teaching and learning, reading and writing, literature and composition. In particular, I would like to thank Lucy Ferris, Catherine Sadow, Roberta Steinberg, and Vivian Zamel for their encouragement and advice as I was preparing this book.

The staff at St. Martin's Press has always given me the support and respect that any author needs. To Naomi Silverman, editor; Denise Quirk, project manager; Emily Berleth, manager of publishing services; Sandy Cohen, permissions assistant; editorial assistants Sarah Crowley and Sarah Picchi: Thank you.

BRIEF CONTENTS

CONTENTS

She was one of those pretty and charming girls who are sometimes, as if by a mistake of destiny, born in a family of clerks.

Nikolai Ilitch Belayeff was a young gentleman of St. Petersburg, aged thirty-two, rosy, well fed, and a patron of the race-tracks.

Alberta having looked not very long into life, had not looked very far.

There is no set rule for the turning of the worm; most worms, however, turn unexpectedly.

North Richmond Street, being blind, was a quiet street except at the hour when the Christian Brothers' School set the boys free.

Chapter Four Discussion Activities   183

Chapter Eight The Editing Process   339

Glossary   345

GEOGRAPHICAL ARRANGEMENT OF THE STORIES

The International Story

An Anthology with Guidelines
for Reading and Writing about Fiction

Introduction: Literature and the Short Story

*L*iterature can be divided into four major categories, known as genres: *poetry* (poems), *drama* (plays), *fiction* (novels and short stories), and *nonfiction* (almost all writing that does not fit into the previous categories, for example, essays and autobiographies). Writers of nonfiction work primarily with the facts as they exist in the real world. Writers of poetry, drama, and fiction re-create events or make up "facts" and create an imaginary world. With the exception of two poems, all of the readings in this book are works of fiction: short stories.

The *short story* is called "short" primarily because it has relatively few pages. But *short* doesn't necessarily mean easy to read. In a short story, what happens usually happens over a brief period of time—often no longer than a day or even an hour. Therefore, the short-story writer must compress the action and description and make the story come alive by implication. One detail must suggest many others. The *short* of *short story*, then, involves much more than just the number of words. Even if a short story is not long, the suggestive use of language can make the story a challenge to read and understand.

PART ONE

Reading Fiction

Chapter One: Developing Effective Reading Strategies: Understanding and Responding

Chapter Two: Developing Effective Reading Strategies: Analyzing and Interpreting

Part One consists of two chapters that are designed to help you find effective strategies for reading and understanding fiction.

Chapter 1 focuses on your initial reactions to what you read. Through a variety of activities, this chapter encourages you to explore your responses to short stories and to recognize that there are many possible responses to a given text.

Chapter 2 focuses on analysis and interpretation of what you read. Learning how a story is composed through various elements such as plot, setting, character, and point of view can help you understand the story's meanings or significance. Activities within this chapter ask you to create scenes and characters as well as to analyze scenes and characters within a short story. Through these activities, you can develop a deeper understanding of how language can be used both to create and to comprehend a story.

CHAPTER ONE

Developing Effective Reading Strategies: Understanding and Responding

Some of the stories in this book may be easy to read; others may be hard. Some will immediately provoke a reaction; others will take more thought and discussion. Some stories may require only one reading before you feel that you understand what is happening and grasp the story's meanings or significance. Others may at first appear easy but in fact involve complex concepts and require careful rereading.

The following guidelines are designed to help you develop effective approaches to reading even the most difficult stories. In time, you will develop your own strategies for productive reading.

BEFORE READING

You may be able to understand what you read better if you have some background knowledge before you begin reading. The following suggestions may be helpful.

1. Read the *title* of the story. The title may give you a clue to the story's focus.
2. Read the *biographical information* ("About the Author") that precedes the story. By reading some background on the author's life and literary history, you may gain some insight into the author's approach. Knowing the date, original language, and country of origin of a work of fiction can help you understand it better.
3. Read any *background information* ("The Context of the Story") that is provided. This information may help you become aware of an unfamiliar concept that is crucial to an understanding of the story.
4. Look at the length of the story. Knowledge of how long a story is can help you plan your reading time.

A FIRST READING

The first time you read, enter the world of the story. Try to feel what the characters feel and to know what they experience. During this first reading, you do not need to understand every word or detail.

GUIDELINES

Guidelines for a First Reading

1. Preview the story by reading the title, the biographical information about the author, and the discussion of the context of the story.
2. Read the story through once to try to grasp what is happening, without using a dictionary.

ACTIVITY: *Reading a short story*

Following the guidelines for a first reading, read "The Story of an Hour" by Kate Chopin (pp. 6–8).   ●

The Story of an Hour
Kate Chopin   United States, 1894

ABOUT THE AUTHOR

Kate Chopin (1851–1904) was born in the United States, in Missouri, the daughter of an Irish Catholic father and a French Creole mother. Her father died in 1855, and she was raised by her mother, grandmother, and great-grandmother. In 1870, she married Oscar Chopin and lived with him and their six children in Louisiana. Her husband died in 1882.

In the early 1890s, Chopin gained national recognition as an outstanding short-story writer. Her major work, the novel The Awakening, *appeared in 1899. Although this novel won the respect of literary critics, its sympathetic treatment of a woman's sensuality shocked readers and reviewers throughout the United States. Her next collection of short stories was rejected by her publisher. Deeply hurt by the negative response to her work, Chopin wrote very little more. Her work remained virtually ignored until the 1960s.*

THE CONTEXT OF THE STORY

In the nineteenth century in Louisiana, where most of Chopin's stories are set, women's rights were limited. Most married women were considered to be the property of their husbands.

Knowing that Mrs. Mallard was afflicted with a heart trouble, great care was taken to break to her as gently as possible the news of her husband's death.

It was her sister Josephine who told her, in broken sentences; veiled hints that revealed in half concealing. Her husband's friend Richards was there, too, near her. It was he who had been in the newspaper office when intelligence of the railroad disaster was received, with Brently Mallard's name leading the list of "killed." He had only taken the time to assure himself of its truth by a second telegram, and had hastened to forestall any less careful, less tender friend in bearing the sad message.

She did not hear the story as many women have heard the same, with a paralyzed inability to accept its significance. She wept at once, with sudden, wild abandonment, in her sister's arms. When the storm of grief had spent itself she went away to her room alone. She would have no one follow her.

There stood, facing the open window, a comfortable, roomy armchair. Into this she sank, pressed down by a physical exhaustion that haunted her body and seemed to reach into her soul.

She could see in the open square before her house the tops of trees that were all aquiver with the new spring life. The delicious breath of rain was in the air. In the street below a peddler was crying his wares. The notes of a distant song which some one was singing reached her faintly, and countless sparrows were twittering in the eaves.

There were patches of blue sky showing here and there through the clouds that had met and piled one above the other in the west facing her window.

She sat with her head thrown back upon the cushion of the chair, quite motionless, except when a sob came up into her throat and shook her, as a child who had cried itself to sleep continues to sob in its dreams.

She was young, with a fair, calm face, whose lines bespoke repression and even a certain strength. But now there was a dull stare in her eyes, whose gaze was fixed away off yonder on one of those patches of blue sky. It was not a glance of reflection, but rather indicated a suspension of intelligent thought.

There was something coming to her and she was waiting for it, fearfully. What was it? She did not know; it was too subtle and elusive to name. But she felt it, creeping out of the sky, reaching toward her through the sounds, the scents, the color that filled the air.

Now her bosom rose and fell tumultuously. She was beginning to recognize this thing that was approaching to possess her, and she was striving to beat it back with her will—as powerless as her two white slender hands would have been.

When she abandoned herself a little whispered word escaped her slightly parted lips. She said it over and over under her breath: "free, free, free!" The vacant stare and the look of terror that had followed it went from her eyes. They stayed keen and bright. Her pulses beat fast, and the coursing blood warmed and relaxed every inch of her body.

She did not stop to ask if it were or were not a monstrous joy that held her. A clear and exalted perception enabled her to dismiss the suggestion as trivial.

She knew that she would weep again when she saw the kind, tender hands folded in death; the face that had never looked save with love upon her, fixed and gray and dead. But she saw beyond that bitter moment a long procession of years to come that would belong to her absolutely. And she opened and spread her arms out to them in welcome.

There would be no one to live for her during those coming years: she would live for herself. There would be no powerful will bending hers in that blind persistence with which men and women believe they have a right to impose a private will upon a fellow-creature. A kind intention or a cruel intention made the act seem no less a crime as she looked upon it in that brief moment of illumination.

And yet she had loved him—sometimes. Often she had not. What did it matter! What could love, the unsolved mystery, count for in face of this possession of self-assertion which she suddenly recognized as the strongest impulse of her being!

"Free! Body and soul free!" she kept whispering.

Josephine was kneeling before the closed door with her lips to the key-hole, imploring for admission. "Louise, open the door! I beg; open the door—you will make yourself ill. What are you doing, Louise? For heaven's sake open the door."

"Go away. I am not making myself ill." No; she was drinking in a very elixir of life through that open window.

Her fancy was running riot along those days ahead of her. Spring days, and summer days, and all sorts of days that would be her own. She breathed a quick prayer that life might be long. It was only yesterday she had thought with a shudder that life might be long.

She arose at length and opened the door to her sister's importunities. There was a feverish triumph in her eyes, and she carried herself unwittingly like a goddess of Victory. She clasped her sister's waist, and together they descended the stairs. Richards stood waiting for them at the bottom.

Some one was opening the front door with a latchkey. It was Brently Mallard who entered, a little travel-stained, composedly carrying his grip-sack and umbrella. He had been far from the scene of accident, and did not even know there had been one. He stood amazed at Josephine's piercing cry; at Richards' quick motion to screen him from the view of his wife.

But Richards was too late.

When the doctors came they said she had died of heart disease—of joy that kills.

SUBSEQUENT READINGS

Because you are reading the short stories in this book to fulfill the demands of an academic course, the way you ultimately read a story will be different from the way you read purely for pleasure. For example, in a second reading of a story, you may read not from beginning to end but rather forwards and backwards, as you predict and remember what you have read before. Details that you hadn't noticed the first time may suddenly appear important. Ideas that seemed to confirm your own beliefs or expectations may now seem to contradict them, and vice versa. Although this reading process can be unsettling, it is a natural process that even the most advanced readers of literature experience.

Establishing a Goal for Rereading

To understand a story fully, you need to read it more than once; and you need to adopt different strategies for different stages of reading. Therefore, when you reread, you should try to establish a goal. The following guidelines can give you an idea of ways to read for different purposes.

- If you are rereading in preparation for a class discussion of the reading, you may want to underline or copy passages that you particularly like or that you find confusing so that you can bring them to the attention of the class.
- If you are rereading for the purpose of answering a question the instructor has posed about the story, you will want to reread the story in an attempt to find an answer.
- If you are rereading in preparation for writing an essay about the story, you will want to look for specific details that will help you develop ideas.

The following guidelines provide some useful suggestions for how to approach a close reading of a story. Activities following the guidelines will help you practice these strategies. However, you may not need to apply every one of the strategies to every story you read or in the order in which they are presented. Your instructor may assign certain tasks for some or all of the stories, or you may discover other strategies that work best for you.

Defining Unfamiliar Vocabulary Words

Even at this stage, you do not need to know the meaning of every word in a story. As you reread, underline or in some other way make note of only the words or expressions that seem to hold a key to comprehension: words whose definitions you need to know in order to achieve a general understanding of the passages in which they occur.

You do not necessarily have to use a dictionary to find the meaning of words. Although a dictionary can be helpful in learning vocabulary, it cannot define all expressions, and the definitions you find may not apply to the reading passage. Furthermore, using a dictionary can be tedious and time-consuming.

Another way to approach unfamiliar vocabulary is to guess at the general meanings of words, using contextual clues. Context will not always give you precise meaning, but it will often give you enough clues about the meaning to understand a passage.

Use a dictionary, or the Glossary, primarily in two circumstances: (1) when you are not satisfied with the meaning you have guessed from context, even after subsequent readings, or (2) when you are assigned to summarize or analyze part or all of the story.

Guidelines for Using Contextual Clues to Guess at Meaning

1. Look at what precedes and follows the word or expression (for example, grammatical forms within the same sentence, other key words or expressions, important ideas, significant scenes, and so on).
2. Try to determine whether the word has a positive or negative connotation.
3. Consider how the word fits into the whole story.

ACTIVITY: Guessing meaning from context

Working in pairs or a small group, read the first four paragraphs of "The Story of an Hour" (pp. 6–7). Identify two or three words or expressions that you find challenging. Following the guidelines for using contextual clues to guess at meaning, discuss those words to infer their meaning in the passages in which they occur.

Consult a dictionary or the Glossary to compare the meanings you have decided upon with the dictionary definitions.   ●

Annotating

A second or third reading can consist simply of reading the story again. But you can achieve a closer reading by making brief notes as you read. Making these notes, either in the margins of the text, within the text itself, or on a separate sheet of paper is known as *annotating*. Annotating is a way to record your reactions to a story. This process not only helps you focus on the reading task but also clarify the action and meanings of the story. Annotating can be practiced in many ways. Each reader has an individual way of making notes. You might write notes about each paragraph or about larger chunks. You might write a brief word or whole sentences. You might underline, highlight, circle, and/or write comments in a notebook.

A Student Reader at Work

Reprinted here is an example of how one student annotated the first four paragraphs of "The Story of an Hour."

Knowing that Mrs. Mallard was afflicted with a (heart trouble,) great care was taken to break to her as gently as possible the news of her husband's death.

It was her sister Josephine who told her, in broken sentences; veiled hints that revealed in half concealing. Her husband's friend Richards was there, too, near her. It was he who had been in the newspaper office when intelligence of the railroad disaster was received, with Brently Mallard's name leading the list of "killed." He had only taken the time to assure himself of its truth by a second telegram, and had hastened to forestall any less careful, less tender friend in bearing the sad message.

she feels different not natural → She did not hear the story as many women have heard the same, with a paralyzed inability to accept its significance. She wept at once, with sudden, wild abandonment, in her sister's arms. When the (storm of grief) had spent itself she went away to her room alone. [She would have no one follow her.]

There stood, facing the open window, a comfortable, roomy armchair. Into this she sank, pressed down by a physical exhaustion that haunted her body and seemed to reach into her soul.

GUIDELINES

Guidelines for Annotating

Among the many possibilities for recording your reactions and clarifying your understanding are these:

1. Express any emotion you feel in response to what you have just read, for example, pleasure, surprise, anger, confusion.
2. Recall personal associations with actions or conversations that take place in the story.
3. Make connections with something else you have read, heard, or seen.
4. Create headings to identify different scenes, for example, "sister," "death," "the view outside her window."
5. Write brief summaries of different scenes.
6. Underline or in some way mark a certain passage or scene that you think is significant.
7. Write definitions of unfamiliar vocabulary words.
8. Ask questions.

ACTIVITY: *Annotating a passage from a short story*

Using whatever approach is most productive for you, annotate the fifth and sixth paragraphs of "The Story of an Hour" (p. 7), following the guidelines above. Your notes should help you clarify the meaning of the passage. Remember that your annotations can include questions if something in the text is unclear.   ●

KEEPING A READING LOG: EXPLORING YOUR INITIAL REACTIONS

One effective way to clarify your understanding of a story is to explore and record your initial reactions in a *reading log*. You can purchase a notebook in which you make regular entries to explore what you feel and think as you read, or just after you read, a particular story. In writing your reaction to a story, you should be honest about your feelings. If you are not sure what the story is about, you can describe your confusion. It may happen that in the process of describing your reaction, you will suddenly realize something you had not realized before.

How you respond to a story is dependent on the way the story is written, the content of the story, its length, and its meaning. Your response also depends on who you are: your background, culture, beliefs, prejudices, experiences, and aspirations. And, of course, your response is also related to how carefully you have read and how fully you understand what happens in the story. You may have a lot to say or you may have very little to say.

Responding to the Whole Story

After you finish reading a story, you can make a brief log entry to help you remember and reflect on your reading experience.

GUIDELINES

Guidelines for Making a Reading Log Entry

The possibilities for responses to a story are numerous. You may write whatever you want or choose among the following:
1. Explore what you like about the story or what interests you most.
2. Explore what you don't like or don't understand about the story.
3. Relate your own experiences or background knowledge to the story.
4. Explore what you find significant about the story.
5. Raise questions if you don't understand all or part of the story.

Student Readers at Work

The following paragraphs show two students' initial reactions to Kate Chopin's "The Story of an Hour."

Note: The students' spelling and grammatical errors have not been corrected, so that you can see that when you write for yourself to explore your own reactions you do not have to focus on grammatical accuracy or correctness.

Sample Student Reading Log Entry on "The Story of an Hour"

At first I was very confused, but after reading three times I got the story.

I like the line "free, free, free" because after those prolonged description of the scenery and her state of feeling, I finally knew reading this line, what the author intended to imply.

The idea of feeling happy at the site of somebody's death was very new and surprising to me. I am reading Bread Givers and in that novel they speak of the death of a spouse as something to wait for, too. It is very scarey to even imagine that unhappy marriage can make somebody to long for his/her spouse to die. How desparate! and deteriorated! Hatred between a couple could bring the most nasty and ugly end.

K.T.

Sample Student Reading Log Entry on "The Story of an Hour"

Sad but very well written. It was so detailed that I felt right there inside the story since the beginning. I liked how vividly she described the scenes, like "the delicious breath of rain was in the air." Death is described in a very original way. As if the power of heaven and the angels were calling on her to take her to the eternal life.

There was a sentence that was similar to one of my sentences in my essay last semester called "Unforgettable Words" — "Her pulses beat fast, and the coursing blood warmed and relaxed every inch of her body." This sentence made me flashback to the time of my tests in my Panamanian high school.

J.C.

ACTIVITY: Reacting to a short story

Write your own response to "The Story of an Hour" (pp. 6–8). Explore what you felt and thought as you read. If there is anything that you don't understand, raise questions about the story. You can write your response as though you are talking to yourself. Focus on your reactions rather than on grammatical accuracy.   ●

Responding to a Particular Passage: Making Double-Entry Notes

Another way to explore your initial reactions to a story is to focus on a particular passage. While you can write about the passage just as you would the whole story (see above), you can instead respond in two different ways, making *double-entry notes*.

A Student Reader at Work

The following paragraphs show one student's double-entry notes on a passage from Kate Chopin's "The Story of an Hour." The passage is written first, with the page number in parentheses. In the left-hand column, the student states what he thinks the passage means. In the right-hand column, he questions his first interpretation.

One Student's Double-Entry Notes

Passage: "There would be no one to live for her during those coming years: she would live for herself" (8).

This thought caused her death, because she suddenly felt empty in the world.	Maybe I didn't get it. She was happy to be free after her husband's death. So maybe here she's happy too, not empty. I wonder if "live for her" means something special. Why would it make her happy to have no one to live for her? Maybe the next line is important: "There would be no powerful will bending hers." So I guess "no one to live for her" means no one to bend her will. "She would live for herself" means that she will control her own will. So I guess that's what makes her happy. I wonder what caused her death.

M.V.

GUIDELINES	## Guidelines for Making Double-Entry Notes

1. Copy a passage (one sentence or a few sentences) from the story onto a sheet of paper.
2. Fold the paper in half.
3. In the left-hand column, write what you think the passage means.
4. In the right-hand column, question your own interpretation of the passage: explore what else the passage might mean.

ACTIVITY: *Making double-entry notes*

Select a passage (one to three or four sentences) from "The Story of an Hour" (pp. 6–8). Rewrite the passage across the top of a piece of notebook paper. Then fold the paper in half. In the left half, write what you think the passage means. In the right half, question your interpretation.   ●

KEEPING A LITERARY JOURNAL: WRITING ABOUT SPECIFIC TOPICS

Another way to explore your responses to your reading is to keep a *literary journal*, in which you write informally about specific topics assigned by your instructor (or about topics suggested in Chapter 4). The purpose of the literary journal is to help you gain confidence in your ability to read literature and to write about it in a meaningful way.

You may be asked to answer a question about a story, for example, "Has the main character changed for the better?" Or you may be asked to write about a specific idea or item, for example, "Explore the significance of the gun in this story." Or you may be asked to raise your own questions or to focus on what you believe is important in the story, for example, "Select a passage from the story that you think is significant, and explain your reasons for your choice." As you respond to the assigned topic, you should select details and quotations from the story to support your ideas.

The literary journal will prepare you to write more formal essays because writing journal entries will give you regular practice in interpretation. Since journal entries are not formal essays, they will enable you to take risks in expressing your ideas. Furthermore, the entries will serve as a source of valid and appropriate approaches to literary works.

How and How Often Do I Write a Journal Entry?

The number of journal entries you write will be determined by your instructor. Since your instructor may be collecting and responding to some or all of the entries, write or type each entry on a separate piece of paper. An entry can then be handed in to the instructor on an assigned date and later kept in a loose-leaf notebook.

How Will My Journal Be Evaluated?

Journal entries are read primarily for meaning. This approach allows you to experiment with words and ideas. The purpose of the journal assignment is to give you the opportunity to use written language informally to explore, develop, and communicate your thoughts.

How Do I Start?

It may be hard for you to get started on a journal entry, especially the first one. Instead of staring for a long time at a blank page, start writing and keep your pen moving, even if you just begin by saying "I don't know what to say." The act of writing will probably generate ideas.

The process of writing a journal entry may be slow at the beginning of the course. But as you gain experience and increasingly trust your own instincts, you will probably find that you can quickly produce even a lengthy entry.

What Do I Say?

It's hard to know what to write in a literary journal entry until you see what one looks like. The following examples of student writing should enable you to envision how your journal entries might look.

Student Readers at Work

Reprinted here are a literary journal assignment on "The Story of an Hour," two student journal entries, and the instructor's comments in response to the journal entries. As you will see, the students' responses are quite different, since they have different reactions to the story.

Note: The journal entries were written after the class had begun to discuss the story. They are reprinted just as they were written, so that you can see that it is acceptable in a journal entry to cross things out or to write over words or even to make inadvertent language errors.

The Journal Assignment

In "The Story of an Hour" by Kate Chopin, a woman reacts to the news of her husband's death. Using details from the story, analyze whether or not Mrs. Mallard can be considered a callous and hard woman. Use at least one quotation to support your point; indicate the page number of the quotation in parentheses. ●

Sample Student Journal Entry on "The Story of an Hour"

This story is a reflection on the 19th century's woman's status as a prisoner to the husband First, she ~~was~~ is happy about her husband's death because she had enough pain under her husband's control. For example, ~~she~~ Chopin describes that "But she saw beyond that bitter moment a long procession of years to come that would belong to her absolutely"... that proves the point that she sufferes from her husband's "cruel intention". As a result, she could say that "Free! Body and soul free!". Secondly, she dies after ~~her hu~~ the great news of her husband. ~~it seems that implyes to the~~ ~~It implies to the life of a woman who usually has longer life than her husband.~~ This story suggests the wife have a ~~few~~ short time of freedom in the house after the husband dies. However, Chopin puts more emphase on the ~~sa~~ sex ~~discrimanation~~ discrimination.

K.L.

Instructor's Comment on K.L.'s Journal Entry

This is fine, showing your understanding of one interpretation of the story.

You use the expression "cruel intention" from the story. But note that the character thinks, "A kind intention or a cruel intention made the act seem no less a crime" (8). By this she means that whether her husband oppressed her intentionally or not makes no difference. (He wasn't necessarily cruel.)

Sample Student Journal Entry on "The Story of an Hour"

Mrs. Mallard exults over the news of her husband's death and I think she certainly is callous, although I understand her hapiness about gaining her freedom to a certain point. However, if a person become so happy about her loving husband's death I think it is definitely callous. "There was a feverish triumph in her eyes, and she carried herself unwittingly like a Goddess of victory" (8). Although I understand that she's maybe first time in her life enjoying life

itself for herself so she ~~might~~
feels free and happy ("she was
drinking in a very elixir of life
through that open window") getting
so happy over one's husband's death
is terribly unkind and insensitive
especially when the husband is
such a kind, tender and loving
man. I feel very controversial
about this story because I
am also pitying the women of those
days because they were supposed to
be so obeying and possesed that
they ~~were~~ didn't have any
individuality or freedom so very few
of them were enjoying their lives
especially the women who were
aware of this were probably in a
worse situation. Even though
I pity those women, getting so
happy over a loving husband's
death is really cruel and egoish.

N.A.

Instructor's Comment on N.A.'s Journal Entry

I can certainly understand the
conflict you feel. Certainly Louise
had the same conflict at first —
"she was striving to beat it back
with her will" (7).

ACTIVITY: *Responding to a student journal*

Working in a small group, respond to the following student journal entry. Discuss how you might comment on the entry. Allow for differences in the group. Discuss the reasons for the differences. Share your comments with the instructor.

Note: Errors have been corrected so that you can focus on content.

Student Journal Entry on "The Story of an Hour"

I don't think Mrs. Mallard should be considered callous and hard. For years she lived her life under the shadow of her husband; he would have the command in everything and she had to obey. She didn't have the chance to develop her will and project her character. So when her husband died, or at least that's what she thought, she cried for a while (a sincere sorrow) but then she realized that she was "free, free, free" (7). "There would be no one to live for her during those coming years: she would live for herself. There would be no powerful will bending hers in that blind persistence with which men and women believe they have a right to impose a private will upon a fellow creature. A kind intention or a cruel intention made the act seem no less a crime as she looked upon it in that brief moment of illumination" (8). Indeed her husband was kind and gentle and treated her well but he was suppressing too much of her; she couldn't take it.

Chopin criticizes her attitude. She wanted too much; she already had a good husband, a good life. She wanted more and that's why she is punished with death.

C.P.

Your Comment on C.P.'s Journal Entry

•

PARTICIPATING IN AND TAKING NOTES ON CLASS DISCUSSIONS

The suggestions in this chapter are designed to help you develop effective reading strategies. Although the activities have focused on *reading* and *writing*, many have involved you in another productive reading strategy: *talking*.

Courses that include literary works as subject matter provide opportunities for you to talk about what you have read with someone else. By speaking and by listening to others, you can come to a deeper understanding of a story. Like the processes of reading and writing, the act of conversation itself can generate ideas.

There are numerous activities connected to each story (see Chapter 4) that will enable you to participate in discussions of the stories with your classmates. For example, sharing what you have written about a story in your reading log can be one way to introduce your ideas into the class discussions. By sharing ideas, you can become actively engaged in the process of understanding literature.

To remember the significant ideas that emerge from class discussions, it is a good idea to take notes in a notebook or in the margins of the stories.

ACTIVITY: *Reading and responding to a short story*

Apply some of the reading strategies discussed in this chapter to the short story "Girl" (pp. 150–51), or to another very short story in Part Two, for example, Luisa Valenzuela's "The Verb *to Kill*" (pp. 147–49). You don't necessarily have to follow all of the suggestions listed here.

1. Preview the story by reading the title, the biographical information, and the discussion of the context of the story.
2. Read the story through once to grasp what is happening, without using a dictionary or the Glossary.
3. Reread and annotate the story.
    - Identify any unfamiliar vocabulary words; try to guess the meaning from the context (see the guidelines on p. 10).
    - Write brief clarifying notes (see the guidelines on p. 11).
4. Write in your reading log to explore your initial reactions to the story (see the guidelines on p. 12).
5. Discuss your reactions with classmates.   ●

CHAPTER TWO

Developing Effective Reading Strategies: Analyzing and Interpreting

The focus in Chapter 1 is on *response* to fiction. In Chapter 2, the focus is on *analysis* and *interpretation* of fiction. Analysis is the process of breaking down something into its parts to examine the parts closely. Interpretation is the process of piecing the parts together to discover a pattern that reveals the story's meanings or significance.

EXAMINING ELEMENTS WITHIN A STORY

The parts of a story that you can examine are elements that exist within the story: plot, setting, character, point of view, imagery, symbolism, tone, irony, speech, structure, and foreshadowing. Each element provides clues to meaning and can help you interpret a story.

In this chapter, the elements are divided into categories for easy explanation. Within a story, they are usually interconnected and sometimes inseparable.

Plot

Plot is a series of events and thoughts arranged to reveal their dramatic and emotional significance. Plot is not just a sequence of chronological events. Rather, plot implies that there is a meaningful relationship among the events.

CONFLICT

Plot is characterized by a *conflict:* a struggle between two or more opposing forces. The conflict may be *internal* (person vs. self) or *external* (person vs. person; person vs. nature; person vs. society; or person vs. fate). A story may have more than one conflict.

PLOT SUMMARY

To summarize a plot, you need to determine what you believe are the key events or happenings in the story and to identify the conflict(s). Ask questions such as these: What is happening? What is the main conflict? Is the conflict resolved (brought to a conclusion)?

In a plot summary, there are primarily four important features:

1. *It should be brief.* Try to summarize the plot in a few sentences, or in only one or two sentences.
2. *It should be accurate.* Use the facts as they are presented in the story.
3. *It should contain the most important details.* Your goal is to tell what is happening in the story, to identify what you perceive to be the main conflict.
   a. Select what you think are the most significant details.
   b. Decide what you are going to include in your summary and what you are going to leave out.
   c. Present the details in the order in which they occur in the story or in another logical order.
   d. Focus on the facts and do as little interpretation as possible.
4. *It should be primarily in your own words.* Retell the story using your own words. Of course, some of the original words of the story must remain, such as the names of people and places. But you can replace many of the words from the original text. Use one of these strategies, or another strategy that you find productive, to find your own words:
   • After reading the story, put it aside and retell the story from memory.
   • After reading, take notes on the story. Then put the story aside and retell the story from the notes.

ACTIVITY: *Evaluating summaries*

Read the following student plot summaries of the story titled "The Story of an Hour" (pp. 6–8).

Answer the following questions about each summary. Allow for differences of opinion in the group.

1. Does the summary briefly tell what is happening in the story? Does it identify the main conflict?
2. Are the details accurate?
3. Are the details presented in the order in which they occur in the story? If not, is the order of presentation logical?
4. Is the summary written primarily in the student's own words?
5. To improve the summary, what suggestions would you have for the writer?

A

In Kate Chopin's "The Story of an Hour," the main character, Mrs. Mallard, is informed of her husband's tragic death through her sister and a close friend, Richards. Mrs. Mallard's first reaction is normal for any loving wife: "She wept at once, with sudden, wild abandonment, in her sister's arms" (7). After spending a short amount of time by herself, Mrs. Mallard's grief turns into a feeling of relief. She is looking forward to a new life of freedom. Just as she begins to enjoy this feeling of freedom, the door bell rings. It is her supposedly dead husband who is not even aware that an accident had occurred. Unable to accept reality, she suffers a heart attack which leads to her immediate death.

T.A.

B

This is the story of a wife who is informed that her husband died. The story develops as she realizes a series of thoughts that she hasn't had before. She abandons herself and sees the things the way they were. Instead of being sad about her husband's death she feels that now she is going to be happier without him. As the story continues, she discovers that her husband is not really dead and dies of a heart attack.

R.G.

ACTIVITY: *Summarizing a plot in one or two sentences*

Working in pairs, try to summarize "The Story of an Hour" (pp. 6–8) in one or two sentences. Then share your summaries with another pair of students or within a larger group. Discuss the difficulty or ease with which you were able to complete this task. If you were unable to summarize the story in one or two sentences, explain why.

Setting

Setting refers to the place, time, social environment, and physical environment of a story.

PLACE

The setting may include details that indicate the geographical location of the story, such as the country or city in which the story takes place, or they may reveal whether the story takes place in a large city or a small village. The details may show whether the story takes place indoors or outdoors, or both.

TIME

The length of time during which the action occurs is a feature of the setting; this may span several years or months or only an hour. Details of the setting may reveal the time of day, not only through actual clock time, but also through descriptions of light, darkness, and shadows. Details of the setting may reveal time of year, through references to the seasons. The period of history in which the action occurs may also be revealed.

SOCIAL ENVIRONMENT

Not all stories include references to social environment, but when they do, such references may include details about the manners, customs, rules, and moral codes of a society. Details may also reveal socioeconomic status or class level.

PHYSICAL ENVIRONMENT

Details of the setting reveal the physical environment in which the story takes place. Such concrete details may include references to or descriptions of objects, clothing, nature, buildings, rooms, weather, sounds, smells, and so on. These physical details often indicate the emotional state of the characters or the relationship between characters.

ACTIVITY: *Creating and analyzing a setting*

Describe a room in your home such as the kitchen or your own bedroom. Include as many concrete details as you can recall. Then analyze those details to discover what they may reflect about you, your family, or your society.   ●

ACTIVITY: *Examining the setting of a story*

Working in a small group or with the whole class, discuss answers to these questions about Kate Chopin's "The Story of an Hour" (pp. 6–8): Where does the story take place? When? How long does it take for the action to occur? Which details reveal the society's manners, customs, rules, moral codes, and/or the socioeconomic level of the characters? Which concrete details reveal a character's emotional state and/or the relationship between the characters?   ●

Character

Characters are the people in stories, or animals or objects that have human traits in stories. The term *character* refers to people's outward appearance and behavior and also to their inner emotional, intellectual, and moral qualities.

Writers of fiction rarely, if ever, directly tell readers what a character is like. Instead, writers suggest what a character is like, relying on indirect methods of characterization. These indirect methods, summarized below, require readers to interpret clues in order to identify character traits and thus understand motivation for or causes of behavior. By piecing together these clues, readers can form a picture of the whole character.

Outer and Inner Characteristics

Character is revealed in a story by how a person is described; by what a person does, says, and thinks; by what others in the story say and think about the person; and by how others in the story react to the person. Character is also revealed by the choices the person makes and the changes the person undergoes.

Central and Minor Characters

Most stories have at least one *central* character (also called *main* or *major* character, *hero/heroine*, or *protagonist*), the person around whom the story revolves. Many stories also have at least one *minor* character, who is not the focus of the story but who still plays an important role. Sometimes characters provide contrasts with one another.

ACTIVITY: *Suggesting a character*

Working in pairs or in a small group, make a list of words or phrases that suggest a character.

A Fifty-Year-Old Man

Outer appearance	Inner qualities
1. graying hair	1. works twelve hours a day
2.	2.
3.	3.
4.	4.
5.	5.

An Eighteen-Year-Old Male College Student

Outer appearance	Inner qualities
1.	1.
2.	2.
3.	3.
4.	4.
5.	5.

A Character of Your Choice

Outer appearance	Inner qualities
1.	1.
2.	2.
3.	3.
4.	4.
5.	5.

ACTIVITY: *Creating a setting for a character*

Create a setting for one or more of the following characters. The setting may be a room, a building, an outdoor scene, and so on. The description of the setting should reveal who the person is.

a college freshman	a famous actress
a Chemistry professor	a fiction writer
a three-year-old boy	a terrorist
a beggar	a wealthy industrialist

ACTIVITY: *Analyzing character*

Working in a small group or with the whole class, discuss answers to the following questions about Kate Chopin's "The Story of an Hour" (pp. 6–8): Who is the central character? What is significant about how the central character is described? Who are the minor characters? What is significant about how they react to the central character? What are the central character's significant actions? What are the central character's inner thoughts and feelings? What choices does the central character have? What changes does the central character undergo? How do those choices and changes help you understand the story?

ACTIVITY: *Analyzing character through a word*

Read the following paragraph from "The Story of an Hour":

> When she abandoned herself a little whispered word escaped her slightly parted lips. She said it over and over under her breath: "free, free, free!" The vacant stare and the look of terror that had followed it went from her eyes. They stayed keen and bright. Her pulses beat fast, and the coursing blood warmed and relaxed every inch of her body (7).

1. Look up the definitions of the word *keen* in the Glossary.
2. Apply the definitions to the story. What different insight into the character does each definition provide?
3. Discuss which definition is most appropriate. Allow for different interpretations.

Point of view

Point of view is a literary term that refers to the perspective from which a story is told. The author creates a *narrator* to tell the story. It is through the narrator's perspective (through the narrator's eyes and mind) that readers learn what is happening in a story.

THE NARRATOR WHO IS A CHARACTER IN THE STORY

The narrator may be one of the characters in the story. If so, the story is told from a first-person perspective, and the character-narrator may use the pronoun "I."

If the story looks back on the narrator's own childhood, there may be a *double* (or *dual*) *point of view*: the perspective of the child *and* the perspective of the adult narrator.

THE NARRATOR WHO IS NOT A CHARACTER IN THE STORY

The narrator may not be one of the characters in the story or may not participate in the events of the story. If so, the story is told primarily from a third-person perspective.

Such a narrator may know almost everything about one character or every character, including inner thoughts. Or the narrator may know everything about one or more of the character(s) *except* inner thoughts. The narrator may comment on the actions and thoughts, or the narrator may just describe them objectively.

THE NARRATOR WHO IS UNRELIABLE

It is easy to be fooled into thinking that the narrator is the author. But it is important to remember that the *narrator* is a device and *point of view* is a technique that an author uses to influence the way a reader perceives what is happening in the story. An easy way to remember that the narrator is not the author is to think of a story in which the narrator and author are of opposite gender. For example, in "Six Feet of the Country" by Nadine Gordimer (pp. 116–25), the author is a woman but the narrator is a man.

Furthermore, the narrator does not necessarily hold or reflect the author's view. What the narrator says may reveal what is true, but the narrator may not be reliable. Even if the narrator knows almost everything about every character, the narrator is still limited in some way (since all human beings are limited in some way). It is only by piecing together several or all of the elements of fiction that you can move toward an understanding of the author's view.

ACTIVITY: *Relating a story from a child's perspective*

Recall a childhood fear or other early memory. Using the present tense, relate the memory in the first person (using the pronoun "I") but use only words and perceptions appropriate to a very young child. Try to select a memory of something that happened during a brief period of time (for example, an hour or a summer) and in one place. Don't analyze what happened, just tell your story. Then exchange stories with another student, and analyze each other's experiences.   ●

ACTIVITY: *Relating a story from two perspectives*

Choose one of the following activities:

1. Relate the childhood memory that you recalled in the previous activity, only this time use your present perspective. In other words, tell the story from the point of view of who you are today. Using the past tense, relate the story in the first person and retain the same details, but add your mature insight into or understanding of the event.
2. Tell two separate versions of the same event (such as your graduation from high school, your first day of college, your first college party).
   - First relate the event in the first person, using "I."
   - Then relate the same event in the third person, referring to yourself as "he" or "she."

Discuss with your classmates the similarities and differences between using different points of view.   ●

ACTIVITY: *Determining point of view in a story*

Working in a small group or with the whole class, discuss answers to the following questions about "The Story of an Hour" (pp. 6–8): Who is telling the story? Is this narrator a character in the story? What does the narrator know about the (other) characters? Why do you think the author has chosen this point of view? How would the story be different if it were told from another point of view?   ●

Imagery

Imagery refers to the collection of *images* in a work of fiction: the mental pictures created by the author's words. These words often carry suggestive meaning in addition to their literal (primary, factual) meaning; writers use concrete images to go beyond physical description in order to express feelings and states of mind. Most images are created through words that appeal to readers' senses of sight, sound, taste, smell, and touch. For example, a pink flower may appeal to a reader's sense of sight or smell and bring forth pleasant associations with springtime or a holiday memory.

ACTIVITY: *Creating images*

Using details related to the senses of sight, sound, smell, sound, taste, or touch, as appropriate, create images of the following:

something with a sweet taste	something soft
something loud	something beautiful
something that smells bad	something frightening

     ●

ACTIVITY: Making associations

What do you think of or remember when you read these words and phrases?

home	a bath filling with warm water
the sun	ice cream
a dog	people linked arm-in-arm
a river	a diamond necklace ●

ACTIVITY: Identifying images in a story

Working in a small group or with the whole class, make note of some of the images in Kate Chopin's "The Story of an Hour" (pp. 6–8). For example, you can make separate lists of words that relate to the senses (sight, sound, taste, smell, touch). Then discuss answers to the following questions. Does one type of image predominate? If so, is this sensory image connected to any feelings or states of mind? If there is a mixture of images, with no one sense predominating, how does this mixture contribute to your understanding of the story? ●

Symbolism

A *symbol* is something that represents something else. Often in a literary work, a symbol is an image of an event or a physical object (a thing, person, or place) that is used to represent something invisible or abstract such as an idea, a value, or an emotion. Authors use symbols to suggest meaning. One symbol may suggest more than one meaning.

The setting can be a major source of symbols. Trees and grain growing near a river, for example, may suggest life or fertility. Areas without any growth may suggest decay or death. A fancy house may suggest wealth; a tiny village may suggest poverty. The sound of dance music may suggest joy; the sound of beating drums may signal fear. Light may suggest knowledge; darkness may suggest ignorance. The possibilities are numerous.

Although there are numerous possibilities, not all objects or events in stories are symbols. Some objects or events are just what they are described or defined to be and have no second or third meaning.

LITERAL MEANING

To determine whether an object is a symbol of something else, begin with the *literal* (factual, dictionary) meaning of the object.

UNIVERSAL MEANING

After you have determined the literal meaning, ask if the object has some *universal* symbolism. For example, rain after a long period of drought can symbolize rebirth or renewal or regeneration in many parts of the world.

CULTURAL MEANING

If you do not recognize universal symbolism, ask if the object has some *cultural* symbolism. For example, a certain style of dress may represent a particular social class in a particular culture.

CONTEXTUAL MEANING

If you do not discover cultural symbolism, ask yourself if the object has some unique meaning within the *context* of the story itself. For example, a flashing light may represent a character's sudden understanding of something.

If you do not discover any second meaning, you may assume that the object is not necessarily a symbol of anything.

ACTIVITY: *Creating a symbol*

Create a scene in which a character learns some wonderful news. Then have the character look out the window and see something—an object, a person, an action—that is upsetting or disturbing. Assume that the upsetting thing acts as a symbol. What could be your hidden purpose in including this thing in your scene?   •

ACTIVITY: *Discovering symbols in a story*

Working in a small group or with the whole class, discuss answers to the following questions about "The Story of an Hour" (pp. 6–8): Does the author use any objects or events that might represent something invisible or abstract? If so, what are those symbols? What meanings might they suggest? Allow for differences of opinion.   •

Tone

Tone is a literary term that refers to the author's attitude or stance toward the action, characters, narrator, subject, and even readers of the story. Tone is conveyed through the language the author uses. Writers of fiction choose every word carefully to create effect or to convey meaning.

ATTITUDE TOWARD ACTIONS OR EVENTS

To understand tone is to understand the author's attitude toward the action or events: whether a story is humorous or tragic or frightening. The author may want you to laugh or cry, to feel happy or sad, to experience anger or fear.

ATTITUDE TOWARD CHARACTERS OR NARRATOR

To understand tone is to understand the author's attitude toward the characters or the narrator; the author may or may not like or trust them. For example, the author may be sympathetic toward, admiring of, hostile toward, critical of, or sentimental about one or more of the characters or the narrator.

ATTITUDE TOWARD SUBJECT MATTER

To understand tone is to understand the author's attitude toward the subject matter of the story: how an author feels about an idea or concept. For example, the author may be sarcastic about, indifferent to, bitter about, curious about, thrilled by, critical of, outraged about, shocked by, frightened about, scornful of, sentimental about, or sad about a subject such as love, death, marriage, family, government, social class, money, religion, or war.

ACTIVITY: *Establishing tone*

Briefly describe a person (real or imaginary) whom you don't like at all or who frightens you. Without stating that you don't like or are frightened by the person, use concrete language that conveys your attitude. You may focus on the personal's physical appearance, emotional state, and/or actions. ●

ACTIVITY: *Determining the tone of a story*

Working in a small group or with the whole class, discuss answers to the following questions about "The Story of an Hour" (pp. 6–8). Allow for differences of opinion about all of these questions. Is this a happy or a sad story? How does this story make you feel? What is the author's attitude toward the main character? The minor characters? How are these attitudes conveyed (which words or groups of words suggest the author's stance)? What ideas or concepts are revealed in the story? What is the author's attitude toward those ideas or concepts? How is that attitude conveyed? ●

Irony

Irony refers to the unexpected incongruity between appearance and truth or between expectation and reality. Irony is apparent when an author uses language to create a deliberate contrast between appearance (what seems to be true) and truth (what is true), or between expectation (what was expected or hoped for) and reality (what actually happens). Often readers know or understand something that a character does not.

IRONIC SITUATIONS

Irony emerges from situations, for example when what happens is different from what the characters or readers hope for or expect (for example, when a character expects that a certain action will result in victory when in fact that action results in defeat).

IRONIC THOUGHTS

Irony emerges from thoughts, for example when a character thinks or believes something that is actually different from the truth (for example, when Character A believes that Character B is a good person, but the truth is that Character B is evil; so that Character A's trust in Character B results in disaster).

IRONIC SPEECH

Irony emerges from spoken words, for example when a character says something that, either intentionally or unintentionally, means the opposite of what it seems to say (for example, when Character A says to Character B, "I understand you now" and Character B interprets that to mean, "I believe you, I trust you" and acts accordingly; but Character A really means, "I understand now that you are a deceitful person and I don't trust you anymore").

ACTIVITY: *Creating an ironic situation*

Describe a situation (real or imaginary) in which you or someone else expected or hoped to achieve something through a certain action but felt disappointed or surprised when the action resulted in the opposite of the goal.   ●

ACTIVITY: *Uncovering irony in a story*

Working in a small group or with the whole class, discuss answers to the following questions about "The Story of an Hour" (pp. 6–8): Is there irony in the story? Is there incongruity between what the characters think is true and what is actually true?

- Does irony emerge from a situation? If so, what happens that is unexpected or different from what is expected or hoped for?
- Does irony emerge from thoughts? If so, what does a character think or believe that is different from the truth?
- Does irony emerge from spoken words? If so, what does a character say that, either intentionally or unintentionally, means the opposite of what it seems to say?

If there is irony, how does irony help you understand the story?   ●

Speech

Characters' *speech* can indicate the intellectual ability, clarity of thought, educational level, social class, national origin, personality, and/or emotional state of the speaker. Therefore, an author may put sophisticated words or nongrammatical expressions or slang in a character's speech to reveal something about the character's background.

There are a number of ways in which authors use characters' speech to communicate meaning.

DIALOGUE

Dialogue refers to the conversation between or among characters. Dialogue can indicate the relationship between characters, revealing whether they are in conflict or in agreement. Thus, a character's words can convey ideas or information important to the story's plot, character development, or tone. However, what characters say is not necessarily true. Sometimes characters can say things that they don't mean. For example, they may want to conceal the truth or mislead someone.

Literary dialogue does not usually sound like real-life conversation because, even when the author uses dialect, the normal pauses, repetitions, and interruptions of daily talk are omitted.

MONOLOGUE

Monologue is a speech by one character. This brief or extended speech can reveal the character's feelings, often previously hidden from the other characters, and can communicate information to other characters and/or to the readers.

DIALECT

Dialect shows the region from which the speaker comes. The dialect may differ from standard literary English in its pronunciation, grammar, and vocabulary (see, for example, "The Man Who Was Almost a Man" by Richard Wright, pp. 103–12).

INDIRECT SPEECH

Sometimes authors do not present conversation directly but rather through *indirect speech*. That is, the conversation is not presented within quotation marks but is revealed through narration or through a character's thoughts. For example, instead of having a character say *"I want to be alone,"* an author can write, *She told her husband that she wanted to be alone.*

ACTIVITY: *Recording and manipulating dialogue*

Listen to a conversation between two people you know. (*Note:* Be sure to obtain permission from both people to do this activity.)

- Tape record or copy down what they say in a few minutes, including every "um," "you know," and cough.
- Then turn the talk into literary dialogue: omit the repetitions, hesitations, and interruptions. Try to retain the essence of the conversation.
- Put each person's contribution to the conversation on a different line, to clarify who is speaking (see pp. 316–21 for instructions on quoting dialogue).

Discuss with your classmates the differences between everyday conversation and literary dialogue.   •

ACTIVITY: *Turning spoken language into indirect speech*

Summarize the literary dialogue you created in the previous activity by turning it into indirect speech. In other words, rewrite the conversation without direct quotations.   •

ACTIVITY: *Examining speech in a story*

Working in a small group or with the whole class, discuss answers to the following questions about "The Story of an Hour" (pp. 6–8): Is there any dialogue in the story? If so, what does it reveal about the plot, characters, and/or tone? Is there a monologue in the story? If so, what does it reveal about the character who is speaking? Is there indirect speech in the story (that is, is any conversation summarized rather than presented within quotation marks)? If so, does it provide clues to meaning?   •

Structure

A traditional story has a predictable *structure:* the plot moves in a direct line from start to finish, from the beginning through the middle to the end. In the beginning of such a story, the author introduces the setting, the characters, and the conflict. In the middle, the conflict intensifies to a crisis. In the end, the conflict is resolved (one of the forces wins out).

In many stories, however, the structure is not predictable. For example, the author may use the technique of *flashback:* switching in time by going back to the past to provide background to character or events. The author may move back and forth between past and present or project into the future. The author may start at the end rather than at the beginning. The story may not even have an identifiable beginning, middle, and end. The conflict may not be resolved.

The structure, whether predictable or unpredictable, may be designed to produce a specific reaction in a reader. For example, if the structure is predictable (with everything in order), the reader may feel a sense of security; if unpredictable (with things in unexpected places), the reader may feel a sense of suspense. The structure may also reflect what the characters are feeling. For example, a predictable structure (with everything the way it should be) could reflect a character's sense of peace; an unpredictable structure (with things out of place) could reflect a character's confusion or anger or lack of control.

ACTIVITY: *Starting at the end*

Read through several newspaper articles to discover reports on violent crimes. Then pick a crime—for example, a murder—and describe the crime, making your description of the crime the first paragraph of a short story you plan to write. Discuss with your classmates what the rest of your story might tell.   ●

ACTIVITY: *Examining the structure of a story*

Working in a small group or with the whole class, discuss answers to the following questions about "The Story of an Hour" (pp. 6–8): Is the structure of the story predictable, moving in a direct line from start to finish, or is the structure unpredictable? (Does the story have a recognizable beginning, middle, and end?) Is the structure of the story connected to the plot or character development or tone of the story? Does the structure provide clues to meaning?   ●

Foreshadowing

Foreshadowing is a technique used by authors to hint at or suggest what is going to happen. For example, authors may hint at the beginning of the story what will happen in the middle. Or they may hint in the middle what will happen in the end. The hints may lie in descriptions of the events, the setting, or the characters; or they may lie in thoughts, dreams, conversations, and so on.

Foreshadowing often adds suspense to a story, creating in readers a feeling of fear or excitement. You may not recognize foreshadowing until you finish a story and then read it again.

ACTIVITY: *Foreshadowing*

Imagine that you are going to write a short story that *ends* with the description of the crime you wrote about in the activity called "Starting at the end" (pp. 36–37). Create a first paragraph of the short story in which you describe a setting or characters. In that first paragraph, give some hint of what will happen later in the story.   ●

ACTIVITY: *Searching for foreshadowing in a story*

Working in a small group or with the whole class, search for answers to the following questions about "The Story of an Hour" (pp. 6–8): Are there any hints, at various stages in the story, about what will happen? If so, how do these hints affect your reaction to or understanding of the story?   ●

RESEARCHING ELEMENTS OUTSIDE A STORY

Sometimes information about *history, literature,* and *biography,* which exists outside the story, can aid in an analysis of a story. You may learn this information from class discussions or lectures, from library research or other outside reading, or from biographical and background material included in this book.

Of course, this outside information is useful only if you know it, and only if it relates directly to the story. For most of the stories in this book, it is not necessary for you to know this information to achieve an understanding. Virtually all of your analysis can be based on elements within the story.

Placement in History

Knowing the historical period in which a story is set can shed some light on the story.

For example, knowing about women's limited rights in the United States in the nineteenth century may help you understand why Louise Mallard, the main character of "The Story of an Hour," reacts as she does after she is told that her husband has died.

Placement in Literature

Knowing how a short story compares to other short stories or other works of literature can help you to understand its effectiveness.

For example, knowing that Kate Chopin was one of the first American female writers who dared to reveal women's inner emotions may enable you to admire "The Story of an Hour" for its honesty.

Link to Biography

Knowing something about the author's life or other literary works can help you understand the significance of certain elements of a story.

For example, knowing that Kate Chopin's husband died when she was only thirty years old may cause you to believe in the validity of her main character's response to death.

DISCOVERING THEMES

A *theme* is a truth that a story reveals. Through the creation of a fictional world, authors reveal what they believe to be true about the real world.

A theme is rarely directly stated by the author. Instead, the reader discovers themes, inferring meaning from the details in the story. Usually themes deal with general areas of human experience, for example: the nature of humanity or society, the relationship of human beings to the environment, or the question of ethical responsibility.

It may help to understand what a theme is by learning what it is not.

Theme versus Subject

A theme is not a subject. A *subject* is what the story is about. A *theme* reveals what the story says about the subject. For example, one subject of "The Story of an Hour" is a woman's response to her husband's death. A theme would reveal the author's view about the woman's response.

Theme versus Topic

A theme is not a topic. A *topic* is what an essay is about. A *theme* reveals a truth about the topic. For example, if you were to write an essay about "The Story of an Hour," your topic might be "love and marriage." A theme would provide the author's ideas about love and marriage.

Theme versus Moral

A theme is not a moral. A *moral* is a statement or lesson that teaches right and wrong behavior. A *theme* reveals how people behave (without telling people how to behave). For example, a story with a moral might teach a lesson such as "Don't do anything immoral," "Never tell a lie," or "Practice what you preach." A story with a theme would not so directly preach a lesson but would instead create characters to examine their behavior and motivation, to try to understand why human beings are the way they are.

It is easier to understand the difference between theme and moral if you read a story with a moral. In the following fable (animal tale), there is a clear statement of the moral at the end.

The Ant and the Grasshopper
Aesop

Aesop, a Greek slave, was probably born about 620 B.C.E. in the ancient Asian country of Phrygia. Although Aesop had no formal education, he knew a great deal about human behavior. He became well known for his ability to weave wonderful tales about animals who spoke and acted just like people.

In a field one summer's day a Grasshopper was hopping about, chirping and singing to its heart's content. An Ant passed by, bearing along with great toil an ear of corn he was taking to the nest.

"Why not come and chat with me," said the Grasshopper, "instead of toiling and moiling in that way?"

"I am helping to lay up food for the winter," said the Ant, "and recommend you to do the same."

"Why bother about winter?" said the Grasshopper; "we have got plenty of food at present." But the Ant went on its way and continued its toil. When the winter came the Grasshopper had no food, and found itself dying of hunger, while it saw the ants distributing every day corn and grain from the stores they had collected in the summer. Then the Grasshopper knew

It is best to prepare for the days of necessity.

The moral of this story is prominently stated at the end, in italics, telling people how to behave to avoid disaster. None of the short-story writers in this book explicitly states a moral as Aesop does. Instead, each story reveals a theme or several themes. Since themes are not clearly stated by the author, you uncover them through a complex reading and thinking process. This process includes examining the "facts" the author provides (plot, setting, character) and the literary devices the author uses (for example, point of view, symbolism, foreshadowing, irony). By piecing together some or all of the elements of fiction, you can disover theme(s) that the details of the story reveal.

ACTIVITY: *Discovering a theme*

Reread the fable by Aesop (p. 39), this time covering up the last line. Then, instead of finding a moral to the story, find a theme or several themes. In other words, decide what Aesop reveals about how people behave.   ●

Student Readers at Work

"The Story of an Hour" (pp. 6–8) is a story that reveals a number of themes. Some of the themes that students have discovered are presented below.

1. Chopin presents life as a series of unexpected events, which may be taken both positively and negatively.

T.A.

2. It is in human nature to seek freedom.

B.L.

3. Chopin suggests that the role of women in the family and society should be changed. However, Chopin also accepts the fact that there are limits to these changes.

N.N.

4. Human striving for freedom is futile. Only in nature can freedom exist.

T.C.

5. Chopin shows that the only way that women can achieve freedom, which is acquiring self-assertion, is through death.

W.J.

ACTIVITY: *Analyzing themes*

Read the above statements of theme that students discovered in "The Story of an Hour" (pp. 6–8). Pick out details from the story that you think may have led the students to their discoveries. If you disagree with their statements, explain why.   •

ACTIVITY: *Discovering a theme*

Working in a small group or with the whole class, read the story "Girl" by Jamaica Kincaid (pp. 150–51) or another very short story in Part Two, such as Luisa Valenzuela's "The Verb *to Kill*" (pp. 147–49).

Go through the list of elements of fiction below (see expanded discussion on pp. 23–37), and apply the questions to the story. While or after you go through the applicable categories, discuss the story as a whole to discover a theme or several themes. Allow for different interpretations.

- *Plot:* What is happening? What is the main conflict?
- *Setting:* Where does the story take place? Over what period of time? What do the physical details reveal about the society or the characters?
- *Character:* Who is the story about? Does the central character have choices or undergo changes? How do the choices or changes (or lack of choice or change) contribute to your understanding of the story?
- *Point of view:* Who is narrating the story? How would the story be different if the narrator were different?
- *Imagery:* What are the dominant images? Are they connected to any feelings or states of mind?
- *Symbolism:* Might any events or objects represent abstract ideas?
- *Tone:* What is the *author's* attitude toward character, event, or subject matter?
- *Irony:* Is there incongruity between what the characters think is true and what is actually true? If so, how does irony contribute to your understanding of the story?
- *Speech:* What does the dialogue, monologue, or indirect speech reveal about plot or character?
- *Structure:* What might the story's structure reveal about the plot or character development?
- *Foreshadowing:* Are there hints in the beginning or the middle as to what will happen at the end?   •

PART TWO
Anthology of Short Stories

Chapter Three: The Stories

Chapter Four: Discussion Activities

P art Two consists of two chapters: Chapter 3, The Stories, and Chapter 4, Discussion Activities.

The stories are presented chronologically, according to the date they were written or originally published. Spanning over one hundred years, they provide a sense of social history as they move from the nineteenth through the twentieth century. Many of the stories reflect the concerns of their times: class distinctions, roles of women, immigration and acculturation, the American dream, social and economic limitations, World War I, racism and colonialism, post–World War II materialism, religious and cultural identity, Communism, poverty, violence, and effects of the Vietnam War. But the stories need not be read in chronological order. For example, they can be read according to geographic origin (see geographical arrangement of stories on p. xix). Or they can be grouped by subject (for example, stories focusing on childhood and adolescence, love and marriage, success and failure, fate and self-determination, and so on). Or you can select stories by level of interest, for example, on the basis of the intrigue of the title and first sentence (see Contents, pp. xi–xvii). Whichever order you read the stories in, you can focus on what is most significant to you in each story.

You may turn to the discussion activities after you have read a story. They provide suggestions for aspects of a story that can be explored. The activities are not meant to be rigid instructions that you must follow. Your instructor may use the activities as a guide for class discussions, and/or you may generate your own discussions.

CHAPTER THREE

The Stories

C hapter 3 consists of twenty-two complete stories from seventeen countries. Although no one story can be representative of a whole culture, together the stories provide a sense of the variety of concerns and traditions of and within many different cultures. While each story raises issues that are significant for all readers, each also has the potential to challenge readers who are unfamiliar with its underlying cultural assumptions.

When you enter another culture through literature, you need an open mind in order to comprehend the complex thoughts and feelings expressed. By looking at the attitudes and behavior patterns through the cultural framework of the story, as well as through your own cultural framework, you can begin to understand why characters think and act as they do. The benefit of recognizing different perspectives is that not only might you understand another literature and culture better, you might also gain a deeper understanding of your own literature and culture.

The Necklace
Guy de Maupassant   France, 1884

ABOUT THE AUTHOR

Guy de Maupassant (1850–1893) was born into an upper bourgeois (middle-class) family in Normandy, France. After serving in the army, without enough money to continue his law studies, he became a civil servant, working in various ministries in Paris. At the same time, he studied writing with the author Gustave Flaubert. The extraordinary success of his earliest published stories convinced him to devote himself full time to his art. Between 1880 and 1890, Maupassant published nearly three hundred stories. He also wrote essays, plays, poetry, and novels, including Pierre et Jean *(1888). His work has influenced countless numbers of writers around the world, including Anton Chekhov and Kate Chopin.*

THE CONTEXT OF THE STORY

"The Necklace" is set in late nineteenth-century Paris. From early times, French society was organized on a class basis; it was extremely difficult for people to change or move from the class into which they were born. After the French Revolution (1789–1799), France became a republic, but class distinctions remained an integral part of French society.

During the time in which the story is set, it was expected that a husband would receive a dowry *(money or property) from the family of his future bride. A man often chose a wife on the basis of how large her fortune was.*

She was one of those pretty and charming girls who are sometimes, as if by a mistake of destiny, born in a family of clerks. She had no dowry, no expectations, no means of being known, understood, loved, wedded by any rich and distinguished man; and she let herself be married to a little clerk at the Ministry of Public Instruction.

She dressed plainly because she could not dress well, but she was as unhappy as though she had really fallen from her proper station, since with women there is neither caste nor rank: and beauty, grace, and charm act instead of family and birth. Natural fineness, instinct for what is elegant, suppleness of wit, are the sole hierarchy, and make from women of the people the equals of the very greatest ladies.

She suffered ceaselessly, feeling herself born for all the delicacies and all the luxuries. She suffered from the poverty of her dwelling, from the wretched look of the walls, from the worn-out chairs, from the ugliness of the curtains. All those things, of which another woman of her rank would

Translated by Marjorie Laurie.

never even have been conscious, tortured her and made her angry. The sight of the little Breton peasant, who did her humble housework aroused in her regrets which were despairing, and distracted dreams. She thought of the silent antechambers hung with Oriental tapestry, lit by tall bronze candelabra, and of the two great footmen in knee breeches who sleep in the big armchairs, made drowsy by the heavy warmth of the hot-air stove. She thought of the long *salons* fitted up with ancient silk, of the delicate furniture carrying priceless curiosities, and of the coquettish perfumed boudoirs made for talks at five o'clock with intimate friends, with men famous and sought after, whom all women envy and whose attention they all desire.

When she sat down to dinner, before the round table covered with a tablecloth three days old, opposite her husband, who uncovered the soup tureen and declared with an enchanted air, "Ah, the good *pot-au-feu*![1] I don't know anything better than that," she thought of dainty dinners, of shining silverware, of tapestry which peopled the walls with ancient personages and with strange birds flying in the midst of a fairy forest; and she thought of delicious dishes served on marvelous plates, and of the whispered gallantries which you listen to with a sphinxlike smile, while you are eating the pink flesh of a trout or the wings of a quail.

She had no dresses, no jewels, nothing. And she loved nothing but that; she felt made for that. She would so have liked to please, to be envied, to be charming, to be sought after.

She had a friend, a former schoolmate at the convent, who was rich, and whom she did not like to go and see any more, because she suffered so much when she came back.

But one evening, her husband returned home with a triumphant air, and holding a large envelope in his hand.

"There," said he. "Here is something for you."

She tore the paper sharply, and drew out a printed card which bore these words:

"The Minister of Public Instruction and Mme. Georges Ramponneau request the honor of M. and Mme. Loisel's company at the palace of the Ministry on Monday evening, January eighteenth."

Instead of being delighted, as her husband hoped, she threw the invitation on the table with disdain, murmuring:

"What do you want me to do with that?"

"But, my dear, I thought you would be glad. You never go out, and this is such a fine opportunity. I had awful trouble to get it. Everyone wants to go; it is very select, and they are not giving many invitations to clerks. The whole official world will be there."

She looked at him with an irritated glance, and said, impatiently:

"And what do you want me to put on my back?"

He had not thought of that; he stammered:

"Why, the dress you go to the theater in. It looks very well, to me."

---

[1] **pot-au-feu:** a broth of beef boiled with carrots

He stopped, distracted, seeing his wife was crying. Two great tears descended slowly from the corners of her eyes toward the corners of her mouth. He stuttered:

"What's the matter? What's the matter?"

But, by violent effort, she had conquered her grief, and she replied, with a calm voice, while she wiped her wet cheeks:

"Nothing. Only I have no dress and therefore I can't go to this ball. Give your card to some colleague whose wife is better equipped than I."

He was in despair. He resumed:

"Come, let us see, Mathilde. How much would it cost, a suitable dress, which you could use on other occasions, something very simple?"

She reflected several seconds, making her calculations and wondering also what sum she could ask without drawing on herself an immediate refusal and a frightened exclamation from the economical clerk.

Finally, she replied, hesitatingly:

"I don't know exactly, but I think I could manage it with four hundred francs."

He had grown a little pale, because he was laying aside just that amount to buy a gun and treat himself to a little shooting next summer on the plain of Nanterre, with several friends who went to shoot larks down there, of a Sunday.

But he said:

"All right. I will give you four hundred francs. And try to have a pretty dress."

The day of the ball drew near, and Mme. Loisel seemed sad, uneasy, anxious. Her dress was ready, however. Her husband said to her one evening:

"What is the matter? Come, you've been so queer these last three days."

And she answered:

"It annoys me not to have a single jewel, not a single stone, nothing to put on. I shall look like distress. I should almost rather not go at all."

He resumed:

"You might wear natural flowers. It's very stylish at this time of the year. For ten francs you can get two or three magnificent roses."

She was not convinced.

"No; there's nothing more humiliating than to look poor among other women who are rich."

But her husband cried:

"How stupid you are! Go look up your friend Mme. Forestier, and ask her to lend you some jewels. You're quite thick enough with her to do that."

She uttered a cry of joy:

"It's true. I never thought of it."

The next day she went to her friend and told of her distress.

Mme. Forestier went to a wardrobe with a glass door, took out a large jewelbox, brought it back, opened it, and said to Mme. Loisel:

"Choose, choose, my dear."

She saw first of all some bracelets, then a pearl necklace, then a Venetian cross, gold and precious stones of admirable workmanship. She tried on the ornaments before the glass, hesitated, could not make up her mind to part with them, to give them back. She kept asking:

"Haven't you any more?"

"Why, yes. Look. I don't know what you like."

All of a sudden she discovered, in a black satin box, a superb necklace of diamonds, and her heart began to beat with an immoderate desire. Her hands trembled as she took it. She fastened it around her throat, outside her high necked dress, and remained lost in ecstasy at the sight of herself.

Then she asked, hesitating, filled with anguish:

"Can you lend me that, only that?"

"Why, yes, certainly."

She sprang upon the neck of her friend, kissed her passionately, then fled with her treasure.

The day of the ball arrived. Mme. Loisel made a great success. She was prettier than them all, elegant, gracious, smiling, and crazy with joy. All the men looked at her, asked her name, endeavored to be introduced. All the attachés of the Cabinet wanted to waltz with her. She was remarked by the minister himself.

She danced with intoxication, with passion, made drunk by pleasure, forgetting all, in the triumph of her beauty, in the glory of her success, in a sort of cloud of happiness composed of all this homage, of all this admiration, of all these awakened desires, and of that sense of complete victory which is so sweet to a woman's heart.

She went away about four o'clock in the morning. Her husband had been sleeping since midnight, in a little deserted anteroom, with three other gentlemen whose wives were having a good time. He threw over her shoulders the wraps which he had brought, modest wraps of common life, whose poverty contrasted with the elegance of the ball dress. She felt this, and wanted to escape so as not to be remarked by the other women, who were enveloping themselves in costly furs.

Loisel held her back.

"Wait a bit. You will catch cold outside. I will go and call a cab."

But she did not listen to him, and rapidly descended the stairs. When they were in the street they did not find a carriage; and they began to look for one, shouting after the cabmen whom they saw passing by at a distance.

They went down toward the Seine, in despair, shivering with cold. At last they found on the quay one of those ancient noctambulant coupés[2] which, exactly as if they were ashamed to show their misery during the day, are never seen round Paris until after nightfall.

It took them to their door in the Rue des Martyrs,[3] and once more, sadly, they climbed up homeward. All was ended, for her. And as to him, he reflected that he must be at the Ministry at ten o'clock.

[2] **coupé:** a four-wheeled enclosed carriage
[3] **Rue des Martyrs:** Street of the Martyrs

She removed the wraps which covered her shoulders before the glass, so as once more to see herself in all her glory. But suddenly she uttered a cry. She no longer had the necklace around her neck!

Her husband, already half undressed, demanded:

"What is the matter with you?"

She turned madly toward him:

"I have—I have—I've lost Mme. Forestier's necklace."

He stood up, distracted.

"What!—how?—impossible!"

And they looked in the folds of her dress, in the folds of her cloak, in her pockets, everywhere. They did not find it.

He asked:

"You're sure you had it on when you left the ball?"

"Yes, I felt it in the vestibule of the palace."

"But if you had lost it in the street we should have heard it fall. It must be in the cab."

"Yes. Probably. Did you take his number?"

"No. And you, didn't you notice it?"

"No."

They looked, thunderstruck, at one another. At last Loisel put on his clothes.

"I shall go back on foot," said he, "over the whole route which we have taken to see if I can find it."

And he went out. She sat waiting on a chair in her ball dress, without strength to go to bed, overwhelmed, without fire, without a thought.

Her husband came back about seven o'clock. He had found nothing.

He went to Police Headquarters, to the newspaper offices, to offer a reward; he went to the cab companies—everywhere, in fact, whither he was urged by the least suspicion of hope.

She waited all day, in the same condition of mad fear before this terrible calamity.

Loisel returned at night with a hollow, pale face; he had discovered nothing.

"You must write to your friend," said he, "that you have broken the clasp of her necklace and that you are having it mended. That will give us time to turn round."

She wrote at his dictation.

At the end of a week they had lost all hope.

And Loisel, who had aged five years, declared:

"We must consider how to replace that ornament."

The next day they took the box which had contained it, and they went to the jeweler whose name was found within. He consulted his books.

"It was not I, madame, who sold that necklace; I must simply have furnished the case."

Then they went from jeweler to jeweler, searching for a necklace like the other, consulting their memories, sick both of them with chagrin and anguish.

They found, in a shop at the Palais Royal,[4] a string of diamonds which seemed to them exactly like the one they looked for. It was worth forty thousand francs. They could have it for thirty-six.

So they begged the jeweler not to sell it for three days yet. And they made a bargain that he should buy it back for thirty-four thousand francs, in case they found the other one before the end of February.

Loisel possessed eighteen thousand francs which his father had left him. He would borrow the rest.

He did borrow, asking a thousand francs of one, five hundred of another, five louis here, three louis there. He gave notes, took up ruinous obligations, dealt with usurers and all the race of lenders. He compromised all the rest of his life, risked his signature without even knowing if he could meet it; and, frightened by the pains yet to come, by the black misery which was about to fall upon him, by the prospect of all the physical privation and of all the moral tortures which he was to suffer, he went to get the new necklace, putting down upon the merchant's counter thirty-six thousand francs.

When Mme. Loisel took back the necklace, Mme. Forestier said to her, with a chilly manner:

"You should have returned it sooner; I might have needed it."

She did not open the case, as her friend had so much feared. If she had detected the substitution, what would she have thought, what would she have said? Would she not have taken Mme. Loisel for a thief?

Mme. Loisel now knew the horrible existence of the needy. She took her part, moreover, all of a sudden, with heroism. That dreadful debt must be paid. She would pay it. They dismissed their servant; they changed their lodgings; they rented a garret under the roof.

She came to know what heavy housework meant and the odious cares of the kitchen. She washed the dishes, using her rosy nails on the greasy pots and pans. She washed the dirty linen, the shirts, and the dishcloths, which she dried upon a line; she carried the slops down to the street every morning, and carried up the water, stopping for breath at every landing. And, dressed like a woman of the people, she went to the fruiterer, the grocer, the butcher, her basket on her arm, bargaining, insulted, defending her miserable money sou by sou.

Each month they had to meet some notes, renew others, obtain more time.

Her husband worked in the evening making a fair copy of some tradesman's accounts, and late at night he often copied manuscript for five sous a page.

And this life lasted for ten years.

At the end of ten years, they had paid everything, everything, with the rates of usury, and the accumulations of the compound interest.

Mme. Loisel looked old now. She had become the woman of impoverished households—strong and hard and rough. With frowsy hair, skirts

---

[4] **Palais Royal:** Royal Palace area

askew, and red hands, she talked loud while washing the floor with great swishes of water. But sometimes, when her husband was at the office, she sat down near the window, and she thought of that gay evening of long ago, of that ball where she had been so beautiful and so fêted.[5]

What would have happened if she had not lost that necklace? Who knows? Who knows? How life is strange and changeful! How little a thing is needed for us to be lost or to be saved!

But, one Sunday, having gone to take a walk in the Champs Elysées[6] to refresh herself from the labor of the week, she suddenly perceived a woman who was leading a child. It was Mme. Forestier, still young, still beautiful, still charming.

Mme. Loisel felt moved. Was she going to speak to her? Yes, certainly. And now that she had paid, she was going to tell her all about it. Why not?

She went up.

"Good-day, Jeanne."

The other, astonished to be familiarly addressed by this plain good-wife, did not recognize her at all, and stammered.

"But—madam!—I do not know—you must be mistaken."

"No. I am Mathilde Loisel."

Her friend uttered a cry.

"Oh, my poor Mathilde! How you are changed!"

"Yes, I have had days hard enough, since I have seen you, days wretched enough—and that because of you!"

"Of me! How so?"

"Do you remember that diamond necklace which you lent me to wear at the ministerial ball?"

"Yes. Well?"

"Well, I lost it."

"What do you mean? You brought it back."

"I brought you back another just like it. And for this we have been ten years paying. You can understand that it was not easy for us, who had nothing. At last it is ended, and I am very glad."

Mme. Forestier had stopped.

"You say that you bought a necklace of diamonds to replace mine?"

"Yes. You never noticed it, then! They were very like."

And she smiled with a joy which was proud and naïve at once.

Mme. Forestier, strongly moved, took her two hands.

"Oh, my poor Mathilde! Why, my necklace was paste. It was worth at most five hundred francs!"

---

[5] **fêted:** celebrated
[6] **Champs Elysées:** fashionable tree-lined boulevard in Paris

A Trifle from Real Life
Anton Chekhov   Russia, 1888

ABOUT THE AUTHOR

Anton Chekhov (1860–1904) was born in Taganrog, Russia. He was the grandson of an emancipated serf and the son of an unsuccessful grocer. While a medical student at Moscow University, he wrote his first short stories (some of which he signed "The Doctor without Patients"), to help support his impoverished family. Chekhov later worked as a doctor in a small town while continuing to write. By the 1880s his stories about the various strata of Russian society had become so popular that he was able to support himself on his writing. He became not only one of Russia's greatest writers of short fiction but also one of the world's great playwrights. Among his masterpieces are The Three Sisters *(1901) and* The Cherry Orchard *(1904). His plays and short stories have had enormous influence on writers everywhere.*

THE CONTEXT OF THE STORY

The story is set in late nineteenth-century St. Petersburg, the capital of Imperial Russia from 1712 to 1918.

Nikolai Ilitch Belayeff was a young gentleman of St. Petersburg, aged thirty-two, rosy, well fed, and a patron of the race-tracks. Once, toward evening, he went to pay a call on Olga Ivanovna with whom, to use his own expression, he was dragging through a long and tedious love-affair. And the truth was that the first thrilling, inspiring pages of this romance had long since been read, and that the story was now dragging wearily on, presenting nothing that was either interesting or novel.

Not finding Olga at home, my hero threw himself upon a couch and prepared to await her return.

"Good evening, Nikolai Ilitch!" he heard a child's voice say. "Mamma will soon be home. She has gone to the dressmaker's with Sonia."

On the divan in the same room lay Aliosha, Olga's son, a small boy of eight, immaculately and picturesquely dressed in a little velvet suit and long black stockings. He had been lying on a satin pillow, mimicking the antics of an acrobat he had seen at the circus. First he stretched up one pretty leg, then another; then, when they were tired, he brought his arms into play, and at last jumped up galvanically, throwing himself on all fours in an effort to stand on his head. He went through all these motions with the most serious face in the world, puffing like a martyr, as if he himself regretted that God had given him such a restless little body.

Translated by Marian Fell.

"Ah, good evening, my boy!" said Belayeff. "Is that you? I did not know you were here. Is mamma well?"

Aliosha seized the toe of his left shoe in his right hand, assumed the most unnatural position in the world, rolled over, jumped up, and peeped out at Belayeff from under the heavy fringes of the lampshade.

"Not very," he said shrugging his shoulders. "Mamma is never really well. She is a woman, you see, and women always have something the matter with them."

From lack of anything better to do, Belayeff began scrutinizing Aliosha's face. During all his acquaintance with Olga he had never bestowed any consideration upon the boy or noticed his existence at all. He had seen the child about, but what he was doing there Belayeff, somehow, had never cared to think.

Now, in the dusk of evening, Aliosha's pale face and fixed, dark eyes unexpectedly reminded Belayeff of Olga as she had appeared in the first pages of their romance. He wanted to pet the boy.

"Come here, little monkey," he said, "and let me look at you!"

The boy jumped down from the sofa and ran to Belayeff.

"Well," the latter began, laying his hand on the boy's thin shoulder. "And how are you? Is everything all right with you?"

"No, not very. It used to be much better."

"In what way?"

"That's easy to answer. Sonia and I used to learn only music and reading before, but now we have French verses, too. You have cut your beard!"

"Yes."

"So I noticed. It is shorter than it was. Please let me touch it—does that hurt?"

"No, not a bit."

"Why does it hurt if you pull one hair at a time, and not a bit if you pull lots? Ha! Ha! I'll tell you something. You ought to wear whiskers! You could shave here on the sides, here, and here you could let the hair grow—"

The boy nestled close to Belayeff and began to play with his watch-chain.

"Mamma is going to give me a watch when I go to school, and I am going to ask her to give me a chain just like yours—Oh, what a lovely locket! Papa has a locket just like that; only yours has little stripes on it, and papa's has letters. He has a portrait of mamma in his locket. Papa wears another watch-chain now made of ribbon."

"How do you know? Do you ever see your papa?"

"I—n-no—I—"

Aliosha blushed deeply at being caught telling a fib and began to scratch the locket furiously with his nail. Belayeff looked searchingly into his face and repeated:

"Do you ever see your papa?"

"N-no!"

"Come, tell me honestly! I can see by your face that you are not telling the truth. It's no use quibbling now that the cat is out of the bag. Tell me, do you see him? Now then, as between friends!"

Aliosha reflected.

"You won't tell mamma?" he said.

"What an idea!"

"Honor bright?"

"Honor bright!"

"Promise!"

"Oh, you insufferable child! What do you take me for?"

Aliosha glanced around, opened his eyes wide, and said:

"For heaven's sake don't tell mamma! Don't tell a soul, because it's a secret. I don't know what would happen to Sonia and Pelagia and me if mamma should find out. Now, listen. Sonia and I see papa every Thursday and every Friday. When Pelagia takes us out walking before dinner we go to Anfel's confectionery and there we find papa already waiting for us. He is always sitting in the little private room with the marble table and the ash-tray that's made like a goose without a back."

"What do you do in there?"

"We don't do anything. First we say how do you do, and then papa orders coffee and pasties for us. Sonia likes pasties with meat, you know, but I can't abide them with meat. I like mine with cabbage or eggs. We eat so much that we have a hard time eating our dinner afterward so that mamma won't guess anything."

"What do you talk about?"

"With papa? Oh, about everything. He kisses us and hugs us and tells us the funniest jokes. Do you know what? He said that when we grow bigger he is going to take us to live with him. Sonia doesn't want to go, but I wouldn't mind. Of course it would be lonely without mamma, but I could write letters to her. Isn't it funny, we might go and see her then on Sundays, mightn't we? Papa says too, he is going to buy me a pony. He is such a nice man! I don't know why mamma doesn't ask him to live with her and why she won't let us see him. He loves mamma very much. He always asks how she is and what she has been doing. When she was ill he took hold of his head just like this—and ran about the room. He always asks us whether we are obedient and respectful to her. Tell me, is it true that we are unfortunate?"

"H'm—why do you ask?"

"Because papa says we are. He says we are unfortunate children, and that he is unfortunate, and that mamma is unfortunate. He tells us to pray to God for her and for ourselves."

Aliosha fixed his eyes on the figure of a stuffed bird, and became lost in thought.

"Well, I declare—" muttered Belayeff. "So, that's what you do, you hold meetings at a confectioner's? And your mamma doesn't know it?"

"N-no. How could she? Pelagia wouldn't tell her for the world. Day before yesterday papa gave us pears. They were as sweet as sugar. I ate two!"

"H'm. But—listen to me, does papa ever say anything about me?"

"About you? What shall I say?" Aliosha looked searchingly into Belayeff's face and shrugged his shoulders. "Nothing special," he answered.

"Well, what does he say, for instance?"

"You won't be angry if I tell you?"

"What an idea! Does he abuse me?"

"No, he doesn't abuse you, but, you know, he is angry with you. He says that it is your fault that mamma is unhappy, and that you have ruined mamma. He is such a funny man! I tell him that you are kind and that you never scold mamma, but he only shakes his head."

"So he says I have ruined her?"

"Yes—don't be angry, Nikolai Ilitch!"

Belayeff rose and began pacing up and down the room.

"How strange this is—and how ridiculous!" he muttered shrugging his shoulders and smiling sarcastically. "It is all *his* fault and yet he says I have ruined her! What an innocent baby this is! And so he told you I had ruined your mother?"

"Yes, but—you promised not to be angry!"

"I'm not angry and—and it is none of your business anyway. Yes, this is—this is really ridiculous! Here I have been caught like a mouse in a trap, and now it seems it is all my fault!"

The door-bell rang. The boy tore himself from Belayeff's arms and ran out of the room. A moment later a lady entered with a little girl. It was Aliosha's mother, Olga Ivanovna. Aliosha skipped into the room behind her, singing loudly and clapping his hands. Belayeff nodded and continued to walk up and down.

"Of course!" he muttered. "Whom should he blame but me? He has right on his side! He is the injured husband."

"What is that you are saying?" asked Olga Ivanovna.

"What am I saying? Just listen to what your young hopeful here has been preaching. It appears that I am a wicked scoundrel and that I have ruined you and your children. You are all unhappy, and I alone am frightfully happy. Frightfully, frightfully happy!"

"I don't understand you, Nikolai. What is the matter?"

"Just listen to what this young gentleman here has to say!" cried Belayeff pointing to Aliosha.

Aliosha flushed and then grew suddenly pale and his face became distorted with fear.

"Nikolai Ilitch!" he whispered loudly. "Hush!"

Olga Ivanovna looked at Aliosha in surprise, and then at Belayeff, and then back again at Aliosha.

"Ask him!" Belayeff continued. "That idiot of yours, Pelagia, takes them to a confectioner's and arranges meetings there between them and their papa. But that isn't the point. The point is that papa is the victim, and that I am an abandoned scoundrel who has wrecked the lives of both of you!"

"Nikolai Ilitch!" groaned Aliosha. "You gave me your word of honor!"

"Leave me alone!" Belayeff motioned to him impatiently. "This is more important than words of honor. This hypocrisy, these lies are intolerable!"

"I don't understand!" cried Olga Ivanovna, the tears glistening in her eyes. "Listen, Aliosha," she asked, turning to her son. "Do you really see your father?"

But Aliosha did not hear her, his eyes were fixed with horror on Belayeff.

"It cannot be possible!" his mother exclaimed, "I must go and ask Pelagia."

Olga Ivanovna left the room.

"But Nikolai Ilitch, you gave me your word of honor!" cried Aliosha trembling all over.

Belayeff made an impatient gesture and went on pacing the floor. He was absorbed in thoughts of the wrong that had been done him, and, as before, was unconscious of the boy's presence: a serious, grown-up person like him could not be bothered with little boys. But Aliosha crept into a corner and told Sonia with horror how he had been deceived. He trembled and hiccoughed and cried. This was the first time in his life that he had come roughly face to face with deceit; he had never imagined till now that there were things in this world besides pasties and watches and sweet pears, things for which no name could be found in the vocabulary of childhood.

Two Portraits
Kate Chopin   United States, 1895

ABOUT THE AUTHOR
See page 6.

THE CONTEXT OF THE STORY

The story takes place in the nineteenth century in the United States.
    The title of Part I of the story is "The Wanton." Three dictionary definitions of wanton *are*

1. *an immoral or unchaste person,*
2. *a person who is playful,*
3. *a person who is undisciplined or spoiled.*

The term is usually reserved for a woman.
    The title of Part II of the story is "The Nun." A nun *is a woman who belongs to a religious order and who has taken vows of* chastity *(virginity),* poverty, *and* obedience. *Other references to the Catholic religion include* the baptismal font *(a receptacle for holy water used to cleanse a person of original sin);* convent *(a building housing a community of nuns);* the Blessed Sacrament *(rite in which bread and wine are received as the body and blood of Jesus);* the bleeding and agonizing Christ *(Jesus Christ dying on the cross); and* the Virgin Mary *(the mother of Jesus Christ).*

I

The Wanton

Alberta having looked not very long into life, had not looked very far. She put out her hands to touch things that pleased her and her lips to kiss them. Her eyes were deep brown wells that were drinking, drinking impressions and treasuring them in her soul. They were mysterious eyes and love looked out of them.

Alberta was very fond of her mama who was really not her mama; and the beatings which alternated with the most amiable and generous indulgence, were soon forgotten by the little one, always hoping that there would never be another, as she dried her eyes.

She liked the ladies who petted her and praised her beauty, and the artists who painted it naked, and the student who held her upon his knee and fondled and kissed her while he taught her to read and spell.

There was a cruel beating about that one day, when her mama happened to be in the mood to think her too old for fondling. And the student had called her mama some very vile names in his wrath, and had asked the woman what else she expected.

There was nothing very fixed or stable about her expectations—whatever they were—as she had forgotten them the following day, and Alberta, consoled with a fantastic bracelet for her plump little arm and a shower of bonbons, installed herself again upon the student's knee. She liked nothing better, and in time was willing to take the beating if she might hold his attentions and her place in his affections and upon his knee.

Alberta cried very bitterly when he went away. The people about her seemed to be always coming and going. She had hardly the time to fix her affections upon the men and women who came into her life before they were gone again.

Her mama died one day—very suddenly; a self-inflicted death, she heard the people say. Alberta grieved sorely, for she forgot the beatings and remembered only the outbursts of a torrid affection. But she really did not belong anywhere then, nor to anybody. And when a lady and gentleman took her to live with them, she went willingly as she would have gone anywhere, with any one. With them she met with more kindness and indulgence than she had ever known before in her life.

There were no more beatings; Alberta's body was too beautiful to be beaten—it was made for love. She knew that herself; she had heard it since she had heard anything. But now she heard many things and learned many more. She did not lack for instruction in the wiles—the ways of stirring a man's desire and holding it. Yet she did not need instruction—the secret was in her blood and looked out of her passionate, wanton eyes and showed in every motion of her seductive body.

At seventeen she was woman enough, so she had a lover. But as for that, there did not seem to be much difference. Except that she had gold now—plenty of it with which to make herself appear more beautiful, and enough to fling with both hands into the laps of those who came whining and begging to her.

Alberta is a most beautiful woman, and she takes great care of her body, for she knows that it brings her love to squander and gold to squander.

Some one has whispered in her ear:

"Be cautious, Alberta. Save, save your gold. The years are passing. The days are coming when youth slips away, when you will stretch out your hands for money and for love in vain. And what will be left for you but—"

Alberta shrunk in horror before the pictured depths of hideous degradation that would be left for her. But she consoles herself with the thought that such need never be—with death and oblivion always within her reach.

Alberta is capricious. She gives her love only when and where she chooses. One or two men have died because of her withholding it. There is a smooth-faced boy now who teases her with his resistance; for Alberta does not know shame or reserve.

One day he seems to half-relent and another time he plays indifference, and she frets and she fumes and rages.

But he had best have a care; for since Alberta has added much wine to her wantonness she is apt to be vixenish; and she carries a knife.

II

The Nun

Alberta having looked not very long into life, had not looked very far. She put out her hands to touch things that pleased her, and her lips to kiss them. Her eyes were deep brown wells that were drinking, drinking impressions and treasuring them in her soul. They were mysterious eyes and love looked out of them.

It was a very holy woman who first took Alberta by the hand. The thought of God alone dwelt in her mind, and his name and none other was on her lips.

When she showed Alberta the creeping insects, the blades of grass, the flowers and trees; the rain-drops falling from the clouds; the sky and the stars and the men and women moving on the earth, she taught her that it was God who had created all; that God was great, was good, was the Supreme Love.

And when Alberta would have put out her hands and her lips to touch the great and all-loving God, it was then the holy woman taught her that it is not with the hands and lips and eyes that we reach God, but with the soul; that the soul must be made perfect and the flesh subdued. And what is the soul but the inward thought? And this the child was taught to keep spotless—pure, and fit as far as a human soul can be, to hold intercourse with the all-wise and all-seeing God.

Her existence became a prayer. Evil things approached her not. The inherited sin of the blood must have been washed away at the baptismal font; for all the things of this world that she encountered—the pleasures, the trials and even temptations, but turned her gaze within, through her soul up to the fountain of all love and every beatitude.

When Alberta had reached the age when with other women the languor of love creeps into the veins and dreams begin, at such a period an overpowering impulse toward the purely spiritual possessed itself of her. She could no longer abide the sights, the sounds, the accidental happenings of life surrounding her, that tended but to disturb her contemplation of the heavenly existence.

It was then she went into the convent—the white convent on the hill that overlooks the river; the big convent whose long, dim corridors echo with the soft tread of a multitude of holy women; whose atmosphere of chastity, poverty and obedience penetrates to the soul through benumbed senses.

But of all the holy women in the white convent, there is none so saintly as Alberta. Any one will tell you that who knows them. Even her pious guide and counsellor does not equal her in sanctity. Because Alberta is endowed with the powerful gift of a great love that lifts her above common mortals, close to the invisible throne. Her ears seem to hear sounds that reach no other ears; and what her eyes see, only God and herself know. When the others are plunged in meditation, Alberta is steeped in an oblivious ecstasy. She kneels before the Blessed Sacrament with stiffened, tireless limbs; with absorbing eyes that drink in the holy mystery till it is a mystery no longer, but a real flood of celestial love deluging her soul. She does not hear the sound of bells nor the soft stir of disbanding numbers. She must be touched upon the shoulder; roused, awakened.

Alberta does not know that she is beautiful. If you were to tell her so she would not blush and utter gentle protest and reproof as might the others. She would only smile, as though beauty were a thing that concerned her not. But she is beautiful, with the glow of a holy passion in her dark eyes. Her face is thin and white, but illumined from within by a light which seems not of this world.

She does not walk upright; she could not, overpowered by the Divine Presence and the realization of her own nothingness. Her hands, slender and blue-veined, and her delicate fingers seem to have been fashioned by God to be clasped and uplifted in prayer.

It is said—not broadcast, it is only whispered—that Alberta sees visions. Oh, the beautiful visions! The first of them came to her when she was rapped in suffering, in quivering contemplation of the bleeding and agonizing Christ. Oh, the dear God! Who loved her beyond the power of man to describe, to conceive. The God-Man, the Man-God, suffering, bleeding, dying for her, Alberta, a worm upon the earth; dying that she might be saved from sin and transplanted among the heavenly delights. Oh, if she might die for him in return! But she could only abandon herself to his mercy and his love. "Into thy hands, Oh Lord! Into thy hands!"

She pressed her lips upon the bleeding wounds and the Divine Blood transfigured her. The Virgin Mary enfolded her in her mantle. She could not describe in words the ecstasy; that taste of the Divine love which only the souls of the transplanted could endure in its awful and complete intensity. She, Alberta, had received this sign of Divine favor; this foretaste of heavenly bliss. For an hour she had swooned in rapture; she had lived in Christ. Oh, the beautiful visions!

The visions come often to Alberta now, refreshing and strengthening her soul; it is being talked about a little in whispers.

And it is said that certain afflicted persons have been helped by her prayers. And others having abounding faith, have been cured of bodily ailments by the touch of her beautiful hands.

The Americanization of Shadrach Cohen
Bruno Lessing   United States, 1903

ABOUT THE AUTHOR

Bruno Lessing (1870–1940) was born in the United States, in New York. His real name was Rudolph Block but he won fame as a short-story writer for magazines under the by-line of Bruno Lessing. He worked first as a news reporter and later became the editor of the comic supplement of the Hearst newspapers. His books include the story collections With the Best Intention *(1914) and* Children of Men, *from which this story is taken. Lessing received high critical praise for his depictions of Jewish life in New York.*

THE CONTEXT OF THE STORY

The story takes place in New York City at the turn into the twentieth century. In the latter part of the nineteenth century, many Jewish immigrants fled their countries primarily to escape religious persecution. Most came to America with little money and had to struggle to survive. They left the ghettos *of Russia (neighborhoods to which Jews were restricted) to live in the ghettos of New York (poor sections of the city occupied by minority groups). In this story, Lessing writes about a family who came to the States with enough money to open a store on* Hester Street, *then the center of Jewish ghetto life on New York's Lower East Side.*

References to the Jewish religion include ringlets *(men's uncut sideburns: a sign of allegiance to God);* a praying cap *(a small head covering that, by symbolically separating man from God, shows reverence and respect);* grace after meals *(a Hebrew prayer said to thank God for the food);* Jehovah *(God); the saying* "Honor your father and your mother" *(one of the Ten Commandments, the fundamental laws of Judaism); the* Pentateuch *(the first five books of the Hebrew Bible); and the* shadchen *(matchmaker, a person who arranges marriages).*

THE FIRST LINE OF THE STORY

The first line of the story reads, "There is no set rule for the turning of the worm; most worms, however, turn unexpectedly." *This line is based on the proverbs,* "Even a worm will turn" *and* "Tread on a worm and it will turn," *which mean that even the humblest persons will resent extreme ill treatment and/or that there are limits to patience.*

There is no set rule for the turning of the worm; most worms, however, turn unexpectedly. It was so with Shadrach Cohen.

He had two sons. One was named Abel and the other Gottlieb. They had left Russia five years before their father, had opened a store on Hester

Street with the money he had given them. For reasons that only business men would understand they conducted the store in their father's name— and, when the business began to prosper and they saw an opportunity of investing further capital in it to good advantage, they wrote to their dear father to come to this country.

"We have a nice home for you here," they wrote. "We will live happily together."

Shadrach came. With him he brought Marta, the serving-woman who had nursed his wife until she died, and whom, for his wife's sake, he had taken into the household. When the ship landed he was met by two dapper-looking young men, each of whom wore a flaring necktie with a diamond in it. It took him some time to realize that these were his two sons. Abel and Gottlieb promptly threw their arms around his neck and welcomed him to the new land. Behind his head they looked at each other in dismay. In the course of five years they had forgotten that their father wore a gaberdine— the loose, baglike garment of the Russian Ghetto—and had a long, straggling grey beard and ringlets that came down over his ears—that, in short, he was a perfect type of the immigrant whose appearance they had so frequently ridiculed. Abel and Gottlieb were proud of the fact that they had become Americanized. And they frowned at Marta.

"Come, father," they said. "Let us go to a barber, who will trim your beard and make you look more like an American. Then we will take you home with us."

Shadrach looked from one to the other in surprise.

"My beard?" he said; "what is the matter with my beard?"

"In this city," they explained to him, "no one wears a beard like yours except the newly landed Russian Jews."

Shadrach's lips shut tightly for a moment. Then he said:

"Then I will keep my beard as it is. I am a newly landed Russian Jew." His sons clinched their fists behind their backs and smiled at him amiably. After all, he held the purse-strings. It was best to humour him.

"What shall we do with Marta?" they asked. "We have a servant. We will not need two."

"Marta," said the old man, "stays with us. Let the other servant go. Come, take me home: I am getting hungry."

They took him home, where they had prepared a feast for him. When he bade Marta sit beside him at the table Abel and Gottlieb promptly turned and looked out of the window. They felt that they could not conceal their feelings. The feast was a dismal affair. Shadrach was racking his brains to find some explanation that would account for the change that had come over his sons. They had never been demonstrative in their affection for him, and he had not looked for an effusive greeting. But he realized immediately that there was a wall between him and his sons; some change had occurred; he was distressed and puzzled. When the meal was over Shadrach donned his praying cap and began to recite the grace after meals. Abel and Gottlieb looked at each other in consternation. Would they have to go through this at every meal? Better—far better—to risk their father's displeasure and acquaint him with the truth at once. When it came to the response Shadrach looked inquiringly at his sons. It was Abel who explained the matter:

"We—er—have grown out of—er—that is—er—done away with—er—sort of fallen into the habit, don't you know, of leaving out the prayer at meals. It's not quite American!"

Shadrach looked from one to the other. Then, bowing his head, he went on with his prayer.

"My sons," he said, when the table had been cleared. "It is wrong to omit the prayer after meals. It is part of your religion. I do not know anything about this America or its customs. But religion is the worship of Jehovah, who has chosen us as His children on earth, and that same Jehovah rules supreme over America even as He does over the country that you came from."

Gottlieb promptly changed the subject by explaining to him how badly they needed more money in their business. Shadrach listened patiently for a while, then said:

"I am tired after my long journey. I do not understand this business that you are talking about. But you may have whatever money you need. After all, I have no one but you two." He looked at them fondly. Then his glance fell upon the serving-woman, and he added, quickly:

"And Marta."

"Thank God," said Gottlieb, when their father had retired, "he does not intend to be stingy."

"Oh, he is all right," answered Abel. "After he gets used to things he will become Americanized like us."

To their chagrin, however, they began to realize, after a few months, that their father was clinging to the habits and customs of his old life with a tenacity that filled them with despair. The more they urged him to abandon his ways the more eager he seemed to become to cling to them. He seemed to take no interest in their business affairs, but he responded, almost cheerfully, to all their requests for money. He began to feel that this, after all, was the only bond between him and his sons. And when they had pocketed the money, they would shake their heads and sigh.

"Ah, father, if you would only not insist upon being so old-fashioned!" Abel would say.

"And let us fix you up a bit," Gottlieb would chime in.

"And become more progressive—like the other men of your age in this country."

"And wear your beard shorter and trimmed differently."

"And learn to speak English."

Shadrach never lost his temper; never upbraided them. He would look from one to the other and keep his lips tightly pressed together. And when they had gone he would look at Marta and would say:

"Tell me what you think, Marta. Tell me what you think."

"It is not proper for me to interfere between father and sons," Marta would say. And Shadrach could never induce her to tell him what she thought. But he could perceive a gleam in her eyes and observed a certain nervous vigor in the way she cleaned the pots and pans for hours after these talks, that fell soothingly upon his perturbed spirit.

As we remarked before, there is no rule for the turning of the worm. Some worms, however, turn with a crash. It was so with Shadrach Cohen.

Gottlieb informed his father that he contemplated getting married.

"She is very beautiful," he said. "The affair is all in the hands of the Shadchen."

His father's face lit up with pleasure.

"Gottlieb," he said, holding out his hand, "God bless you! It's the very best thing you could do. Marta, bring me my hat and coat. Come, Gottlieb. Take me to see her. I cannot wait a moment. I want to see my future daughter-in-law at once. How happy your mother would be if she were alive to-day!"

Gottlieb turned red and hung back.

"I think, father," he said, "you had better not go just yet. Let us wait a few days until the Shadchen has made all the arrangements. She is an American girl. She—she won't—er—understand your ways—don't you know? And it may spoil everything."

Crash! Marta had dropped an iron pot that she was cleaning. Shadrach was red in the face with suppressed rage.

"So!" he said. "It has come to this. You are ashamed of your father!" Then he turned to the old servant:

"Marta," he said, "to-morrow we become Americanized—you and I."

There was an intonation in his voice that alarmed his son.

"You are not angry—" he began, but with a fierce gesture his father cut him short.

"Not another word. To bed! Go to bed at once."

Gottlieb was dumbfounded. With open mouth he stared at his father. He had not heard that tone since he was a little boy.

"But, father—" he began.

"Not a word. Do you hear me? Not a word will I listen to. In five minutes if you are not in bed you go out of this house. Remember, this is my house."

Then he turned to Abel. Abel was calmly smoking a cigar.

"Throw that cigar away," his father commanded, sternly.

Abel gasped and looked at his father in dismay.

"Marta, take that cigar out of his mouth and throw it into the fire. If he objects he goes out of the house."

With a smile of intense delight Marta plucked the cigar from Abel's unresisting lips, and incidentally trod heavily upon his toes. Shadrach gazed long and earnestly at his sons.

"To-morrow, my sons," he said, slowly, "you will begin to lead a new life."

In the morning Abel and Gottlieb, full of dread forebodings, left the house as hastily as they could. They wanted to get to the store to talk matters over. They had hardly entered the place, however, when the figure of their father loomed up in the doorway. He had never been in the place before. He looked around him with great satisfaction at the many evidences of prosperity which the place presented. When he beheld the name "Shadrach Cohen, Proprietor" over the door he chuckled. Ere his sons had recovered from the shock of his appearance a pale-faced clerk, smoking a cigarette, approached Shadrach, and in a sharp tone asked:

"Well, sir, what do you want?" Shadrach looked at him with considerable curiosity. Was he Americanized, too? The young man frowned impatiently.

"Come, come! I can't stand here all day. Do you want anything?"

Shadrach smiled and turned to his sons.

"Send him away at once. I don't want that kind of young man in my place." Then turning to the young man, upon whom the light of revelation had quickly dawned, he said, sternly:

"Young man, whenever you address a person who is older than you, do it respectfully. Honour your father and your mother. Now go away as fast as you can. I don't like you."

"But, father," interposed Gottlieb, "we must have someone to do his work."

"Dear me," said Shadrach, "is that so? Then, for the present, you will do it. And that young man over there—what does he do?"

"He is also a salesman."

"Let him go. Abel will take his place."

"But, father, who is to manage the store? Who will see that the work is properly done?"

"I will," said the father. "Now, let us have no more talking. Get to work."

Crestfallen, miserable, and crushed in spirit, Abel and Gottlieb began their humble work while their father entered upon the task of familiarizing himself with the details of the business. And even before the day's work was done he came to his sons with a frown of intense disgust.

"Bah!" he exclaimed. "It is just as I expected. You have both been making as complete a mess of this business as you could without ruining it. What you both lack is sense. If becoming Americanized means becoming stupid, I must congratulate you upon the thoroughness of your work. To-morrow I shall hire a manager to run this store. He will arrange your hours of work. He will also pay you what you are worth. Not a cent more. How late have you been keeping this store open?"

"Until six o'clock," said Abel.

"H'm! Well, beginning to-day, you both will stay here until eight o'clock. Then one of you can go. The other will stay until ten. You can take turns. I will have Marta send you some supper."

To the amazement of Abel and Gottlieb the business of Shadrach Cohen began to grow. Slowly it dawned upon them that in the mercantile realm they were as children compared with their father. His was the true money-maker spirit; there was something wonderful in the swiftness with which he grasped the most intricate phases of trade; and where experience failed him some instinct seemed to guide him aright. And gradually, as the business of Shadrach Cohen increased, and even the sons saw vistas of prosperity beyond their wildest dreams, they began to look upon their father with increasing respect. What they had refused to the integrity of his character, to the nobility of his heart, they promptly yielded to the shrewdness of his brain. The sons of Shadrach Cohen became proud of their father. He, too, was slowly undergoing a change. A new life was unfolding itself before his eyes, he became broader-minded, more tolerant, and, above all, more flexible in his tenets. Contact with the outer world had quickly impressed him with the vast differences between his present surroundings and his old life in Russia. The charm of American life, of liberty, of democracy, appealed to him strongly. As the field of his business operations widened he came more and more in contact with American business men, from whom he learned many things—principally the faculty of adaptibility. And as his sons began to perceive that all these business men whom, in former days, they had looked upon with feelings akin to reverence, seemed to show to their father an amount of deference and respect which they had never evinced toward the sons, their admiration for their father increased.

And yet it was the same Shadrach Cohen.

From that explosive moment when he had rebelled against his sons he demanded from them implicit obedience and profound respect. Upon that point he was stern and unyielding. Moreover, he insisted upon a strict observance of every tenet of their religion. This, at first, was the bitterest pill of all. But they soon became accustomed to it. When life is light and free from care, religion is quick to fly; but when the sky grows dark and life becomes earnest, and we feel its burden growing heavy upon our shoulders, then we welcome the consolation that religion brings, and we cling to it. And Shadrach Cohen had taught his sons that life was earnest. They were earning their bread by the sweat of their brow. No prisoner, with chain and ball, was subjected to closer supervision by his keeper than were Gottlieb and Abel.

"You have been living upon my charity," their father said to them: "I will teach you how to earn your own living."

And he taught them. And with the lesson they learned many things; learned the value of discipline, learned the beauty of filial reverence, learned the severe joy of the earnest life.

One day Gottlieb said to his father:

"May I bring Miriam to supper to-night? I am anxious that you should see her."

Shadrach turned his face away so that Gottlieb might not see the joy that beamed in his eyes.

"Yes, my son," he answered. "I, too, am anxious to see if she is worthy of you."

Miriam came, and in a stiff, embarrassed manner Gottlieb presented her to his father. The girl looked in surprise at the venerable figure that stood before her—a picture of a patriarch from the Pentateuch, with a long, straggling beard, and ringlets of hair falling over the ears, and clad in the long gaberdine of the Russian Ghettos. And she saw a pair of grey eyes bent keenly upon her—eyes of shrewdness, but soft and tender as a woman's— the eyes of a strong man with a kind heart. Impulsively she ran toward him and seized his hands. And, with a smile upon her lips, she said:

"Will you not give me your blessing?"

When the evening meal had ended, Shadrach donned his praying cap, and with bowed head intoned the grace after meals:

"We will bless Him from whose wealth we have eaten!" And in fervent tones rose from Gottlieb's lips the response:

"Blessed be He!"

Araby
James Joyce   Ireland, 1914

ABOUT THE AUTHOR

James Joyce (1882–1941) was born and grew up in Dublin, Ireland, with his parents, three brothers, and six sisters. Partly because of the difficulty of getting his work published in Ireland, Joyce left his native land in 1904 and lived and wrote in Trieste, Zurich, and Paris. His novels, including A Portrait of the Artist as a Young Man *(1916) and* Ulysses *(1922), have established him as one of the most significant writers of modern times. "Araby" is one of fifteen stories published in* Dubliners.

THE CONTEXT OF THE STORY

The story takes place in Dublin, Ireland, in the late nineteenth century. Over 90 percent of the population of the Republic of Ireland is Roman Catholic. References to religion include priest *(member of the clergy who has taken vows of poverty and celibacy) and* Freemason *(connected to a secret group believed to be an enemy of the Catholic church).*

THE TITLE OF THE STORY

The name Araby *refers to the name of an actual traveling bazaar that featured exotic goods from the East.*

North Richmond Street, being blind, was a quiet street except at the hour when the Christian Brothers' School set the boys free. An uninhabited house of two storeys stood at the blind end, detached from its neighbours in a square ground. The other houses of the street, conscious of decent lives within them, gazed at one another with brown imperturbable faces.

The former tenant of our house, a priest, had died in the back drawing-room. Air, musty from having been long enclosed, hung in all the rooms, and the waste room behind the kitchen was littered with old useless papers. Among these I found a few paper-covered books, the pages of which were curled and damp: *The Abbot*, by Walter Scott,[1] *The Devout Communicant*,[2] and *The Memoirs of Vidocq*.[3] I liked the last best because its leaves were yellow. The wild garden behind the house contained a central apple-tree and a few straggling bushes under one of which I found the late tenant's rusty bicycle-pump. He had been a very charitable priest; in his will he had left all his money to institutions and the furniture of his house to his sister.

---

[1] *The Abbot* by **Walter Scott:** a historical romance by a famous English novelist (an *abbot* is a man who heads a religious community)

[2] *The Devout Communicant:* a Protestant religious pamphlet

[3] *The Memoirs of Vidocq:* a volume of shocking and often sexually suggestive memoirs by a notorious imposter

When the short days of winter came dusk fell before we had well eaten our dinners. When we met in the street the houses had grown sombre. The space of sky above us was the colour of ever-changing violet and towards it the lamps of the street lifted their feeble lanterns. The cold air stung us and we played till our bodies glowed. Our shouts echoed in the silent street. The career of our play brought us through the dark muddy lanes behind the houses where we ran the gauntlet of the rough tribes from the cottages, to the back doors of the dark dripping gardens where odours arose from the ashpits, to the dark odorous stables where a coachman smoothed and combed the horse or shook music from the buckled harness. When we returned to the street light from the kitchen windows had filled the areas. If my uncle was seen turning the corner we hid in the shadow until we had seen him safely housed. Or if Mangan's sister came out on the doorstep to call her brother in to his tea we watched her from our shadow peer up and down the street. We waited to see whether she would remain or go in and, if she remained, we left our shadow and walked up to Mangan's steps resignedly. She was waiting for us, her figure defined by the light from the half-opened door. Her brother always teased her before he obeyed and I stood by the railings looking at her. Her dress swung as she moved her body and the soft rope of her hair tossed from side to side.

Every morning I lay on the floor in the front parlour watching her door. The blind was pulled down to within an inch of the sash so that I could not be seen. When she came out on the doorstep my heart leaped. I ran to the hall, seized my books, and followed her. I kept her brown figure always in my eye and, when we came near the point at which our ways diverged, I quickened my pace and passed her. This happened morning after morning. I had never spoken to her, except for a few casual words, and yet her name was like a summons to all my foolish blood.

Her image accompanied me even in places the most hostile to romance. On Saturday evenings when my aunt went marketing I had to go to carry some of the parcels. We walked through the flaring streets, jostled by drunken men and bargaining women, amid the curses of labourers, the shrill litanies of shop-boys who stood on guard by the barrel of pigs' cheeks, the nasal chanting of street-singers, who sang a *come-all-you* about O'Donovan Rossa,[4] or a ballad about the troubles in our native land. These noises converged in a single sensation of life for me: I imagined that I bore my chalice[5] safely through a throng of foes. Her name sprang to my lips at moments in strange prayers and praises which I myself did not understand. My eyes were often full of tears (I could not tell why) and at times a flood from my heart seemed to pour itself out into my bosom. I thought little of the future. I did not know whether I would ever speak to her or not or, if I spoke to her, how I could tell her of my confused adoration. But my body

[4] *come-all-you* about O'Donovan Rossa: a street ballad about a nineteenth-century Irish patriot known as O'Donovan Rossa, which describes Irish traitors

[5] chalice: sacred cup for wine. In medieval legend, the chalice known as the Holy Grail was used by Christ and was subsequently the object of many chivalrous quests.

was like a harp and her words and gestures were like fingers running upon the wires.

One evening I went into the back drawing-room in which the priest had died. It was a dark rainy evening and there was no sound in the house. Through one of the broken panes I heard the rain impinge upon the earth, the fine incessant needles of water playing in the sodden beds. Some distant lamp or lighted window gleamed below me. I was thankful that I could see so little. All my senses seemed to desire to veil themselves and, feeling that I was about to slip from them, I pressed the palms of my hands together until they trembled, murmuring: *"O love! O love!"* many times.

At last she spoke to me. When she addressed the first words to me I was so confused that I did not know what to answer. She asked me was I going to *Araby*. I forgot whether I answered yes or no. It would be a splendid bazaar, she said she would love to go.

"And why can't you?" I asked.

While she spoke she turned a silver bracelet round and round her wrist. She could not go, she said, because there would be a retreat that week in her convent. Her brother and two other boys were fighting for their caps and I was alone at the railings. She held one of the spikes, bowing her head towards me. The light from the lamp opposite our door caught the white curve of her neck, lit up her hair that rested there and, falling, lit up the hand upon the railing. It fell over one side of her dress and caught the white border of a petticoat, just visible as she stood at ease.

"It's well for you," she said.

"If I go," I said, "I will bring you something."

What innumerable follies laid waste my waking and sleeping thoughts after that evening! I wished to annihilate the tedious intervening days. I chafed against the work of school. At night in my bedroom and by day in the classroom her image came between me and the page I strove to read. The syllables of the word *Araby* were called to me through the silence in which my soul luxuriated and cast an Eastern enchantment over me. I asked for leave to go to the bazaar on Saturday night. My aunt was surprised and hoped it was not some Freemason affair. I answered few questions in class. I watched my master's face pass from amiability to sternness; he hoped I was not beginning to idle. I could not call my wandering thoughts together. I had hardly any patience with the serious work of life which, now that it stood between me and my desire, seemed to me child's play, ugly monotonous child's play.

On Saturday morning I reminded my uncle that I wished to go to the bazaar in the evening. He was fussing at the hallstand, looking for the hat-brush, and answered me curtly:

"Yes, boy, I know."

As he was in the hall I could not go into the front parlour and lie at the window. I left the house in bad humour and walked slowly towards the school. The air was pitilessly raw and already my heart misgave me.

When I came home to dinner my uncle had not yet been home. Still it was early. I sat staring at the clock for some time and, when its ticking began to irritate me, I left the room. I mounted the staircase and gained the upper part of the house. The high cold empty gloomy rooms liberated me and I went from room to room singing. From the front window I saw my companions playing below in the street. Their cries reached me weakened and indistinct and, leaning my forehead against the cool glass, I looked over at the dark house where she lived. I may have stood there for an hour, seeing nothing but the brown-clad figure cast by my imagination, touched discreetly by the lamplight at the curved neck, at the hand upon the railings and at the border below the dress.

When I came downstairs again I found Mrs. Mercer sitting at the fire. She was an old garrulous woman, a pawnbroker's widow, who collected used stamps for some pious purpose. I had to endure the gossip of the tea-table. The meal was prolonged beyond an hour and still my uncle did not come. Mrs. Mercer stood up to go: she was sorry she couldn't wait any longer, but it was after eight o'clock and she did not like to be out late, as the night air was bad for her. When she had gone I began to walk up and down the room, clenching my fists. My aunt said:

"I'm afraid you may put off your bazaar for this night of Our Lord."

At nine o'clock I heard my uncle's latchkey in the halldoor. I heard him talking to himself and heard the hallstand rocking when it had received the weight of his overcoat. I could interpret these signs. When he was midway through his dinner I asked him to give me the money to go to the bazaar. He had forgotten.

"The people are in bed and after their first sleep now," he said.

I did not smile. My aunt said to him energetically:

"Can't you give him the money and let him go? You've kept him late enough as it is."

My uncle said he was very sorry he had forgotten. He said he believed in the old saying: "All work and no play makes Jack a dull boy." He asked me where I was going and, when I had told him a second time he asked me did I know *The Arab's Farewell to his Steed.*[6] When I left the kitchen he was about to recite the opening lines of the piece to my aunt.

I held a florin[7] tightly in my hand as I strode down Buckingham Street towards the station. The sight of the streets thronged with buyers and glaring with gas[8] recalled to me the purpose of my journey. I took my seat in a third-class carriage of a deserted train. After an intolerable delay the train moved out of the station slowly. It crept onward among ruinous houses and over the twinkling river. At Westland Row Station a crowd of people pressed to the carriage doors; but the porters moved them back, saying that it was a special train for the bazaar. I remained alone in the bare carriage. In a few minutes the train drew up beside an improvised wooden platform. I

[6] *The Arab's Farewell to His Steed:* a popular poem about a beautiful, beloved horse that has been sold
[7] **florin:** a piece of silver money
[8] **gas:** fuel used to light streetlamps

passed out on to the road and saw by the lighted dial of a clock that it was ten minutes to ten. In front of me was a large building which displayed the magical name.

I could not find any sixpenny entrance and, fearing that the bazaar would be closed, I passed in quickly through a turnstile, handing a shilling[9] to a weary-looking man. I found myself in a big hall girdled at half its height by a gallery. Nearly all the stalls were closed and the greater part of the hall was in darkness. I recognised a silence like that which pervades a church after a service. I walked into the centre of the bazaar timidly. A few people were gathered about the stalls which were still open. Before a curtain, over which the words *Café Chantant*[10] were written in coloured lamps, two men were counting money on a salver. I listened to the fall of the coins.

Remembering with difficulty why I had come I went over to one of the stalls and examined porcelain vases and flowered tea-sets. At the door of the stall a young lady was talking and laughing with two young gentlemen. I remarked their English accents and listened vaguely to their conversation.

"O, I never said such a thing!"

"O, but you did!"

"O, but I didn't!"

"Didn't she say that?"

"Yes. I heard her."

"O, there's a . . . fib!"

Observing me the young lady came over and asked me did I wish to buy anything. The tone of her voice was not encouraging; she seemed to have spoken to me out of a sense of duty. I looked humbly at the great jars that stood like eastern guards at either side of the dark entrance to the stall and murmured:

"No, thank you."

The young lady changed the position of one of the vases and went back to the two young men. They began to talk of the same subject. Once or twice the young lady glanced at me over her shoulder.

I lingered before her stall, though I knew my stay was useless, to make my interest in her wares seem the more real. Then I turned away slowly and walked down the middle of the bazaar. I allowed the two pennies to fall against the sixpence in my pocket. I heard a voice call from one end of the gallery that the light was out. The upper part of the hall was now completely dark.

Gazing up into the darkness I saw myself as a creature driven and derided by vanity; and my eyes burned with anguish and anger.

---

[9] **shilling:** a former coin of the United Kingdom worth about twelve pence.
[10] *Café Chantant:* a cafe with music

War
Luigi Pirandello   Italy, 1918

ABOUT THE AUTHOR

Luigi Pirandello (1867–1936) was born near Girgenti, on the island of Sicily. He left Sicily at the age of twenty to study law. His interest changed to literature and, following further study in Germany, Pirandello returned to Rome to become a writer. After his family lost their fortune in 1903, he found it necessary to become a teacher to support his wife and children. To add to his income, he began to write prolifically. From 1916 to 1924, he wrote twenty-eight works for the theater. His plays, including Six Characters in Search of an Author *(1921), have had a profound influence on modern drama. In 1926, he established his own touring theater company. In 1934, he was awarded the Nobel Prize for Literature.*

THE CONTEXT OF THE STORY

The story takes place on a train in Italy during World War I (1914–1918). Italy entered the war in 1915.

The passengers who had left Rome by the night express had had to stop until dawn at the small station of Fabriano in order to continue their journey by the small old-fashioned local joining the main line with Sulmona.

At dawn, in a stuffy and smoky second-class carriage in which five people had already spent the night, a bulky woman in deep mourning was hoisted in—almost like a shapeless bundle. Behind her, puffing and moaning, followed her husband—a tiny man, thin and weakly, his face death-white, his eyes small and bright and looking shy and uneasy.

Having at last taken a seat he politely thanked the passengers who had helped his wife and who had made room for her; then he turned round to the woman trying to pull down the collar of her coat, and politely inquired:

"Are you all right, dear?"

The wife, instead of answering, pulled up her collar again to her eyes, so as to hide her face.

"Nasty world," muttered the husband with a sad smile.

And he felt it his duty to explain to his traveling companions that the poor woman was to be pitied, for the war was taking away from her her only son, a boy of twenty to whom both had devoted their entire life, even breaking up their home at Sulmona to follow him to Rome, where he had to go as a student, then allowing him to volunteer for war with an assurance, however, that at least for six months he would not be sent to the front and now, all of a sudden, receiving a wire saying that he was due to leave in three days' time and asking them to go and see him off.

Translated by Michele Pettinati.

The woman under the big coat was twisting and wriggling, at times growling like a wild animal, feeling certain that all those explanations would not have aroused even a shadow of sympathy from those people who—most likely—were in the same plight as herself. One of them, who had been listening with particular attention, said:

"You should thank God that your son is only leaving now for the front. Mine has been sent there the first day of the war. He has already come back twice wounded and been sent back again to the front."

"What about me? I have two sons and three nephews at the front," said another passenger.

"Maybe, but in our case it is our *only* son," ventured the husband.

"What difference can it make? You may spoil your only son with excessive attentions, but you cannot love him more than you would all your other children if you had any. Paternal love is not like bread that can be broken into pieces and split amongst the children in equal shares. A father gives *all* his love to each one of his children without discrimination, whether it be one or ten, and if I am suffering now for my two sons, I am not suffering half for each of them but double . . ."

"True . . . true . . ." sighed the embarrassed husband, "but suppose (of course we all hope it will never be your case) a father has two sons at the front and he loses one of them, there is still one left to console him . . . while . . ."

"Yes," answered the other, getting cross, "a son left to console him but also a son left for whom he must survive, while in the case of the father of an only son if the son dies the father can die too and put an end to his distress. Which of the two positions is the worse? Don't you see how my case would be worse than yours?"

"Nonsense," interrupted another traveler, a fat, red-faced man with bloodshot eyes of the palest gray.

He was panting. From his bulging eyes seemed to spurt inner violence of an uncontrolled vitality which his weakened body could hardly contain.

"Nonsense," he repeated, trying to cover his mouth with his hand so as to hide the two missing front teeth. "Nonsense. Do we give life to our children for our own benefit?"

The other travelers stared at him in distress. The one who had had his son at the front since the first day of the war sighed: "You are right. Our children do not belong to us, they belong to the Country. . . ."

"Bosh," retorted the fat traveler. "Do we think of the Country when we give life to our children? Our sons are born because . . . well, because they must be born and when they come to life they take our own life with them. This is the truth. We belong to them but they never belong to us. And when they reach twenty they are exactly what we were at their age. We too had a father and mother, but there were so many other things as well . . . girls, cigarettes, illusions, new ties . . . and the Country, of course, whose call we would have answered—when we were twenty—even if father and mother had said no. Now at our age, the love of our Country is still great, of course, but stronger than it is the love for our children. Is there any one of us here who wouldn't gladly take his son's place at the front if he could?"

There was a silence all around, everybody nodding as to approve.

"Why then," continued the fat man, "shouldn't we consider the feelings of our children when they are twenty? Isn't it natural that at their age they should consider the love for their Country (I am speaking of decent boys, of course) even greater than the love for us? Isn't it natural that it should be so, as after all they must look upon us as upon old boys who cannot move any more and must stay at home? If Country exists, if Country is a natural necessity, like bread, of which each of us must eat in order not to die of hunger, somebody must go to defend it. And our sons go, when they are twenty, and they don't want tears, because if they die, they die inflamed and happy (I am speaking, of course, of decent boys). Now, if one dies young and happy, without having the ugly sides of life, the boredom of it, the pettiness, the bitterness of disillusion . . . what more can we ask for him? Everyone should stop crying; everyone should laugh, as I do . . . or at least thank God—as I do—because my son, before dying, sent me a message saying that he was dying satisfied at having ended his life in the best way he could have wished. That is why, as you see, I do not even wear mourning. . . ."

He shook his light fawn coat as to show it; his livid lip over his missing teeth was trembling, his eyes were watery and motionless, and soon after he ended with a shrill laugh which might well have been a sob.

"Quite so . . . quite so . . ." agreed the others.

The woman who, bundled in a corner under her coat, had been sitting and listening had—for the last three months—tried to find in the words of her husband and her friends something to console her in her deep sorrow, something that might show her how a mother should resign herself to send her son not even to death but to a probably dangerous life. Yet not a word had she found amongst the many which had been said . . . and her grief had been greater in seeing that nobody—as she thought—could share her feelings.

But now the words of the traveler amazed and almost stunned her. She suddenly realized that it wasn't the others who were wrong and could not understand her but herself who could not rise up to the same height of those fathers and mothers willing to resign themselves, without crying, not only to the departure of their sons but even to their death.

She lifted her head, she bent over from her corner trying to listen with great attention to the details which the fat man was giving to his companions about the way his son had fallen as a hero, for his King and his Country, happy and without regrets. It seemed to her that she had stumbled into a world she had never dreamt of, a world so far unknown to her and she was so pleased to hear everyone joining in congratulating that brave father who could so stoically speak of his child's death.

Then suddenly, just as if she had heard nothing of what had been said and almost as if waking up from a dream, she turned to the old man, asking him:

"Then . . . is your son really dead?"

Everybody stared at her. The old man, too, turned to look at her, fixing his great, bulging, horribly watery light gray eyes, deep in her face. For some little time he tried to answer, but words failed him. He looked and looked at her, almost as if only then—at that silly, incongruous question—he had suddenly realized at last that his son was really dead—gone for ever—for ever. His face contracted, became horribly distorted, then he snatched in haste a handkerchief from his pocket and, to the amazement of everyone, broke into harrowing, heart-rending, uncontrollable sobs.

The Egg
Sherwood Anderson   United States, 1920

ABOUT THE AUTHOR

*Sherwood Anderson (1876–1941) was born in the United States, in
Ohio. He quit high school before graduation, partly because of his need to
keep several jobs to help support his family. Anderson worked as an adver-
tising copywriter for twelve years until he published his first novel at the
age of forty. He won literary acclaim in 1919 when* Winesburg, Ohio
was published. His other works include Death in the Woods and Other
Stories *(1933). Anderson's writing influenced numerous American
writers.*

THE CONTEXT OF THE STORY

*The story takes place in Ohio at a time when that area of the country was
being transformed from a largely agricultural to an industrial society.*

My father was, I am sure, intended by nature to be a cheerful, kindly
man. Until he was thirty-four years old he worked as a farm-hand for a man
named Thomas Butterworth whose place lay near the town of Bidwell,
Ohio. He had then a horse of his own and on Saturday evenings drove into
town to spend a few hours in social intercourse with other farm-hands. In
town he drank several glasses of beer and stood about in Ben Head's saloon—crowded on Saturday evenings with visiting farmhands. Songs were
sung and glasses thumped on the bar. At ten o'clock father drove home
along a lonely country road, made his horse comfortable for the night and
himself went to bed, quite happy in his position in life. He had at that time
no notion of trying to rise in the world.

It was in the spring of his thirty-fifth year that father married my
mother, then a country school-teacher, and in the following spring I came
wriggling and crying into the world. Something happened to the two people. They became ambitious. The American passion for getting up in the
world took possession of them.

It may have been that mother was responsible. Being a school-teacher
she had no doubt read books and magazines. She had, I presume, read of
how Garfield,[1] Lincoln,[2] and other Americans rose from poverty to fame
and greatness and as I lay beside her—in the days of her lying-in—she may
have dreamed that I would some day rule men and cities. At any rate she
induced father to give up his place as a farm-hand, sell his horse and embark
on an independent enterprise of his own. She was a tall silent woman with a

---

[1] **James Garfield (1831–81):** twentieth president of the United States (1881); assassinated
[2] **Abraham Lincoln (1809–65):** sixteenth president of the United States (1861–1865); assassinated

long nose and troubled grey eyes. For herself she wanted nothing. For father and myself she was incurably ambitious.

The first venture into which the two people went turned out badly. They rented ten acres of poor stony land on Grigg's Road, eight miles from Bidwell, and launched into chicken raising. I grew into boyhood on the place and got my first impressions of life there. From the beginning they were impressions of disaster and if, in my turn, I am a gloomy man inclined to see the darker side of life, I attribute it to the fact that what should have been for me the happy joyous days of childhood were spent on a chicken farm.

One unversed in such matters can have no notion of the many and tragic things that can happen to a chicken. It is born out of an egg, lives for a few weeks as a tiny fluffy thing such as you will see pictured on Easter cards, then becomes hideously naked, eats quantities of corn and meal bought by the sweat of your father's brow, gets diseases called pip, cholera, and other names, stands looking with stupid eyes at the sun, becomes sick and dies. A few hens and now and then a rooster, intended to serve God's mysterious ends, struggle through to maturity. The hens lay eggs out of which come other chickens and the dreadful cycle is thus made complete. It is all unbelievably complex. Most philosophers must have been raised on chicken farms. One hopes for so much from a chicken and is so dreadfully disillusioned. Small chickens, just setting out on the journey of life, look so bright and alert and they are in fact so dreadfully stupid. They are so much like people they mix one up in one's judgments of life. If disease does not kill them they wait until your expectations are thoroughly aroused and then walk under the wheels of a wagon—to go squashed and dead back to their maker. Vermin infest their youth, and fortunes must be spent for curative powders. In later life I have seen how a literature has been built up on the subject of fortunes to be made out of the raising of chickens. It is intended to be read by the gods who have just eaten of the tree of the knowledge of good and evil.[3] It is a hopeful literature and declares that much may be done by simple ambitious people who own a few hens. Do not be led astray by it. It was not written for you. Go hunt for gold on the frozen hills of Alaska, put your faith in the honesty of a politician, believe if you will that the world is daily growing better and that good will triumph over evil, but do not read and believe the literature that is written concerning the hen. It was not written for you.

I, however, digress. My tale does not primarily concern itself with the hen. If correctly told it will centre on the egg. For ten years my father and mother struggled to make our chicken farm pay and then they gave up that struggle and began another. They moved into the town of Bidwell, Ohio and embarked in the restaurant business. After ten years of worry with incubators that did not hatch, and with tiny—and in their own way lovely—

---

[3] **tree of the knowledge of good and evil:** the biblical tree from which Adam and Eve gained knowledge after eating a forbidden apple

balls of fluff that passed on into semi-naked pullethood and from that into dead henhood, we threw all aside and packing our belongings on a wagon drove down Grigg's Road toward Bidwell, a tiny caravan of hope looking for a new place from which to start on our upward journey through life.

We must have been a sad-looking lot, not, I fancy, unlike refugees flee-ing from a battlefield. Mother and I walked in the road. The wagon that contained our goods had been borrowed for the day from Mr. Albert Griggs, a neighbor. Out of its sides stuck the legs of cheap chairs and at the back of the pile of beds, tables, and boxes filled with kitchen utensils was a crate of live chickens, and on top of that the baby carriage in which I had been wheeled about in my infancy. Why we stuck to the baby carriage I don't know. It was unlikely other children would be born and the wheels were broken. People who have few possessions cling tightly to those they have. That is one of the facts that make life so discouraging.

Father rode on top of the wagon. He was then a bald-headed man of forty-five, a little fat and from long association with mother and the chickens he had become habitually silent and discouraged. All during our ten years on the chicken farm he had worked as a laborer on neighboring farms and most of the money he had earned had been spent for remedies to cure chicken diseases, on Wilmer's White Wonder Cholera Cure or Pro-fessor Bidlow's Egg Producer or some other preparations that mother found advertised in the poultry papers. There were two little patches of hair on father's head just above his ears. I remember that as a child I used to sit looking at him when he had gone to sleep in a chair before the stove on Sunday afternoons in the winter. I had at that time already begun to read books and have notions of my own and the bald path that led over the top of his head was, I fancied, something like a broad road, such a road as Caesar might have made on which to lead his legions out of Rome and into the wonders of an unknown world. The tufts of hair that grew above fa-ther's ears were, I thought, like forests. I fell into a half-sleeping, half-waking state and dreamed I was a tiny thing going along the road into a far beautiful place where there were no chicken farms and where life was a happy eggless affair.

One might write a book concerning our flight from the chicken farm into town. Mother and I walked the entire eight miles—she to be sure that nothing fell from the wagon and I to see the wonders of the world. On the seat of the wagon beside father was his greatest treasure. I will tell you of that.

On a chicken farm where hundreds and even thousands of chickens come out of eggs, surprising things sometimes happen. Grotesques are born out of eggs as out of people. The accident does not often occur—perhaps once in a thousand births. A chicken is, you see, born that has four legs, two pairs of wings, two heads or what not. The things do not live. They go quickly back to the hand of their maker that has for a moment trembled. The fact that the poor little things could not live was one of the tragedies of life to father. He had some sort of notion that if he could but bring into henhood or roosterhood a five-legged hen or a two-headed rooster his fortune would be made. He dreamed of taking the wonder about to county fairs and of growing rich by exhibiting it to other farm-hands.

At any rate he saved all the little monstrous things that had been born on our chicken farm. They were preserved in alcohol and put each in its own glass bottle. These he had carefully put into a box and on our journey into town it was carried on the wagon seat beside him. He drove the horses with one hand and with the other clung to the box. When we got to our destination the box was taken down at once and the bottles removed. All during our days as keepers of a restaurant in the town of Bidwell, Ohio, the grotesques in their little glass bottles sat on a shelf back of the counter. Mother sometimes protested but father was a rock on the subject of his treasure. The grotesques were, he declared, valuable. People, he said, liked to look at strange and wonderful things.

Did I say that we embarked in the restaurant business in the town of Bidwell, Ohio? I exaggerated a little. The town itself lay at the foot of a low hill and on the shore of a small river. The railroad did not run through the town and the station was a mile away to the north at a place called Pickleville. There had been a cider mill and pickle factory at the station, but before the time of our coming they had both gone out of business. In the morning and in the evening busses came down to the station along a road called Turner's Pike from the hotel on the main street of Bidwell. Our going to the out-of-the-way place to embark in the restaurant business was mother's idea. She talked of it for a year and then one day went off and rented an empty store building opposite the railroad station. It was her idea that the restaurant would be profitable. Travelling men, she said, would be always waiting around to take trains out of town and town people would come to the station to await incoming trains. They would come to the restaurant to buy pieces of pie and drink coffee. Now that I am older I know that she had another motive in going. She was ambitious for me. She wanted me to rise in the world, to get into a town school and become a man of the towns.

At Pickleville father and mother worked hard as they always had done. At first there was the necessity of putting our place into shape to be a restaurant. That took a month. Father built a shelf on which he put tins of vegetables. He painted a sign on which he put his name in large red letters. Below his name was the sharp command—"EAT HERE"—that was so seldom obeyed. A showcase was brought and filled with cigars and tobacco. Mother scrubbed the floor and the walls of the room. I went to school in the town and was glad to be away from the farm and from the presence of the discouraged, sad-looking chickens. Still I was not very joyous. In the evening I walked home from school along Turner's Pike and remembered the children I had seen playing in the town school yard. A troop of little girls had gone hopping about and singing. I tried that. Down along the frozen road I went hopping solemnly on one leg. "Hippity Hop To The Barber Shop," I sang shrilly. Then I stopped and looked doubtfully about. I was afraid of being seen in my gay mood. It must have seemed to me that I was doing a thing that should not be done by one who, like myself, had been raised on a chicken farm where death was a daily visitor.

Mother decided that our restaurant should remain open at night. At ten in the evening a passenger train went north past our door followed by a local freight. The freight crew had switching to do in Pickleville and when the work was done they came to our restaurant for hot coffee and food. Sometimes one of them ordered a fried egg. In the morning at four they returned north-bound and again visited us. A little trade began to grow up. Mother slept at night and during the day tended the restaurant and fed our boarders while father slept. He slept in the same bed mother had occupied during the night and I went off to the town of Bidwell and to school. During the long nights, while mother and I slept, father cooked meats that were to go into sandwiches for the lunch baskets of our boarders. Then an idea in regard to getting up in the world came into his head. The American spirit took hold of him. He also became ambitious.

In the long nights when there was little to do father had time to think. That was his undoing. He decided that he had in the past been an unsuccessful man because he had not been cheerful enough and that in the future he would adopt a cheerful outlook on life. In the early morning he came upstairs and got into bed with mother. She woke and the two talked. From my bed in the corner I listened.

It was father's idea that both he and mother should try to entertain the people who came to eat at our restaurant. I cannot now remember his words, but he gave the impression of one about to become in some obscure way a kind of public entertainer. When people, particularly young people from the town of Bidwell, came into our place, as on very rare occasions they did, bright entertaining conversation was to be made. From father's words I gathered that something of the jolly inn-keeper effect was to be sought. Mother must have been doubtful from the first, but she said nothing discouraging it. It was father's notion that a passion for the company of himself and mother would spring up in the breasts of the younger people of the town of Bidwell. In the evening bright happy groups would come singing down Turner's Pike. They would troop shouting with joy and laughter into our place. There would be song and festivity. I do not mean to give the impression that father spoke so elaborately of the matter. He was as I have said an uncommunicative man. "They want some place to go. I tell you they want some place to go," he said over and over. That was as far as he got. My own imagination has filled in the blanks.

For two or three weeks this notion of father's invaded our house. We did not talk much, but in our daily lives tried earnestly to make smiles take the place of glum looks. Mother smiled at the boarders and I, catching the infection, smiled at our cat. Father became a little feverish in his anxiety to please. There was no doubt, lurking somewhere in him, a touch of the spirit of the showman. He did not waste much of his ammunition on the railroad men he served at night but seemed to be waiting for a young man or woman from Bidwell to come in to show what he could do. On the counter in the restaurant there was a wire basket kept always filled with eggs, and it must have been before his eyes when the idea of being entertaining was born in his brain. There was something pre-natal about the way eggs kept themselves connected with the development of his idea. At any rate an egg ruined his new impulse in life. Late one night I was awakened by a roar of anger coming from father's throat. Both mother and I sat upright in our beds. With trembling hands she lighted a lamp that stood on a table by her head. Downstairs the front door of our restaurant went shut with a bang and in a few minutes father tramped up the stairs. He held an egg in his hand and his hand trembled as though he were having a chill. There was a half insane light in his eyes. As he stood glaring at us I was sure he intended throwing the egg at either mother or me. Then he laid it gently on the table beside the lamp and dropped on his knees beside mother's bed. He began to cry like a boy and I, carried away by his grief, cried with him. The two of us filled the little upstairs room with our wailing voices. It is ridiculous, but of the picture we made I can remember only the fact that mother's hand continually stroked the bald patch that ran across the top of his head. I have forgotten what mother said to him and how she induced him to tell her of what had happened downstairs. His explanation also has gone out of my mind. I remember only my own grief and fright and the shiny path over father's head glowing in the lamp light as he knelt by the bed.

As to what happened downstairs. For some unexplainable reason I know the story as well as though I had been a witness to my father's discomfiture. One in time gets to know many unexplainable things. On that evening young Joe Kane, son of a merchant of Bidwell, came to Pickleville to meet his father, who was expected on the ten o'clock evening train from the South. The train was three hours late and Joe came into our place to loaf about and to wait for its arrival. The local freight train came in and the freight crew were fed. Joe was left alone in the restaurant with father.

From the moment he came into our place the Bidwell young man must have been puzzled by my father's actions. It was his notion that father was angry at him for hanging around. He noticed that the restaurant keeper was apparently disturbed by his presence and he thought of going out. However, it began to rain and he did not fancy the long walk to town and back. He bought a five-cent cigar and ordered a cup of coffee. He had a newspaper in his pocket and took it out and began to read. "I'm waiting for the evening train. It's late," he said apologetically.

For a long time father, whom Joe Kane had never seen before, remained silently gazing at his visitor. He was no doubt suffering an attack of stage fright. As so often happens in life he had thought so much and so often of the situation that now confronted him that he was somewhat nervous in its presence.

For one thing, he did not know what to do with his hands. He thrust one of them nervously over the counter and shook hands with Joe Kane. "How-de-do," he said. Joe Kane put his newspaper down and stared at him.

Father's eyes lighted on the basket of eggs that sat on the counter and he began to talk. "Well," he began hesitatingly, "well, you have heard of Christopher Columbus, eh?" He seemed to be angry. "That Christopher Columbus was a cheat," he declared emphatically. "He talked of making an egg stand on its end. He talked, he did and then he went and broke the end of the egg."

My father seemed to his visitor to be beside himself at the duplicity of Christopher Columbus. He muttered and swore. He declared it was wrong to teach children that Christopher Columbus was a great man when, after all, he cheated at the critical moment. He had declared he would make an egg stand on end and then when his bluff had been called he had done a trick. Still grumbling at Columbus, father took an egg from the basket on the counter and began to walk up and down. He rolled the egg between the palms of his hands. He smiled genially. He began to mumble words regarding the effect to be produced on an egg by the electricity that comes out of the human body. He declared that without breaking its shell and by virtue of rolling it back and forth in his hands he could stand the egg on its end. He explained that the warmth of his hands and the gentle rolling movement he gave the egg created a new centre of gravity, and Joe Kane was mildly interested. "I have handled thousands of eggs," father said. "No one knows more about eggs than I do."

He stood the egg on the counter and it fell on its side. He tried the trick again and again, each time rolling the egg between the palms of his hands and saying the words regarding the wonders of electricity and the laws of gravity. When after a half hour's effort he did succeed in making the egg stand for a moment he looked up to find that his visitor was no longer watching. By the time he had succeeded in calling Joe Kane's attention to the success of his effort the egg had again rolled over and lay on its side.

Afire with the showman's passion and at the same time a good deal disconcerted by the failure of his first effort, father now took the bottles containing the poultry monstrosities down from their place on the shelf and began to show them to his visitor. "How would you like to have seven legs and two heads like this fellow?" he asked, exhibiting the most remarkable of his treasures. A cheerful smile played over his face. He reached over the counter and tried to slap Joe Kane on the shoulder as he had seen men do in Ben Head's saloon when he was a young farmhand and drove to town on Saturday evenings. His visitor was made a little ill by the sight of the body of the terribly deformed bird floating in the alcohol in the bottle and got up to go. Coming from behind the counter father took hold of the young man's arm and led him back to his seat. He grew a little angry and for a moment had to turn his face away and force himself to smile. Then he put the bottles back on the shelf. In an outburst of generosity he fairly compelled Joe Kane to have a fresh cup of coffee and another cigar at his expense. Then he took a pan and filling it with vinegar, taken from a jug that sat beneath the counter, he declared himself about to do a new trick. "I will heat this egg in this pan of vinegar," he said. "Then I will put it through the neck of a bottle without breaking the shell. When the egg is inside the bottle it will resume its normal shape and the shell will become hard again. Then I will give the bottle with the egg in it to you. You can take it about with you wherever you go. People will want to know how you got the egg in the bottle. Don't tell them. Keep them guessing. This is the way to have fun with this trick."

Father grinned and winked at his visitor. Joe Kane decided that the man who confronted him was mildly insane but harmless. He drank the cup of coffee that had been given him and began to read his paper again. When the egg had been heated in vinegar father carried it on a spoon to the counter and going into a back room got an empty bottle. He was angry because his visitor did not watch him as he began to do his trick, but nevertheless went cheerfully to work. For a long time he struggled, trying to get the egg to go through the neck of the bottle. He put the pan of vinegar back on the stove, intending to reheat the egg, then picked it up and burned his fingers. After a second bath in the hot vinegar the shell of the egg had been softened a little but not enough for his purpose. He worked and worked and a spirit of desperate determination took possession of him. When he thought that at last the trick was about to be consummated the delayed train came in at the station and Joe Kane started to go nonchalantly out at the door. Father made a last desperate effort to conquer the egg and make it do the things that would establish his reputation as one who knew how to entertain guests who came into his restaurant. He worried the egg. He attempted to be somewhat rough with it. He swore and the sweat stood out on his forehead. The egg broke under his hand. When the contents spurted over his clothes, Joe Kane, who had stopped at the door, turned and laughed.

A roar of anger rose from my father's throat. He danced and shouted a string of inarticulate words. Grabbing another egg from the basket on the counter, he threw it, just missing the head of the young man as he dodged through the door and escaped.

Father came upstairs to mother and me with an egg in his hand. I do not know what he intended to do. I imagine he had some idea of destroying it, of destroying all eggs, and that he intended to let mother and me see him begin. When, however, he got into the presence of mother something happened to him. He laid the egg gently on the table and dropped to his knees by the bed as I have already explained. He later decided to close the restaurant for the night and to come upstairs and get into bed. When he did so he blew out the light and after much muttered conversation both he and mother went to sleep. I suppose I went to sleep also, but my sleep was troubled. I awoke at dawn and for a long time looked at the egg that lay on the table. I wondered why eggs had to be and why from the egg came the hen who again laid the egg. The question got into my blood. It has stayed there, I imagine, because I am the son of my father. At any rate, the problem remains unsolved in my mind. And that, I conclude, is but another evidence of the complete and final triumph of the egg—at least as far as my family is concerned.

Babylon Revisited
F. Scott Fitzgerald   United States, 1931

ABOUT THE AUTHOR

F. Scott Fitzgerald (1896–1940) was born in the United States, in Minnesota. He began to write fiction and poetry while a student at Princeton University. In 1920, when his first novel, This Side of Paradise, *was published, he became instantly famous. His early stories established him as the spokesperson for the decade of the 1920s, known as the "Jazz Age," a time of relative prosperity for the United States. His most famous work is the novel* The Great Gatsby *(1925).*

THE CONTEXT OF THE STORY

The story takes place in Paris in 1931. During the 1920s, many Americans had become wealthy through investments in the stock market; and Paris had been a favorite playground for the rich. But in 1929, the stock market collapsed, leaving many of these Americans poor or even penniless. The crash of the stock market ushered in worldwide economic depression.

References to the financial world include bull market *(period of optimism in the stock market when prices rose);* the boom *(time of prosperity); and* selling short *(not owning the stocks or commodities one is selling).*

THE TITLE

Fitzgerald draws on a biblical source for his title. The Old Testament city of Babylon was well known for its luxurious and often immoral way of life.

I

"And where's Mr. Campbell?" Charlie asked.

"Gone to Switzerland. Mr. Campbell's a pretty sick man, Mr. Wales."

"I'm sorry to hear that. And George Hardt?" Charlie inquired.

"Back in America, gone to work."

"And where is the Snow Bird?"

"He was in here last week. Anyway, his friend, Mr. Schaeffer, is in Paris."

Two familiar names from the long list of a year and a half ago. Charlie scribbled an address in his notebook and tore out the page.

"If you see Mr. Schaeffer, give him this," he said. "It's my brother-in-law's address. I haven't settled on a hotel yet."

He was not really disappointed to find Paris was so empty. But the stillness in the Ritz bar was strange and portentous. It was not an American bar any more—he felt polite in it, and not as if he owned it. It had gone back into France. He felt the stillness from the moment he got out of the taxi and saw the doorman, usually in a frenzy of activity at this hour, gossiping with a *chasseur*[1] by the servants' entrance.

Passing through the corridor, he heard only a single, bored voice in the once-clamorous women's room. When he turned into the bar he traveled the twenty feet of green carpet with his eyes fixed straight ahead by old habit; and then, with his foot firmly on the rail, he turned and surveyed the room, encountering only a single pair of eyes that fluttered up from a newspaper in the corner. Charlie asked for the head barman, Paul, who in the latter days of the bull market had come to work in his own custom-built car—disembarking, however, with due nicety at the nearest corner. But Paul was at his country house today and Alix giving him information.

"No, no more," Charlie said, "I'm going slow these days."

Alix congratulated him: "You were going pretty strong a couple of years ago."

"I'll stick to it all right," Charlie assured him. "I've stuck to it for over a year and a half now."

"How do you find conditions in America?"

"I haven't been to America for months. I'm in business in Prague, representing a couple of concerns there. They don't know about me down there."

Alix smiled.

"Remember the night of George Hardt's bachelor dinner here?" said Charlie. "By the way, what's become of Claude Fessenden?"

Alix lowered his voice confidentially: "He's in Paris, but he doesn't come here any more. Paul doesn't allow it. He ran up a bill of thirty thousand francs, charging all his drinks and his lunches, and usually his dinner, for more than a year. And when Paul finally told him he had to pay, he gave him a bad check."

Alix shook his head sadly.

"I don't understand it, such a dandy fellow. Now he's all bloated up—" He made a plump apple of his hands.

Charlie watched a group of strident queens installing themselves in a corner.

"Nothing affects them," he thought. "Stocks rise and fall, people loaf or work, but they go on forever." The place oppressed him. He called for the dice and shook with Alix for the drink.

"Here for long, Mr. Wales?"

"I'm here for four or five days to see my little girl."

"Oh-h! You have a little girl?"

Outside, the fire-red, gas-blue, ghost-green signs shone smokily through the tranquil rain. It was late afternoon and the streets were in movement; the *bistros*[2] gleamed. At the corner of the Boulevard des Ca-

---

[1] *chasseur:* bellhop
[2] *bistros:* small bars, taverns, or nightclubs

pucines he took a taxi. The Place de la Concorde moved by in pink majesty; they crossed the logical Seine, and Charlie felt the sudden provincial quality of the Left Bank.

Charlie directed his taxi to the Avenue de l'Opera, which was out of his way. But he wanted to see the blue hour spread over the magnificent façade, and imagine that the cab horns, playing endlessly the first few bars of *La Plus que Lente*, were the trumpets of the Second Empire.[3] They were closing the iron grill in front of Brentano's Book-store, and people were already at dinner behind the trim little bourgeois hedge of Duval's. He had never eaten at a really cheap restaurant in Paris. Five-course dinner, four francs fifty, eighteen cents, wine included. For some odd reason he wished that he had.

As they rolled on to the Left Bank and he felt its sudden provincialism, he thought, "I spoiled this city for myself. I didn't realize it, but the days came along one after another, and then two years were gone, and everything was gone, and I was gone."

He was thirty-five, and good to look at. The Irish mobility of his face was sobered by a deep wrinkle between his eyes. As he rang his brother-in-law's bell in the Rue Palatine, the wrinkle deepened till it pulled down his brows; he felt a cramping sensation in his belly. From behind the maid who opened the door darted a lovely little girl of nine who shrieked "Daddy!" and flew up, struggling like a fish, into his arms. She pulled his head around by one ear and set her cheek against his.

"My old pie," he said.

"Oh, daddy, daddy, daddy, daddy, dads, dads, dads!"

She drew him into the salon, where the family waited, a boy and a girl his daughter's age, his sister-in-law and her husband. He greeted Marion with his voice pitched carefully to avoid either feigned enthusiasm or dislike, but her response was more frankly tepid, though she minimized her expression of unalterable distrust by directing her regard toward his child. The two man clasped hands in a friendly way and Lincoln Peters rested his for a moment on Charlie's shoulder.

The room was warm and comfortably American. The three children moved intimately about, playing through the yellow oblongs that led to other rooms; the cheer of six o'clock spoke in the eager smacks of the fire and the sounds of French activity in the kitchen. But Charlie did not relax; his heart sat up rigidly in his body and he drew confidence from his daughter, who from time to time came close to him, holding in her arms the doll he had brought.

"Really extremely well," he declared in answer to Lincoln's question. "There's a lot of business there that isn't moving at all, but we're doing even better than ever. In fact, damn well. I'm bringing my sister over from America next month to keep house for me. My income last year was bigger than it was when I had money. You see, the Czechs—"

[3] **Second Empire:** period of rule under Napoleon III, 1852–70

His boasting was for a specific purpose; but after a moment, seeing a faint restiveness in Lincoln's eye, he changed the subject:

"Those are fine children of yours, well brought up, good manners."

"We think Honoria's a great little girl too."

Marion Peters came back from the kitchen. She was a tall woman with worried eyes, who had once possessed a fresh American loveliness. Charlie had never been sensitive to it and was always surprised when people spoke of how pretty she had been. From the first there had been an instinctive antipathy between them.

"Well, how do you find Honoria?" she asked.

"Wonderful. I was astonished how much she's grown in ten months. All the children are looking well."

"We haven't had a doctor for a year. How do you like being back in Paris?"

"It seems very funny to see so few Americans around."

"I'm delighted," Marion said vehemently. "Now at least you can go into a store without their assuming you're a millionaire. We've suffered like everybody, but on the whole it's a good deal pleasanter."

"But it was nice while it lasted," Charlie said. "We were a sort of royalty, almost infallible, with a sort of magic around us. In the bar this afternoon"—he stumbled, seeing his mistake—"there wasn't a man I knew."

She looked at him keenly. "I should think you'd have had enough of bars."

"I only stayed a minute. I take one drink every afternoon, and no more."

"Don't you want a cocktail before dinner?" Lincoln asked.

"I take only one drink every afternoon, and I've had that."

"I hope you keep to it," said Marion.

Her dislike was evident in the coldness with which she spoke, but Charlie only smiled; he had larger plans. Her very aggressiveness gave him an advantage, and he knew enough to wait. He wanted them to initiate the discussion of what they knew had brought him to Paris.

At dinner he couldn't decide whether Honoria was most like him or her mother. Fortunate if she didn't combine the traits of both that had brought them to disaster. A great wave of protectiveness went over him. He thought he knew what to do for her. He believed in character; he wanted to jump back a whole generation and trust in character again as the eternally valuable element. Everything else wore out.

He left soon after dinner, but not to go home. He was curious to see Paris by night with clearer and more judicious eyes than those of other days. He bought a *strapontin*[4] for the Casino and watched Josephine Baker[5] go through her chocolate arabesques.

After an hour he left and strolled toward Montmartre, up the Rue Pi-

---

[4] *strapontin:* inexpensive seat
[5] **Josephine Baker:** a well-known dancer of African-American descent

galle into the Place Blanche. The rain had stopped and there were a few
people in evening clothes disembarking from taxis in front of cabarets, and
cocottes[6] prowling singly or in pairs, and many Negroes. He passed a lighted
door from which issued music, and stopped with the sense of familiarity; it
was Bricktop's, where he had parted with so many hours and so much
money. A few doors farther on he found another ancient rendezvous and
incautiously put his head inside. Immediately an eager orchestra burst into
sound, a pair of professional dancers leaped to their feet and a maître d'hôtel[7] swooped toward him, crying, "Crowd just arriving, sir!" But he with-
drew quickly.

"You have to be damn drunk," he thought.

Zelli's was closed, the bleak and sinister cheap hotels surrounding it
were dark; up in the Rue Blanche there was more light and a local, colloquial French crowd. The Poet's Cave had disappeared, but the two great
mouths of the Café of Heaven and the Café of Hell still yawned—even
devoured, as he watched, the meager contents of a tourist bus—a German,
a Japanese, and an American couple who glanced at him with frightened
eyes.

So much for the effort and ingenuity of Montmartre. All the catering to
vice and waste was on an utterly childish scale, and he suddenly realized the
meaning of the word "dissipate"—to dissipate into thin air; to make nothing out of something. In the little hours of the night every move from place
to place was an enormous human jump, an increase of paying for the privilege of slower and slower motion.

He remembered thousand-franc notes given to an orchestra for playing
a single number, hundred-franc notes tossed to a doorman for calling a cab.

But it hadn't been given for nothing.

It had been given, even the most wildly squandered sum, as an offering
to destiny that he might not remember the things most worth remembering, the things that now he would always remember—his child taken from
his control, his wife escaped to a grave in Vermont.

In the glare of a *brasserie*[8] a woman spoke to him. He bought her some
eggs and coffee, and then, eluding her encouraging stare, gave her a twenty-
franc note and took a taxi to his hotel.

II

He woke upon a fine fall day—football weather. The depression of
yesterday was gone and he liked the people on the streets. At noon he sat
opposite Honoria at Le Grand Vatel, the only restaurant he could think of
not reminiscent of champagne dinners and long luncheons that began at
two and ended in a blurred and vague twilight.

"Now, how about vegetables? Oughtn't you to have some vegetables?"

[6] *cocottes:* prostitutes
[7] **maître de'hôtel:** head waiter
[8] *brasserie:* ale-house; pub

"Well, yes."

"Here's *épinards* and *chou-fleur* and carrots and *haricots.*"[9]

"I'd like *chou-fleur.*"

"Wouldn't you like to have two vegetables?"

"I usually only have one at lunch."

The waiter was pretending to be inordinately fond of children. *"Qu'elle est mignonne la petite! Elle parle exactement comme une Française."*[10]

"How about dessert? Shall we wait and see?"

The waiter disappeared. Honoria looked at her father expectantly.

"What are we going to do?"

"First, we're going to that toy store in the Rue Saint-Honoré and buy you anything you like. And then we're going to the vaudeville at the Empire."

She hesitated. "I like it about the vaudeville, but not the toy store."

"Why not?"

"Well, you brought me this doll." She had it with her. "And I've got lots of things. And we're not rich any more, are we?"

"We never were. But today you are to have anything you want."

"All right," she agreed resignedly.

When there had been her mother and a French nurse he had been inclined to be strict; now he extended himself, reached out for a new tolerance; he must be both parents to her and not shut any of her out of communication.

"I want to get to know you," he said gravely. "First let me introduce myself. My name is Charles J. Wales, of Prague."

"Oh, daddy!" her voice cracked with laughter.

"And who are you, please?" he persisted, and she accepted a rôle immediately: "Honoria Wales, Rue Palatine, Paris."

"Married or single?"

"No, not married. Single."

He indicated the doll. "But I see you have a child, madame."

Unwilling to disinherit it, she took it to her heart and thought quickly: "Yes, I've been married, but I'm not married now. My husband is dead."

He went on quickly, "And the child's name?"

"Simone. That's after my best friend at school."

"I'm very pleased that you're doing so well at school."

"I'm third this month," she boasted. "Elsie"—that was her cousin—"is only about eighteenth, and Richard is at the bottom."

"You like Richard and Elsie, don't you?"

"Oh, yes. I like Richard quite well and I like her all right."

Cautiously and casually he asked: "And Aunt Marion and Uncle Lincoln—which do you like best?"

"Oh, Uncle Lincoln, I guess."

[9] *épinards; chou-fleur; haricots:* spinach; cauliflower; beans
[10] *"Qu'elle . . . Française":* "What a darling little girl! She speaks exactly like a French girl."

He was increasingly aware of her presence. As they came in, a murmur of ". . . adorable" followed them, and now the people at the next table bent all their silences upon her, staring as if she were something no more conscious than a flower.

"Why don't I live with you?" she asked suddenly. "Because mamma's dead?"

"You must stay here and learn more French. It would have been hard for daddy to take care of you so well."

"I don't really need much taking care of any more. I do everything for myself."

Going out of the restaurant, a man and a woman unexpectedly hailed him.

"Well, the old Wales!"

"Hello there, Lorraine. . . . Dunc."

Sudden ghosts out of the past: Duncan Schaeffer, a friend from college. Lorraine Quarrles, a lovely, pale blonde of thirty; one of a crowd who had helped them make months into days in the lavish times of three years ago.

"My husband couldn't come this year," she said, in answer to his question. "We're poor as hell. So he gave me two hundred a month and told me I could do my worst on that. . . . This your little girl?"

"What about coming back and sitting down?" Duncan asked.

"Can't do it." He was glad for an excuse. As always, he felt Lorraine's passionate, provocative attraction, but his own rhythm was different now.

"Well, how about dinner?" she asked.

"I'm not free. Give me your address and let me call you."

"Charlie, I believe you're sober," she said judicially. "I honestly believe he's sober, Dunc. Pinch him and see if he's sober."

Charlie indicated Honoria with his head. They both laughed.

"What's your address?" said Duncan skeptically.

He hesitated, unwilling to give the name of his hotel.

"I'm not settled yet. I'd better call you. We're going to see the vaudeville at the Empire."

"There! That's what I want to do," Lorraine said. "I want to see some clowns and acrobats and jugglers. That's just what we'll do, Dunc."

"We've got to do an errand first," said Charlie. "Perhaps we'll see you there."

"All right, you snob. . . . Good-by, beautiful little girl."

"Good-by."

Honoria bobbed politely.

Somehow, an unwelcome encounter. They liked him because he was functioning, because he was serious; they wanted to see him, because he was stronger than they were now, because they wanted to draw a certain sustenance from his strength.

At the Empire, Honoria proudly refused to sit upon her father's folded coat. She was already an individual with a code of her own, and Charlie was more and more absorbed by the desire of putting a little of himself into her before she crystallized utterly. It was hopeless to try to know her in so short a time.

Between the acts they came upon Duncan and Lorraine in the lobby where the band was playing.

"Have a drink?"

"All right, but not up at the bar. We'll take a table."

"The perfect father."

Listening abstractedly to Lorraine, Charlie watched Honoria's eyes leave their table, and he followed them wistfully about the room, wondering what they saw. He met her glance and she smiled.

"I liked that lemonade," she said.

What had she said? What had he expected? Going home in a taxi afterward, he pulled her over until her head rested against his chest.

"Darling, do you ever think of your mother?"

"Yes, sometimes," she answered vaguely.

"I don't want you to forget her. Have you got a picture of her?"

"Yes, I think so. Anyhow, Aunt Marion has. Why don't you want me to forget her?"

"She loved you very much."

"I loved her too."

They were silent for a moment.

"Daddy, I want to come and live with you," she said suddenly.

His heart leaped; he had wanted it to come like this.

"Aren't you perfectly happy?"

"Yes, but I love you better than anybody. And you love me better than anybody, don't you, now that mummy's dead?"

"Of course I do. But you won't always like me best, honey. You'll grow up and meet somebody your own age and go marry him and forget you ever had a daddy."

"Yet, that's true," she agreed tranquilly.

He didn't go in. He was coming back at nine o'clock and he wanted to keep himself fresh and new for the thing he must say then.

"When you're safe inside, just show yourself in that window."

"All right. Good-by, dads, dads, dads, dads."

He waited in the dark street until she appeared, all warm and glowing, in the window above and kissed her fingers out into the night.

III

They were waiting. Marion sat behind the coffee service in a dignified black dinner dress that just faintly suggested mourning. Lincoln was walking up and down with the animation of one who had already been talking. They were as anxious as he was to get into the question. He opened it almost immediately:

"I suppose you know what I want to see you about—why I really came to Paris."

Marion played with the black stars on her necklace and frowned.

"I'm awfully anxious to have a home," he continued. "And I'm awfully anxious to have Honoria in it. I appreciate your taking in Honoria for her mother's sake, but things have changed now"—he hesitated and then continued more forcibly—"changed radically with me, and I want to ask you to reconsider the matter. It would be silly for me to deny that about three years ago I was acting badly—"

Marion looked up at him with hard eyes.

"—but all that's over. As I told you, I haven't had more than a drink a day for over a year, and I take that drink deliberately, so that the idea of alcohol won't get too big in my imagination. You see the idea?"

"No," said Marion succinctly.

"It's a sort of stunt I set myself. It keeps the matter in proportion."

"I get you," said Lincoln. "You don't want to admit it's got any attraction for you."

"Something like that. Sometimes I forget and don't take it. But I try to take it. Anyhow, I couldn't afford to drink in my position. The people I represent are more than satisfied with what I've done, and I'm bringing my sister over from Burlington to keep house for me, and I want awfully to have Honoria too. You know that even when her mother and I weren't getting along well we never let anything that happened touch Honoria. I know she's fond of me and I know I'm able to take care of her and—well, there you are. How do you feel about it?"

He knew that now he would have to take a beating. It would last an hour or two hours, and it would be difficult, but if he modulated his inevitable resentment to the chastened attitude of the reformed sinner, he might win his point in the end.

Keep your temper, he told himself. You don't want to be justified. You want Honoria.

Lincoln spoke first: "We've been talking it over ever since we got your letter last month. We're happy to have Honoria here. She's a dear little thing, and we're glad to be able to help her, but of course that isn't the question—"

Marion interrupted suddenly. "How long are you going to stay sober, Charlie?" she asked.

"Permanently, I hope."

"How can anybody count on that?"

"You know I never did drink heavily until I gave up business and came over here with nothing to do. Then Helen and I began to run around with—"

"Please leave Helen out of it. I can't bear to hear you talk about her like that."

He stared at her grimly; he had never been certain how fond of each other the sisters were in life.

"My drinking only lasted about a year and a half—from the time we came over until I—collapsed."

"It was time enough."

"It was time enough," he agreed.

"My duty is entirely to Helen," she said. "I try to think what she would have wanted me to do. Frankly, from the night you did that terrible thing you haven't really existed for me. I can't help that. She was my sister."

"Yes."

"When she was dying she asked me to look out for Honoria. If you hadn't been in a sanitarium then, it might have helped matters."

He had no answer.

"I'll never in my life be able to forget the morning when Helen knocked at my door, soaked to the skin and shivering and said you'd locked her out."

Charlie gripped the sides of the chair. This was more difficult than he expected; he wanted to launch out into a long expostulation and explanation, but he only said: "The night I locked her out—" and she interrupted, "I don't feel up to going over that again."

After a moment's silence Lincoln said: "We're getting off the subject. You want Marion to set aside her legal guardianship and give you Honoria. I think the main point for her is whether she has confidence in you or not."

"I don't blame Marion," Charlie said slowly, "but I think she can have entire confidence in me. I had a good record up to three years ago. Of course, it's within human possibilities I might go wrong any time. But if we wait much longer I'll lose Honoria's childhood and my chance for a home." He shook his head, "I'll simply lose her, don't you see?"

"Yes, I see," said Lincoln.

"Why didn't you think of all this before?" Marion asked.

"I suppose I did, from time to time, but Helen and I were getting along badly. When I consented to the guardianship, I was flat on my back in a sanitarium and the market had cleaned me out. I knew I'd acted badly, and I thought if it would bring any peace to Helen, I'd agree to anything. But now it's different. I'm functioning, I'm behaving damn well, so far as—"

"Please don't swear at me," Marion said.

He looked at her, startled. With each remark the force of her dislike became more and more apparent. She had built up all her fear of life into one wall and faced it toward him. This trivial reproof was possibly the result of some trouble with the cook several hours before. Charlie became increasingly alarmed at leaving Honoria in this atmosphere of hostility against himself; sooner or later it would come out, in a word here, a shake of the head there, and some of that distrust would be irrevocably implanted in Honoria. But he pulled his temper down out of his face and shut it up inside him; he had won a point, for Lincoln realized the absurdity of Marion's remark and asked her lightly since when she had objected to the word "damn."

"Another thing," Charlie said: "I'm able to give her certain advantages now. I'm going to take a French governess to Prague with me. I've got a lease on a new apartment—"

He stopped, realizing that he was blundering. They couldn't be expected to accept with equanimity the fact that his income was again twice as large as their own.

"I suppose you can give her more luxuries than we can," said Marion. "When you were throwing away money we were living along watching every ten francs. . . . I suppose you'll start doing it again."

"Oh, no," he said. "I've learned. I worked hard for ten years, you know—until I got lucky in the market, like so many people. Terribly lucky. It won't happen again."

There was a long silence. All of them felt their nerves straining, and for the first time in a year Charlie wanted a drink. He was sure now that Lincoln Peters wanted him to have his child.

Marion shuddered suddenly; part of her saw that Charlie's feet were planted on the earth now, and her own maternal feeling recognized the naturalness of his desire; but she had lived for a long time with a prejudice—a prejudice founded on a curious disbelief in her sister's happiness, and which, in the shock of one terrible night, had turned to hatred for him. It had all happened at a point in her life where the discouragement of ill health and adverse circumstances made it necessary for her to believe in tangible villainy and an tangible villain.

"I can't help what I think!" she cried out suddenly. "How much you were responsible for Helen's death, I don't know. It's something you'll have to square with your own conscience."

An electric current of agony surged through him; for a moment he was almost on his feet, an unuttered sound echoing in his throat. He hung on to himself for a moment, another moment.

"Hold on there," said Lincoln uncomfortably. "I never thought you were responsible for that."

"Helen died of heart trouble," Charlie said dully.

"Yes, heart trouble." Marion spoke as if the phrase had another meaning for her.

Then, in the flatness that followed her outburst, she saw him plainly and she knew he had somehow arrived at control over the situation. Glancing at her husband, she found no help from him, and as abruptly as if it were a matter of no importance, she threw up the sponge.

"Do what you like!" she cried, springing up from her chair. "She's your child. I'm not the person to stand in your way. I think if it were my child I'd rather see her—" She managed to check herself. "You two decide it. I can't stand this. I'm sick. I'm going to bed."

She hurried from the room; after a moment Lincoln said:

"This has been a hard day for her. You know how strongly she feels—" His voice was almost apologetic: "When a woman gets an idea in her head."

"Of course."

"It's going to be all right. I think she sees now that you—can provide for the child, and so we can't very well stand in your way or Honoria's way."

"Thank you, Lincoln."

"I'd better go along and see how she is."

"I'm going."

He was still trembling when he reached the street, but a walk down the Rue Bonaparte to the *quais*[11] set him up, and as he crossed the Seine, fresh and new by the *quai* lamps, he felt exultant. But back in his room he couldn't sleep. The image of Helen haunted him. Helen whom he had loved so until they had senselessly begun to abuse each other's love, tear it into shreds. On that terrible February night that Marion remembered so vividly, a slow quarrel had gone on for hours. There was a scene at the Florida, and then he attempted to take her home, and then she kissed young Webb at a table; after that there was what she had hysterically said. When he arrived home alone he turned the key in the lock in wild anger. How could he know she would arrive an hour later alone, that there would be a snowstorm in which she wandered about in slippers, too confused to find a taxi? Then the aftermath, her escaping pneumonia by a miracle, and all the attendant horror. They were "reconciled," but that was the beginning of the end, and Marion, who had seen with her own eyes and who imagined it to be one of many scenes from her sister's martyrdom, never forgot.

Going over it again brought Helen nearer, and in the white, soft light that steals upon half sleep near morning he found himself talking to her again. She said that he was perfectly right about Honoria and that she wanted Honoria to be with him. She said she was glad he was being good and doing better. She said a lot of other things—very friendly things—but she was in a swing in a white dress, and swinging faster and faster all the time, so that at the end he could not hear clearly all that she said.

IV

He woke up feeling happy. The door of the world was open again. He made plans, vistas, futures for Honoria and himself, but suddenly he grew sad, remembering all the plans he and Helen had made. She had not planned to die. The present was the thing—work to do and someone to love. But not to love too much, for he knew the injury that a father can do to a daughter or a mother to a son by attaching them too closely: afterward, out in the world, the child would seek in the marriage partner the same blind tenderness and, failing probably to find it, turn against love and life.

It was another bright, crisp day. He called Lincoln Peters at the bank where he worked and asked if he could count on taking Honoria when he left for Prague. Lincoln agreed that there was no reason for delay. One thing—the legal guardianship. Marion wanted to retain that a while longer. She was upset by the whole matter, and it would oil things if she felt that the situation was still in her control for another year. Charlie agreed, wanting only the tangible, visible child.

---

[11] *quai:* wharf; embankment along a river

Then the question of a governess. Charles sat in a gloomy agency and talked to a cross Béarnaise and to a buxom Breton peasant, neither of whom he could have endured. There were others whom he would see tomorrow.

He lunched with Lincoln Peters at Griffons, trying to keep down his exultation.

"There's nothing quite like your own child," Lincoln said. "But you understand how Marion feels too."

"She's forgotten how hard I worked for seven years there," Charlie said. "She just remembers one night."

"There's another thing." Lincoln hesitated. "While you and Helen were tearing around Europe throwing money away, we were just getting along. I didn't touch any of the prosperity because I never got ahead enough to carry anything but my insurance. I think Marion felt there was some kind of injustice in it—you not even working toward the end, and getting richer and richer."

"It went just as quick as it came," said Charlie.

"Yes, a lot of it stayed in the hands of *chasseurs* and saxophone players and maîtres d'hôtel—well, the big party's over now. I just said that to explain Marion's feeling about those crazy years. If you drop in about six o'clock tonight before Marion's too tired, we'll settle the details on the spot."

Back at his hotel, Charlie found a *pneumatique*[12] that had been redirected from the Ritz bar where Charlie had left his address for the purpose of finding a certain man.

Dear Charlie: You were so strange when we saw you the other day that I wondered if I did something to offend you. If so, I'm not conscious of it. In fact, I have thought about you too much for the last year, and it's always been in the back of my mind that I might see you if I came over here. We *did* have such good times that crazy spring, like the night you and I stole the butcher's tricycle, and the time we tried to call on the president and you had the old derby rim and the wire cane. Everybody seems so old lately, but I don't feel old a bit. Couldn't we get together some time today for old time's sake? I've got a vile hangover for the moment, but will be feeling better this afternoon and will look for you about five in the sweatshop at the Ritz.

Always devotedly,
Lorraine

His first feeling was one of awe that he had actually, in his mature years, stolen a tricycle and pedaled Lorraine all over the Étoile between the small hours and dawn. In retrospect it was a nightmare. Locking out Helen didn't fit in with any other act of his life, but the tricycle incident did—it was one of many. How many weeks or months of dissipation to arrive at that condition of utter irresponsibility?

[12] *pneumatique:* express letter, sent through a system of tubes

He tried to picture how Lorraine had appeared to him then—very attractive; Helen was unhappy about it, though she said nothing. Yesterday, in the restaurant, Lorraine had seemed trite, blurred, worn away. He emphatically did not want to see her, and he was glad Alix had not given away his hotel address. It was a relief to think, instead, of Honoria, to think of Sundays spent with her and of saying good morning to her and of knowing she was there in his house at night, drawing her breath in the darkness.

At five he took a taxi and bought presents for all the Peters—a piquant cloth doll, a box of Roman soldiers, flowers for Marion, big linen handkerchiefs for Lincoln.

He saw, when he arrived in the apartment, that Marion had accepted the inevitable. She greeted him now as though he were a recalcitrant member of the family, rather than a menacing outsider. Honoria had been told she was going; Charlie was glad to see that her tact made her conceal her excessive happiness. Only on his lap did she whisper her delight and the question "When?" before she slipped away with the other children.

He and Marion were alone for a minute in the room, and on an impulse he spoke out boldly:

"Family quarrels are bitter things. They don't go according to any rules. They're not like aches or wounds; they're more like splits in the skin that won't heal because there's not enough material. I wish you and I could be on better terms."

"Some things are hard to forget," she answered. "It's a question of confidence." There was no answer to this and presently she asked, "When do you propose to take her?"

"As soon as I can get a governess. I hoped the day after tomorrow."

"That's impossible. I've got to get her things in shape. Not before Saturday."

He yielded. Coming back into the room, Lincoln offered him a drink.

"I'll take my daily whiskey," he said.

It was warm here, it was a home, people together by a fire. The children felt very safe and important; the mother and father were serious, watchful. They had things to do for the children more important than his visit here. A spoonful of medicine was, after all, more important than the strained relations between Marion and himself. They were not dull people, but they were very much in the grip of life and circumstances. He wondered if he couldn't do something to get Lincoln out of his rut at the bank.

A long peal at the door-bell; the *bonne à tout faire*[13] passed through and went down the corridor. The door opened upon another long ring, and then voices, and the three in the salon looked up expectantly; Richard moved to bring the corridor within his range of vision, and Marion rose. Then the maid came back along the corridor, closely followed by the voices, which developed under the light into Duncan Schaeffer and Lorraine Quarrles.

They were gay, they were hilarious, they were roaring with laughter.

[13] *bonne à tout faire:* maid

For a moment Charlie was astounded; unable to understand how they ferreted out the Peters' address.

"Ah-h-h!" Duncan wagged his finger roguishly at Charlie. "Ah-h-h!"

They both slid down another cascade of laughter. Anxious and at a loss, Charlie shook hands with them quickly and presented them to Lincoln and Marion. Marion nodded, scarcely speaking. She had drawn back a step toward the fire; her little girl stood beside her, and Marion put an arm about her shoulder.

With growing annoyance at the intrusion, Charlie waited for them to explain themselves. After some concentration Duncan said:

"We came to invite you out to dinner. Lorraine and I insist that all this shishi, cagy business 'bout your address got to stop."

Charlie came closer to them, as if to force them backward down the corridor.

"Sorry, but I can't. Tell me where you'll be and I'll phone you in half an hour."

This made no impression. Lorraine sat down suddenly on the side of a chair, and focusing her eyes on Richard, cried, "Oh, what a nice little boy! Come here, little boy." Richard glanced at his mother, but did not move. With a perceptible shrug of her shoulders, Lorraine turned back to Charlie:

"Come and dine. Sure your cousins won' mine. See you so sel'om.[14] Or solemn."

"I can't," said Charlie sharply. "You two have dinner and I'll phone you."

Her voice became suddenly unpleasant. "All right, we'll go. But I remember once when you hammered on my door at four A.M. I was enough of a good sport to give you a drink. Come on, Dunc."

Still in slow motion, with blurred, angry faces, with uncertain feet, they retired along the corridor.

"Good night," Charlie said.

"Good night!" responded Lorraine emphatically.

When he went back into the salon Marion had not moved, only now her son was standing in the circle of her other arm. Lincoln was still swinging Honoria back and forth like a pendulum from side to side.

"What an outrage!" Charlie broke out. "What an absolute outrage!"

Neither of them answered. Charlie dropped into an armchair, picked up his drink, set it down again and said:

"People I haven't seen for two years having the colossal nerve—"

He broke off. Marion had made the sound "Oh!" in one swift, furious breath, turned her body from him with a jerk and left the room.

Lincoln set down Honoria carefully.

"You children go in and start your soup," he said, and when they obeyed, he said to Charlie:

"Marion's not well and she can't stand shocks. That kind of people make her really physically sick."

[14] **sel'om:** seldom (the drunk speaker is slurring her words)

"I didn't tell them to come here. They wormed your name out of somebody. They deliberately—"

"Well, it's too bad. It doesn't help matters. Excuse me a minute."

Left alone, Charlie sat tense in his chair. In the next room he could hear the children eating, talking in monosyllables, already oblivious to the scene between their elders. He heard a murmur of conversation from a farther room and then the ticking bell of a telephone receiver picked up, and in a panic he moved to the other side of the room and out of earshot.

In a minute Lincoln came back. "Look here, Charlie. I think we'd better call off dinner for tonight. Marion's in bad shape."

"Is she angry with me?"

"Sort of," he said, almost roughly. "She's not strong and—"

"You mean she's changed her mind about Honoria?"

"She's pretty bitter right now. I don't know. You phone me at the bank tomorrow."

"I wish you'd explain to her I never dreamed these people would come here. I'm just as sore as you are."

"I couldn't explain anything to her now."

Charlie got up. He took his coat and hat and started down the corridor. Then he opened the door of the dining room and said in a strange voice, "Good night, children."

Honoria rose and ran around the table to hug him.

"Good night, sweetheart," he said vaguely, and then trying to make his voice more tender, trying to conciliate something, "Good night, dear children."

V

Charlie went directly to the Ritz bar with the furious idea of finding Lorraine and Duncan, but they were not there, and he realized that in any case there was nothing he could do. He had not touched his drink at the Peters', and now he ordered a whiskey-and-soda. Paul came over to say hello.

"It's a great change," he said sadly. "We do about half the business we did. So many fellows I hear about back in the States lost everything, maybe not in the first crash, but then in the second. Your friend George Hardt lost every cent, I hear. Are you back in the States?"

"No, I'm in business in Prague."

"I heard that you lost a lot in the crash."

"I did," and he added grimly, "but I lost everything I wanted in the boom."

"Selling short."

"Something like that."

Again the memory of those days swept over him like a nightmare—the people they had met travelling; then people who couldn't add a row of figures or speak a coherent sentence. The little man Helen had consented to dance with at the ship's party, who had insulted her ten feet from the table; the women and girls carried screaming with drink or drugs out of public places—

—The men who locked their wives out in the snow, because the snow of twenty-nine wasn't real snow. If you didn't want it to be snow, you just paid some money.

He went to the phone and called the Peters' apartment; Lincoln answered.

"I called up because this thing is on my mind. Has Marion said anything definite?"

"Marion's sick," Lincoln answered shortly. "I know this thing isn't altogether your fault, but I can't have her go to pieces about it. I'm afraid we'll have to let it slide for six months; I can't take the chance of working her up to this state again."

"I see."

"I'm sorry, Charlie."

He went back to his table. His whisky glass was empty, but he shook his head when Alix looked at it questioningly. There wasn't much he could do now except send Honoria some things; he would send her a lot of things tomorrow. He thought rather angrily that this was just money—he had given so many people money. . . .

"No, no more," he said to the waiter. "What do I owe you?"

He would come back some day; they couldn't make him pay forever. But he wanted his child, and nothing was much good now, beside that fact. He wasn't young any more, with a lot of nice thoughts and dreams to have by himself. He was absolutely sure Helen wouldn't have wanted him to be so alone.

The Man Who Was Almost a Man
Richard Wright   United States, 1940

ABOUT THE AUTHOR

Richard Wright (1908–1960) was born in the United States, in Missis-
sippi. His father deserted the family when Wright was only five. When
his mother became ill a few years later, he was sent to live with a variety
of relatives, who often beat him. He moved constantly from town to town,
rarely able to complete a year of school. When he was seventeen, he fled to
Tennessee, worked at menial jobs, and educated himself by reading books.
When he left with his family for Chicago in 1927, he became part of
what is now called the Great Migration, a movement of more than a mil-
lion African-American southerners to Northern cities in search of better
jobs and more education. By the 1930s, Wright had established himself as
a prize-winning writer in New York. Writing about the difficulties of
growing up poor in a racist society, Wright produced a classic autobiogra-
phy, Black Boy *(1945). His most well-known novel is* Native Son
(1940).

THE CONTEXT OF THE STORY

The story takes place in the 1930s on a rural farm in the South. It
reflects the historical truth that African Americans were economically
exploited by white landowners. Although slavery had been abolished,
restrictions dictating where and how black people could live, eat, travel,
and speak were enforced in the North as well as in the South.

Dave struck out across the fields, looking homeward through paling
light. Whut's the use talkin wid em niggers in the field? Anyhow, his
mother was putting supper on the table. Them niggers can't understan
nothing. One of these days he was going to get a gun and practice shooting,
then they couldn't talk to him as though he were a little boy. He slowed,
looking at the ground. Shucks, Ah ain scareda them even ef they are biggern
me! Aw, Ah know whut Ahma do. Ahm going by ol Joe's sto n git that Sears
Roebuck catlog n look at them guns. Mebbe Ma will lemme buy one when
she gits mah pay from ol man Hawkins. Ahma beg her t gimme some
money. Ahm ol ernough to hava gun. Ahm seventeen. Almost a man. He
strode, feeling his long loose-jointed limbs. Shucks, a man oughta hava little
gun aftah he done worked hard all day.

He came in sight of Joe's store. A yellow lantern glowed on the front
porch. He mounted steps and went through the screen door, hearing it
bang behind him. There was a strong smell of coal oil and mackerel fish.
He felt very confident until he saw fat Joe walk in through the rear door,
then his courage began to ooze.

"Howdy, Dave! Whutcha want?"

"How yuh, Mistah Joe? Aw, Ah don wanna buy nothing. Ah jus wanted t see ef yuhd lemme look at tha catlog erwhile."

"Sure! You wanna see it here?"

"Nawsuh. Ah wants t take it home wid me. Ah'll bring it back termorrow when Ah come in from the fiels."

"You plannin on buying something?"

"Yessuh."

"Your ma lettin you have your own money now?"

"Shucks. Mistah Joe, Ahm gittin t be a man like anybody else!"

Joe laughed and wiped his greasy white face with a red bandanna.

"Whut you plannin on buyin?"

Dave looked at the floor, scratched his head, scratched his thigh, and smiled. Then he looked up shyly.

"Ah'll tell yuh, Mistah Joe, ef yuh promise yuh won't tell."

"I promise."

"Waal, Ahma buy a gun."

"A gun? What you want with a gun?"

"Ah wanna keep it."

"You ain't nothing but a boy. You don't need a gun."

"Aw, lemme have the catlog, Mistah Joe. Ah'll bring it back."

Joe walked through the rear door. Dave was elated. He looked around at barrels of sugar and flour. He heard Joe coming back. He craned his neck to see if he were bringing the book. Yeah, he's got it. Gawddog, he's got it!

"Here, but be sure you bring it back. It's the only one I got."

"Sho, Mistah Joe."

"Say, if you wanna buy a gun, why don't you buy one from me? I gotta gun to sell."

"Will it shoot?"

"Sure it'll shoot."

"Whut kind is it?"

"Oh, it's kinda old . . . a left-hand Wheeler. A pistol. A big one."

"Is it got bullets in it?"

"It's loaded."

"Kin Ah see it?"

"Where's your money?"

"What yuh wan fer it?"

"I'll let you have it for two dollars."

"Just two dollahs? Shucks, Ah could buy tha when Ah git mah pay."

"I'll have it here when you want it."

"Awright, suh. Ah be in fer it."

He went through the door, hearing it slam again behind him. Ahma git some money from Ma n buy me a gun! Only two dollahs! He tucked the thick catalogue under his arm and hurried.

"Where yuh been, boy?" His mother held a steaming dish of black-eyed peas.

"Aw, Ma, Ah just stopped down the road t talk wid the boys."

"Yuh know bettah t keep suppah waitin."

He sat down, resting the catalogue on the edge of the table.

"Yuh git up from there and git to the well n wash yosef! Ah ain feedin no hogs in mah house!"

She grabbed his shoulder and pushed him. He stumbled out of the room, then came back to get the catalogue.

"Whut this?"

"Aw, Ma, it's jusa catlog."

"Who yuh git it from?"

"From Joe, down at the sto."

"Waal, thas good. We kin use it in the outhouse."

"Naw, Ma." He grabbed for it. "Gimme ma catlog, Ma."

She held onto it and glared at him.

"Quit hollerin at me! Whut's wrong wid yuh? Yuh crazy?"

"But Ma, please. It ain mine! It's Joe's! He tol me t bring it back t im termorrow."

She gave up the book. He stumbled down the back steps, hugging the thick book under his arm. When he had splashed water on his face and hands, he groped back to the kitchen and fumbled in a corner for the towel. He bumped into a chair; it clattered to the floor. The catalogue sprawled at his feet. When he had dried his eyes he snatched up the book and held it again under his arm. His mother stood watching him.

"Now, ef yuh gonna act a fool over that ol book, Ah'll take it n burn it up."

"Naw, Ma, please."

"Waal, set down n be still!"

He sat down and drew the oil lamp close. He thumbed page after page, unaware of the food his mother set on the table. His father came in. Then his small brother.

"Whutcha got there, Dave?" his father asked.

"Jusa catlog," he answered, not looking up.

"Yeah, here they is!" His eyes glowed at blue-and-black revolvers. He glanced up, feeling sudden guilt. His father was watching him. He eased the book under the table and rested it on his knees. After the blessing was asked, he ate. He scooped up peas and swallowed fat meat without chewing. Buttermilk helped to wash it down. He did not want to mention money before his father. He would do much better by cornering his mother when she was alone. He looked at his father uneasily out of the edge of his eye.

"Boy, how come yuh don quit foolin wid tha book n eat yo suppah?"

"Yessuh."

"How you n ol man Hawkins gitten erlong?"

"Suh?"

"Can't yuh hear? Why don yuh lissen? Ah ast yu how wuz yuh n ol man Hawkins gitten erlong?"

"Oh, swell, Pa. Ah plows mo lan than anybody over there."

"Waal, yuh oughta keep you mind on whut yuh doin."

"Yessuh."

He poured his plate full of molasses and sopped it up slowly with a chunk of cornbread. When his father and brother had left the kitchen, he still sat and looked again at the guns in the catalogue, longing to muster courage enough to present his case to his mother. Lawd, ef Ah only had tha pretty one! He could almost feel the slickness of the weapon with his fingers. If he had a gun like that he would polish it and keep it shining so it would never rust. N Ah'd keep it loaded, by Gawd!

"Ma?" His voice was hesitant.

"Hunh?"

"Ol man Hawkins give yuh mah money yit?"

"Yeah, but ain no usa yuh thinking bout throwin nona it erway. Ahm keeping tha money sos yuh kin have cloes t go to school this winter."

He rose and went to her side with the open catalogue in his palms. She was washing dishes, her head bent low over a pan. Shyly he raised the book. When he spoke, his voice was husky; faint.

"Ma, Gawd knows Ah wans one of these."

"One of whut?" she asked, not raising her eyes.

"One of these," he said again, not daring even to point. She glanced up at the page, then at him with wide eyes.

"Nigger, is yuh gone plumb crazy?"

"Aw, Ma—"

"Git outta here! Don yuh talk t me bout no gun! Yuh a fool!"

"Ma, Ah kin buy one fer two dollahs."

"Not ef Ah knows it, yuh ain!"

"But yuh promised me one—"

"Ah don care what Ah promised! Yuh ain nothing but a boy yit!"

"Ma, ef yuh lemme buy one Ah'll *never* ast yuh fer nothing no mo."

"Ah tol yuh t git outta here! Yuh ain gonna toucha penny of tha money fer no gun! Thas how come Ah has Mistah Hawkins t pay yo wages t me, cause Ah knows yuh ain got no sense."

"But, Ma, we needa gun. Pa ain got no gun. We needa gun in the house. Yuh kin never tell whut might happen."

"Now don yuh try to maka fool outta me, boy! Ef we did hava gun, yuh wouldn't have it!"

He laid the catalogue down and slipped his arm around her waist.

"Aw, Ma, Ah done worked hard alla summer n ain ast yuh fer nothing, is Ah, now?"

"Thas whut yuh spose to do!"

"But Ma, Ah wans a gun. Yuh kin lemme have two dollahs outta mah money. Please, Ma. I kin give it to Pa. . . . Please, Ma! Ah loves yuh, Ma."

When she spoke her voice came soft and low.

"What yu wan wida gun, Dave? Yuh don need no gun. Yuh'll git in trouble. N ef yo pa jus thought Ah let yuh have money t buy a gun he'd hava fit."

"Ah'll hide it, Ma. It ain but two dollahs."

"Lawd, chil, whut's wrong wid yuh?"

"Ain nothin wrong, Ma. Ahm almos a man now. Ah wans a gun."

"Who gonna sell yuh a gun?"

"Ol Joe at the sto."

"N it don cos but two dollahs?"

"Thas all, Ma. Jus two dollahs. Please, Ma."

She was stacking the plates away; her hands moved slowly, reflectively. Dave kept an anxious silence. Finally, she turned to him.

"Ah'll let yuh git tha gun ef yuh promise me one thing."

"What's tha, Ma?"

"Yuh bring it straight back t me, yuh hear? It be fer Pa."

"Yessum! Lemme go now, Ma."

She stooped, turned slightly to one side, raised the hem of her dress, rolled down the top of her stocking, and came up with a slender wad of bills.

"Here," she said. "Lawd knows yuh don need no gun. But yer pa does. Yuh bring it right back t me, yuh hear? Ahma put it up. Now ef yuh don, Ahma have yuh pa lick yuh so hard yuh won fergit it."

"Yessum."

He took the money, ran down the steps, and across the yard.

"Dave! Yuuuuuh Daaaaave!"

He heard, but he was not going to stop now. "Now, Lawd!"

The first movement he made the following morning was to reach under his pillow for the gun. In the gray light of dawn he held it loosely, feeling a sense of power. Could kill a man with a gun like this. Kill anybody, black or white. And if he were holding his gun in his hand, nobody could run over him; they would have to respect him. It was a big gun, with a long barrel and a heavy handle. He raised and lowered it in his hand, marveling at its weight.

He had not come straight home with it as his mother had asked; instead he had stayed out in the fields, holding the weapon in his hand, aiming it now and then at some imaginary foe. But he had not fired it; he had been afraid that his father might hear. Also he was not sure he knew how to fire it.

To avoid surrendering the pistol he had not come into the house until he knew that they were all asleep. When his mother had tiptoed to his bedside late that night and demanded the gun, he had first played possum; then he had told her that the gun was hidden outdoors, that he would bring it to her in the morning. Now he lay turning it slowly in his hands. He broke it, took out the cartridges, felt them, and then put them back.

He slid out of bed, got a long strip of old flannel from a trunk, wrapped the gun in it, and tied it to his naked thigh while it was still loaded. He did not go in to breakfast. Even though it was not yet daylight, he started for Jim Hawkins' plantation. Just as the sun was rising he reached the barns where the mules and plows were kept.

"Hey! That you, Dave?"

He turned. Jim Hawkins stood eyeing him suspiciously.

"What're yuh doing here so early?"

"Ah didn't know Ah wuz gittin up so early, Mistah Hawkins. Ah was fixin t hitch up ol Jenny n take her t the fiels."

"Good. Since you're so early, how about plowing that stretch down by the woods?"

"Suits me, Mistah Hawkins."

"O.K. Go to it!"

He hitched Jenny to a plow and started across the fields. Hot dog! This was just what he wanted. If he could get down by the woods, he could shoot his gun and nobody would hear. He walked behind the plow, hearing the traces creaking, feeling the gun tied tight to his thigh.

When he reached the woods, he plowed two whole rows before he decided to take out the gun. Finally, he stopped, looked in all directions, then untied the gun and held it in his hand. He turned to the mule and smiled.

"Know whut this is, Jenny? Naw, yuh wouldn know! Yuhs jusa ol mule! Anyhow, this is a gun, n it kin shoot, by Gawd!"

He held the gun at arm's length. Whut t hell, Ahma shoot this thing! He looked at Jenny again.

"Lissen here, Jenny! When Ah pull this ol trigger, Ah don wan yuh t run n acka fool now!"

Jenny stood with head down, her short ears pricked straight. Dave walked off about twenty feet, held the gun far out from him at arm's length, and turned his head. Hell, he told himself, Ah ain afraid. The gun felt loose in his fingers; he waved it widely for a moment. Then he shut his eyes and tightened his forefinger. Bloom! A report half deafened him and he thought his right hand was torn from his arm. He heard Jenny whinnying and galloping over the field, and he found himself on his knees, squeezing his fingers hard between his legs. His hand was numb; he jammed it into his mouth, trying to warm it, trying to stop the pain. The gun lay at his feet. He did not quite know what had happened. He stood up and stared at the gun as though it were a living thing. He gritted his teeth and kicked the gun. Yuh almos broke mah arm! He turned to look for Jenny; she was far over the fields, tossing her head and kicking wildly.

"Hol on there, ol mule!"

When he caught up with her she stood trembling, walling her big white eyes at him. The plow was far away; the traces had broken. Then Dave stopped short, looking, not believing. Jenny was bleeding. Her left side was red and wet with blood. He went closer. Lawd, have mercy! Wondah did Ah shoot this mule? He grabbed for Jenny's mane. She flinched, snorted, whirled, tossing her head.

"Hol on now! Hol on."

Then he saw the hole in Jenny's side, right between the ribs. It was round, wet, red. A crimson stream streaked down the front leg, flowing fast. Good Gawd! Ah wuzn't shootin at tha mule. He felt panic. He knew he had to stop that blood, or Jenny would bleed to death. He had never seen so much blood in all his life. He chased the mule for half a mile, trying to catch her. Finally she stopped, breathing hard, stumpy tail half arched. He caught her mane and led her back to where the plow and gun lay. Then he stopped and grabbed handfuls of damp black earth and tried to plug the bullet hole. Jenny shuddered, whinnied, and broke from him.

"Hol on! Hol on now!"

He tried to plug it again, but blood came anyhow. His fingers were hot and sticky. He rubbed dirt into his palms, trying to dry them. Then again he attempted to plug the bullet hole, but Jenny shied away, kicking her heels high. He stood helpless. He had to do something. He ran at Jenny; she dodged him. He watched a red stream of blood flow down Jenny's leg and form a bright pool at her feet.

"Jenny . . . Jenny," he called weakly.

His lips trembled. She's bleeding t death! He looked in the direction of home, wanting to go back, wanting to get help. But he saw the pistol lying in the damp black clay. He had a queer feeling that if he only did something, this would not be; Jenny would not be there bleeding to death.

When he went to her this time, she did not move. She stood with sleepy, dreamy eyes; and when he touched her she gave a low-pitched whinny and knelt to the ground, her front knees slopping in blood.

"Jenny . . . Jenny . . ." he whispered.

For a long time she held her neck erect; then her head sank, slowly. Her ribs swelled with a mighty heave and she went over.

Dave's stomach felt empty, very empty. He picked up the gun and held it gingerly between his thumb and forefinger. He buried it at the foot of a tree. He took a stick to cover the pool of blood with dirt—but what was the use? There was Jenny lying with her mouth open and her eyes walled and glassy. He could not tell Jim Hawkins he had shot his mule. But he had to tell something. Yeah, Ah'll tell em Jenny started gittin wil n fell on the joint of the plow. . . . But that would hardly happen to a mule. He walked across the field slowly, head down.

It was sunset. Two of Jim Hawkins' men were over near the edge of the woods digging a hole in which to bury Jenny. Dave was surrounded by a knot of people, all of whom were looking down at the dead mule.

"I don't see how in the world it happened," said Jim Hawkins for the tenth time.

The crowd parted and Dave's mother, father, and small brother pushed into the center.

"Where Dave?" his mother called.

"There he is," said Jim Hawkins.

His mother grabbed him.

"Whut happened, Dave? Whut yuh done?"

"Nothin."

"C mon, boy, talk," his father said.

Dave took a deep breath and told the story he knew nobody believed.

"Waal," he drawled. "Ah brung ol Jenny down here sos Ah could do mah plowin. Ah plowed bout two rows, just like yuh see." He stopped and pointed at the long rows of upturned earth. "Then somethin musta been wrong wid ol Jenny. She wouldn ack right a-tall. She started snortin n kickin her heels. Ah tried t hol her, but she pulled erway, rearin n goin in. Then when the point of the plow was stickin up in the air, she swung erroun n twisted herself back on it. . . . She stuck hersef n started t bleed. N fo Ah could do anything, she wuz dead."

"Did you ever hear of anything like that in all your life?" asked Jim Hawkins.

There were white and black standing in the crowd. They murmured. Dave's mother came close to him and looked hard into his face. "Tell the truth, Dave," she said.

"Looks like a bullet hole to me," said one man.

"Dave, whut yuh do wid the gun?" his mother asked.

The crowd surged in, looking at him. He jammed his hands into his pockets, shook his head slowly from left to right, and backed away. His eyes were wide and painful.

"Did he hava gun?" asked Jim Hawkins.

"By Gawd, Ah tol yuh tha wuz a gun wound," said a man, slapping his thigh.

His father caught his shoulders and shook him till his teeth rattled.

"Tell whut happened, yuh rascal! Tell whut. . . ."

Dave looked at Jenny's stiff legs and began to cry.

"Whut yuh do wid tha gun?" his mother asked.

"What wuz he doin wida gun?" his father asked.

"Come on and tell the truth," said Hawkins. "Ain't nobody going to hurt you. . . ."

His mother crowded close to him.

"Did yuh shoot tha mule, Dave?"

Daved cried, seeing blurred white and black faces.

"Ahh ddinn gggo tt sshooot hher. . . . Ah ssswear ffo Gawd Ahh ddin. . . . Ah wuz a-tryin t sssee ef the old gggun would sshoot—"

"Where yuh git the gun from?" his father asked.

"Ah got it from Joe, at the sto."

"Where yuh git the money?"

"Ma give it t me."

"He kept worryin me, Bob. Ah had t. Ah tol im t bring the gun right back t me. . . . It was fer yuh, the gun."

"But how yuh happen to shoot that mule?" asked Jim Hawkins.

"Ah wuzn shootin at the mule, Mistah Hawkins. The gun jumped when Ah pulled the trigger. . . . N fo Ah knowed anythin Jenny was there a-bleedin."

Somebody in the crowd laughed. Jim Hawkins walked close to Dave and looked into his face.

"Well, looks like you have bought you a mule, Dave."

"Ah swear fo Gawd, Ah didn go t kill the mule, Mistah Hawkins!"

"But you killed her!"

All the crowd was laughing now. They stood on tiptoe and poked heads over one another's shoulders.

"Well, boy, looks like yuh done bought a dead mule! Hahaha!"

"Ain tha ershame."

"Hohohohoho."

Dave stood, head down, twisting his feet in the dirt.

"Well, you needn't worry about it, Bob," said Jim Hawkins to Dave's father. "Just let the boy keep on working and pay me two dollars a month."

"Whut yuh wan fer yo mule, Mistah Hawkins?"

Jim Hawkins screwed up his eyes.

"Fifty dollars."

"Whut yuh do wid tha gun?" Dave's father demanded.

Dave said nothing.

"Yuh wan me t take a tree n beat yuh till yuh talk!"

"Nawsuh!"

"Whut yuh do wid it?"

"Ah throwed it erway."

"Where?"

"Ah . . . Ah throwed it in the creek."

"Waal, c mon home. N firs thing in the mawnin git to tha creek n fin tha gun."

"Yessuh."

"Whut yuh pay fer it?"

"Two dollahs."

"Take tha gun n git yo money back n carry it to Mistah Hawkins, yuh hear? N don fergit Ahma lam you black bottom good fer this! Now march yosef on home, suh!"

Dave turned and walked slowly. He heard people laughing. Dave glared, his eyes welling with tears. Hot anger bubbled in him. Then he swallowed and stumbled on.

That night Dave did not sleep. He was glad that he had gotten out of killing the mule so easily, but he was hurt. Something hot seemed to turn over inside him each time he remembered how they had laughed. He tossed on his bed, feeling his hard pillow. N Pa says he's gonna beat me. . . . He remembered other beatings, and his back quivered. Naw, naw, Ah sho don wan im t beat me tha way no mo. Dam em all! Nobody ever gave him anything. All he did was work. They treat me like a mule, n then they beat me. He gritted his teeth. N Ma had t tell on me.

Well, if he had to, he would take old man Hawkins that two dollars. But that meant selling the gun. And he wanted to keep that gun. Fifty dollars for a dead mule.

He turned over, thinking how he had fired the gun. He had an itch to fire it again. Ef other men kin shoota gun, by Gawd, Ah kin! He was still, listening. Mebbe they all sleepin now. The house was still. He heard the soft breathing of his brother. Yes, now! He would go down and get that gun and see if he could fire it! He eased out of bed and slipped into overalls.

The moon was bright. He ran almost all the way to the edge of the woods. He stumbled over the ground, looking for the spot where he had buried the gun. Yeah, here it is. Like a hungry dog scratching for a bone, he pawed it up. He puffed his black cheeks and blew dirt from the trigger and barrel. He broke it and found four cartridges unshot. He looked around; the fields were filled with silence and moonlight. He clutched the gun stiff and hard in his fingers. But, as soon as he wanted to pull the trigger, he shut his eyes and turned his head. Naw, Ah can't shoot wid mah eyes closed n mah head turned. With effort he held his eyes open; then he squeezed. *Blooooom!* He was stiff, not breathing. The gun was still in his hands. Dammit, he'd done it! He fired again. *Blooooom!* He smiled. *Bloooom! Blooooom! Click, click.* There! It was empty. If anybody could shoot a gun, he could. He put the gun into his hip pocket and started across the fields.

When he reached the top of a ridge he stood straight and proud in the moonlight, looking at Jim Hawkins' big white house, feeling the gun sagging in his pocket. Lawd, ef Ah had just one mo bullet Ah'd taka shot at tha house. Ah'd like t scare ol man Hawkins jusa little. . . . Jusa enough t let im know Dave Saunders is a man.

To his left the road curved, running to the tracks of the Illinois Central. He jerked his head, listening. From far off came a faint *hoooof-hoooof; hoooof-hoooof.* . . . He stood rigid. Two dollahs a mont. Les see now. . . . Tha means it'll take bout two years. Shucks! Ah'll be dam!

He started down the road, toward the tracks. Yeah, here she comes! He stood beside the track and held himself stiffly. Here she comes, erroun the ben. . . . C mon, yuh slow poke! C mon! He had his hand on his gun; something quivered in his stomach. Then the train thundered past, the gray and brown box cars rumbling and clinking. He gripped the gun tightly; then he jerked his hand out of his pocket. Ah betcha Bill wouldn't do it! Ah betcha. . . . The cars slid past, steel grinding upon steel. Ahm ridin yuh ternight, so hep me Gawd! He was hot all over. He hesitated just a moment; then he grabbed, pulled atop of a car, and lay flat. He felt his pocket; the gun was still there. Ahead the long rails were glinting in the moonlight, stretching away, away to somewhere, somewhere where he could be a man. . . .

Dead Men's Path
Chinua Achebe   Nigeria, 1953

ABOUT THE AUTHOR

Chinua Achebe (b. 1930) was born and raised in the Igbo village of Ogidi, in eastern Nigeria. His first language was Igbo. As a Christian, Achebe was excluded from certain traditional practices of non-Christians. Nevertheless, he was always fascinated by the folktales and rituals of tribal life. After attending a mission school, where he learned English, Achebe entered college. After graduating in 1953, he worked for several years for the Nigerian Broadcasting Service. He has traveled extensively and taught in the United States. Achebe's work, including award-winning novels such as Things Fall Apart *(1958), are written in English, a language he uses to reveal both universal and peculiarly African experiences.*

THE CONTEXT OF THE STORY

The British gained control of Nigeria at the turn of the twentieth century. Viewing Igbo culture and beliefs as inferior and barbaric, their missionaries introduced Christianity and Western education. Christianity ultimately weakened tribal affiliations. (Note: Nigeria achieved independence in 1960.)

Michael Obi's hopes were fulfilled much earlier than he had expected. He was appointed headmaster of Ndume Central School in January 1949. It had always been an unprogressive school, so the Mission authorities decided to send a young and energetic man to run it. Obi accepted this responsibility with enthusiasm. He had many wonderful ideas and this was an opportunity to put them into practice. He had had sound secondary school education which designated him a "pivotal teacher" in the official records and set him apart from the other headmasters in the mission field. He was outspoken in his condemnation of the narrow views of these older and often less-educated ones.

"We shall make a good job of it, shan't we?" he asked his young wife when they first heard the joyful news of his promotion.

"We shall do our best," she replied. "We shall have such beautiful gardens and everything will be just *modern* and delightful . . ." In their two years of married life she had become completely infected by his passion for "modern methods" and his denigration of "these old and superannuated people in the teaching field who would be better employed as traders in the Onitsha market." She began to see herself already as the admired wife of the young headmaster, the queen of the school.

The wives of the other teachers would envy her position. She would set the fashion in everything . . . Then, suddenly, it occurred to her that there might not be other wives. Wavering between hope and fear, she asked her husband, looking anxiously at him.

"All our colleagues are young and unmarried," he said with enthusiasm which for once she did not share. "Which is a good thing," he continued.

"Why?"

"Why? They will give all their time and energy to the school."

Nancy was downcast. For a few minutes she became sceptical about the new school; but it was only for a few minutes. Her little personal misfortune could not blind her to her husband's happy prospects. She looked at him as he sat folded up in a chair. He was stoop-shouldered and looked frail. But he sometimes surprised people with sudden bursts of physical energy. In his present posture, however, all his bodily strength seemed to have retired behind his deep-set eyes, giving them an extraordinary power of penetration. He was only twenty-six, but looked thirty or more. On the whole, he was not unhandsome.

"A penny for your thoughts, Mike," said Nancy after a while, imitating the woman's magazine she read.

"I was thinking what a grand opportunity we've got at last to show these people how a school should be run."

Ndume School was backward in every sense of the word. Mr. Obi put his whole life into the work, and his wife hers too. He had two aims. A high standard of teaching was insisted upon, and the school compound was to be turned into a place of beauty. Nancy's dream-gardens came to life with the coming of the rains, and blossomed. Beautiful hibiscus and allamanda hedges in brilliant red and yellow marked out the carefully tended school compound from the rank neighbourhood bushes.

One evening as Obi was admiring his work he was scandalized to see an old woman from the village hobble right across the compound, through a marigold flower-bed and the hedges. On going up there he found faint signs of an almost disused path from the village across the school compound to the bush on the other side.

"It amazes me," said Obi to one of his teachers who had been three years in the school, "that you people allowed the villagers to make use of this footpath. It is simply incredible." He shook his head.

"The path," said the teacher apologetically, "appears to be very important to them. Although it is hardly used, it connects the village shrine with their place of burial."

"And what has that got to do with the school?" asked the headmaster.

"Well, I don't know," replied the other with a shrug of the shoulders. "But I remember there was a big row some time ago when we attempted to close it."

"That was some time ago. But it will not be used now," said Obi as he walked away. "What will the Government Education Officer think of this when he comes to inspect the school next week? The villagers might, for all I know, decide to use the schoolroom for a pagan ritual during the inspection."

Heavy sticks were planted closely across the path at the two places where it entered and left the school premises. These were further strengthened with barbed wire.

Three days later the village priest of *Ani*[1] called on the headmaster. He was an old man and walked with a slight stoop. He carried a stout walking-stick which he usually tapped on the floor, by way of emphasis, each time he made a new point in his argument.

"I have heard," he said after the usual exchange of cordialities, "that our ancestral footpath has recently been closed . . ."

"Yes," replied Mr. Obi. "We cannot allow people to make a highway of our school compound."

"Look here, my son," said the priest bringing down his walking-stick, "this path was here before you were born and before your father was born. The whole life of this village depends on it. Our dead relatives depart by it and our ancestors visit us by it. But most important, it is the path of children coming in to be born . . ."

Mr. Obi listened with a satisfied smile on his face.

"The whole purpose of our school," he said finally, "is to eradicate just such beliefs as that. Dead men do not require footpaths. The whole idea is just fantastic. Our duty is to teach your children to laugh at such ideas."

"What you say may be true," replied the priest, "but we follow the practices of our fathers. If you reopen the path we shall have nothing to quarrel about. What I always say is: let the hawk perch and let the eagle perch." He rose to go.

"I am sorry," said the young headmaster. "But the school compound cannot be a thoroughfare. It is against our regulations. I would suggest your constructing another path, skirting our premises. We can even get our boys to help in building it. I don't suppose the ancestors will find the little detour too burdensome."

"I have no more words to say," said the old priest, already outside.

Two days later a young woman in the village died in childbed. A diviner was immediately consulted and he prescribed heavy sacrifices to propitiate ancestors insulted by the fence.

Obi woke up the next morning among the ruins of his work. The beautiful hedges were torn up not just near the path but right round the school, the flowers trampled to death and one of the school buildings pulled down . . . That day, the white Supervisor came to inspect the school and wrote a nasty report on the state of the premises but more seriously about the "tribal-war situation developing between the school and the village, arising in part from the misguided zeal of the new headmaster."

---

[1] *Ani:* the goddess of the earth and judge of morality, who also controls the coming and going of the ancestors

Six Feet of the Country
Nadine Gordimer   South Africa, 1953

ABOUT THE AUTHOR

Nadine Gordimer (b. 1923) was born in the Transvaal, South Africa, the daughter of immigrants. Her mother was English, her father Eastern European. She published her first short story at the age of fifteen, and made writing her career while she was still a student at the University of Witwatersrand. For a period of time, some of her books were banned in her country, until she became active in an anticensorship movement and embarrassed the government. Gordimer has been awarded many literary honors, including the Nobel Prize for Literature in 1991. Among her many novels are July's People *(1981) and* My Son's Story *(1990). "Six Feet of the Country" originally appeared in the* New Yorker *magazine.*

THE CONTEXT OF THE STORY

Dutch settlers (Boers) arrived in South Africa in the seventeenth century; their descendants are known as Afrikaners. By the beginning of the twentieth century, black Africans had lost their independence and come under white British or Afrikaner rule. In 1931, Britain gave South Africa independence.

In 1948, the Afrikaner Nationalist party formalized the system of apartheid: it passed laws that segregated racial groups. Apartheid is based on master-race *theory (the theory that one race is superior to and therefore should rule other races). Apartheid separated whites from nonwhites and separated nonwhites—Coloreds (of mixed descent), Asiatics (mainly of Indian ancestry), and Black Africans (called* Bantu*)—from each other. Outside their assigned* townships, *the activities of the Bantu were strictly limited. At the time in which the story is set, they could not vote, own land, travel, or work without permits; and spouses were often forbidden to accompany workers to urban areas.*

My wife and I are not real farmers—not even Lerice, really. We bought our place, ten miles out of Johannesburg[1] on one of the main roads, to change something in ourselves, I suppose; you seem to rattle about so much within a marriage like ours. You long to hear nothing but a deep satisfying silence when you sound a marriage. The farm hasn't managed that for us, of course, but it has done other things, unexpected, illogical. Lerice, who I thought would retire there in Chekhovian sadness for a month or two, and then leave the place to the servants while she tried yet again to get a part she wanted and become the actress she would like to be, has sunk into the

---

[1] **Johannesburg:** largest city of South Africa

business of running the farm with all the serious intensity with which she once imbued the shadows in a playwright's mind. I should have given it up long ago if it had not been for her. Her hands, once small and plain and well-kept—she was not the sort of actress who wears red paint and diamond rings—are hard as a dog's pads.

I, of course, am there only in the evenings and on weekends. I am a partner in a luxury-travel agency, which is flourishing—needs to be, as I tell Lerice, in order to carry the farm. Still, though I know we can't afford it, and though the sweetish smell of the fowls Lerice breeds sickens me, so that I avoid going past their runs, the farm is beautiful in a way I had almost forgotten—especially on a Sunday morning when I get up and go out into the paddock and see not the palm trees and fishpond and imitation-stone bird bath of the suburbs but white ducks on the dam, the lucerne field brilliant as window dresser's grass, and the little, stocky, mean-eyed bull, lustful but bored, having his face tenderly licked by one of his ladies. Lerice comes out with her hair uncombed, in her hand a stick dripping with cattle dip. She will stand and look dreamily for a moment, the way she would pretend to look sometimes in those plays. "They'll mate tomorrow," she will say. "This is their second day. Look how she loves him, my little Napoleon." So that when people come out to see us on Sunday afternoon, I am likely to hear myself saying as I pour out the drinks, "When I drive back home from the city every day, past those rows of suburban houses, I wonder how the devil we ever did stand it. . . . Would you care to look around?" And there I am, taking some pretty girl and her young husband stumbling down to our riverbank, the girl catching her stockings on the mealie-stooks and stepping over cow-turds humming with jewel-green flies while she says, ". . . the *tensions* of the damned city. And you're near enough to get into town to a show, too! I think it's wonderful. Why, you've got it both ways!"

And for a moment I accept the triumph as if I *had* managed it—the impossibility that I've been trying for all my life—just as if the truth was that you could get it "both ways," instead of finding yourself with not even one way or the other but a third, one you had not provided for at all.

But even in our saner moments, when I find Lerice's earthy enthusiasms just as irritating as I once found her histrionical ones, and she finds what she calls my "jealousy" of her capacity for enthusiasm as big a proof of my inadequacy for her as a mate as ever it was, we do believe that we have at least honestly escaped those tensions peculiar to the city about which our visitors speak. When Johannesburg people speak of "tension," they don't mean hurrying people in crowded streets, the struggle for money, or the general competitive character of city life. They mean the guns under the white men's pillows and the burglar bars on the white men's windows. They mean those strange moments on city pavements when a black man won't stand aside for a white man.

Out in the country, even ten miles out, life is better than that. In the country, there is a lingering remnant of the pretransitional stage; our relationship with the blacks is almost feudal. Wrong, I suppose, obsolete, but more comfortable all round. We have no burglar bars, no gun. Lerice's farm boys have their wives and their piccanins living with them on the land. They brew their sour beer without the fear of police raids. In fact, we've always rather prided ourselves that the poor devils have nothing much to fear, being with us; Lerice even keeps an eye on their children, with all the competence of a woman who has never had a child of her own, and she certainly doctors them all—children and adults—like babies whenever they happen to be sick.

It was because of this that we were not particularly startled one night last winter when the boy Albert came knocking at our window long after we had gone to bed. I wasn't in our bed but sleeping in the little dressing-room-*cum*-linen-room next door, because Lerice had annoyed me and I didn't want to find myself softening toward her simply because of the sweet smell of the talcum powder on her flesh after her bath. She came and woke me up. "Albert says one of the boys is very sick," she said. "I think you'd better go down and see. He wouldn't get us up at this hour for nothing."

"What time is it?"

"What does it matter?" Lerice is maddeningly logical.

I got up awkwardly as she watched me—How is it I always feel a fool when I have deserted her bed? After all, I know from the way she never looks at me when she talks to me at breakfast the next day that she is hurt and humiliated at my not wanting her—and I went out, clumsy with sleep.

"Which of the boys is it?" I asked Albert as we followed the dance of my torch.

"He's too sick. Very sick, *Baas*,"[2] he said.

"But who? Franz?" I remembered Franz had had a bad cough for the past week.

Albert did not answer; he had given me the path, and was walking along beside me in the tall dead grass. When the light of the torch caught his face, I saw that he looked acutely embarrassed. "What's this all about?" I said.

He lowered his head under the glance of the light. "It's not me, *Baas*. I don't know. Petrus he send me."

Irritated, I hurried him along to the huts. And there, on Petrus's iron bedstead, with its brick stilts, was a young man, dead. On his forehead there was still a light, cold sweat; his body was warm. The boys stood around as they do in the kitchen when it is discovered that someone has broken a dish—uncoöperative, silent. Somebody's wife hung about in the shadows, her hands wrung together under her apron.

I had not seen a dead man since the war. This was very different. I felt like the others—extraneous, useless. "What was the matter?" I asked.

The woman patted at her chest and shook her head to indicate the painful impossibility of breathing.

He must have died of pneumonia.

I turned to Petrus. "Who was this boy? What was he doing here?" The

---

[2] ***Baas:*** an Afrikaans word meaning master or boss

light of the candle on the floor showed that Petrus was weeping. He followed me out the door.

When we were outside, in the dark, I waited for him to speak. But he didn't. "Now, come on, Petrus, you must tell me who this boy was. Was he a friend of yours?"

"He's my brother, *Baas*. He come from Rhodesia[3] to look for work."

The story startled Lerice and me a little. The young boy had walked down from Rhodesia to look for work in Johannesburg, had caught a chill from sleeping out along the way, and had lain ill in his brother Petrus's hut since his arrival three days before. Our boys had been frightened to ask us for help for him because we had never been intended ever to know of his presence. Rhodesian natives are barred from entering the Union unless they have a permit; the young man was an illegal immigrant. No doubt our boys had managed the whole thing successfully several times before; a number of relatives must have walked the seven or eight hundred miles from poverty to the paradise of zoot suits, police raids, and black slum townships that is their *Egoli*, City of Gold—the Bantu name for Johannesburg. It was merely a matter of getting such a man to lie low on our farm until a job could be found with someone who would be glad to take the risk of prosecution for employing an illegal immigrant in exchange for the services of someone as yet untainted by the city.

Well, this was one who would never get up again.

"You would think they would have felt they could tell *us*," said Lerice next morning. "Once the man was ill. You would have thought at least—" When she is getting intense over something, she has a way of standing in the middle of a room as people do when they are shortly to leave on a journey, looking searchingly about her at the most familiar objects as if she had never seen them before. I had noticed that in Petrus's presence in the kitchen, earlier, she had had the air of being almost offended with him, almost hurt.

In any case, I really haven't the time or inclination any more to go into everything in our life that I know Lerice, from those alarmed and pressing eyes of hers, would like us to go into. She is the kind of woman who doesn't mind if she looks plain, or odd; I don't suppose she would even care if she knew how strange she looks when her whole face is out of proportion with urgent uncertainty. I said, "Now I'm the one who'll have to do all the dirty work, I suppose."

She was still staring at me, trying me out with those eyes—wasting her time, if she only knew.

"I'll have to notify the health authorities," I said calmly. "They can't just cart him off and bury him. After all, we don't really know what he died of."

---

[3] **Rhodesia:** now Zimbabwe and Zambia

She simply stood there, as if she had given up—simply ceased to see me at all.

I don't know when I've been so irritated. "It might have been something contagious," I said. "God knows?" There was no answer.

I am not enamored of holding conversations with myself. I went out to shout to one of the boys to open the garage and get the car ready for my morning drive to town.

As I had expected, it turned out to be quite a business. I had to notify the police as well as the health authorities, and answer a lot of tedious questions: How was it I was ignorant of the boy's presence? If I did not supervise my native quarters, how did I know that that sort of thing didn't go on all the time? Et cetera, et cetera. And when I flared up and told them that so long as my natives did their work, I didn't think it my right or concern to poke my nose into their private lives, I got from the coarse, dull-witted police sergeant one of those looks that come not from any thinking process going on in the brain but from that faculty common to all who are possessed by the master-race theory—a look of insanely inane certainty. He grinned at me with a mixture of scorn and delight at my stupidity.

Then I had to explain to Petrus why the health authorities had to take away the body for a post-mortem—and, in fact, what a post-mortem was. When I telephoned the health department some days later to find out the result, I was told that the cause of death was, as we had thought, pneumonia, and that the body had been suitably disposed of. I went out to where Petrus was mixing a mash for the fowls and told him that it was all right, there would be no trouble; his brother had died from that pain in his chest. Petrus put down the paraffin tin and said, "When can we go to fetch him, *Baas?*"

"To fetch him?"

"Will the *Baas* please ask them when we must come?"

I went back inside and called Lerice, all over the house. She came down the stairs from the spare bedrooms, and I said, "*Now* what am I going to do? When I told Petrus, he just asked calmly when they could go and fetch the body. They think they're going to bury him themselves."

"Well, go back and tell him," said Lerice. "You must tell him. Why didn't you tell him then?"

When I found Petrus again, he looked up politely. "Look, Petrus," I said. "You can't go to fetch your brother. They've done it already—they've *buried* him, you understand?"

"Where?" he said slowly, dully, as if he thought that perhaps he was getting this wrong.

"You see, he was a stranger. They knew he wasn't from here, and they didn't know he had some of his people here, so they thought they must bury him." It was difficult to make a pauper's grave sound like a privilege.

"Please, *Baas*, the *Baas* must ask them?" But he did not mean that he wanted to know the burial place. He simply ignored the incomprehensible

machinery I told him had set to work on his dead brother; he wanted the
brother back.

"But, Petrus," I said, "how can I? Your brother is buried already. I can't
ask them now."

"Oh, *Baas!*" he said. He stood with his bran-smeared hands uncurled at
his sides, one corner of his mouth twitching.

"Good God, Petrus, they won't listen to me! They can't, anyway. I'm
sorry, but I can't do it. You understand?"

He just kept on looking at me, out of his knowledge that white men
have everything, can do anything; if they don't, it is because they won't.

And then, at dinner, Lerice started. "You could at least phone," she
said.

"Christ, what d'you think I am? Am I supposed to bring the dead back
to life?"

But I could not exaggerate my way out of this ridiculous responsibility
that had been thrust on me. "Phone them up," she went on. "And at least
you'll be able to tell him you've done it and they've explained that it's impossible."

She disappeared somewhere into the kitchen quarters after coffee. A
little later she came back to tell me, "The old father's coming down from
Rhodesia to be at the funeral. He's got a permit and he's already on his
way."

Unfortunately, it was not impossible to get the body back. The authorities said that it was somewhat irregular, but that since the hygiene conditions had been fulfilled, they could not refuse permission for exhumation. I
found out that, with the undertaker's charges, it would cost twenty pounds.
Ah, I thought, that settles it. On five pounds a month, Petrus won't have
twenty pounds—and just as well, since it couldn't do the dead any good.
Certainly I should not offer it to him myself. Twenty pounds—or anything
else within reason, for that matter—I would have spent without grudging it
on doctors or medicines that might have helped the boy when he was alive.
Once he was dead, I had no intention of encouraging Petrus to throw away,
on a gesture, more than he spent to clothe his whole family in a year.

When I told him, in the kitchen that night, he said, "Twenty pounds?"

I said, "Yes, that's right, twenty pounds."

For a moment, I had the feeling, from the look on his face, that he was
calculating. But when he spoke again I thought I must have imagined it.
"We must pay twenty pounds!" he said in the faraway voice in which a
person speaks of something so unattainable that it does not bear thinking
about.

"All right, Petrus," I said in dismissal, and went back to the living room.

The next morning before I went to town, Petrus asked to see me.
"Please, *Baas,*" he said, awkwardly handing me a bundle of notes. They're so
seldom on the giving rather than the receiving side, poor devils, that they
don't really know how to hand money to a white man. There it was, the
twenty pounds, in ones and halves, some creased and folded until they were

soft as dirty rags, others smooth and fairly new—Franz's money, I suppose, and Albert's, and Dora the cook's, and Jacob the gardener's, and God knows who else's besides, from all the farms and small holdings round about. I took it in irritation more than in astonishment, really—irritation at the waste, the uselessness of this sacrifice by people so poor. Just like the poor everywhere, I thought, who stint themselves the decencies of life in order to insure themselves the decencies of death. So incomprehensible to people like Lerice and me, who regard life as something to be spent extravagantly and, if we think about death at all, regard it as the final bankruptcy.

The servants don't work on Saturday afternoon anyway, so it was a good day for the funeral. Petrus and his father had borrowed our donkey cart to fetch the coffin from the city, where, Petrus told Lerice on their return, everything was "nice"—the coffin waiting for them, already sealed up to save them from what must have been a rather unpleasant sight after two weeks' interment. (It had taken all that time for the authorities and the undertaker to make the final arrangements for moving the body.) All morning, the coffin lay in Petrus's hut, awaiting the trip to the little old burial ground, just outside the eastern boundary of our farm, that was a relic of the days when this was a real farming district rather than a fashionable rural estate. It was pure chance that I happened to be down there near the fence when the procession came past; once again Lerice had forgotten her promise to me and had made the house uninhabitable on a Saturday afternoon. I had come home and been infuriated to find her in a pair of filthy old slacks and with her hair uncombed since the night before, having all the varnish scraped off the living-room floor, if you please. So I had taken my No. 8 iron and gone off to practice my approach shots. In my annoyance, I had forgotten about the funeral, and was reminded only when I saw the procession coming up the path along the outside of the fence toward me; from where I was standing, you can see the graves quite clearly, and that day the sun glinted on bits of broken pottery, a lopsided homemade cross, and jam jars brown with rain water and dead flowers.

I felt a little awkward, and did not know whether to go on hitting my golf ball or stop at least until the whole gathering was decently past. The donkey cart creaks and screeches with every revolution of the wheels and it came along in a slow, halting fashion somehow peculiarly suited to the two donkeys who drew it, their little potbellies rubbed and rough, their heads sunk between the shafts, and their ears flattened back with an air submissive and downcast; peculiarly suited, too, to the group of men and women who came along slowly behind. The patient ass. Watching, I thought, You can see now why the creature became a Biblical symbol. Then the procession drew level with me and stopped, so I had to put down my club. The coffin was taken down off the cart—it was a shiny, yellow-varnished wood, like cheap furniture—and the donkeys twitched their ears against the flies. Petrus, Franz, Albert, and the old father from Rhodesia hoisted it on their shoulders and the procession moved on, on foot. It was really a very awkward moment. I stood there rather foolishly at the fence, quite still, and slowly they filed past, not looking up, the four men bent beneath the shiny wooden box, and the straggling troop of mourners. All of them were servants or neighbors' servants whom I knew as casual, easygoing gossipers about our lands or kitchen. I heard the old man's breathing.

I had just bent to pick up my club again when there was a sort of jar in the flowing solemnity of their processional mood; I felt it at once, like a wave of heat along the air, or one of those sudden currents of cold catching at your legs in a placid stream. The old man's voice was muttering something; the people had stopped, confused, and they bumped into one another, some pressing to go on, others hissing them to be still. I could see that they were embarrassed, but they could not ignore the voice; it was much the way that the mumblings of a prophet, though not clear at first, arrest the mind. The corner of the coffin the old man carried was sagging at an angle; he seemed to be trying to get out from under the weight of it. Now Petrus expostulated with him.

The little boy who had been left to watch the donkeys dropped the reins and ran to see. I don't know why—unless it was for the same reason people crowd round someone who has fainted in a cinema—but I parted the wires of the fence and went through, after him.

Petrus lifted his eyes to me—to anybody—with distress and horror. The old man from Rhodesia had let go of the coffin entirely, and the three others, unable to support it on their own, had laid it on the ground, in the pathway. Already there was a film of dust lightly wavering up its shiny sides. I did not understand what the old man was saying; I hesitated to interfere. But now the whole seething group turned on my silence. The old man himself came over to me, with his hands outspread and shaking, and spoke directly to me, saying something that I could tell from the tone, without understanding the words, was shocking and extraordinary.

"What is it, Petrus? What's wrong?" I appealed.

Petrus threw up his hands, bowed his head in a series of hysterical shakes, then thrust his face up at me suddenly. "He says, 'My son was not so heavy.'"

Silence. I could hear the old man breathing; he kept his mouth a little open, as old people do.

"My son was young and thin," he said at last, in English.

Again silence. Then babble broke out. The old man thundered against everybody; his teeth were yellowed and few, and he had one of those fine, grizzled, sweeping mustaches that one doesn't often see nowadays, which must have been grown in emulation of early Empire builders. It seemed to frame all his utterances with a special validity, perhaps merely because it was the symbol of the traditional wisdom of age—an idea so fearfully rooted that it carries still something awesome beyond reason. He shocked them; they thought he was mad, but they had to listen to him. With his own hands he began to prize the lid off the coffin and three of the men came forward to help him. Then he sat down on the ground; very old, very weak, and unable to speak, he merely lifted a trembling hand toward what was there. He abdicated, he handed it over to them; he was no good any more.

They crowded round to look (and so did I), and now they forgot the nature of this surprise and the occasion of grief to which it belonged, and for a few minutes were carried up in the delightful astonishment of the surprise itself. They gasped and flared noisily with excitement. I even noticed the little boy who had held the donkeys jumping up and down, almost weeping with rage because the backs of the grownups crowded him out of his view.

In the coffin was someone no one had ever seen before: a heavily built, rather light-skinned native with a neatly stitched scar on his forehead—perhaps from a blow in a brawl that had also dealt him some other, slower-working injury, which had killed him.

I wrangled with the authorities for a week over that body. I had the feeling that they were shocked, in a laconic fashion, by their own mistake, but that in the confusion of their anonymous dead they were helpless to put it right. They said to me, "We are trying to find out," and "We are still making inquiries." It was as if at any moment they might conduct me into their mortuary and say, "There! Lift up the sheets; look for him—your poultry boy's brother. There are so many black faces—surely one will do?"

And every evening when I got home, Petrus was waiting in the kitchen. "Well, they're trying. They're still looking. The *Baas* is seeing to it for you, Petrus," I would tell him. "God, half the time I should be in the office I'm driving around the back end of the town chasing after this affair," I added aside, to Lerice, one night.

She and Petrus both kept their eyes turned on me as I spoke, and, oddly, for those moments they looked exactly alike, though it sounds impossible: my wife, with her high, white forehead and her attenuated Englishwoman's body, and the poultry boy, with his horny bare feet below khaki trousers tied at the knee with string and the peculiar rankness of his nervous sweat coming from his skin.

"What makes you so indignant, so determined about this now?" said Lerice suddenly.

I stared at her. "It's a matter of principle. Why should they get away with a swindle? It's time these officials had a jolt from someone who'll bother to take the trouble."

She said, "Oh." And as Petrus slowly opened the kitchen door to leave, sensing that the talk had gone beyond him, she turned away, too.

I continued to pass on assurances to Petrus every evening, but although what I said was the same and the voice in which I said it was the same, every evening it sounded weaker. At last, it became clear that we would never get Petrus's brother back, because nobody really knew where he was. Somewhere in a graveyard as uniform as a housing scheme, somewhere under a number that didn't belong to him, or in the medical school, perhaps, laboriously reduced to layers of muscle and strings of nerve? Goodness knows. He had no identity in this world anyway.

It was only then, and in a voice of shame, that Petrus asked me to try and get the money back.

"From the way he asks, you'd think he was robbing his dead brother," I said to Lerice later. But as I've said, Lerice had got so intense about this business that she couldn't even appreciate a little ironic smile.

I tried to get the money; Lerice tried. We both telephoned and wrote and argued, but nothing came of it. It appeared that the main expense had been the undertaker, and after all he had done his job. So the whole thing was a complete waste, even more of a waste for the poor devils than I had thought it would be.

The old man from Rhodesia was about Lerice's father's size, so she gave him one of her father's old suits, and he went back home rather better off, for the winter, than he had come.

Like a Bad Dream
Heinrich Böll   *Germany, 1966*

ABOUT THE AUTHOR

*Heinrich Böll (1917–1985) was born in Cologne, Germany. After gradu-
ating from high school, he became an apprentice to a book dealer and then
was inducted into the labor service, a semi-military obligation. Following
his service, he enrolled in college, but his studies were interrupted when, at
the age of twenty-one, he was drafted into the army. Böll witnessed cruelty
and injustice during his youth and military service; and in his autobiogra-
phy and other writings, he expressed his outrage at the Nazis. His many
works treat every significant phase in West German history from the nation's establishment in 1949 to the mid-1980s. Among his novels are* Bil-
liards at Half-Past Nine *(1962) and* The Clown *(1965). Böll was
awarded the Nobel Prize for Literature in 1972.*

THE CONTEXT OF THE STORY

*The story takes place in Germany after World War II. References to the
characters' Christian religion include* nuns *(women who belong to a religious order); artwork representing the* Madonna *(the mother of Jesus
Christ) and the* crucifix *(the image of Christ dying on the cross).*

That evening we had invited the Zumpens over for dinner, nice people;
it was through my father-in-law that we had got to know them: ever since
we have been married he has helped me to meet people who can be useful
to me in business, and Zumpen can be useful: he is chairman of a committee which places contracts for large housing projects, and I have married
into the excavating business.

I was tense that evening, but Bertha, my wife, reassured me. "The fact,"
she said, "that he's coming at all is promising. Just try and get the conversation round to the contract. You know it's tomorrow they're going to be
awarded."

I stood looking through the net curtains of the glass front door, waiting
for Zumpen. I smoked, ground the cigarette butts under my foot, and
shoved them under the mat. Next I took up a position at the bathroom
window and stood there wondering why Zumpen had accepted the invitation; he couldn't be that interested in having dinner with us, and the fact
that the big contract I was involved in was going to be awarded tomorrow
must have made the whole thing as embarrassing to him as it was to me.

I thought about the contract too: it was a big one, I would make 20,000
marks on the deal, and I wanted the money.

Translated by Leila Vennewitz.

Bertha had decided what I was to wear: a dark jacket, trousers a shade lighter, and a conservative tie. That's the kind of thing she learned at home, and at boarding school from the nuns. Also what to offer guests: when to pass the cognac, and when the vermouth, how to arrange dessert. It is comforting to have a wife who knows all about such things.

But Bertha was tense too: as she put her hands on my shoulders, they touched my neck, and I felt her thumbs damp and cold against it.

"It's going to be all right," she said. "You'll get the contract."

"Christ," I said, "it means 20,000 marks to me, and you know how we need the money."

"One should never," she said gently, "mention Christ's name in connection with money!"

A dark car drew up in front of our house, a make I didn't recognize, but it looked Italian. "Take it easy," Bertha whispered, "wait till they've rung, let them stand there for a couple of seconds, then walk slowly to the door and open it."

I watched Mr. and Mrs. Zumpen come up the steps: he is slender and tall, with graying temples, the kind of man who fifty years ago would have been known as a "ladies' man"; Mrs. Zumpen is one of those thin dark women who always make me think of lemons. I could tell from Zumpen's face that it was a frightful bore for him to have dinner with us.

Then the doorbell rang, and I waited one second, two seconds, walked slowly to the door and opened it.

"Well," I said, "how nice of you to come!"

Cognac glasses in hand, we went from room to room in our apartment, which the Zumpens wanted to see. Bertha stayed in the kitchen to squeeze some mayonnaise out of a tube onto the appetizers; she does this very nicely: hearts, loops, little houses. The Zumpens complimented us on our apartment; they exchanged smiles when they saw the big desk in my study, at that moment it seemed a bit too big even to me.

Zumpen admired a small rococo cabinet, a wedding present from my grandmother, and a baroque Madonna in our bedroom.

By the time we got back to the dining room, Bertha had dinner on the table; she had done this very nicely too, it was all so attractive yet so natural, and dinner was pleasant and relaxed. We talked about movies and books, about the recent elections, and Zumpen praised the assortment of cheeses, and Mrs. Zumpen praised the coffee and the pastries. Then we showed the Zumpens our honeymoon pictures: photographs of the Breton coast, Spanish donkeys, and street scenes from Casablanca.

After that we had some more cognac, and when I stood up to get the box with the photos of the time when we were engaged, Bertha gave me a sign, and I didn't get the box. For two minutes there was absolute silence, because we had nothing more to talk about, and we all thought about the contract; I thought of the 20,000 marks, and it struck me that I could deduct the bottle of cognac from my income tax. Zumpen looked at his watch and said: "Too bad, it's ten o'clock; we have to go. It's been such a pleasant evening!" And Mrs. Zumpen said: "It was really delightful, and I hope you'll come to us one evening."

"We would love to," Bertha said, and we stood around for another half-minute, all thinking again about the contract, and I felt Zumpen was waiting for me to take him aside and bring up the subject. But I didn't. Zumpen kissed Bertha's hand, and I went ahead, opened the doors, and held the car door open for Mrs. Zumpen down below.

"Why," said Bertha gently, "didn't you mention the contract to him? You know it's going to be awarded tomorrow."

"Well," I said. "I didn't know how to bring the conversation round to it."

"Now look," she said in a quiet voice, "you could have used any excuse to ask him into your study, that's where you should have talked to him. You must have noticed how interested he is in art. You ought to have said: I have an eighteenth-century crucifix in there you might like to have a look at, and then . . ."

I said nothing, and she sighed and tied on her apron. I followed her into the kitchen; we put the rest of the appetizers back in the refrigerator, and I crawled about on the floor looking for the top of the mayonnaise tube. I put away the remains of the cognac, counted the cigars: Zumpen had smoked only one. I emptied the ashtrays, ate another pastry, and looked to see if there was any coffee left in the pot. When I went back to the kitchen, Bertha was standing there with the car key in her hand.

"What's up?" I asked.

"We have to go over there, of course," she said.

"Over where?"

"To the Zumpens'," she said, "where do you think?"

"It's nearly half past ten."

"I don't care if it's midnight," Bertha said, "all I know is, there's 20,000 marks involved. Don't imagine they're squeamish."

She went into the bathroom to get ready, and I stood behind her watching her wipe her mouth and draw in new outlines, and for the first time I noticed how wide and primitive that mouth is. When she tightened the knot of my tie I could have kissed her, the way I always used to when she fixed my tie, but I didn't.

Downtown the cafés and restaurants were brightly lit. People were sitting outside on the terraces, and the light from the street lamps was caught in the silver ice-cream dishes and ice buckets. Bertha gave me an encouraging look; but she stayed in the car when we stopped in front of the Zumpens' house, and I pressed the bell at once and was surprised how quickly the door was opened. Mrs. Zumpen did not seem surprised to see me; she had on some black lounging pajamas with loose full trousers embroidered with yellow flowers, and this made me think more than ever of lemons.

"I beg your pardon," I said, "I would like to speak to your husband."

"He's gone out again," she said, "he'll be back in half an hour."

In the hall I saw a lot of Madonnas, gothic and baroque, even rococo Madonnas, if there is such a thing.

"I see," I said, "well then, if you don't mind, I'll come back in half an hour."

Bertha had bought an evening paper; she was reading it and smoking, and when I sat down beside her she said: "I think you could have talked about it to her too."

"But how do you know he wasn't there?"

"Because I know he is at the Gaffel Club playing chess, as he does every Wednesday evening at this time."

"You might have told me that earlier."

"Please try and understand," said Bertha, folding the newspaper. "I am trying to help you, I want you to find out for yourself how to deal with such things. All we had to do was call up Father and he would have settled the whole thing for you with one phone call, but I want you to get the contract on your own."

"All right," I said, "then what'll we do: wait here half an hour, or go up right away and have a talk with her?"

"We'd better go up right away," said Bertha.

We got out of the car and went up in the elevator together. "Life," said Bertha, "consists of making compromises and concessions."

Mrs. Zumpen was no more surprised now than she had been earlier, when I had come alone. She greeted us, and we followed her into her husband's study. Mrs. Zumpen brought some cognac, poured it out, and before I could say anything about the contract she pushed a yellow folder toward me: "Housing Project Fir Tree Haven," I read, and looked up in alarm at Mrs. Zumpen, at Bertha, but they both smiled, and Mrs. Zumpen said: "Open the folder," and I opened it; inside was another one, pink, and on this I read: "Housing Project Fir Tree Haven—Excavation Work." I opened this too, saw my estimate lying there on top of the pile; along the upper edge someone had written in red: "Lowest bid."

I could feel myself flushing with pleasure, my heart thumping, and I thought of the 20,000 marks.

"Christ," I said softly, and closed the file, and this time Bertha forgot to rebuke me.

"*Prost,*"[1] said Mrs. Zumpen with a smile, "let's drink to it then."

We drank, and I stood up and said: "It may seem rude of me, but perhaps you'll understand that I would like to go home now."

"I understand perfectly," said Mrs. Zumpen, "there's just one small item to be taken care of." She took the file, leafed through it, and said: "Your price per square meter is thirty pfennigs below that of the next-lowest bidder. I suggest you raise your price by fifteen pfennigs: that way you'll still be lowest and you'll have made an extra four thousand five hun-

---

[1] *Prost:* "Your health"

dred marks. Come on, do it now!" Bertha took her pen out of her purse and offered it to me, but I was in too much of turmoil to write; I gave the file to Bertha and watched her alter the price with a steady hand, rewrite the total, and hand the file back to Mrs. Zumpen.

"And now," said Mrs. Zumpen, "just one more little thing. Get out your check book and write a check for three thousand marks; it must be a cash check and endorsed by you."

She had said this to me, but it was Bertha who pulled our check book out of her purse and made out the check.

"It won't be covered," I said in a low voice.

"When the contract is awarded, there will be an advance, and then it will be covered," said Mrs. Zumpen.

Perhaps I failed to grasp what was happening at the time. As we went down the elevator, Bertha said she was happy, but I said nothing.

Bertha chose a different way home, we drove through quiet residential districts, I saw lights in open windows, people sitting on balconies drinking wine; it was a clear, warm night.

"I suppose the check was for Zumpen?" was all I said, softly, and Bertha replied, just as softly: "Of course."

I looked at Bertha's small, brown hands on the steering wheel, so confident and quiet. Hands, I thought, that sign checks and squeeze mayonnaise tubes, and I looked higher—at her mouth, and still felt no desire to kiss it.

That evening I did not help Bertha put the car away in the garage, nor did I help her with the dishes. I poured myself a large cognac, went up to my study, and sat down at my desk, which was much too big for me. I was wondering about something. I got up, went into the bedroom, and looked at the baroque Madonna, but even there I couldn't put my finger on the thing I was wondering about.

The ringing of the phone interrupted my thoughts; I lifted the receiver and was not surprised to hear Zumpen's voice.

"Your wife," he said, "made a slight mistake. She raised the price by twenty-five pfennigs instead of fifteen."

I thought for a moment and then said: "That wasn't a mistake, she did it with my consent."

He was silent for a second or two, then said with a laugh: "So you had already discussed the various possibilities?"

"Yes," I said.

"All right, then make out another check for a thousand."

"Five hundred," I said, and I thought: It's like a bad dream—that's what it's like.

"Eight hundred," he said, and I said with a laugh: "Six hundred," and I knew, although I had no experience to go on, that he would now say seven hundred and fifty, and when he did I said "Yes" and hung up.

It was not yet midnight when I went downstairs and over to the car to give Zumpen the check; he was alone and laughed as I reached in to hand him the folded check. When I walked slowly back into the house, there was no sign of Bertha; she didn't appear when I went back into my study; she didn't appear when I went downstairs again for a glass of milk from the refrigerator, and I knew what she was thinking; she was thinking: he has to get over it, and I have to leave him alone; this is something he has to understand.

But I never did understand. It is beyond understanding.

Swaddling Clothes
Mishima Yukio   Japan, 1966

ABOUT THE AUTHOR
*Mishima Yukio (1925–1970) is the pen name of Kimitake Hiraoka.
Born in Tokyo, Japan, he began to publish his writing when he was in his
twenties. In addition to writing fiction and drama, Mishima directed and
acted in films. Among his novels are* Confessions of a Mask *(1949),*
The Temple of the Golden Pavilion *(1959), and* The Sailor Who
Fell from Grace with the Sea *(1965). He won numerous literary
awards and was nominated three times for the Nobel Prize for Literature.
Mishima is remembered not only for his work but also for his public ritual
suicide.*

THE CONTEXT OF THE STORY
*The story takes place in Tokyo after World War II. References to Japa-
nese life include* kimono *(a traditional long, wide-sleeved robe); the* Imperial Palace *(home of the Japanese emperor);* cherry trees *(trees that
blossom in April and are the central feature of one of Japan's major cele-
brations, the Cherry Blossom Festival); and* paper lanterns *(traditional
lighting of Japan used for special festivals).*

THE TITLE OF THE STORY
The phrase swaddling clothes *refers to the cloth wrapped around a newborn infant to hold its legs and arms still, for security.*

He was always busy, Toshiko's husband. Even tonight he had to dash
off to an appointment, leaving her to go home alone by taxi. But what else
could a woman expect when she married an actor—an attractive one? No
doubt she had been foolish to hope that he would spend the evening with
her. And yet he must have known how she dreaded going back to their
house, unhomely with its Western-style furniture and with the bloodstains
still showing on the floor.

Toshiko had been oversensitive since girlhood: that was her nature. As
the result of constant worrying she never put on weight, and now, an adult
woman, she looked more like a transparent picture than a creature of flesh
and blood. Her delicacy of spirit was evident to her most casual acquaintance.

Earlier that evening, when she had joined her husband at a night club,
she had been shocked to find him entertaining friends with an account of
"the incident." Sitting there in his American-style suit, puffing at a cigarette, he had seemed to her almost a stranger.

Translated by Ivan Morris.

"It's a fantastic story," he was saying, gesturing flamboyantly as if in an attempt to outweigh the attractions of the dance band. "Here this new nurse for our baby arrives from the employment agency, and the very first thing I notice about her is her stomach. It's enormous—as if she had a pillow stuck under her kimono! No wonder, I thought, for I soon saw that she could eat more than the rest of us put together. She polished off the contents of our rice bin like that. . . ." He snapped his fingers. "'Gastric dilation'—that's how she explained her girth and her appetite. Well, the day before yesterday we heard groans and moans coming from the nursery. We rushed in and found her squatting on the floor, holding her stomach in her two hands, and moaning like a cow. Next to her our baby lay in his cot, scared out of his wits and crying at the top of his lungs. A pretty scene, I can tell you!"

"So the cat was out of the bag?" suggested one of their friends, a film actor like Toshiko's husband.

"Indeed it was! And it gave me the shock of my life. You see, I'd completely swallowed that story about 'gastric dilation.' Well, I didn't waste any time. I rescued our good rug from the floor and spread a blanket for her to lie on. The whole time the girl was yelling like a stuck pig. By the time the doctor from the maternity clinic arrived, the baby had already been born. But our sitting room was a pretty shambles!"

"Oh, that I'm sure of!" said another of their friends, and the whole company burst into laughter.

Toshiko was dumbfounded to hear her husband discussing the horrifying happening as though it were no more than an amusing incident which they chanced to have witnessed. She shut her eyes for a moment and all at once she saw the newborn baby lying before her: on the parquet floor the infant lay, and his frail body was wrapped in bloodstained newspapers.

Toshiko was sure that the doctor had done the whole thing out of spite. As if to emphasize his scorn for this mother who had given birth to a bastard under such sordid conditions, he had told his assistant to wrap the baby in some loose newspapers, rather than proper swaddling. This callous treatment of the newborn child had offended Toshiko. Overcoming her disgust at the entire scene, she had fetched a brand-new piece of flannel from her cupboard and, having swaddled the baby in it, had lain him carefully in an armchair.

This all had taken place in the evening after her husband had left the house. Toshiko had told him nothing of it, fearing that he would think her oversoft, oversentimental; yet the scene had engraved itself deeply in her mind. Tonight she sat silently thinking back on it, while the jazz orchestra brayed and her husband chatted cheerfully with his friends. She knew that she would never forget the sight of the baby, wrapped in stained newspapers and lying on the floor—it was a scene fit for a butchershop. Toshiko, whose own life had been spent in solid comfort, poignantly felt the wretchedness of the illegitimate baby.

I am the only person to have witnessed its shame, the thought occurred to her. The mother never saw her child lying there in its newspaper wrappings, and the baby itself of course didn't know. I alone shall have to preserve that terrible scene in my memory. When the baby grows up and wants to find out about his birth, there will be no one to tell him, so long as I preserve silence. How strange that I should have this feeling of guilt! After all, it was I who took him up from the floor, swathed him properly in flannel, and laid him down to sleep in the armchair.

They left the night club and Toshiko stepped into the taxi that her husband had called for her. "Take this lady to Ushigomé," he told the driver and shut the door from the outside. Toshiko gazed through the window at her husband's smiling face and noticed his strong, white teeth. Then she leaned back in the seat, oppressed by the knowledge that their life together was in some way too easy, too painless. It would have been difficult for her to put her thoughts into words. Through the rear window of the taxi she took a last look at her husband. He was striding along the street toward his Nash[1] car, and soon the back of his rather garish tweed coat had blended with the figures of the passers-by.

The taxi drove off, passed down a street dotted with bars and then by a theatre, in front of which the throngs of people jostled each other on the pavement. Although the performance had only just ended, the lights had already been turned out and in the half dark outside it was depressingly obvious that the cherry blossoms decorating the front of the theatre were merely scraps of white paper.

Even if that baby should grow up in ignorance of the secret of his birth, he can never become a respectable citizen, reflected Toshiko, pursuing the same train of thoughts. Those soiled newspaper swaddling clothes will be the symbol of his entire life. But why should I keep worrying about him so much? Is it because I feel uneasy about the future of my own child? Say twenty years from now, when our boy will have grown up into a fine, carefully educated young man, one day by a quirk of fate he meets the other boy, who then will also have turned twenty. And say that the other boy, who has been sinned against, savagely stabs him with a knife. . . .

It was a warm, overcast April night, but thoughts of the future made Toshiko feel cold and miserable. She shivered on the back seat of the car.

No, when the time comes I shall take my son's place, she told herself suddenly. Twenty years from now I shall be forty-three. I shall go to that young man and tell him straight out about everything—about his newspaper swaddling clothes, and about how I went and wrapped him in flannel.

The taxi ran along the dark wide road that was bordered by the park and by the Imperial Palace moat. In the distance Toshiko noticed the pinpricks of light which came from the blocks of tall office buildings.

Twenty years from now that wretched child will be in utter misery. He will be living a desolate, hopeless, poverty-stricken existence—a lonely rat. What else could happen to a baby who has had such a birth? He'll be

---

[1] **Nash:** an American-made automobile

wandering through the streets by himself, cursing his father, loathing his mother.

No doubt Toshiko derived a certain satisfaction from her somber thoughts: she tortured herself with them without cease. The taxi approached Hanzomon and drove past the compound of the British Embassy. At that point the famous rows of cherry trees were spread out before Toshiko in all their purity. On the spur of the moment she decided to go and view the blossoms by herself in the dark night. It was a strange decision for a timid and unadventurous young woman, but then she was in a strange state of mind and she dreaded the return home. That evening all sorts of unsettling fancies had burst open in her mind.

She crossed the wide street—a slim, solitary figure in the darkness. As a rule when she walked in the traffic Toshiko used to cling fearfully to her companion, but tonight she darted alone between the cars and a moment later had reached the long narrow park that borders the Palace moat. Chidorigafuchi, it is called—the Abyss of the Thousand Birds.

Tonight the whole park had become a grove of blossoming cherry trees. Under the calm cloudy sky the blossoms formed a mass of solid whiteness. The paper lanterns that hung from wires between the trees had been put out; in their place electric light bulbs, red, yellow, and green, shone dully beneath the blossoms. It was well past ten o'clock and most of the flower-viewers had gone home. As the occasional passers-by strolled through the park, they would automatically kick aside the empty bottles or crush the waste paper beneath their feet.

Newspapers, thought Toshiko, her mind going back once again to those happenings. Bloodstained newspapers. If a man were ever to hear of that piteous birth and know that it was he who had lain there, it would ruin his entire life. To think that I, a perfect stranger, should from now on have to keep such a secret—the secret of a man's whole existence. . . .

Lost in these thoughts, Toshiko walked on through the park. Most of the people still remaining there were quiet couples; no one paid her any attention. She noticed two people sitting on a stone bench beside the moat, not looking at the blossoms, but gazing silently at the water. Pitch black it was, and swathed in heavy shadows. Beyond the moat the somber forest of the Imperial Palace blocked her view. The trees reached up, to form a solid dark mass against the night sky. Toshiko walked slowly along the path beneath the blossoms hanging heavily overhead.

On a stone bench, slightly apart from the others, she noticed a pale object—not, as she had at first imagined, a pile of cherry blossoms, nor a garment forgotten by one of the visitors to the park. Only when she came closer did she see that it was a human form lying on the bench. Was it, she wondered, one of those miserable drunks often to be seen sleeping in public places? Obviously not, for the body had been systematically covered with newspapers, and it was the whiteness of those papers that had attracted Toshiko's attention. Standing by the bench, she gazed down at the sleeping figure.

It was a man in a brown jersey who lay there, curled up on layers of newspapers, other newspapers covering him. No doubt this had become his normal night residence now that spring had arrived. Toshiko gazed down at the man's dirty, unkempt hair, which in places had become hopelessly matted. As she observed the sleeping figure wrapped in its newspapers, she was inevitably reminded of the baby who had lain on the floor in its wretched swaddling clothes. The shoulder of the man's jersey rose and fell in the darkness in time with his heavy breathing.

It seemed to Toshiko that all her fears and premonitions had suddenly taken concrete form. In the darkness the man's pale forehead stood out, and it was a young forehead, though carved with the wrinkles of long poverty and hardship. His khaki trousers had been slightly pulled up; on his sockless feet he wore a pair of battered gym shoes. She could not see his face and suddenly had an overmastering desire to get one glimpse of it.

She walked to the head of the bench and looked down. The man's head was half buried in his arms, but Toshiko could see that he was surprisingly young. She noticed the thick eyebrows and the fine bridge of his nose. His slightly open mouth was alive with youth.

But Toshiko had approached too close. In the silent night the newspaper bedding rustled, and abruptly the man opened his eyes. Seeing the young woman standing directly beside him, he raised himself with a jerk, and his eyes lit up. A second later a powerful hand reached out and seized Toshiko by her slender wrist.

She did not feel in the least afraid and made no effort to free herself. In a flash the thought had struck her. Ah, so the twenty years have already gone by! The forest of the Imperial Palace was pitch dark and utterly silent.

A Handful of Dates
Tayeb Salih   Sudan, 1968

ABOUT THE AUTHOR

Tayeb Salih (b. 1929) was born in a northern province of Sudan and grew up in a farming community. He studied at Khartoum and London universities. In England, he worked for the British Broadcasting Company's Arabic Service. He later worked for the Sudan Broadcasting Service, UNESCO in Paris, and the Information Services in Qatar. His novel, Season of Migration to the North *(1969), is partly set in the same village as the stories in his collection* The Wedding of Zein, *from which "A Handful of Dates" is taken. Critics rate him among the best authors of Arabic literature.*

THE CONTEXT OF THE STORY

The story takes place in a village in a northern province of Sudan, the inhabitants of which are Muslim. The Koran *(the holy book of Islam) directs Muslims to pray to* Allah *(God) five times a day, either by going to the* mosque *(a Moslem house of worship) or by kneeling on a* prayer-rug. *Before prayer, Muslims are expected to take part in* ablutions *(ceremonial washing of face, hands, and feet), using water poured from an* ewer *(a pitcher or jug).*

I must have been very young at the time. While I don't remember exactly how old I was, I do remember that when people saw me with my grandfather they would pat me on the head and give my cheek a pinch—things they didn't do to my grandfather. The strange thing was that I never used to go out with my father, rather it was my grandfather who would take me with him whenever he went, except for the mornings when I would go to the mosque to learn the Koran. The mosque, the river and the fields—these were the landmarks in our life. While most of the children of my age grumbled at having to go to the mosque to learn the Koran, I used to love it. The reason was, no doubt, that I was quick at learning by heart and the Sheikh[1] always asked me to stand up and recite the *Chapter of the Merciful* whenever we had visitors, who would pat me on my head and cheek just as people did when they saw me with my grandfather.

Yes, I used to love the mosque, and I loved the river too. Directly we finished our Koran reading in the morning I would throw down my wooden slate and dart off, quick as a genie, to my mother, hurriedly swallow down my breakfast, and run off for a plunge in the river. When tired of swimming about I would sit on the bank and gaze at the strip of water that wound

Translated by Denys Johnson-Davies.
[1] **Sheikh:** a Moslem religious official

away eastwards and hid behind a thick wood of acacia trees. I loved to give rein to my imagination and picture to myself a tribe of giants living behind that wood, a people tall and thin with white beards and sharp noses, like my grandfather. Before my grandfather ever replied to my many questions he would rub the tip of his nose with his forefinger; as for his beard, it was soft and luxuriant and as white as cotton-wool—never in my life have I seen anything of a purer whiteness or greater beauty. My grandfather must also have been extremely tall, for I never saw anyone in the whole area address him without having to look up at him, nor did I see him enter a house without having to bend so low that I was put in mind of the way the river wound round behind the wood of acacia trees. I loved him and would imagine myself, when I grew to be a man, tall and slender like him, walking along with great strides.

I believe I was his favorite grandchild: no wonder, for my cousins were a stupid bunch and I—so they say—was an intelligent child. I used to know when my grandfather wanted me to laugh, when to be silent; also I would remember the times for his prayers and would bring him his prayer-rug and fill the ewer for his ablutions without his having to ask me. When he had nothing else to do he enjoyed listening to me reciting to him from the Koran in a lilting voice, and I could tell from his face that he was moved.

One day I asked him about our neighbour Masood. I said to my grandfather: "I fancy you don't like our neighbour Masood?"

To which he answered, having rubbed the tip of his nose: "He's an indolent man and I don't like such people."

I said to him: "What's an indolent man?"

My grandfather lowered his head for a moment, then looking across at the wide expanse of field, he said: "Do you see it stretching out from the edge of the desert up to the Nile bank? A hundred feddans.[2] Do you see all those date palms? And those trees—*sant,* acacia, and *sayal?* All this fell into Masood's lap, was inherited by him from his father."

Taking advantage of the silence that had descended upon my grandfather, I turned my gaze from him to the vast area defined by his words. "I don't care," I told myself, "who owns those date palms, those trees or this black, cracked earth—all I know is that it's the arena for my dreams and my playground."

My grandfather then continued: "Yes, my boy, forty years ago all this belonged to Masood—two-thirds of it is now mine."

This was news to me, for I had imagined that the land had belonged to my grandfather ever since God's Creation.

"I didn't own a single feddan when I first set foot in this village. Masood was then the owner of all these riches. The position has changed now, though, and I think that before Allah calls me to Him I shall have bought the remaining third as well."

---

[2] **feddan:** approximately an acre

I do not know why it was I felt fear at my grandfather's words—and pity for our neighbour Masood. How I wished my grandfather wouldn't do what he'd said! I remembered Masood's singing, his beautiful voice and powerful laugh that resembled the gurgling of water. My grandfather never used to laugh.

I asked my grandfather why Masood had sold his land.

"Women," and from the way my grandfather pronounced the word I felt that "women" was something terrible. "Masood, my boy, was a much-married man. Each time he married he sold me a feddan or two." I made the quick calculation that Masood must have married some ninety women. Then I remembered his three wives,[3] his shabby appearance, his lame donkey and its dilapidated saddle, his *galabia*[4] with the torn sleeves. I had all but rid my mind of the thoughts that jostled in it when I saw the man approaching us, and my grandfather and I exchanged glances.

"We'll be harvesting the dates today," said Masood. "Don't you want to be there?"

I felt, though, that he did not really want my grandfather to attend. My grandfather, however, jumped to his feet and I saw that his eyes sparkled momentarily with an intense brightness. He pulled me by the hand and we went off to the harvesting of Masood's dates.

Someone brought my grandfather a stool covered with an ox-hide, while I remained standing. There was a vast number of people there, but though I knew them all, I found myself for some reason watching Masood: aloof from that great gathering of people he stood as though it were no concern of his, despite the fact that the date palms to be harvested were his own. Sometimes his attention would be caught by the sound of a huge clump of dates crashing down from on high. Once he shouted up at the boy perched on the very summit of the date palm who had begun hacking at a clump with his long, sharp sickle: "Be careful you don't cut the heart of the palm."

No one paid any attention to what he said and the boy seated at the very summit of the date palm continued, quickly and energetically, to work away at the branch with his sickle till the clump of dates began to drop like something descending from the heavens.

I, however, had begun to think about Masood's phrase "the heart of the palm." I pictured the palm tree as something with feeling, something possessed of a heart that throbbed. I remembered Masood's remark to me when he had once seen me playing about with the branch of a young palm tree: "Palm trees, my boy, like humans, experience joy and suffering." And I had felt an inward and unreasoned embarrassment.

When I again looked at the expanse of ground stretching before me I saw my young companions swarming like ants around the trunks of the

---

[3] So that every woman would have someone to take care of her, traditional Muslim law allows men to have as many as four wives simultaneously.

[4] *galabia:* long, sacklike garment

palm trees, gathering up dates and eating most of them. The dates were collected into high mounds. I saw people coming along and weighing them into measuring bins and pouring them into sacks, of which I counted thirty. The crowd of people broke up, except for Hussein the merchant, Mousa the owner of the field next to ours on the east, and two men I'd never seen before.

I heard a low whistling sound and saw that my grandfather had fallen asleep. Then I noticed that Masood had not changed his stance, except that he had placed a stalk in his mouth and was munching at it like someone surfeited with food who doesn't know what to do with the mouthful he still has.

Suddenly my grandfather woke up, jumped to his feet and walked towards the sacks of dates. He was followed by Hussein the merchant, Mousa the owner of the field next to ours, and the two strangers. I glanced at Masood and saw that he was making his way towards us with extreme slowness, like a man who wants to retreat but whose feet insist on going forward. They formed a circle round the sacks of dates and began examining them, some taking a date or two to eat. My grandfather gave me a fistful, which I began munching. I saw Masood filling the palms of both hands with dates and bringing them up close to his nose, then returning them.

Then I saw them dividing up the sacks between them. Hussein the merchant took ten; each of the strangers took five. Mousa the owner of the field next to ours on the eastern side took five, and my grandfather took five. Understanding nothing, I looked at Masood and saw that his eyes were darting about to left and right like two mice that have lost their way home.

"You're still fifty pounds in debt to me," said my grandfather to Masood. "We'll talk about it later."

Hussein called his assistants and they brought along donkeys, the two strangers produced camels, and the sacks of dates were loaded on to them. One of the donkeys let out a braying which set the camels frothing at the mouth and complaining noisily. I felt myself drawing close to Masood, felt my hand stretch out towards him as though I wanted to touch the hem of his garment. I heard him make a noise in his throat like the rasping of a lamb being slaughtered. For some unknown reason, I experienced a sharp sensation of pain in my chest.

I ran off into the distance. Hearing my grandfather call after me, I hesitated a little, then continued on my way. I felt at that moment that I hated him. Quickening my pace, it was as though I carried within me a secret I wanted to rid myself of. I reached the river bank near the bend it made behind the wood of acacia trees. Then, without knowing why, I put my finger into my throat and spewed up the dates I'd eaten.

The Plane Reservation
Massud Farzan   Iran, 1969

ABOUT THE AUTHOR

Massud Farzan (b. 1936) was born and raised in Tabriz, Iran. After graduating from Tabriz University, he earned two graduate degrees in the United States. He was chairperson of the English department at Pahlavi University (now Shiraz University) and has taught literature and writing at several universities in the United States; currently, he is a professor of English in Belgium. A poet, critic, short-story writer, and translator, Farzan has published widely in a number of British and American journals. His five books include The Tale of the Reed Pipe *(1974) and* From Kashan to Kalamazoo *(1974).*

THE CONTEXT OF THE STORY

The story takes place in Iran, the dominant religion of which is Islam. References to the teachings of Islam include Allah *(God);* Mecca *(the holy city in Saudi Arabia that Muslims face when they pray); a* rosary *(a string of prayer beads); a* prayer-spread *(a shawl or rug on which Muslims stand and then kneel as they pray); and* chador *(a veil traditionally worn by religious women over the head, part of the face, and shoulders or whole body, to comply with the Islamic prescription of modesty).*

At the time the story was written, Iran was ruled by a constitutional monarchy supported by the United States. In the 1960s, the shah (king) initiated a modernization program designed to improve social and economic conditions, opening the way for many Iranians to come to the United States to study.

We lived on 23 Sadness Street. But it was a narrow street—cars couldn't enter—so I asked the cabdriver to drop me on the corner of Sadness and Pomegranate Blossoms. I paid the fare we had settled at the airport, plus a generous tip. The driver asked for more, speaking slowly and with funny gestures. I said no, and why do you speak like that, I am not a foreigner: I am just a Persian like yourself. He became embarrassed and I paid him a little more. He then helped me carry the heavy suitcase as far as 23 Sadness Street.

I knocked the horseshoe knocker that dangled in the afternoon breeze. An old woman opened the door a crack, peeped and immediately ran back into the house. "Khanom,[1] my baksheesh![2] Mr. Morad come!" I recognized the voice of the old laundress and remembered how I used to eavesdrop her

---

[1] **Khanom:** Lady; Madame
[2] **baksheesh:** reward or gift of money (for carrying good news)

conversations with herself. I passed the dark vestibule, knocked my head on the transom overhead and figured out how much taller I must have gotten since I had last passed under it. The little brick-covered yard, surrounded by four big walls, had been watered for coolness. In front of the yard stood the two little flowerbeds with flowers of many colors and with assorted vegetables. In the middle there was the little pond. A goldfish hung from the water surface, eating bubbles.

My mother rushed through the sitting room window to the yard, her prayer chador safety-pinned under her chin. "My son! Thanks Allah!" She opened her arms. My head down, I saw her shoulders shake. I stood wordless, without tears of happiness. I did not feel happy.

"Have you lost some weight, Morad? You look so different. Come through the window. That's all right, you needn't take off your shoes."

The living room was covered with thick native rugs, from wall to wall. There was no furniture except for a chair in a corner. Against the wall facing the yard and the flowerbeds there were two cushions. In the middle of the room my mother's prayer-spread lay open on the floor.

"You aren't through with your prayer, Mom. Go ahead and finish it first."

"I am going to. But first let me fix you a glass of quince sharbat,[3] it is good for the heart. Why did you sit on the floor? We have put the chair for you."

"I don't need to sit on the chair, Mom. It feels so good to spread my legs on these thick rugs."

"Drink your sharbat, it is good for the heart."

"All right. You go ahead and finish your prayer now."

She stood before her prayer-spread, facing Mecca, and began to move her lips. I noticed that she was saying her prayer slowly and deliberately and that her chador reached the floor, covering her entire feet. I remembered that she didn't used to wear her chador so long. Nor was her rosary so big. Mother must be getting old.

Outside, a man was selling ice. And in a distance a voice called out: THIS EVENING! IT WILL HAPPEN THIS EVENING AT EIGHT!

I sipped the quince sharbat and watched the yard. The flowerbeds were certainly my father's work; carefully cultivated and yet going wild and wayward. So many things in that ten by fifteen feet. Vivid green spotted with flowers red and yellow, pink and blue. Red roses surrounded by lettuce. Little violets at the foot of delpheniums. Petunias everywhere.

Four walls, thick and tall, surrounded the yard, keeping out whatever rays there were left of the setting sun.

A little clay-roofed closet huddled back in the corner, on the other side of the flowerbeds. It was the toilet. It had no stool, no toilet seat. You merely squatted over a funnel-shaped pit, dark and deep. You could keep

---

[3] **quince sharbat:** fruit juice

the door open, if you wished, watching the flowers, the rooftops, and the sky. Nobody to see you except maybe a couple of sparrows or a lone pigeon. I remembered how my father used to sit there, sometimes for half an hour or more. My mother would then go to wash her hands in the pond and call out, "Aren't you going to come out of that toilet?" Or, "Do you know you have been sitting in there for forty minutes?" My father wouldn't say anything. I knew that he didn't want to come out. He liked very much to think or meditate without being disturbed. My mother would make snide remarks whenever she caught him in deep reflection. "Inventing again, eh?" she would say and disturb his thoughts.

My father was an inventor. He had invented many things, although none of them had worked out. With each invention, he thought that he would make lots of money. He never told anybody what he would do once he got rich. But I knew what he would do. He would buy a house with a bigger yard, perhaps a garden, with a big pond; have a lot of goldfish; cultivate a great variety of flowers and vegetables. He would go on pilgrimage to Mecca and give to the poor. He would elicit respect from those he didn't like. He would cease to worry about his future in this world and beyond. But with each invention something would go wrong at the last moment, and he would abandon it only to start inventing something else. That would make my mother bolder and warier. She thought that whenever my father was silent and staring into the blank, he was conceiving a new invention. So she was always on the watch for those moments.

One day my father had come home with a big box under his arms. He had bought a radio. We all rejoiced. Every evening we sat on the rugs and listened. My father seemed to listen more attentively than everyone else. But it did not take long before my mother discovered what he was really doing. I think what gave him away was the faraway look in his eyes and the faint motionless smile on his face. My mother called him a sneak, a hopeless dreamer and other names. My father looked quite embarrassed. From then on he used to spend more time in the toilet at the corner of the yard.

That was many years ago. My mother was getting old: my father must be getting older. Maybe now they understood their common lot and forgave each other's foibles.

Once again the voice outside called out: IT WILL HAPPEN THIS EVENING AT EIGHT!

My mother finished her prayer. She carefully folded the prayer-spread and put it away on the shelf by the radio. "Tell me what you'd like to eat and I'll cook it for you. You really look so dark and thin."

I didn't know what to answer. "Am I? Maybe that's because I am now taller than I was when I left."

"As a boy you were so good looking," she went on. "We were all thinking you would come back from America fat and white."

Suddenly it occurred to me that she was blaming me.

"Look at that picture of your brother over your head. See the belly, *mashallah?*[4] Isn't that something? He's married, that's right. Maybe that is the reason. Which reminds me, you haven't gotten married, have you?"

"No, Mom, not yet. As a matter of fact, I may get married here."

"Good, I tell everybody that you are my wisest son. Is that why you came back?"

"Well, not really. To be frank, Mom, I came back in order to see what I can do for, I mean to have a close look at you and Pop and make sure that you are happy together. Now tell me, how are you getting along? How is Pop?"

"Don't worry about him. The bad vessel is seldom broken, as the saying goes."

THIS EVENING. . . .

My mother turned to the door. "He's not inventing anymore, if that's what you mean, but he's taken something else."

I listened.

"He's now buying lottery tickets *every* week. He also writes poetry. He thinks that—"

Just then the door opened and my father came in, holding a full grocery bag under his chin and a melon in the curve of his arm. The melon rolled on the floor; we salaamed[5] and embraced.

"You've kept yourself pretty well," I lied. "You look good, Pop."

"Do I really?" He smiled diffidently and watched my mother from the corner of his eye. "How do you find our little house? I mean next to American houses. Modest, eh?"

"I never saw flowerbeds like this anywhere," I said. My father smiled with mild contentment. "You should've seen it last month, Morad, we had roses as big as sunflowers." He walked to the window and gently threw the melon into the pond to get cool there.

THIS EVENING AT EIGHT! The voice was now very close, loud and clear.

"What does that mean?" I asked.

My father's face lit up. My mother looked at him reproachfully. "He's selling lottery tickets," he finally said. "The draw is this evening at eight." He stole a look at the clock on the radio.

My mother went out to the kitchen. I thought it was time to ask him if he was happy in his job and at home, whether he got along well with Mom. But just then he took his ashtray and cushion and sat beside me. "There is something I wanted to tell you," he began in a low, confidential tone, "I hope you won't mind it. What I wanted to say, Morad, you see, maybe you've forgotten all this time you were abroad, but in this country people look at your appearance and judge you accordingly; as the poet said: Feel the skin of a melon/Before thou purchaseth one. You see, if you were fat

[4] *mashallah:* knock on wood (literally, Praise be God)
[5] **salaamed:** bowed respectfully

and white, if you had a nice double chin and a potbelly, then there wouldn't be any problem and I wouldn't take up your time telling you all this. I mean people would then think that you're rich; you would be respected wherever you went in the country. But unfortunately you and I are the wiry type and rather dark. It would be a blasphemy to complain about it. Allah must have wanted it to be that way and we just can't do anything about it. But there is something we *can* do."

He leaned over and whispered, "Buy yourself a nice new suit and change your necktie. What is that you're wearing? As the poet said: What is in my weary heart/That while I'm quiet, it's in turmoil? Maybe that is not the appropriate poem; there is a better one in Sa'di's *Rose Garden*. I can't remember it now, but it doesn't matter. What I am trying to tell you, Morad, I'm really ashamed to mention it, but the barber on the corner of Pomegranate Street wears a better tie than yours. I always watch him closely when he cuts my hair, he wears genuine Silka ties, I am not lying to you. And his shoes are always polished. I myself can't afford to be very well dressed, but at least I can have a crease in my trousers, I can afford to have a shoeshine once in a while. I'll be darned if I can tell when it was last you got a shoeshine."

His face was quite somber. Apparently he wasn't any more pleased with his returning son than my mother was. Why did they keep asking me to go back? What made them believe that I would return someone other than I was, fatter and whiter than I was, as young as I was ten years ago? One thing was clear—they were disillusioned at the one who had returned. But I didn't resent that at all. If only I could make sure that they got along to-gether, that they were a bit happier than I remembered them to be.

My father put half a cigarette in a cigarette holder. "That's all I wanted to say, Morad. But I am not a narrow-minded old man; you'll of course do whatever you choose. As the poet has said: I advise whatever methinks fit/ You either profit by it or resent it."

Just then my mother came, hugging the big copper tray of supper. "What were you whispering to each other?" she asked.

"I was just telling Morad how he would look like a real gentleman if he had his shoes shined."

She said she agreed with him on that. I fetched the melon from the pond.

After supper my mother went to the kitchen to do the dishes. My father took a pencil and a piece of paper. He then turned on the radio. "I have a little lottery ticket. Who knows, Morad, maybe you've brought good luck to our house tonight."

At eight o'clock the radio chimed eight times, followed by a minute of silence. Then the announcer said that the draw procedures were being broadcast live from the Horizon Hall. My father took out his ticket and put it upside down on the floor beside his cigarette case and abacus. He then began to jot down the winning numbers on the sheet of paper.

My mother finished the dishes while the draw was still going on. She came in with a small tray of green beans and sat down to string them. I noticed that she was watching my father from the corner of her eye.

Having written all the winning numbers, my father turned over the ticket and began to check its number against the winning numbers. He started with the top prize and went down. His hand hovered over each number for a second before going to the next. The pencil trembled a little. My mother held a bean and forgot to string it. My eyes raced from him to her and back to him.

Suddenly my father threw the pencil up in the air. "Ten tumans! won ten tumans!" Immediately I made a mental calculation: one dollar and twenty-five cents. My mother was now bending over the tray, stringing rapidly; she didn't want father to see the broad smile that had spread all over her face.

I found myself outside in the yard. The night had fallen. I had to think. I sat over the deep pit. I left the door open. There was a full moon and the crickets sang. I sat there for several minutes, my chin propped in my hand. I wanted to sit more, but I thought that they might wonder where I was and get worried. I went back to the living room. My father was now sitting beside my mother, helping her string the beans; I dropped a bulb into my Agfa and snapped a picture. They smiled. I hurried back to the yard. The goldfish was motionless at the bottom of the pond. The night smelled of petunias. I sat over the pit again. I thought, what a marvelous picture that will be. Stringing beans together in peace and harmony!

In the morning I would get my shoes shined. I would also buy a few fish for the pond and make a plane reservation.

The Verb *to Kill*

Luisa Valenzuela   Argentina, 1975

ABOUT THE AUTHOR

Luisa Valenzuela (b. 1938) was born in Buenos Aires, Argentina. The daughter of a well-known Argentinian writer, Luisa Mercedes Levinson, she published her first short story when she was seventeen. After graduating from the University of Buenos Aires, she worked as a freelance writer and lived in France for three years. She returned to Argentina but later moved to the United States to flee the state terrorism and general paranoia that permeated Argentina in the 1970s and early 1980s. Among her awards are a Fulbright grant and a Guggenheim Foundation Fellowship. Her works of fiction include a novel, The Lizard's Tail *(1983) and the short-story collection,* Open Door *(1988).*

THE CONTEXT OF THE STORY

The story is set in Argentina.

He kills—he killed—he will kill—he has killed—he had killed—he will have killed—he would have killed—he is killing—he was killing—he has been killing—he would have been killing—he will have been killing—he will be killing—he would be killing—he may kill.

We decided that none of these tenses or moods suited him. Did he kill, will he kill, will he have killed? We think he *is* killing, with every step, with every breath, with every . . . We don't like him to get close to us but we come across him when we go clam-digging on the beach. We walk from north to south, and he comes from south to north, closer to the dunes, as if looking for pebbles. He looks at us and we look at him—did he kill, will he kill, would he have killed, is he killing? We put down the sack with the clams and hold each other's hand till he passes. He doesn't throw so much as one little pebble at us, he doesn't even look at us, but afterward we're too weak in the knees to go on digging clams.

The other day he walked by us and right afterward we found an injured sea gull on the beach. We took the poor thing home and on the way we told it that we were good, not like him, that it didn't have to be afraid of us, and we even covered it up with my jacket so the cold wind wouldn't hurt its broken wing. Later we ate it in a stew. A little tough, but tasty.

The next day we went back to run on the beach. We didn't see him and we didn't find a single injured sea gull. He may be bad, but he's got something that attracts animals. For example, when we were fishing: hours without a bite until he suddenly showed up and then we caught a splendid sea

Translated by Helen Lane.

bass. He didn't look at our catch or smile, and it's good he didn't because he looked more like a murderer than ever with his long bushy hair and gleaming eyes. He just went on gathering his pebbles as though nothing were wrong, thinking about the girls that he has killed, will kill, kills.

When he passes by we're petrified—will it be our turn someday? In school we conjugate the verb *to kill* and the shiver that goes up our spine isn't the same as when we see him passing on the beach, all puffed up with pride and gathering his pebbles. The shiver on the beach is lower down in our bodies and more stimulating, like sea air. He gathers all those pebbles to cover up the graves of his victims—very small, transparent pebbles that he holds up to the sun and looks through from time to time so as to make certain that the sun exists. Mama says that if he spends all day looking for pebbles, it's because he *eats* them. Mama can't think about anything but food, but I'm sure he eats something else. The last breath of his victims, for example. There's nothing more nourishing than the last sigh, the one that brings with it everything that a person has gathered over the years. He must have some secret for trapping this essence that escapes his victims, and that's why he doesn't need vitamins. My sister and I are afraid he'll catch us some night and kill us to absorb everything that we've been eating over the last few years. We're terribly afraid because we're well nourished, Mama has always seen to it that we eat balanced meals and we've never lacked for fruit or vegetables even though they're very expensive in this part of the country. And clams have lots of iodine, Mama says, and fish are the healthiest food there is even though the taste of it bores us but why should he be bored because while he kills his victims (always girls, of course) he must do those terrible things to them that my sister and I keep imagining, just for fun. We spend hours talking about the things that he does to his victims before killing them just for fun. The papers often talk about degenerates like him but he's one of the worst because that's all he eats. The other day we spied on him while he was talking to the lettuce he has growing in his garden (he's crazy as well as degenerate). He was saying affectionate things to it and we were certain it was poisoned lettuce. For our part we don't say anything to lettuce, we have to eat it with oil and lemon even though it's disgusting, all because Mama says it has lots of vitamins. And now we have to swallow vitamins for him, what a bother, because the better fed we are the happier we'll make him and the more he'll like doing those terrible things the papers talk about and we imagine, just before killing us so as to gulp down our last breath full of vitamins in one big mouthful. He's going to do a whole bunch of things so repulsive we'll be ashamed to tell anybody, and we only say them in a whisper when we're on the beach and there's nobody within miles. He's going to take our last breath and then he'll be as strong as a bull to go kill other girls like us. I hope he catches Pocha. But I hope he doesn't do any of those repulsive things to her before killing her because she might like it, the dirty thing. I hope he kills her straightaway by plunging a knife in her belly. But he'll have his fun with us for a long time because we're pretty and he'll like our bodies and our voices when we scream. And we will scream and scream but nobody will hear us because he's going to take us to a place very far away and then he will put in our mouths that terrible thing we know he has. Pocha already told us about it—he must have an enormous thing that he uses to kill his victims.

An enormous one, even though we've never seen it. To show how brave we are, we tried to watch him while he made peepee, but he saw us and chased us away. I wonder why he didn't want to show it to us. Maybe it's because he wants to surprise us on our last day here and catch us while we're pure so's to get more pleasure. That must be it. He's saving himself for our last day and that's why he doesn't try to get close to us.

Not anymore.

Papa finally lent us the rifle after we asked and asked for it to hunt rabbits. He told us we were big girls now, that we can go out alone with the rifle if we want to, but to be careful, and he said it was a reward for doing so well in school. It's true we're doing well in school. It isn't hard at all to learn to conjugate verbs:

He will be killed—he is killed—he has been killed.

Girl
Jamaica Kincaid   Antigua, 1978

ABOUT THE AUTHOR

Jamaica Kincaid (b. 1949) was born Elaine Potter Richardson in St. Johns, Antigua, in the British West Indies. At the age of sixteen, she left Antigua and took jobs in New York working as a housekeeper and then babysitter. Her attempt to study in college was unsuccessful, and instead she educated herself. By the early 1970s, Kincaid had published several articles in teen magazines and had committed herself to becoming a writer. Her first book, a collection of stories titled At the Bottom of the River, *was published in 1984 and won the Morton Dauwen Zabel Award of the American Academy and Institute of Arts and Letters. Her novels* Annie John *(1985) and* Lucy *(1990) have received high praise.*

THE CONTEXT OF THE STORY

The story is set in Antigua. References to Antiguan life include benna *(popular Calypso music); tropical plants such as* dasheen *and* okra; *and foods such as* doukona *(a spicy pudding) and* pepper pot *(a thick stew).*

Wash the white clothes on Monday and put them on the stone heap; wash the color clothes on Tuesday and put them on the clothesline to dry; don't walk barehead in the hot sun; cook pumpkin fritters in very hot sweet oil; soak your little clothes right after you take them off; when buying cotton to make yourself a nice blouse, be sure that it doesn't have gum on it, because that way it won't hold up well after a wash; soak salt fish overnight before you cook it; is it true that you sing benna in Sunday School?; always eat your food in such a way that it won't turn someone else's stomach; on Sundays try to walk like a lady and not like the slut you are so bent on becoming; don't sing benna in Sunday School; you mustn't speak to wharf-rat boys, not even to give directions; don't eat fruits on the street—flies will follow you; *but I don't sing benna on Sundays at all and never in Sunday school;* this is how to sew on a button; this is how to make a buttonhole for the button you have just sewed on; this is how to hem a dress when you see the hem coming down and so to prevent yourself from looking like the slut I know you are so bent on becoming; this is how you iron your father's khaki shirt so that it doesn't have a crease; this is how you iron your father's khaki pants so that they don't have a crease, this is how you grow okra—far from the house, because okra tree harbors red ants; when you are growing dasheen, make sure it gets plenty of water or else it makes your throat itch when you are eating it; this is how you sweep a corner; this is how you sweep a whole house; this is how you sweep a yard; this is how you smile to someone you don't like too much; this is how you smile to someone you don't like at all; this is how you smile to someone you like completely; this is how you set a table for tea; this is how you set a table for dinner; this is how you set a table for dinner with an important guest; this is how you set a table for lunch; this is how you set a table for breakfast; this is how to behave in the presence of men who don't know you very well, and this way they won't recognize immediately the slut I have warned you against becoming; be sure to wash every day, even if it is with your own spit; don't squat down to play marbles—you are not a boy, you know; don't pick people's flowers—you might catch something; don't throw stones at blackbirds, because it might not be a blackbird at all; this is how to make a bread pudding; this is how to make doukona; this is how to make pepper pot; this is how to make a good medicine for a cold; this is how to make a good medicine to throw away a child before it even becomes a child; this is how to catch a fish; this is how to throw back a fish you don't like, and that way something bad won't fall on you; this is how to bully a man; this is how a man bullies you; this is how to love a man, and if this doesn't work there are other ways, and if they don't work don't feel too bad about giving up; this is how to spit up in the air if you feel like it, and this is how to move quick so that it doesn't fall on you; this is how to make ends meet; always squeeze bread to make sure it's fresh; *but what if the baker won't let me feel the bread?*; you mean to say that after all you are really going to be the kind of woman who the baker won't let near the bread?

A Woman Like Me
Xi Xi

Hong Kong, 1982

ABOUT THE AUTHOR

Xi Xi (b. 1938) is the pen name of Cheung Yin. She was born in Canton, China, and moved to Hong Kong in 1950, where she graduated from the Normal College. Xi Xi has worked as a teacher and editor of a literary magazine. Although she lives in Hong Kong, she publishes most of her work in Taiwan. She has influenced a number of Taiwan's contemporary writers. Her publications include the novel The Hunter Who Whistles to Bait a Deer *(1983) and the short-story collection* Beard with a Face *(1986).*

THE CONTEXT OF THE STORY

The story is set in twentieth-century Hong Kong.

A woman like me is actually unsuitable for any man's love. So the fact that the emotional involvement between Xia and me has reached this point fills even me with wonder. I feel that the blame for my having fallen into this trap, from which there is no escape, rests solely with Fate, which has played a cruel trick on me. I am totally powerless to resist Fate. I've heard others say that when you truly like someone what may be nothing more than an innocent smile directed your way as you sit quietly in a corner can cause your very soul to take wing. That's exactly how I feel about Xia. So when he asked me: Do you like me? I expressed my feelings toward him without holding back a thing. I'm a person who has no concept of self-protection, and my words and deeds will always conspire to make me a laughing stock in the eyes of others. Sitting in a coffee shop with Xia, I had the appearance of a happy person, but my heart was filled with a hidden sorrow; I was so terribly unhappy because I knew where Fate was about to take me, and now the fault would be mine alone. I made a mistake at the very beginning by agreeing to accompany Xia on a trip to visit a schoolmate he hadn't seen for a long time, then later on, by not declining any of his invitations to go to the movies. It's too late for regret now, and, besides, the difference between regretting and not regretting is too slight to be important, since at this very moment I am sitting in the corner of a coffee shop waiting for him. I agreed to show him where I work, and that will be the final chapter. I had already been out of school for a long time when I first met Xia, so when he asked me if I had a job, I told him that I had been working for several years.

What sort of job do you have?

He asked.

Translated by Howard Goldblatt.

I'm a cosmetician.

I said.

Oh, a cosmetician.

He remarked.

But your face is so natural.

He said.

He said that he didn't like women who used cosmetics, and preferred the natural look. I think that the reason his attention had been drawn to my face, on which I never use makeup, was not my response to his question, but because my face is paler than most people's. My hands too. Both my hands and my face are paler than most people's because of my job. I knew that as soon as I divulged my occupation to him, he would jump to the same erroneous conclusion that all my former friends had. He has already assumed that my job is to beautify the appearance of girls in general, such as adding just the right touch of color to the face of a bride-to-be on her wedding day. And so when I told him that there were no days off in my job, that I was often busy Sundays, he was more convinced than ever that his assumption was correct. There were always so many brides on Sundays and holidays. But making brides-to-be beautiful is not what I do; my job is to apply the final cosmetic touches to people whose lives have already come to an end, to make them appear gentle and at peace during their final moments before leaving the world of man. In days past I had brought up the subject of my occupation to friends, and I always immediately corrected their momentary misconception, so that they would know exactly what sort of person I am. But all my honesty ever brought me was the loss of virtually all my friends. I frightened them all off; it was as though the me who was sitting across from them drinking coffee was actually the ghost of their own inner fears. And I never blamed them, for we all have an inborn, primitive timidity where the unknown mysteries of life are concerned. The main reason I didn't give a fuller answer to Xia's question was my concern that the truth would frighten him; I could no longer allow my unusual occupation to unsettle the friends around me, something for which I could never forgive myself. The other reason was my natural inability to express what I think and feel, which, over a long period of time, has led to my habit of being uncommunicative.

But your face is so natural.

He said.

When Xia said that, I knew that it was a bad omen for the emotional road he and I were taking; but at that moment he was so happy—happy because I was a woman who didn't use makeup on herself. Yet my heart was filled with sadness.

I don't know who will someday be applying makeup to my face—will it be Aunt Yifen? Aunt Yifen and I have one hope in common: that in our lifetimes we will never have to make up the face of a loved one. I don't know why, after the appearance of this unlucky omen, I continued going on pleasure excursions with Xia, but maybe, since I'm only human, I lack self-

control and merely go where Fate takes me, one ordained step after another. I have no logical explanation for my behavior, and I think that this
might just be what humans are all about: much of our behavior is inexplicable, even to ourselves.

Can I come and see you work?

Xia asked.

That shouldn't be a problem.

I said.

Will they mind?

He asked.

I don't imagine any of them will.

I said.

The reason Xia asked if he could see how I worked was that every
Sunday morning I have to go to my workplace, and on those days he never
has anything else to do. He offered to walk me to work, and since he'd be
there already, he might as well hang around and take a look. He said he
wanted to look at the brides-to-be and their maids-of-honor and all the
hustle and bustle; he also wanted to watch me as I made the pretty ones
prettier or the attractive ones plain. I agreed without a second's thought. I
knew that Fate had already led me up to the starting line, and what was
about to happen was a foregone conclusion. So here I am, sitting in a small
coffee shop waiting for Xia; and from here we'll go together to my workplace. As soon as we get there he'll understand everything. Xia will know
then that the perfume he thought I was wearing for him actually serves to
mask the smell of formaldehyde on my body. He'll also know then that the
reason I wear white so often is not a conscious effort to produce an appearance of purity, but merely as a convenience in going to and coming from
work. The strange medicinal odor that clings to my body has already penetrated my bones, and all of my attempts to wash it off have failed. Eventually, I gave up trying, and even got to the point where I no longer even
notice the smell. Xia knows nothing of all this, and he once even commented to me: That's a very unusual perfume you wear. But everything will
soon become crystal clear. I've always been a technician who can fashion
elegant hairdos and tie a bowtie with the very best. But so what? Look at
these hands of mine; how many haircuts and trims have they completed on
people who could no longer speak, and how many bowties have they tied
around the necks of totally solemn people? Would Xia allow me to cut his
hair with them? Would he allow me to carefully tie his tie for him? In the
eyes of others, these soft, warm hands have become cold; in the eyes of
others, these hands, which were made to cradle a newborn infant, have
already become the hands for touching the white bones of skeletons.

There may have been many reasons why Aunt Yifen passed her skills on
to me and they can be clearly perceived through her normal daily remarks.
Sure, with these skills, no one would ever have to worry about being out of
work and would be assured of a good living. So how can a woman like me,
with little schooling and not much knowledge, compete with others in this

greed-consumed, dog-eat-dog world? Aunt Yifen was willing to pass the consummate knowledge of her lifework on to me solely because I was her niece. She had never let anyone watch her when she was working until the day she took me on as her apprentice, when she kept me by her side instructing me in every detail, until I lost my fear of being alone with the cold, naked corpses. I even learned how to sew up the sundered bodies and split skulls as though they were nothing more than theatrical costumes. I lost my parents when I was very young and was reared by Aunt Yifen. The strange thing is that I began to resemble her more and more, even becoming as taciturn as she, as pale of hand and face as she, and as slow in my movements as she. There were times when I couldn't shake my doubts that instead of being me, I had become another Aunt Yifen; the two of us were, in fact, one person—I had become a continuation of Aunt Yifen.

From today on, you'll not have to worry about your livelihood.

Aunt Yifen had said.

And you'll never have to rely upon anyone else to get through life, like other women do.

She had said.

I really didn't understand what she had meant by that. I couldn't figure out why I wouldn't have to worry about my livelihood if I learned what she had to teach me, or why I wouldn't have to rely upon anyone else to get through life, like other women do. Was it possible that no other profession in the world could free me from worrying about my livelihood or let me avoid having to rely upon others to get through life? But I was only a woman with little knowledge, so of course I would not be able to compete with other women. Therefore, it was strictly for my own good that Aunt Yifen had taken such pains to pass her special skills on to me. Actually, there is not a single person in this city who doesn't need help from someone in our profession. No matter who they are—rich or poor, high or low— once Fate has brought them to us, we are their final consolation; it is we who will give them a calm, good-natured appearance and make them seem incomparably gentle. Both Aunt Yifen and I have our individual hopes, but in addition to these, we share the common hope that in our lifetimes we will never have to make up the face of a loved one. That's why I was so sorrowful last week: I had a nagging feeling that something terrible had happened, and that it had happened to my own younger brother. From what I heard, my younger brother had met a young woman whose appearance and temperament made her the envy of all, a woman of talent and beauty. They were so happy together, and to me it was a stroke of joyous good fortune. But the happiness was all too short-lived, for I soon learned that for no apparent reason, that delightful young woman had married a man she didn't love. Why is it that two people who are in love cannot marry, but wind up spending the rest of their lives as the bitter victims of unrequited love? My younger brother changed into a different person; he even said to me: I don't want to live anymore. I didn't know what to do. Would I someday be making up the face of my own younger brother?

I don't want to live any more.

My younger brother had said.

I couldn't understand how things could have reached that stage. Neither could my younger brother. If she had merely said: I don't like you anymore. He would have had nothing more to say. But the two of them were clearly in love. It was not to pay a debt of gratitude, nor was it due to economic hardships, so could it be that in this modern, civilized society of ours there are still parents who arrange their daughters' marriages? A lifetime covers many long years, why must one bow to Fate? *Ai,* I only hope that during my lifetime I will never have to make up the face of a loved one. But who can say for sure? When Aunt Yifen formally took me on as an apprentice and began passing her consummate skills on to me, she said: You must follow my wishes in one respect before I will take you on as my apprentice. I didn't know why she was being so solemn about it. But she continued with extreme seriousness: When it is my turn to lie down, you must personally make up my face; you are not to permit any stranger to so much as touch my body. I didn't feel that this would present any problems, but I was surprised by her inflexibility in the matter. Take me, for example: when it is my turn to lie down, what will the body I leave behind have to do with me? But that was Aunt Yifen's one and only personal wish, and it is up to me to help her fulfill it, if I am still around when that day comes. On this long road of life, Aunt Yifen and I are alike in that we harbor no grandiose wishes; Aunt Yifen hopes that I will be her cosmetician, and I only hope to use my talents to create the "most perfectly serene cadaver," one that will be gentler and calmer than all others, just as though death were truly the most beautiful sleep of all. Actually, even if I am successful, it will be nothing more than a game to kill a little time amidst the boredom of life; isn't the entirety of human existence meaningless anyway? All my efforts constitute nothing more than an exercise in futility; if I someday manage to create the "most perfectly serene cadaver," will I gain any rewards from it? The dead know nothing, and my efforts will surely go unnoticed by the family of the deceased. Clearly, I will not hold an exhibition to display to the public my cosmetic skills and innovations. Even less likely is the prospect that anyone will debate, compare, analyze, or hold a forum to discuss my cosmetic job on the deceased; and even if they did, so what? It would cause as much of a stir as the buzzing of insects. My work is purely and simply a game played for the benefit of myself in my workroom. Why then have I bothered to form this hope in the first place? More than likely to provide a stimulus for me to go on working, because mine is a lonely profession: no peers, no audience, and naturally, no applause. When I'm working, I can only hear the faint sound of my own breathing; in a room filled with supine bodies—male and female—I alone am breathing softly. It's gotten to the point where I imagine I can hear the sound of my own heart grieving and sighing, and when the hearts of others cease producing sounds of lament, the sounds of my own heart intensify. Yesterday I decided to do the cosmetic work on a young couple who had died in a love-inspired suicide pact, and as I gazed into the sleeping face of the young man, I realized that this was my chance to create the "most perfectly serene cadaver." His eyes were closed, his lips were pressed lightly together, and there was a pale scar on his left temple. He truly looked as though he were only sleeping very peacefully. In all my years of working on thousands of faces, many of which had fretful, distressed looks on them, the majority appearing quite hideous, I had done what I felt was most appropriate to improve their looks, using needle and thread or makeup to give them an appearance of unlimited gentleness. But words cannot describe the peaceful look on the face of the boy I saw yesterday, and I wondered if his suicide should be viewed as an act of joy. But then I felt that I was being deceived by appearances, and I believed instead that his had been an act of extreme weakness: I knew that, considering my position, I should have nothing to do with anyone who lacked the courage to resist the forces of Fate. So not only did I abandon all thoughts of using him to create the "most perfectly serene cadaver," I refused to even work on him, turning both him and the girl who had joined him in stupidly resigning themselves to Fate's whims over to Aunt Yifen to let her carefully repair the cheeks that had been scalded by the force of the powerful poison they had ingested.

Everyone is familiar with Aunt Yifen's past, because there are some around who personally witnessed it. Aunt Yifen was still young at the time, and she not only liked to sing as she worked, but she talked to the cadavers who lay in front of her, as though they were her friends. It wasn't until later that she became so uncommunicative. Aunt Yifen was in the habit of telling her sleeping friends everything that was in her heart—she never kept a diary—letting her monologues stand as a daily record of her life. The people who slept in her presence were mankind's finest audience: they listened to her voluble outpourings for the longest time, yet her secrets were always completely safe with them. She told them how she had met a young man and how they had shared the happiness of all young lovers whenever they were together, even though there were times when they had occasional ups and downs. In those days Aunt Yifen went to a school of cosmetics once a week, rain or shine, fifty weeks a year, to learn new techniques, until she had mastered all that the instructor could teach her. But even when the school informed her that there was nothing left for her to study, she persisted in asking if there weren't some new techniques that they could pass on to her. Her interest in cosmetology was that keen, almost as though it were inborn, and her friends were sure that someday she would open a grand salon somewhere. But no, she merely applied this knowledge of hers to the bodies of people who slept in front of her. Her young lover knew nothing of any of this, for he was convinced that physical beauty was a natural desire of all girls, and that this particular one was simply fonder of cosmetics than most. That is, until that fateful day when she brought him along and showed him where she worked, pointing out the bodies that lay in the room and telling him that although hers was a lonely profession, in a place like this one encountered no worldly bickerings, and that no petty jealousies, hatreds, or disputes over personal fame or gain existed; when these people entered the world of darkness, peace and gentleness settled over each and every one of them. He was shocked beyond belief; never in his wildest dreams had he thought that she could be a woman like this, one engaged in this sort of occupation. He had loved her, had been willing to do anything for her, vowing that he would never leave her, no matter what, and that they would grow old together, their mutual love enduring until death. But his courage failed him, his nerve abandoned him there among the bodies of people who could no longer speak and who had lost the ability to breathe. He let out a loud yell, turned on his heel and ran, flinging open every door that stood in his way. Many people saw him in a state of complete shock as he fled down the street. Aunt Yifen never saw him again. People sometimes overheard her talking to her silent friends in her workroom: Didn't he say he loved me? Didn't he say he would never leave me? What was it that suddenly frightened him so? Later on, Aunt Yifen grew more and more uncommunicative. Maybe she had already said everything she wanted to say, or maybe since her silent friends already knew all about her, there was no need to say anything more—there truly are many things that never need to be spoken. When Aunt Yifen was teaching me her consummate skills, she told me what had happened. It was I whom she had chosen as her apprentice, not my younger brother, and although there were other factors involved, the major reason had been that I was not a timid person.

Are you afraid?
She asked.
Not at all.
I said.
Are you timid?
She asked.
Not at all.
I said.

Aunt Yifen selected me as her successor because I was not afraid. She had a premonition that my fate would be the same as hers, and neither of us could explain how we grew to be so much alike, although it may have had its origins in the fact that neither of us was afraid. There was no fear in either one of us. When Aunt Yifen was telling me about what had happened to her, she said: I will always believe that there have to be others somewhere who are like us, people who are unafraid. This was before she had become so uncommunicative; she told me to stand by her side and watch how she reddened lips that had already become rigid, and how she worked gently on a pair of long-staring eyes until she had coaxed them into restful sleep. At that time she still talked now and then to her sleeping friends: And you, why were you afraid? Why do people who are falling in love have so little faith in love? Why do they not have courage in their love? Among Aunt Yifen's sleeping friends were many who had been timid and cowardly, and they were even quieter than the others. She knew certain things about her sleeping friends, and sometimes, as she powdered the face of a girl with bangs on her forehead, she would say to me: *Ai! Ai!* What a weak girl she was. She gave up the man she loved just so she would be considered a filial daughter. Aunt Yifen knew that this girl over here had placed herself into Fate's hands, of her own accord, out of a sense of gratitude, while that one over there had done the same by meekly accepting her lot. She talked about them not as though they had been living, feeling, thinking, human beings, but merely pieces of merchandise.

What a horrible job!

My friends said.

Making up the faces of dead people! My God!

My friends said.

I wasn't the least bit afraid, but my friends were. They disliked my eyes because I often used them to look into the eyes of the dead, and they disliked my hands because I often used them to touch the hands of the dead. At first it was just dislike, but it gradually evolved into fear, pure and simple; not only that, the dislike and fear that at first involved only my eyes and hands later on included everything about me. I watched every one of them drift away from me, like wild animals before a forest fire or farmers before a swarm of locusts. Why are you afraid? I asked them. It's a job that someone has to do. Is it that I'm not good enough at what I do, or that I'm not professional enough? But I gradually grew to accept my situation—I got used to being lonely. So many people search for jobs that promise sweetness and warmth, wanting their lives to be filled with flowers and stars. But how does a life of flowers and stars give one the chance to take firm strides in life? I have virtually no friends left today: a touch of my hands reminds them of a deep and distant land of ice and cold, while a look into my eyes produces innumerable images of silent floating spirits, and so they have become afraid. There is nothing that can make them look back, not even the possibility that there is warmth in my hands, that my eyes can shed tears, or that I am warmhearted. And so I began to be more and more like Aunt Yifen, my only remaining friends being the bodies of the deceased lying in front of me. I surprised myself by breaking the silence around me as I said to them: Have I told you that tomorrow I'm going to bring someone named Xia here to meet you? He asked me if you would object, and I told him you wouldn't. Was I right in saying that? So tomorrow Xia will be here, and I think I know how it's going to end, because my fate and Aunt Yifen's are one and the same. I expect to see Xia as his very soul will take wing the moment he steps foot in here. *Ai!* We cause each other's souls to take wing, but in different ways. I will not be startled by what happens, because the outcome has already been made clear to me by a variety of omens. Xia once said to me: Your face is so natural. Yes, my face is natural, and a natural face lacks the power to remove someone else's fear of things.

I once entertained the thought of changing my occupation; is it possible that I am incapable of doing the kinds of work that other women do? Granted that I'm not qualified to be a teacher, a nurse, or a secretary or clerk in an office building, but does that mean I can't work as a saleswoman in a shop, or sell bakery products, or even be a maid in someone's home? A woman like me needs only a roof over her head and three square meals a day, so there must be some place I could fit in. Honestly speaking, with my skills I could easily find work as a cosmetician for brides-to-be, but the very thought that lips I was applying color to could open to reveal a smile stops me cold. What would be going through my mind at a time like that? Too many memories keep me from working at that occupation, which is so similar to the one I have now. I wonder, if I did change jobs, would the color return to my pale face and hands? Would the smell of formaldehyde that has penetrated to my very bones completely disappear? And what about the job I have now, should I keep Xia completely in the dark about it? Hiding the past from a loved one is dishonest, even though there are countless girls in the world who will do anything to cover up their loss of chastity and the authentic number of years they have lived. But I find people like that despicable. I would have to tell Xia that for a long time I had done cosmetic work on the sleeping bodies of the deceased. Then he would know and would have to acknowledge what sort of woman I am. He'd know that the unusual odor on my body is not perfume, but formaldehyde, and that the reason I wear white so often is not symbolic of purity, but a means of making it more convenient for going to and coming from work. But all of this is as significant as a few drops of water in a vast ocean. Once Xia learns that my hands often touch the bodies of the deceased, will he still be willing to hold my hand as we cross a fast-flowing stream? Will he let me cut his hair for him, or tie his tie? Will he be able to bear my gazing intently at him? Will he be able to lie down in my presence without fear? I think he will be afraid, extremely afraid, and like all my friends, his initial shock will turn into dislike and then fear, and he will turn away from me. Aunt Yifen once said: There can be no fear where love is concerned. But I know that although what many people call love is unyielding and indomitable on the surface, it is actually extraordinarily fragile and pliable; puffed-up courage is really nothing but a layer of sugar-coating. Aunt Yifen said to me: Maybe Xia is not a timid person. That's one of the reasons why I never went into detail with him about my occupation. Naturally, another reason was that I'm not very good at expressing myself, and maybe I'd botch what I wanted to say, or I'd distort what I hoped to express to him by choosing the wrong place or time or mood. My not making it clear to Xia that it is not brides-to-be whom I make up is, in actuality, a sort of test: I want to observe his reaction when he sees the subjects I work on. If he is afraid, then he'll just have to be afraid. If he turns and flees, then I'll just tell my sleeping friends: Nothing ever really happened at all.

Can I see how you work?

He asked.

That shouldn't be a problem.

I said.

So here I am, sitting in the corner of a coffee shop waiting for Xia to arrive.

I spent some of this time carefully thinking things over. Maybe I'm not being fair to Xia by doing it this way: If he feels frightened by the work I do, is that his fault? Why should he be more courageous than the others? Why does there have to be any relationship between a fear of the dead and timidity where love is concerned? The two may be totally unrelated. My parents died while I was still young, and I was reared by Aunt Yifen. Both my younger brother and I were orphans. I don't know very much about my parents, and the few things I have learned were told to me later by Aunt Yifen. I remember her telling me that my father was a cosmetician for the deceased before he married my mother. When they were making their plans to get married, he asked her: Are you afraid? No, I'm not, she said. I believe that the reason I'm not afraid is that I take after my mother—her blood flows in my veins. Aunt Yifen said to me that my mother lives on in her memory because of what she had once said: I'm not afraid, and love is the reason. Perhaps that's why my mother lives on in my memory too, however faintly, even though I can no longer recall what she looked or sounded like. But I believe that just because she was my mother and that she said that love had kept her from being afraid does not mean that I have the right to demand the same attitude of everyone else. Maybe I ought to be hardest on myself for accepting my fate from the time I was a child, and for making this occupation that others find so hard to accept my life's work. Men everywhere like women who are gentle, warm, and sweet, and such women are expected to work at jobs that are intimate, graceful, and elegant. But my job is cold and ghostly dark, and I'm sure that my entire body has long been tainted by that sort of shadowy cast. Why would a man who exists in a world of brightness want to be friendly with a woman surrounded by darkness? When he lies down beside her, could he avoid thinking that this is a person who regularly comes into contact with cadavers, and that when her hands brush up against his skin, would that remind him that these are hands that for a long time have rubbed the hands of the dead? *Ai! Ai!* A woman like me is actually unsuitable for any man's love. I think that I myself am to blame for all that has happened, so why don't I just get up and leave and return to my workplace; I have never known anyone by the name of Xia, and he will forget that he once had such a woman for a friend, a cosmetician who made up the faces of brides-to-be. But it's probably too late for that now. I see him there through the window, crossing the street and walking this way. What's that in his hand? What a large bouquet of flowers! What's the occasion? It is someone's birthday? I see him enter the coffee shop; he spots me sitting in this shadowy corner. The sun is shining brightly outside, and he has brought some of it in with him, for the sun's rays are reflected off of his white shirt. He is just like his name, Xia—eternal summer.

Hey, happy Sunday!

He says.

These flowers are for you.

He says.

He is so happy. He sits down and has a cup of coffee. We have had so many happy days together. But what is happiness, after all? Happiness is fleeting. There is such sadness in my heart. From here it is only a walk of three hundred paces before we arrive at my workplace. After that the same thing will happen that happened years ago. A man will come flying through that door as thought his very soul had taken leave of him, and he will be followed by the eyes of the curious until he disappears from view. Aunt Yifen said: Maybe somewhere there is a man of true courage who is unafraid. But I know that this is just an assumption, and when I saw Xia crossing the street heading this way, a huge bouquet of flowers in his hand, I already knew, for this was truly a bad omen. *Ai! Ai!* A woman like me is actually unsuitable for any man's love; perhaps I should say to my sleeping friends: Aren't we all the same, you and I? The decades fly by in the blink of an eye, and no matter what the reason, there's no need for anyone to shock anyone else out of their senses. The bouquet of flowers Xia brought into the coffee shop with him is so very, very beautiful; he is happy, but I am laden with grief. He doesn't know that in our profession flowers symbolize eternal parting.

The Street-Sweeping Show
Feng Jicai   China, 1982

ABOUT THE AUTHOR

*Feng Jicai (b. 1942) was born into a wealthy family in Tianjin, China.
A prize-winning painter, he studied and collected local folk art. In 1966,
at the beginning of the Cultural Revolution (the Communist leadership's
three-year effort to rid the country of liberal and bourgeois elements), his
collection of books and art was destroyed. He was forced to give up his
work and instead to make products for the government. Feng began secretly to write fiction as a way to express his feelings about the social and
political situation in China. He was not able to publish his work until
1977 because no one was permitted to criticize the government. His many
works include the novel* The Boxers *(1977) and* Voices from the
Whirlwind: An Oral History of the Chinese Cultural Revolution
(1991). He is one of China's best known contemporary writers.

THE CONTEXT OF THE STORY

*The story takes place in the People's Republic of China. References to Chi-
nese Communism include the* Mao suit *(the uniform worn by Mao Tse-
tung [1893–1976], leader of Communist China, and by his followers) and*
red armband *(symbol of a dedicated communist). Other references to
China include* dragon dancers *(traditional dancers who perform at a festival under a cloth in the shape and design of a dragon).*

"National Cleanup Week starts today," said Secretary Zhao, "and officials everywhere are going out to join in the street sweeping. Here's our list
of participants—all top city administrators and public figures. We've just
had it mimeographed over at the office for your approval."

He looked like a typical upper-echelon secretary: the collar of his well-
worn, neatly pressed Mao suit was buttoned up military style; his complex-
ion was pale; his glasses utilitarian. His gentle, deferential manner and
pleasantly modulated voice concealed a shrewd, hard-driving personality.

The mayor pored over the list, as if the eighty names on it were those
of people selected to go abroad. From time to time he glanced thoughtfully
at the high white ceiling.

"Why isn't there anyone from the Women's Federation?" he asked.

Secretary Zhao thought for a moment. "Oh, you're right—there isn't!
We've got the heads of every office in the city—the Athletic Committee,
the Youth League Committee, the Federation of Trade Unions, the Feder-

Translated by Susan Wilf Chen.

ation of Literary and Art Circles—even some famous university professors. The only group we forgot is the Women's Federation."

"Women are the pillars of society. How can we leave out the women's representatives?" The mayor sounded smug rather than reproachful. Only a leader could think of everything. This was where true leadership ability came into play.

Secretary Zhao was reminded of the time when the mayor had pointed out that the fish course was missing from the menu for a banquet in honor of some foreign guests.

"Add two names from the Women's Federation, and make sure you get people in positions of authority or who are proper representatives of the organization. 'March 8 Red Banner Pacesetters,'[1] 'Families of Martyrs,' or 'Model Workers' would be fine." Like an elementary school teacher returning a poor homework paper to his student, the mayor handed the incomplete list back to his secretary.

"Yes, your honor, I'll do it right away. A complete list will be useful the next time something like this comes up. And I must contact everyone at once. The street sweeping is scheduled for two this afternoon in Central Square. Will you be able to go?"

"Of course. As mayor of the city, I have to set an example."

"The car will be at the gate for you at one-thirty. I'll go with you."

"All right," the mayor answered absentmindedly, scratching his forehead and looking away.

Secretary Zhao hurried out.

At one-thirty that afternoon the mayor was whisked to the square in his limousine. All office workers, shop clerks, students, housewives, and retirees were out sweeping the streets, and the air was thick with dust. Secretary Zhao hastily rolled up the window. Inside the car there was only a faint, pleasant smell of gasoline and leather.

At the square they pulled up beside a colorful assortment of limousines. In front of them a group of top city administrators had gathered to wait for the mayor's arrival. Someone had arranged for uniformed policemen to stand guard on all sides.

Secretary Zhao sprang out of the limousine and opened the door for his boss. The officials in the waiting crowd stepped forward with smiling faces to greet the mayor. Everyone knew him and hoped to be the first to shake his hand.

"Good afternoon—oh, nice to see you—good afternoon—" the mayor repeated as he shook hands with each of them.

An old policeman approached, followed by two younger ones pushing wheelbarrows full of big bamboo brooms. The old policeman selected one of the smaller neater brooms and presented it respectfully to the mayor, like a Tibetan offering a *hada*[2] to an honored guest. When the other dignitaries

[1] March 8 is International Working Women's Day.
[2] **hada:** a piece of silk used in Tibet as a gift of greeting

had gotten their brooms, a marshal with a red armband led them all the center of the square. Naturally the mayor walked at the head.

Groups of people had come from their workplaces to sweep the huge square. At the sight of this majestic, broom-carrying procession, with its marshal, police escort, and retinue of shutter-clicking photographers, they realized that they were in the presence of no ordinary mortals and gathered closer for a look. How extraordinary for a mayor to be sweeping the streets, thought Secretary Zhao, swelling with unconscious pride as he strutted along beside the mayor with his broom on his shoulder.

"Here we are," the marshal said when they had reached the designated spot.

All eighty-two dignitaries began to sweep.

The swelling crowd of onlookers, which was kept back by a police cordon, was buzzing with excitement:

"Look, he's the one over there."

"Which one? The one in black?"

"No. The bald fat one in blue."

"Cut the chitchat!" barked a policeman.

The square was so huge that no one knew where to sweep. The concrete pavement was clean to begin with; they pushed what little grit there was back and forth with their big brooms. The most conspicuous piece of litter was a solitary popsicle wrapper, which they all pursued like children chasing a dragonfly.

The photographers surrounded the mayor. Some got down on one knee to shoot from below, while others ran from side to side trying to get a profile. Like a cloud in a thunderstorm, the mayor was constantly illuminated by silvery flashes. Then a man in a visored cap, with a video camera, approached Secretary Zhao.

"I'm from the TV station," he said. "Would you please ask them to line up single file so they'll look neat on camera?"

Secretary Zhao consulted with the mayor, who agreed to this request. The dignitaries formed a long line and began to wield their brooms for the camera, regardless of whether there was any dirt on the ground.

The cameraman was about to start shooting, when he stopped and ran over to the mayor.

"I'm sorry, your honor," he said, "but you're all going to have to face the other way because you've got your backs to the sun. And I'd also like the entire line to be reversed so that you're at the head."

"All right," the mayor agreed graciously, and he led his entourage, like a line of dragon dancers, in a clumsy turnaround. Once in place, everyone began sweeping again.

Pleased, the cameraman ran to the head of the line, pushed his cap up, and aimed at the mayor. "All right," he said as the camera started to whir, "swing those brooms. All together now—put your hearts into it—that's it! Chin up please, your honor. Hold it—that's fine—all right!"

He stopped the camera, shook the mayor's hand, and thanked him for helping an ordinary reporter carry out his assignment.

"Let's call it a day," the marshal said to Secretary Zhao. Then he turned to the mayor. "You have victoriously accomplished your mission," he said.

"Very good—thank you for your trouble," the mayor replied routinely, smiling and shaking hands again.

Some reporters came running up to the mayor. "Do you have any instructions, your honor?" asked a tall, thin, aggressive one.

"Nothing in particular." The mayor paused for a moment. "Everyone should pitch in to clean up our city."

The reporters scribbled his precious words in their notebooks.

The policemen brought the wheelbarrows back, and everyone returned the brooms. Secretary Zhao replaced the mayor's for him.

It was time to go. The mayor shook hands with everyone again.

"Good-bye—good-bye—good-bye—"

The others waited until the mayor had gotten into his limousine before getting into theirs.

The mayor's limousine delivered him to his house, where his servant had drawn his bathwater and set out scented soap and fresh towels. He enjoyed a leisurely bath and emerged from the bathroom with rosy skin and clean clothes, leaving his grime and exhaustion behind him in the tub.

As he descended the stairs to eat dinner, his grandson hurriedly led him into the living room.

"Look, Granddad, you're on TV!"

There he was on the television screen, like an actor, putting on a show of sweeping the street. He turned away and gave his grandson a casual pat on the shoulder.

"It's not worth watching. Let's go have dinner."

The Grass-Eaters
Krishnan Varma   India, 1985

ABOUT THE AUTHOR

Krishnan Varma was born in Kerala, a southwestern state of India. He writes in English as well as in Malayalam. In many of his stories, Krishnan shares his observations of the life of the poorest people in his country.

THE CONTEXT OF THE STORY

The story takes place in Calcutta, one of the largest cities in India, with a population of over nine million. The characters in the story are Hindus. *Hinduism is a religion and philosophy characterized by a belief in reincarnation: the transfer of the soul into another body after death. According to this belief, every action influences how the soul will be born in the next reincarnation. For example, if a person leads a good life, the soul will be born into a higher state.*

Other references to Indian life include sari *(traditional outer garment of Hindu women: a long cloth wrapped around the body).*

For some time several years ago I was tutor to a spherical boy (now a spherical youth). One day his ovoid father, Ramaniklal Misrilal, asked me where I lived. I told him.

Misrilal looked exceedingly distressed. "A pipe, Ajit Babu? Did you say—a *pipe*, Ajit Babu?"

His cuboid wife was near to tears. "A *pipe*, Ajit Babu? How can you live in a pipe?"

It was true: at that time I was living in a pipe with my wife, Swapna. It was long and three or four feet across. With a piece of sack cloth hung at either end, we had found it far more comfortable than any of our previous homes.

The first was a footpath of Chittaranjan Avenue. We had just arrived in Calcutta from East Bengal[1] where Hindus and Muslims were killing one another. The footpath was so crowded with residents, refugees like us and locals, that if you got up at night to relieve yourself you could not be sure of finding your place again. One cold morning I woke to find that the woman beside me was not Swapna at all but a bag of bones instead. And about fifty or sixty or seventy years old. I had one leg over her too. I paid bitterly for my mistake. The woman very nearly scratched out my eyes. Then came Swapna, fangs bared, claws out . . . I survived, but minus one ear. Next came the woman's husband, a hill of a man, whirling a tree over his head, roaring. That was my impression, anyway. I fled.

---

[1] **East Bengal:** primarily Muslim. East Bengal became East Pakistan in 1947 and gained independence as Bangladesh in 1971.

Later in the day Swapna and I moved into an abandoned-looking freight wagon at the railway terminus. A whole wagon to ourselves—a place with doors which could be opened and shut—we did nothing but open and shut them for a full hour—all the privacy a man and wife could want—no fear of waking up with a complete stranger in your arms . . . it was heaven. I felt I was God.

Then one night we woke to find that the world was running away from us: we had been coupled to a freight train. There was nothing for it but to wait for the train to stop. When it did, miles from Calcutta, we got off, took a passenger train back, and occupied another unwanted-looking wagon. That was not the only time we went to bed in Calcutta and woke up in another place. I found it an intensely thrilling experience, but not Swapna.

She wanted a stationary home; she insisted on it. But she would not say why. If I persisted in questioning her she snivelled. If I tried to persuade her to change her mind, pointing out all the advantages of living in a wagon—four walls, a roof and door absolutely free of charge, and complete freedom to make love day or night—she still snivelled. If I ignored her nagging, meals got delayed, the rice undercooked, the curry over-salted. In the end I gave in. We would move, I said, even if we had to occupy a house by force, but couldn't she tell me the reason, however irrelevant, why she did not like the wagon?

For the first time in weeks Swapna smiled, a very vague smile. Then, slowly, she drew the edge of her sari over her head, cast her eyes down, turned her face from me, and said in a tremulous, barely audible whisper that she (short pause) did (long pause) not want (very long pause) her (at jet speed) baby-to-be-born-in-a-running-train. And she buried her face in her hands. Our fourth child. One died of diphtheria back home (no longer our home) in Dacca; two, from fatigue, on our long trek on foot to Calcutta. Would the baby be a boy? I felt no doubt about it; it would be. Someone to look after us in our old age, to do our funeral rites when we died. I suddenly kissed Swapna, since her face was hidden in her hands, on her elbow, and was roundly chided. Kissing, she holds, is a western practice, unclean also, since it amounts to licking, and should be eschewed by all good Hindus.

I lost no time in looking for a suitable place for her confinement. She firmly rejected all my suggestions: the railway station platform (too many residents); a little-used overbridge (she was not a kite to live so high above the ground); a water tank that had fallen down and was empty (Did I think that she was a frog?). I thought of suggesting the municipal primary school where I was teaching at the time, but felt very reluctant. Not that the head-master would have objected if we had occupied one end of the back ve- randa: a kindly man, father of eleven, all girls, he never disturbed the cat that regularly kittened in his in-tray. My fear was: suppose Swapna came running into my class, saying, "Hold the baby for a moment, will you? I'm going to the l-a-t-r-i-n-e." Anyway, we set out to the school. On the way, near the Sealdah railway station, we came upon a cement concrete pipe left over from long-ago repairs to underground mains. Unbelievably, it was not occupied and, with no prompting from me, she crept into it. That was how we came to live in a pipe.

"It is not proper," said Misrilal, "not at all, for a school master to live in a pipe." He sighed deeply. "Why don't you move into one of my buildings, Ajit Babu?"

The house I might occupy, if I cared to, he explained, was in Entally, not far from where the pipe lay; I should have no difficulty in locating it; it was an old building and there were a number of old empty coal tar drums on the roof; I could live on the roof if I stacked the drums in two rows and put a tarpaulin over them.

We have lived on that roof ever since. It is not as bad as it sounds. The roof is flat, not gabled, and it is made of cement concrete, not corrugated iron sheets. The rent is far less than that of other tenants below us—Bijoy Babu, Akhanda Chatterjee and Sagar Sen. We have far more light and ventilation than they. We don't get nibbled by rats and mice and rodents as often as they do. And our son, Prodeep, has far more room to play than the children below.

Prodeep is not with us now; he is in the Naxalite[2] underground. We miss him, terribly. But there is some compensation, small though it is. Had he been with us, we would have had to wear clothes. Now, we don't. Not much, that is. I make do with a loin cloth and Swapna with a piece slightly wider to save our few threadbare clothes from further wear and tear. I can spare little from my pension for new clothes. Swapna finds it very embarrassing to be in my presence in broad daylight so meagerly clad and so contrives to keep her back turned to me. Like a chimp in the sulks, I am fed up with seeing her backside and tell her that she has nothing that I have not seen. But she is adamant; she will not turn around. After nightfall, however, she relents: we are both nightblind.

When we go out—to the communal lavatory, to pick up pieces of coal from the railway track, to gather grass—we do wear clothes. Grass is our staple food now: a mound of green grass boiled with green peppers and salt, and a few ladles of very thin rice gruel. We took to eating it when the price of rice started soaring. I had a good mind to do as Bijoy Babu below us is believed to be doing. He has a theory that if you reduce your consumption of food by five grams each day, you will not only not notice that you are eating less but after some time you can do without any food at all. One day I happened to notice that he was not very steady on his feet. That gave me pause. He can get around, however badly he totters, because he has two legs; but I have only one. I lost the other after a fall from the roof of a tram. In Calcutta the trams are always crowded and if you can't get into a carriage you may get up on its roof. The conductor will not stop you. If he tries to, the passengers beat him up, set fire to the tram and any other vehicles parked in the vicinity, loot nearby shops, break street lamps, take out a

[2] **Naxalite:** the Naxalite movement aimed to change India's social structure by liquidating estates and distributing land among the rural poor

procession, hold a protest meeting, denounce British imperialism, American neo-colonialism, the central government, capitalism and socialism, and set off crackers. I don't mind my handicap at all; I need wear only one sandal and thereby save on footwear.

So, on the whole, our life together has been very eventful. The events, of course, were not always pleasant. But, does it matter? We have survived them. And now, we have no fears or anxieties. We have a home made of coal tar drums. We eat two square meals of grass every day. We don't need to wear clothes. We have a son to do our funeral rites when we die. We live very quietly, content to look at the passing scene: a tram burning, a man stabbing another man, a woman dropping her baby in a garbage bin.

Las papas
Julio Ortega   Peru, 1988

ABOUT THE AUTHOR

Julio Ortega (b. 1942) was born in Casma, Peru, and has lived in the United States since 1979. He has taught Latin American Literature at universities in Texas, California, and Massachusetts, and is currently a professor of Hispanic Studies at Brown University in Rhode Island. A writer of poetry, fiction, and essays, he has published in both Spanish and English. His first book of short fiction, Diario imaginario (1988), *was published in Colombia.*

THE CONTEXT OF THE STORY

Set in the United States, the story focuses on a Peruvian emigrant. References to Peru include Andean *(from the Andes Mountains) and* hacienda *(large estate or plantation, or the house of the owner of the* hacienda). *Peru is a diverse nation, populated by Peru's original Indian peoples and descendants of Europeans, Africans, and Asians. The Europeans are mostly of Spanish descent.*

THE TITLE OF THE STORY

Las papas is Spanish for "potatoes."

He turned on the faucet of the kitchen sink and washed off the knife. As he felt the splashing water, he looked up through the front window and saw the September wind shaking the tender shoots of the trees on his street, the first hint of fall.

He quickly washed the potatoes one by one. Although their coloring was light and serene, they were large and heavy. When he started to peel them, slowly, using the knife precisely and carefully, the child came into the kitchen.

"What are you going to cook?" he asked. He stood there waiting for an answer.

"Chicken cacciatore,"[1] the man answered, but the child didn't believe him. He was only six, but he seemed capable of objectively discerning between one chicken recipe and another.

"Wait and see," he promised.

"Is it going to have onions in it?" asked the child.

"Very few," he said.

The child left the kitchen unconvinced.

Translated by Regina Harrison.
[1] **cacciatore:** an Italian dish made with a spicy red sauce

He finished peeling the potatoes and started to slice them. Through the window he saw the growing brightness of midday. That strong light seemed to paralyze the brilliant foliage on the trees. The inside of the potatoes had the same clean whiteness, and the knife penetrated it, as if slicing through soft clay.

Then he rinsed the onions and cut into them, chopping them up. He glanced at the recipe again and looked for seasonings in the pantry. The child came back in.

"Chicken is really boring," the child said, almost in protest.

"Not this recipe," he said. "It'll be great. You'll see."

"Put a lot of stuff in it," the child recommended.

"It's going to have oregano, pepper, and even some sugar," he said.

The child smiled, approvingly.

He dried the potato slices. The pulp was crisp, almost too white, more like an apple, perhaps. Where did these potatoes come from? Wyoming or Idaho, probably. The potatoes from his country, on the other hand, were grittier, with a heavy flavor of the land. There were dark ones, almost royal purple like fruit, and delicate yellow ones, like the yolk of an egg. They say there used to be more than a thousand varieties of potato. Many of them have disappeared forever.

The ones that were lost, had they been less firmly rooted in the soil? Were they more delicate varieties? Maybe they disappeared when control of the cultivated lands was deteriorating. Some people say, and it's probably true, that the loss of even one domesticated plant makes the world a little poorer, as does the destruction of a work of art in a city plundered by invaders. If a history of the lost varieties were written it might prove that no one would ever have gone hungry.

Boiled, baked, fried, or stewed: the ways of cooking potatoes were a long story in themselves. He remembered what his mother had told him as a child: at harvest time, the largest potatoes would be roasted for everybody, and, in the fire, they would open up—just like flowers. That potato was probably one of the lost varieties, the kind that turned into flowers in the flames.

Are potatoes harvested at night in the moonlight? He was surprised how little he knew about something that came from his own country. As he thought about it, he believed *harvest* wasn't even the correct term. *Gathering? Digging?* What do you call this harvest from under the earth?

For a long time he had avoided eating them. Even their name seemed unpleasant to him, *papas*. A sign of the provinces, one more shred of evidence of the meager resources, of underdevelopment—a potato lacked protein and was loaded with carbohydrates. French-fried potatoes seemed more tolerable to him: they were, somehow, in a more neutralized condition.

At first, when he began to care for the child all by himself, he tried to simplify the ordeal of meals by going out to the corner restaurant. But he soon found that if he tried to cook something it passed the time, and he also amused himself with the child's curiosity.

He picked up the cut slices. There wasn't much more to discover in them. It wasn't necessary to expect anything more of them than the density they already possessed, a crude cleanliness that was the earth's flavor. But that same sense transformed them right there in his hands, a secret flowering, uncovered by him in the kitchen. It was as if he discovered one of the lost varieties of the Andean potato: the one that belonged to him, wondering, at noon.

When the chicken began to fry in the skillet, the boy returned, attracted by its aroma. The man was in the midst of making the salad.

"Where's this food come from?" the child asked, realizing it was a different recipe.

"Peru," he replied.

"Not Italy?" said the child, surprised.

"I'm cooking another recipe now," he explained. "Potatoes come from Peru. You know that, right?"

"Yeah, but I forgot it."

"They're really good, and there are all kinds and flavors. Remember mangoes? You really used to like them when we went to see your grandparents."

"I don't remember them either. I only remember the lion in the zoo."

"You don't remember the tree in Olivar Park?"

"Uh-huh. I remember that."

"We're going back there next summer, to visit the whole family."

"What if there's an earthquake?"

The boy went for his Spanish reader and sat down at the kitchen table. He read the resonant names out loud, names that were also like an unfinished history, and the man had to go over to him every once in a while to help explain one thing or another.

He tasted the sauce for the amount of salt, then added a bit of tarragon, whose intense perfume was delightful, and a bit of marjoram, a sweeter aroma.

He noticed how, outside, the light trapped by a tree slipped out from the blackened greenness of the leaves, now spilling onto the grass on the hill where their apartment house stood. The grass, all lit up, became an oblique field, a slope of tame fire seen from the window.

He looked at the child, stuck on a page in his book; he looked at the calm, repeated blue of the sky; and he looked at the leaves of lettuce in his hands, leaves that crackled as they broke off and opened up like tender shoots, beside the faucet of running water.

As if it suddenly came back to him, he understood that he must have been six or seven when his father, probably forty years old, as he was now, used to cook at home on Sundays. His father was always in a good mood as be cooked, boasting beforehand about how good the Chinese recipes were that he had learned in a remote hacienda in Peru. Maybe his father had made these meals for him, in this always incomplete past, to celebrate the meeting of father and son.

Unfamiliar anxiety, like a question without a subject, grew in him as he understood that he had never properly acknowledged his father's gesture; he hadn't even understood it. Actually, he had rejected his father's cooking one time, saying that it was too spicy. He must have been about fifteen then, a recent convert devoutly practicing the religion of natural foods, when he left the table with the plate of fish in his hands. He went out to the kitchen to turn on the faucet and quickly washed away the flesh boiled in soy sauce and ginger. His mother came to the kitchen and scolded him for what he had just done, a seemingly harmless act, but from then on an irreparable one. He returned to the table in silence, sullen, but his father didn't appear to be offended. Or did he suspect that one day his son's meal would be refused by his own son when he served it?

The emotion could still wound him, but it could also make him laugh. There was a kind of irony in this repeating to a large extent his father's gestures as he concocted an unusual flavor in the kitchen. However, like a sigh that only acquires some meaning by turning upon itself, he discovered a symmetry in the repetitions, a symmetry that revealed the agony of emotions not easily understood.

Just like animals that feed their young, we feed ourselves with a promise that food will taste good, he said to himself. We prepare a recipe with painstaking detail so that our children will recognize us in a complete history of flavor.

He must have muttered this out loud because the child looked up.

"What?" he said, "Italian?"

"Peruvian," he corrected. "With a taste of the mountains, a mixture of Indian, Chinese, and Spanish."

The child laughed, as if he'd heard a private joke in the sound of the words.

"When we go to Lima, I'll take you around to the restaurants," he promised.

The child broke into laughter again.

"It tastes good," said the child.

"It tastes better than yesterday's," the man said.

He poured some orange juice. The boy kneeled in the chair and ate a bit of everything. He ate more out of curiosity than appetite.

He felt once again that brief defenselessness that accompanies the act of eating one's own cooking. Behind that flavor, he knew, lurked the raw materials, the separate foods cooked to render them neutral, a secret known only to the cook, who combined ingredients and proportions until something different was presented to eyes and mouth. This culinary act could be an adventure, a hunting foray. And the pleasure of creating a transformation must be shared, a kind of brief festival as the eaters decipher the flavors, knowing that an illusion has taken place.

Later, he looked for a potato in the pantry and he held it up against the unfiltered light in the window. It was large, and it fit perfectly in his barely closed hand. He was not surprised that the misshapen form of this swollen tuber adapted to the contour of his hand; he knew the potato adapted to different lands, true to its own internal form, as if it occupied stolen space. The entire history of his people was here, he said to himself, surviving in a territory overrun and pillaged several times, growing in marginal spaces, under siege and waiting.

He left the apartment, went down the stairs and over to the tree on the hillock. It was a perfect day, as if the entire history of daytime were before him. The grass was ablaze, standing for all the grass he had ever seen. With both hands, he dug, and the earth opened up to him, cold. He placed the potato there, and he covered it up quickly. Feeling slightly embarrassed, he looked around. He went back up the stairs, wiping his hands, almost running.

The boy was standing at the balcony, waiting for him; he had seen it all.

"A tree's going to grow there!" said the boy, alarmed.

"No," he said soothingly, "potatoes aren't trees. If it grows, it will grow under the ground."

The child didn't seem to understand everything, but then suddenly he laughed.

"Nobody will even know it's there," he said, excited by such complicity with his father.

Village
Estela Portillo Trambley   United States, 1989

ABOUT THE AUTHOR

Estela Portillo Trambley (b. 1936) was born in the United States, in Texas. A teacher and radio talk-show host, she published her first stories and poems in the early 1970s in El Grito, *a literary review devoted to publishing works by Mexican Americans. In 1972, she received the Quinto Sol Award for literature. Portillo Trambley was the first Mexican-American woman to publish a collection of stories,* Rain of Scorpions and Other Writings *(1976). Among her other published writings are the play* The Day of the Swallows *(1971) and the novel* Trini *(1986).*

THE CONTEXT OF THE STORY

The story takes place in Vietnam during the Vietnam War. The Vietnam War (1954–1975) was fought with the aid of the United States (from 1961 on), to keep the government of South Vietnam independent of pro-Communist North Vietnam. References to Vietnam include the Delta *(area formed at the mouth of the Mekong River); the* Viet Cong *(Communist-led guerrillas, also referred to as* VC*);* napalm *(compound used in flame throwers that sticks to a target as it burns); and* Saigon *(the capital city, which served as military headquarters for U.S. and South Vietnamese forces during the war).*

The story focuses on a Mexican-American soldier. References to the character's Mexican background include barrio *(a chiefly Spanish-speaking community, village, or neighborhood);* Indian *(a member of one of the original peoples of Central America);* Tarahumara chieftain *(leader of an Indian tribe in Mexico); and* gringos *(derisive Spanish word for Anglo-Americans).*

Rico stood on top of a bluff overlooking Mai Cao. The whole of the wide horizon was immersed in a rosy haze. His platoon was returning from an all-night patrol. They had scoured the area in a radius of thirty-two miles, following the length of the canal system along the Delta, furtively on the lookout for an enemy attack. On their way back, they had stopped to rest, smoke, drink warm beer after parking the carry-alls along the edge of the climb leading to the top of the bluff. The hill was good cover, seemingly safe.

Harry was behind him on the rocky slope. Then, the sound of thunder overhead. It wasn't thunder, but a squadron of their own helicopters on the usual run. Rico and Harry sat down to watch the planes go by. After that, a stillness, a special kind of silence. Rico knew it well, the same kind of stillness that was a part of him back home, the kind of stillness that makes a man part of his world—river, clearing, sun, wind. The stillness of a village early in the morning—barrio stillness, the first stirrings of life that come with dawn. Harry was looking down at the village of Mai Cao.

"Makes me homesick . . ." Harry lighted a cigarette.

Rico was surprised. He thought Harry was a city dude. Chicago, no less. "I don't see no freeway or neon lights."

"I'm just sick of doing nothing in this goddamned war."

No action yet. But who wanted action? Rico had been transformed into a soldier, but he knew he was no soldier. He had been trained to kill the enemy in Vietnam. He watched the first curl of smoke coming out of one of the chimneys. They were the enemy down there. Rico didn't believe it. He would never believe it. Perhaps because there had been no confrontation with Viet Cong soldiers or village people. Harry flicked away his cigarette and started down the slope. He turned, waiting for Rico to follow him. "Coming?"

"I'll be down after a while."

"Suit yourself." Harry walked swiftly down the bluff, his feet carrying with them the dirt yieldings in a flurry of small pebbles and loose earth. Rico was relieved. He needed some time by himself, to think things out. But Harry was right. To come across an ocean just to do routine checks, to patrol ground where there was no real danger . . . it could get pretty shitty. The enemy was hundreds of miles away.

The enemy! He remembered the combat bible—kill or be killed. Down a man—the lethal lick: a garotte strangling is neater and more quiet than the slitting of a throat; grind your heel against a face to mash the brains. Stomp the ribcage to carve the heart with bone splinters. Kill . . .

Hey, who was kidding who? They almost made him believe it back at boot camp in the States. In fact, only a short while ago, only that morning he had crouched down along the growth following a mangrove swamp, fearing an unseen enemy, ready to kill. Only that morning. But now, looking down at the peaceful village with its small rice field, its scattered huts, something had struck deep, something beyond the logic of war and enemy, something deep in his guts.

He had been cautioned. The rows of thatched huts were not really peoples' homes, but "hootches," makeshift temporary stays built by the makeshift enemy. But then they were real enemies. There were too many dead Americans to prove it. The "hootches" didn't matter. The people didn't matter. These people knew how to pick up their sticks and go. Go where? Then how many of these villages had been bulldozed? Flattened by gunfire? Good pyre for napalm, these Vietnamese villages. A new kind of battleground.

Rico looked down and saw huts that were homes, clustered in an intimacy that he knew well. The village of Mai Cao was no different than Valverde, the barrio where he had grown up. A woman came out of a hut, walking straight and with a certain grace, a child on her shoulder. She was walking toward a stream east of the slope. She stopped along the path and looked up to say something to the child. It struck him again, the feeling—a bond—people all the same everywhere.

The same scent from the earth, the same warmth from the sun, a woman walking with a child—his mother, Trini. His little mother who had left Tarahumara country and crossed the Barranca del Cobre, taking with her seeds from the hills of Batopilas, withstanding suffering, danger—for what? A dream—a piece of ground in the land of plenty, the United States of America. She had waded across the Rio Grande from Juárez, Mexico, to El Paso, Texas, when she felt the birth pangs of his coming. He had been born a citizen because his mother had had a dream. She had made the dream come true—an acre of riverland in Valverde on the edge of the border. His mother, like the earth and sun, mattered. The woman with the child on her shoulder mattered. Every human life in the village mattered. He knew this not only with the mind but with the heart.

Rico remembered a warning from combat training, from the weary, wounded soldiers who had fought and killed and survived, soldiers sent to Saigon, waiting to go home. His company had been flown to Saigon before being sent to the front. And this was the front, villages like Mai Cao. He felt relieved knowing that the fighting was hundreds of miles away from the people in Mai Cao—but the warning was still there:

Watch out for pregnant women with machine guns. Toothless old women are experts with the knife between the shoulders. Begging children with hidden grenades, the unseen VC hiding in the hootches—village people were not people; they were the enemy. The woman who knew the child on her shoulder, who knew the path to her door, who knew the coming of the sun—she was the enemy.

It was a discord not to be believed by instinct or intuition. And Rico was an Indian, the son of a Tarahumara chieftain. Theirs was a world of instinct and intuitive decisions. Suddenly he heard the sounds of motors. He looked to the other side of the slope, down to the road where the carry-alls had started queuing their way back to the post. Rico ran down the hill to join his company.

In his dream, Sergeant Keever was shouting, "Heller, heller . . ." Rico woke with a start. It wasn't a dream. The men around him were scrambling out of the pup tent. Outside most of the men were lining up in uneven formation. Rico saw a communiqué in the sergeant's hand. Next to Keever was a lieutenant from communications headquarters. Keever was reading the communiqué:

"Special mission 72 . . . for Company C, platoon 2, assigned at 22 hours. Move into the village of Mai Cao, field manual description—hill 72. Destroy the village."

No! It was crazy. Why? Just words on a piece of paper. Keever had to tell him why. There had to be a reason. Had the enemy come this far? It was impossible. Only that morning he had stood on the slope. He caught up with Keever, blurting out, "Why? I mean—why must we destroy it?"

Sergeant Keever stopped in his tracks and turned steel-blue eyes at Rico. "What you say?"

"Why?"

"You just follow orders, savvy?"

"Are the Viet Cong . . ."

"Did you hear me? You want trouble, private?"

"There's people . . ."

"I don't believe you, soldier. But OK. Tell you as much as I know. We gotta erase the village in case the Viet Cong come this way. That way they won't use it as a stronghold. Now move your ass . . ."

Keever walked away from him, his lips tight in some kind of disgust. Rico did not follow this time. He went to get his gear and join the men in one of the carry-alls. Three carry-alls for the assault—three carry-alls moving up the same road. Rico felt the weight and hardness of his carbine. Now it had a strange, hideous meaning. The machine guns were some kind of nightmare. The mission was to kill and burn and erase all memories. Rico swallowed a guilt that rose from the marrow—with it, all kinds of fear. He had to do something, something to stop it, but he didn't know what. And with all these feelings, a certain reluctance to do anything but follow orders. In the darkness, his lips formed words from the anthem, "My country, 'tis of thee . . ."

They came to the point where the treelines straggled between two hills that rose darkly against the moon. Rico wondered if all the men were of one mind—one mind to kill . . . Was he a coward? No! It was not killing the enemy that his whole being was rejecting, but firing machine guns into a village of sleeping people . . . people. Rico remembered only the week before, returning from their usual patrol, the men from the company had stopped at the stream, mingling with the children, old men, and women of the village. There had been an innocence about the whole thing. His voice broke the silence in the carry-all, a voice harsh and feverish. "We can get the people out of there. Help them evacuate . . ."

"Shut up." Harry voice was tight, impatient.

The carry-alls traveled through tall, undulant grass following the dirt road that led to the edge of the bluff. It was not all tall grass. Once in a while trees appeared again, clumped around scrub bushes. Ten miles out the carry-alls stopped. It was still a mile's walk to the bluff in the darkness, but they had to avoid detection. Sergeant Keever was leading the party. Rico, almost at the rear, knew he had to catch up to him. He had to stop him. Harry was ahead of him, a silent black bundle walking stealthily through rutted ground to discharge his duty. For a second, Rico hesitated. That was the easy thing to do—to carry out his duty—to die a hero, to do his duty blindly and survive. Hell, why not? He knew what happened to men who backed down in battle. But he wasn't backing down. Hell, what else was it? How often had he heard it among the gringos in his company.

"You Mexican? Hey, you Mexicans are real fighters. I mean, everybody knows Mexicans have guts . . ."

A myth perhaps. But no. He thought of the old guys who had fought in World War II. Many of them were on welfare back in the barrio. But, man! did they have metals! He had never seen so many purple hearts.[1] He remembered old Toque, the wino, who had tried to pawn his metals to buy a bottle. No way, man. They weren't worth a nickle.

He quickly edged past Harry, pushing the men ahead of him to reach the sergeant. He was running, tall grass brushing his shoulder, tall grass that had swayed peacefully like wheat. The figure of Sergeant Keever was in front of him now. There was a sudden impulse to reach out and hold him back. But the sergeant had stopped. Rico did not touch him, but whispered hoarsely, desperately in the dark. "Let's get the people out—evacuate . . ."

"What the hell . . ." Keever's voice was ice. He recognized Rico, and hissed, "Get back to your position soldier or I'll shoot you myself."

Rico did as he was told, almost unaware of the men around him. But at a distance he heard something splashing in the water of the canal, in his nostrils the smell of sweet burnt wood. He looked toward the clearing and saw the cluster of huts bathed in moonlight. In the same moonlight, he saw Keever giving signals. In the gloom he saw figures of the men carrying machine guns. They looked like dancing grasshoppers as they ran ahead to position themselves on the bluff. He felt like yelling, "For Christ's sake! Where is the enemy?"

The taste of blood in his mouth—he suddenly realized he had bitten his quivering lower lip. As soon as Sergeant Keever gave the signal, all sixteen men would open fire on the huts—machine guns, carbines—everything would be erased. No more Mai Cao—the execution of duty without question, without alternative. They were positioned on the south slope, Sergeant Keever up ahead, squatting on his heels, looking at his watch. He raised himself, after a quick glance at the men. As Sergeant Keever raised his hand to give the signal for attack, Rico felt the cold metallic deadness of his rifle. His hands began to tremble as he released the safety catch. Sergeant Keever was on the rise just above him. Rico stared at the sergeant's arm, raised, ready to fall—the signal to fire. The crossfire was inside Rico, a heavy-dosed tumult—destroy the village, erase all memory. There was ash in his mouth. Once the arm came down, there was no turning back.

In a split second, Rico turned his rifle at a forty-degree angle and fired at the sergeant's arm. Keever half-turned with the impact of the bullet, then fell to his knees. In a whooping whisper the old-time soldier blew out the words, "That fucking bastard—get him." He got up and signaled the platoon back to the carry-alls, as two men grabbed Rico, one hitting him on the side of the head with the butt of his rifle. Rico felt the sting of the blow, as they pinned his arm back and forced him to walk the path back to the carry-all. He did not resist. There was a lump in his throat, and he blinked back tears, tears of relief. The memory of the village would not be erased.

---

[1] **purple hearts:** U.S. military medals awarded to soldiers wounded in action

Someone shouted in the dark, "They're on to us. There's an old man with a lantern and others coming out of the hootches . . ."

"People—just people . . ." Rico whispered, wanting to shout it, wanting to tell them that he had done the right thing. But the heaviness that filled his senses was the weight of the truth. He was a traitor—a maniac. He had shot his superior in a battle crisis. He was being carried almost bodily back to the truck. He glanced at the thick brush along the road, thinking that somewhere beyond it was a rice field, and beyond that a mangrove swamp. There was a madman inside his soul that made him think of rice fields and mangrove swamps instead of what he had done. Not once did he look up. Everyone around him was strangely quiet and remote. Only the sound of trudging feet.

In the carry-all, the faces of the men sitting around Rico were indiscernible in the dark, but he imagined their eyes, wide, confused, peering through the dark at him with a wakefulness that questioned what he had done. Did they know his reason? Did they care? The truck suddenly lurched. Deep in the gut, Rico felt a growing fear. He choked back a hysteria rising from the diaphragm. The incessant bumping of the carry-alls as they moved unevenly on the dirt road accused him too. He looked up into a night sky and watched the moon eerily weave in and out of tree branches. The darkness was like his fear. It had no solutions.

Back on the post, Sergeant Keever and a medic passed by Rico, already handcuffed, without any sign of recognition. Sergeant Keever had already erased him from existence. The wheels of justice would take their course. Rico had been placed under arrest, temporarily shackled to a cot in one of the tents. Three days later he was moved to a makeshift bamboo hut, with a guard in front of the hut at all times. His buddies brought in food like strangers, awkward in their silence, anxious to leave him alone. He felt like some kind of poisonous bug. Only Harry came by to see him after a week.

"You dumb ass, were you on loco weed?" Harry asked in disgust.

"I didn't want people killed, that's all."

"Hell, that's no reason, those chinks aren't even—even . . ."

"Even what?" Rico demanded. He almost screamed it a second time. "Even what?"

"Take it easy, will you? You better go for a Section eight."[2] Harry was putting him aside like every one else. "They're sending you back to the States next week. You'll have to face Keever sometime this afternoon. I thought I'd better let you know."

"Thanks." Rico knew the hopelessness of it all. There was still that nagging question he had to ask. "Listen, nobody tells me anything. Did you all go back to Mai Cao? I mean, is it still there?"

"Still there. Orders from headquarters to forget it. The enemy were

[2] **Section eight:** discharge from the U.S. army for military inaptitude or undesirable habits or traits of character

spotted taking an opposite direction. But nobody's going to call you a hero, you understand? What you did was crud. You're no soldier. You'll never be a soldier."

Rico said nothing to defend himself. He began to scratch the area around the steel rings on his ankles. Harry was scowling at him. He said it again, almost shouting, "I said, you'll never be a soldier."

"So?" There was soft disdain in Rico's voice.

"You blew it, man. You'll be locked up for a long, long time."

"Maybe . . ." Rico's voice was without concern.

"Don't you care?"

"I'm free inside, Harry." Rico laughed in relief. "Free . . ."

Harry shrugged, peering at Rico unbelievingly, then turned and walked out of the hut.

CHAPTER FOUR

Discussion Activities

The discussion activities in Chapter 4 are designed to help you become engaged in the processes of reading and responding to the stories in Chapter 3. Ideally, the activities will lead you to make your own discoveries and to trust your reactions to what you read. At the same time, they provide strategies for analysis and interpretation. These strategies are expanded on in Chapter 6.

To activate class discussions, you can share what you have written in your reading log and literary journal entries and continue exploring the significance of what you have read. Multiple responses to the stories will reveal that there are many possible interpretations. There is no one "right" view.

Discussion Activities: "The Necklace" by Guy de Maupassant (pp. 46–52)

Write after You Read

Explore your response to "The Necklace" by recording your initial reactions in your reading log, following the guidelines on page 12. ●

Responding to, Analyzing, and Interpreting the Story

Working with a partner, in a small group, or with the whole class, share in some or all of the following activities. You can decide the order in which to cover the material and the amount of time to spend on each activity. Allow for different reactions to and interpretations of the various aspects of the story.

1. Share your initial reaction to the story (for example, you may share the responses you have recorded in your reading log entry). Raise any questions you may have.
2. Make sure that everyone understands what happens in the story.
3. Without looking at the story, try to remember and describe one scene that stands out in your mind. Take turns describing the scenes you remember. Then, looking at the text, read the scenes

aloud and analyze why each scene is particularly memorable. You might want to ask questions such as these:

    a. Is the scene memorable because you can identify with it? If so, what similar experience have you had?

    b. Is the scene memorable because it is so different from your own experience? If so, how has the author succeeded in capturing your attention?

    c. Is this scene memorable because of your positive reaction to it? If so, which images account for your positive reaction?

    d. Is this scene memorable because of your negative reaction to it? If so, which images account for your negative reaction?

4. Read aloud specific passages that reveal the place, time, social environment, and physical environment of the story. Begin by focusing on the first sentence of the story. Then continue to discuss the first six paragraphs.

    a. Determine where and over what period of time this part of the story takes place.

    b. Examine the manners, customs, rules, and/or moral codes of the society in which the story is set.

    c. Examine concrete details that reveal the characters' socio-economic status.

5. Read aloud the scene in which M. Loisel brings home the large envelope (beginning with the seventh paragraph). One student can read the narration, one can play the part of M. Loisel, and one can play the part of Mme. Loisel. Characterize the relationship between this husband and wife.

6. Read aloud the scene in which Mme. Loisel visits Mme. Forestier (beginning on page 48). One student can read the narration, one student can play the part of Mme. Loisel, and one student can play the part of Mme. Forestier. Characterize the relationship between the two women.

7. Referring to specific passages, analyze the character of Mathilde Loisel up to and including the time of the ball.

    a. Examine her outward appearance and behavior.

    b. Examine her inner emotional and moral qualities.

       • Explore her positive and negative characteristics.

       • Explore her values.

       • Explore her conflicts (internal or external).

       • Explore her choices.

       • Explore her changes.

8. Analyze the character of Mathilde Loisel after the ball. Use the guidelines in activity 7, above.

9. Analyze the character of M. Loisel before and after the ball. Use the guidelines in activity 7, above.

10. Analyze the character of Mme. Forestier before and after the ball. Use the guidelines in activity 7, above.

11. "How little a thing is needed for us to be lost or to be saved!" Provide various interpretations of this line from page 52. You might want to ask questions such as these:
    a. Whose words are these?
    b. What is the "little" thing?
    c. What does it mean "to be lost or to be saved"?
    d. Is a character in the story "lost" or "saved"?

12. The adjective *proud* is used in the story to describe Mme. Loisel on page 52. The word *proud* has several meanings. The following definitions are adapted from *The Oxford English Dictionary*. Apply the definitions to different scenes in the story and determine whether the definitions apply to any or all of the characters. You can divide into groups, with each group examining one or two definitions, and then share your findings with the entire class.
    a. *proud*: having a high opinion of one's own qualities and attainments, which makes one feel superior to and contemptuous of others.
    b. *proud*: conscious of what is due to oneself because of social position, which prevents one from doing what is perceived to be unworthy of or beneath oneself
       1. as a good quality, this is self-respect: proper pride
       2. as a mistaken or misapplied feeling, this is false pride
    c. *proud*: feeling pleasure, high satisfaction, or increased self-esteem from some action or possession
    d. *proud*: having great dignity
    e. *proud*: being in the best, highest, most excellent state or condition, the prime

13. Mathilde is referred to as "naïve" on page 52.
    a. Look up the definitions of the word *naïve* in the Glossary.
    b. Apply the five definitions to the story and decide whether any or all of the definitions are appropriate.

14. Go through different scenes to find incongruities between what seems to be true or real and what is actually true or real. You might want to ask questions such as these:
    a. Does anything happen that is unexpected or different from what is expected or hoped for?
    b. Does a character think or believe something that is different from the truth?
    c. Does a character say something that, either intentionally or unintentionally, means the opposite of what it seems to say?

15. Looking back at the whole story, can you say what, precisely, is the "point of no return," that is, that point at which the characters' actions make the outcome inevitable? If you do not think there is such a point, give your reasons for thinking that a different outcome could have been possible.

16. What might the necklace symbolize?

17. Compare the marriage of the Loisels with the marriage of another couple in one or more stories (for example, "The Story of an Hour," "Babylon Revisited," "Like a Bad Dream," or "Swaddling Clothes").
    a. Examine similarities and differences.
    b. Explore the authors' attitudes toward marriage.
18. Compare the exploration of the role and identity of women in this story with the exploration of the role and identity of women in one or more stories (for example, "The Story of an Hour," "Two Portraits," "Swaddling Clothes," "Girl," "A Woman Like Me").
    a. Examine similarities and differences.
    b. Examine the authors' attitudes toward the role and identity of women. ●

Suggested Literary Journal Topic

What might have been the quality of Mme. Loisel's life if she had not lost the necklace? Is her life better or worse now? Use at least one quotation to support your point; include the page number of the quotation in parentheses. ●

Discussion Activities: "A Trifle From Real Life" by Anton Chekhov (pp. 53–57)

Write after You Read

Explore your response to "A Trifle from Real Life" by recording your initial reactions in your reading log, following the guidelines on page 12. ●

Responding to, Analyzing, and Interpreting the Story

Working with a partner, in a small group, or with the whole class, share in some or all of the following activities. You can decide the order in which to cover the material and the amount of time to spend on each activity. Allow for different reactions to and interpretations of the various aspects of the story.

1. Share your initial reaction to the story (for example, you may share the responses you have recorded in your reading log entry). Raise any questions you may have.
2. Make sure that everyone understands what happens in the story.
3. Discuss how well you are able to keep a secret, and why. Compare your experiences with Aliosha's.

4. Read the first four paragraphs of the story aloud.
   a. Focus on words or phrases or figures of speech that enable you to create mental pictures of what is described.
   b. Then analyze the images to discover the author's possible purpose in creating them.
5. Read aloud the scene between Belayeff and Aliosha that begins with the fifth paragraph of the story, ending with the line, "What do you talk about?" on pages 54–55. One student can read the narration, one can play the part of Belayeff, and one can play the part of Aliosha. Referring to specific details in this scene, characterize their relationship.
6. Read the following passage from page 55, in which Aliosha tells Belayeff about his father. Then, analyzing the passage, characterize the father.

   He kisses us and hugs us and tells us the funniest jokes. Do you know what? He says that when we grow bigger he is going to take us to live with him. Sonia doesn't want to go, but I wouldn't mind. Of course it would be lonely without mamma, but I could write letters to her. Isn't it funny, we might go and see her then on Sundays, mightn't we? Papa says, too, he is going to buy me a pony. He is such a nice man! I don't know why mamma doesn't ask him to live with her and why she won't let us see him. He loves mamma very much. He always asks how she is and what she has been doing. When she was ill he took hold of his head just like this—and ran about the room. He always asks us whether we are obedient and respectful to her. Tell me, is it true that we are unfortunate?

7. Read aloud the scene on pages 55–56 between Aliosha and Belayeff that begins, "H'm—why do you ask?" and ends with " . . . and now it seems it is all my fault!" One student can play the part of Aliosha and another of Belayeff. Characterize their relationship in this scene.
8. Read aloud and act out the last scene of the story, beginning with the moment when Aliosha's mother, Olga Ivanova, enters the room. One student can read the narration (starting with, "The door-bell rang," p. 56), and other students can read the parts of Belayeff, Olga, and Aliosha. Then discuss Olga's reaction.
   a. Explain why she behaves as she does.
   b. Evaluate her behavior. How would you have reacted in her place?
9. Referring to specific passages, analyze the character of Belayeff.
   a. Examine his outward appearance and behavior.
   b. Examine his inner emotional and moral qualities.
      • Explore his positive and negative characteristics.
      • Explore his values.

- Explore his conflicts (internal or external).
- Explore his choices.
- Explore his changes.

10. Analyze the character of Aliosha, using the guidelines in activity 9, above.
11. Explain the title in reference to the story.
12. Analyze the author's attitude toward Belayeff, Olga, the father, and Aliosha.
13. Analyze the author's attitude toward parenthood and childhood.
14. Compare the experience of the child in this story with the experience of growing up in one or more other stories (for example, "Two Portraits," "Araby," "The Egg," "A Handful of Dates," "The Verb *to Kill*," "Girl").
    a. Examine similarities and differences.
    b. Examine the authors' attitudes toward the experience of children.
15. Compare the family relationships in this story with family relationships in one or more other stories (for example, "Two Portraits," "The Egg," "Babylon Revisited," "War," "Swaddling Clothes," "A Handful of Dates," "The Plane Reservation," "Las papas").
    a. Examine similarities and differences.
    b. Examine the authors' attitudes toward family relationships. •

Suggested Literary Journal Topic

What is the "deceit" that Aliosha "had come roughly face to face with" on page 57? Consider various interpretations. •

Discussion Activities: "Two Portraits" by Kate Chopin (pp. 58–61)

Write after You Read

Explore your response to "Two Portraits" by recording your initial reactions in your reading log, following the guidelines on page 12. •

Responding to, Analyzing, and Interpreting the Story

Working with a partner, in a small group, or with the whole class, share in some or all of the following activities. You can decide the order in which to cover the material and the amount of time to spend on each activity. Allow for different reactions to and interpretations of the various aspects of the story.

1. Share your initial reaction to the story (for example, you may share the responses you have recorded in your reading log). Raise any questions you may have.
2. Make sure that everyone understands what happens in the story.
3. Discuss your own preconceived views of wantons and nuns. Compare your views with those presented in the story.
4. Looking at the text, select one or two significant quotations. The quotation may be one you like, one you think best illustrates an idea, or one you found difficult to understand. After you have selected the quotation(s), follow these guidelines:
   a. Take turns reading quotations aloud.
   b. Discuss what you perceive to be the meaning and significance of each quotation.
5. Referring to specific passages, analyze the character of the wanton (pp. 58–60).
   a. Examine her outward appearance and behavior.
   b. Examine her inner emotional and moral qualities.
      • Explore her positive and negative characteristics.
      • Explore her values.
      • Explore her choices.
      • Explore her conflicts (internal or external).
      • Explore her changes.
6. Analyze the character of the nun (pp. 60–61). Use the guidelines for activity 5, above.
7. Compare and contrast the wanton and the nun.
   a. Explore their differences.
   b. Explore their similarities.
   c. Discuss the significance of the differences and similarities.
8. Read aloud the first paragraph of each of the two sections of the story.
   a. Do any words or phrases appeal to your sense of sight? sound? taste? smell? touch?
   b. Does one type of image predominate?
   c. If you perceive a change from one type of image to another, what might the change reveal about the story's meaning?
   d. If you perceive no change from one type of image to another, what might the lack of change reveal about the story's meaning?
9. Analyze the author's view of the wanton and the nun.
10. Compare the main character in this story to an important female character in another story (for example, "The Story of an Hour," "The Necklace," "Swaddling Clothes," "Girl," "A Woman Like Me").
    a. Examine similarities and differences between the characters.
    b. Examine the authors' attitudes toward the role and identity of women.

11. Compare the role of religion in this story with the role of religion in one or more stories (for example, "The Americanization of Shadrach Cohen," "Araby," "Like a Bad Dream," "A Handful of Dates," "The Plane Reservation," "The Grass-Eaters").
    a. Examine similarities and differences.
    b. Examine the authors' attitudes toward religion. ●

Suggested Literary Journal Topic

Which life is better for Alberta, life as a wanton or life as a nun? Use at least one quotation from each part of the story in your answer; include the page numbers of the quotations within parentheses. ●

Discussion Activities: "The Americanization of Shadrach Cohen" by Bruno Lessing (pp. 62–68).

Write after You Read

Explore your response to "The Americanization of Shadrach Cohen" by recording your reactions in your reading log, following the guidelines on page 12. ●

Responding to, Analyzing, and Interpreting the Story

Working with a partner, in a small group, or with the whole class, share in some or all of the following activities. You can decide the order in which to cover the material and the amount of time to spend on each activity. Allow for different reactions to and interpretations of the various aspects of the story.

1. Share your initial reaction to the story (for example, you may share the responses you have recorded in your reading log entry). Raise any questions you may have.
2. Make sure that everyone understands what happens in the story.
3. What does the term *Americanization* mean to you? Compare your definitions with those of the story's characters.
4. Characterize Abel and Gottlieb. Read aloud relevant passages.
    a. Explore the significance of the way they dress.
    b. Explore the significance of the way they initially react and speak to their father (and to Marta).
    c. Analyze their father's reaction to them.
5. Referring to specific passages, analyze the character of Shadrach.
    a. Examine his attitude toward his own outward appearance and behavior.

b. Examine his relationship with Marta.

c. Analyze his qualities as a father.

d. Analyze his qualities as a businessman.

e. Explore his values.

f. Explore his choices.

g. Explore his changes.

6. On page 67, the narrator says,

> When life is light and free from care, religion is quick to fly; but when the sky grows dark and life becomes earnest and we feel its burden growing heavy upon our shoulders, then we welcome the consolation that religion brings, and we cling to it.

  a. Discuss what you think this statement means and whether you agree with it.

  b. Discuss how the statement applies to the story.

7. If you were to choose one or two words to describe your impression of the tone of the story as a whole, what might the word(s) be?

8. If you were to choose one or two words to describe the author's attitude toward each of the characters, what might those words be?

9. Read the following quotations about parents and children. Discuss some or all of the quotations to uncover their meaning or significance. Then, where appropriate, apply your discussion to the story.

  a. "When I was a boy of fourteen, my father was so ignorant I could hardly stand to have the old man around. But when I got to be twenty-one, I was astonished at how much he had learned in seven years." (Mark Twain, 1835–1910)

  b. "There may be some doubt as to who are the best people to have charge of children, but there can be no doubt that parents are the worst." (George Bernard Shaw, 1856–1950)

  c. "It is a wise father that knows his own child." (William Shakespeare, 1564–1616)

  d. "It is a wise child that knows its own father, and an unusual one that unreservedly approves of him." (Mark Twain, 1835–1910)

  e. "Children begin by loving their parents; after a time they judge them; rarely, if ever, do they forgive them." (Oscar Wilde, 1854–1900)

  f. "There must always be a struggle between a father and a son; while one aims at power and the other at independence." (Samuel Johnson, 1709–1784)

  g. "The finest legacy any parent can leave his child is the ability to do his own thinking when the parent is no longer around to make decisions." (Dorothy Clifton, b. 1922)

10. Compare the father-son relationship with the (grand)parent-child relationship in one or more stories (for example, "A Trifle from Real Life," "The Egg," "War," "Babylon Revisited," "The Man

Who Was Almost a Man," "A Handful of Dates," "The Plane Reservation," "Las papas").

a. Examine the similarities and differences between the relationships.

b. Examine the authors' attitudes toward parent-child relationships.

11. Compare the striving-for-success experience in this story with the striving-for-success experience in one or more stories (for example, "The Egg," "Babylon Revisited," "Dead Men's Path," "Like a Bad Dream").

a. Examine the similarities and differences between the experiences.

b. Examine the authors' attitudes toward success.   ●

Suggested Literary Journal Topic

Write an interior monologue (conversation with herself) for Marta, providing what you think are her thoughts at different stages of this entire experience.   ●

Discussion Activities: "Araby" by James Joyce (pp. 69–73)

Write after You Read

Explore your response to "Araby" by recording your reactions in your reading log, following the guidelines on page 12.   ●

Responding to, Analyzing, and Interpreting the Story

Working with a partner, in a small group, or with the whole class, share in some or all of the following activities. You can decide the order in which to cover the material and the amount of time to spend on each activity. Allow for different reactions to and interpretations of the various aspects of the story.

1. Share your initial reaction to the story (for example, you may share the responses you have recorded in your reading log entry). Raise any questions you may have.

2. Make sure that everyone understands what happens in the story.

3. Share experiences you have had involving expectation and disappointment or illusion and disillusionment. Compare your experiences with those of the boy.

4. Read aloud the first and second paragraphs to find words or images that may suggest hidden meanings. Stop after every sentence or

two. Determine the literal meaning; then analyze the words or phrases for possible symbolic intent.

5. Read aloud the third paragraph and focus on the words or phrases that enable you to create mental pictures of what the author describes. Analyze the images to speculate on the author's purpose in creating them.

6. Continue focusing on and analyzing images on pages 69–71. You might want to take turns reading paragraphs aloud and to stop after each paragraph to discuss its contents.

7. Read the paragraph on page 71 that begins, "What innumerable follies laid waste my waking and sleeping thoughts after that evening!" Then, imagine that you are the boy's schoolmaster and compose an oral or written progress report about his schoolwork and attitude, to be delivered to his aunt and uncle. You may include other relevant details from the story in your report.

8. Referring to specific passages in the story, characterize the uncle and aunt.
    a. Explore the significance of how they react to the boy and what they say to him.
    b. Explore the significance of how the boy reacts to them.

9. Read aloud the scene in the train (p. 72). Look for hints that suggest what is ahead for the boy.

10. The narrator says, "I could not find any sixpenny entrance and, fearing that the bazaar would be closed, I passed in quickly through a turnstile, handing a shilling to a weary-looking man" (p. 73). Literally, a *sixpenny* is worth six cents and a *shilling* is worth twice that amount. Speculate on what the "sixpenny entrance" might be and why he could not find such an entrance to the bazaar.

11. Characterize the bazaar, gathering details from the last few paragraphs of the story (p. 73). You might want to make a list of words or phrases that depict the place. Then read over the list to discover a pattern that emerges from the details.

12. Read aloud the scene in which the boy overhears the young lady talking and laughing with two young gentlemen, with three students taking the parts of the lady and the two men. Read the lines as you think the characters would actually say them (you may need to practice more than once).
    a. Speculate on why this scene is included in the story.
    b. Explore the connection between this scene and earlier events in the story.
    Read the lines that immediately follow this scene to determine what effect it has on the boy.

13. At the end, the boy see himself as "a creature driven and derided by vanity" and his eyes burn "with anguish and anger." Why might that be?

14. Looking back at the whole story, can you say what, precisely, was

the "point of no return," that is, that point at which the outcome became inevitable? If you do not think there was such a point, give your reasons for thinking that the outcome was not inevitable.

15. The point of view of the story (the perspective through which the story is told) is that of an adult narrator looking back on his earlier life. With this dual point of view, there are two characters to analyze: the boy in the story and the adult that he grew up to be.
    a. Using clues from the story, determine the approximate age of the boy. What do you know about boys of that age that might help you understand this story?
    b. Is there anything unique or special about the way the adult narrator presents the information that suggests something about the narrator's character? Can you tell what kind of man the boy turned out to be?
    c. Why do you think the author has chosen this point of view? How would the story be different if it were told from another point of view?

16. Compare the process of growing up as explored in this story with the exploration of this subject in one or more other stories (for example, "Two Portraits," "A Trifle from Real Life," "The Man Who Was Almost a Man," "A Handful of Dates," "The Plane Reservation," "The Verb *to Kill*," "Girl").
    a. Examine the similarities and differences.
    b. Examine the authors' attitudes toward the process of growing up.

17. Compare the role of religion in this story with the role of religion in one or more stories (for example, "Two Portraits," "The Americanization of Shadrach Cohen," "Dead Men's Path," "Like a Bad Dream," "A Handful of Dates," "The Plane Reservation," "The Grass-Eaters").
    a. Examine similarities and differences.
    b. Examine the authors' attitudes toward religion.   •

Suggested Literary Journal Topic

Select one aspect of the setting (for example, neighborhood, darkness, light, rain, school, train, bazaar) and relate it to the emotional state or character development of the boy. Use at least two quotations in your response; put the page numbers of the quotations within parentheses.   •

Discussion Activities: "War" by Luigi Pirandello (pp. 74–77)

Write after You Read

Explore your response to "War" by recording your reactions in your reading log, following the guidelines on page 12.   •

Responding to, Analyzing, and Interpreting the Story

Working with a partner, in a small group, or with the whole class, share in some or all of the following activities. You can decide the order in which to cover the material and the amount of time to spend on each activity. Allow for different reactions to and interpretations of the various aspects of the story.

1. Share your initial reaction to the story (for example, you may share the responses you have recorded in your reading log entry). Raise any questions you may have.
2. Make sure that everyone understands what happens in the story.
3. Discuss your knowledge of and attitude toward military service and war. You might want to answer questions such as these:
   a. If you have served in the military, will have to serve in the military, or know a family member or friend who has served or will serve in the military, share your knowledge of the military service with the class. For example, answer such questions as: Is the military service voluntary? mandatory? At what age does it start? How long does it last?
   b. If you are not required to serve in the military, under what circumstances, if any, would you volunteer?
   c. Under what circumstances do you think war is justified?
      • If you were drafted to fight in a war that you considered unjustified, what would you do?
      • If you were asked to volunteer to fight in a war that you considered justified, what would you do?
4. Read aloud specific passages that reveal the place, time, and social environment of the story.
   a. Determine where and over what period of time the story takes place.
   b. Examine the manners, customs, rules, and/or moral codes of the society in which the story is set.
5. Read aloud the conversation among the passengers, pages 75–77. Different class members can play the roles of the woman, the husband, the fat man, and the other passengers. Stop periodically to

discuss the characters' different responses to having sons at war, deciding whether you agree or disagree with what they are saying.

6. Referring to specific passages, analyze the character of the fat man.
   a. Explore the significance of his physical appearance.
   b. Explore the significance of how the other passengers relate to him.
   c. Examine his conflicts.

7. Read aloud the poem on page 197, "Dulce et Decorum Est," by Wilfred Owen. Discuss the ways in which it is different from and similar to the story, "War."

8. Discuss some or all of the following quotations about war to uncover their meaning and significance. Allow for different interpretations of the quotations. Then, where appropriate, apply your discussion to the story.
   a. "In war, whichever side may call itself the victor, there are no winners, but all are losers." (Neville Chamberlain, 1869–1940)
   b. "For what can war but endless war still breed?" (John Milton, 1608–1674)
   c. "Let him who desires peace, prepare for war." (Vegetius, c. A.D. 300–400)
   d. "There is such a thing as legitimate warfare: war has its laws; there are things which may be fairly done, and things which may not be done." (John Henry Cardinal Newman, 1801–1890)
   e. "War is much too serious a thing to be left to the military." (Georges Clemenceau, 1841–1929)
   f. "The first casualty when war comes is truth." (Hiram Johnson, 1866–1945).

9. Compare the parent-child relationship explored in this story with the exploration of the subject in one or more other stories (for example, "A Trifle from Real Life," "The Egg," "Babylon Revisited," "A Handful of Dates," "The Plane Reservation," "Las papas").
   a. Examine similarities and differences.
   b. Explore the authors' attitudes toward parent-child relationships.

10. Compare the exploration of war in this story with the exploration of war in the story "The Village" and in the poem "Dulce et Decorum Est" (p. 197).
    a. Examine similarities and differences.
    b. Examine the authors' attitude toward war.   ●

Suggested Literary Journal Topic

The fat traveler says of children, "We [parents] belong to them but they never belong to us" (p. 75). Explain what he means, and then discuss whether or not you agree with him.

Dulce et Decorum Est
Wilfred Owen   England, 1918?

ABOUT THE AUTHOR

Wilfred Owen (1893–1918) was born in Shropshire, England. Among the most celebrated of the English war poets, he was killed in action in World War I.

THE TITLE OF THE POEM

The title, "Dulce et Decorum Est," is taken from the Latin poet Horace's statement, "Dulce et decorum est pro patria mori": "It is sweet and fitting to die for one's country."

Bent double, like old beggars under sacks,
Knock-kneed, coughing like hags, we cursed through sludge,
Till on the haunting flares we turned our backs,
And towards our distant rest began to trudge.
Men marched asleep. Many had lost their boots.
But limped on, blood-shod. All went lame, all blind;
Drunk with fatigue; deaf even to the hoots
Of gas-shells dropping softly behind.

Gas! GAS! Quick, boys!—An ecstasy of fumbling,
Fitting the clumsy helmets just in time,
But someone still was yelling out and stumbling
And flound'ring like a man in fire or lime.—
Dim through the misty panes and thick green light,
As under a green sea, I saw him drowning.
In all my dreams before my helpless sight
He plunges at me, guttering, choking, drowning.

If in some smothering dreams, you too could pace
Behind the wagon that we flung him in,
And watch the white eyes writhing in his face,
His hanging face, like a devil's sick of sin,
If you could hear, at every jolt, the blood
Come gargling from the froth-corrupted lungs
Bitter as the cud
Of vile, incurable sores on innocent tongues,—
My friend, you would not tell with such high zest
To children ardent for some desperate glory,
The old lie: *Dulce et decorum est
Pro patria mori.*

Discussion Activities: "The Egg" by Sherwood Anderson (pp. 78–85)

Write after You Read

Explore your response to "The Egg" by recording your reactions in your reading log, following the guidelines on page 12.   •

Responding to, Analyzing, and Interpreting the Story

Working with a partner, in a small group, or with the whole class, share in some or all of the following activities. You can decide the order in which to cover the material and the amount of time to spend on each activity. Allow for different reactions to and interpretations of the various aspects of the story.

1. Share your initial reaction to the story (for example, you may share the responses you have recorded in your reading log entry). Raise any questions you may have.
2. Establish the facts: Make sure that everyone understands what happens in the story.
3. The story refers to the "American passion for getting up in the world" (p. 78). What does this expression mean to you? Apply your definitions to the story.
4. Read the first paragraph of the story aloud. Characterize the father before he got married and had a child.
   a. Examine his work and social life.
   b. Examine his attitude.
5. Read the second and third paragraphs of the story aloud. Characterize the mother.
   a. Examine her background.
   b. Examine her relationship with her husband.
   c. Examine her attitude toward her son.
6. As in "Araby" by James Joyce (pp. 69–73), the point of view of this story (the perspective through which the story is told) is that of an adult narrator looking back on his earlier life. With this dual point of view, there are two characters to analyze: the boy in the story and the adult that he grew up to be.
   a. Using clues from the story, determine the approximate ages of the boy at different stages. Characterize him at these stages.
   b. Read the fourth and fifth paragraphs aloud. Characterize the adult narrator on the basis of the information provided in these passages.
      • If you were to use two words to describe the adult narrator, what might they be?

    • Discuss his philosophy of life.

7. Discuss all or some of the following quotations about chickens and eggs to uncover their meaning or significance. Then, where appropriate, apply your discussion to the material in the fourth and fifth paragraphs and to the whole story. Allow for different interpretations of the quotations.

    a. "Which came first, the chicken or the egg?"

    b. "It has, I believe, often been remarked, that a hen is only an egg's way of making another egg." (Samuel Butler, 1835–1902)

    c. "See this egg. It is with this that all the schools of theology and all the temples of the earth are to be overturned." (Denis Diderot, 1713–1784)

    d. "I want there to be no peasant in my kingdom so poor that he is unable to have a chicken in his pot every Sunday." (Henri IV of France, 1553–1610)

    e. "Republican prosperity has reduced hours and increased earning capacity, silenced discontent, put the proverbial 'chicken in every pot.'" (Republican campaign newspaper advertisement, 1920s)

8. Referring to specific passages, analyze the character of the father.

    a. Discuss his positive and negative qualities.

    b. Discuss his values.

    c. Discuss his conflicts (internal and external).

    d. Discuss the choices he makes in life.

    e. Discuss whether he changes.

9. On page 84, the father expresses his anger at Christopher Columbus (1451–1506), the Italian explorer who has been mythologized as the discoverer of America. The father calls Columbus a "cheat" because of a trick he did with an egg. Read the following description of Columbus's trick, and apply the lesson that Columbus taught to the father's situation in "The Egg."

[Pedro Gonzalez de Mendoza, the Grand Cardinal of Spain] invited Columbus to a banquet where he assigned him the most honorable place at table. . . . At this repast is said to have occurred the well-known anecdote of the egg. A shallow courtier present, impatient of the honors paid Columbus and meanly jealous of him as a foreigner, abruptly asked him whether he thought that in case he had not discovered the Indies, there were not other men in Spain who would have been capable of the enterprise? To this Columbus made no reply, but taking an egg, invited the company to make it stand on one end. Every one attempted it, but in vain; whereupon he struck it upon the table so as to break the end, and left it standing on the broken part; illustrating in this simple manner, that when he had once shown the way to the New World, nothing was easier than to follow it.

    —from Washington Irving, *The Life and Voyages of Columbus*

10. Referring to specific passages, analyze the character of the young boy. Compare him with the adult narrator that he has become (see activity 6, above).

11. In the last paragraph of the story, the father "gently" lays an egg on the table instead of destroying it. Speculate on why he does not destroy this egg.

12. What might be "the complete and final triumph of the egg" (p. 85)?

13. Compare the difficulties of growing up as explored in this story with the exploration of this subject in one or more other stories (for example, "A Trifle from Real Life," "Araby," "The Man Who Was Almost a Man," "A Handful of Dates," "The Verb *to Kill*," "Girl").
    a. Examine the similarities and differences.
    b. Examine the authors' attitudes toward the process of growing up.

14. Compare the desire for success as explored in this story with the exploration of this subject in one or more stories (for example, "The Necklace," "The Americanization of Shadrach Cohen," "Babylon Revisited," "Dead Men's Path," "Like a Bad Dream").
    a. Examine the similarities and differences.
    b. Examine the authors' attitudes toward success.   •

Suggested Literary Journal Topic

What might the egg symbolize? Use at least one quotation in your answer; include the page number of the quotation within parentheses.   •

Discussion Activities: "Babylon Revisited" by F. Scott Fitzgerald (pp. 86–102)

Write after You Read

Explore your response to "Babylon Revisited" by recording your reactions in your reading log, following the guidelines on page 12.   •

Responding to, Analyzing, and Interpreting the Story

Working with a partner, in a small group, or with the whole class, share in some or all of the following activities. You can decide the order in which to cover the material and the amount of time to spend on each activity. Allow for different reactions to and interpretations of the various aspects of the story.

1. Share your initial reaction to the story (for example, you may share the responses you have recorded in your reading log entry). Raise any questions you may have.
2. Make sure that everyone understands what happens in the story. Take care to determine the chronology of the story: the order in which events have taken place in the characters' lives. You might want to make a time line of the key events.
3. Discuss under what circumstances you believe a child should be kept from his or her biological parents. Compare your conclusions with the story.
4. Looking at the text, select a passage that you found difficult to understand or that you particularly like.
   a. Take turns reading your passages aloud.
   b. Explain why you are confused by a passage or why you like it. Discuss the meaning of each passage. Remember that each reader may have a different response. Be ready to accept different interpretations of the same passage.
5. Read aloud specific passages that reveal the place, time, and social environment of the story.
   a. Determine where and over what period of time the story takes place.
   b. Examine the manners, customs, rules, and/or moral codes of the society in which the story is set.
   c. Analyze the description of the Peters' home (p. 88).
6. Referring to specific passages, analyze the character of Marion.
   a. Examine her outward appearance and behavior.
   b. Explore her inner emotional and moral qualities.
      • Examine her positive and negative characteristics.
      • Examine her values.
      • Examine her conflicts (internal and external).
      • Examine her choices.
      • Examine her changes.
7. Create a classroom debate to discuss the question, "Has Charlie changed?" Divide the class into two teams. (Teams can be further subdivided to cover different sections of the story.)
   a. Team A's task is to look at the text to find evidence to prove that Charlie has changed. Assign one person in the team to keep a list of the evidence, including quotations and page numbers.
   b. Team B's task is to look at the text to find evidence to prove that Charlie has not changed. Assign one person in the group to keep a list of the evidence, including quotations and page numbers.
   c. After the evidence is gathered, regroup as a whole class so that Team A can debate Team B.
8. Based on the evidence presented in the debate (see activity 7), discuss whether you would have made the same decision Marion makes at the end of the story.

9. If you were the judge in a custody battle between Charlie and Marion, what decision would you make?

10. If you were Charlie, what would you do now?

11. Gather together the references to *money*. Examine any details that reveal the characters' emotional or moral state.

12. Gather together the references to *time*. Examine the details that reveal the characters' emotional or moral state.

13. Read the following quotations and excerpts from poems about time and the past. Discuss what you think they mean. Then, if appropriate, compare and contrast them to various scenes in the story.

    a. "Remember, that time is money." (Benjamin Franklin, 1706–1790)

    b. "The past is a foreign country: they do things differently there." (L. P. Hartley, 1895–1957)

    c. "When to the sessions of sweet silent thought
    I summon up remembrance of things past,
    I sigh the lack of many a thing I sought,
    And with old woes new wail my dear times' waste."
                                (William Shakespeare, 1564–1616)

    d. "Time present and time past
    Are both perhaps present in time future,
    And time future contained in time past."
                                (T. S. Eliot, 1888–1965)

14. Compare the issue of success as explored in this story with the exploration of this subject in one or more other stories (for example, "The Necklace," "The Americanization of Shadrach Cohen," "The Egg," "Dead Men's Path," "Like a Bad Dream").

    a. Examine similarities and differences.

    b. Explore the authors' attitudes toward success.

15. Compare the parent-child relationship explored in this story with the exploration of the subject in one or more other stories (for example, "A Trifle from Real Life," "The Egg," "War," "A Handful of Dates," "The Plane Reservation," "Las papas").

    a. Examine similarities and differences.

    b. Explore the authors' attitudes toward parent-child relationships.

Suggested Literary Journal Topic

Read the following passage from page 89. Explain what you think Charlie means, and discuss whether you agree with him.

> He believed in character; he wanted to jump back a whole generation and trust in character again as the eternally valuable element. Everything else wore out.

Discussion Activities: "The Man Who Was Almost a Man" by Richard Wright (pp. 103–13)

Write after You Read

Explore your response to "The Man Who Was Almost a Man" by recording your reactions in your reading log, following the guidelines on page 12. •

Responding to, Analyzing, and Interpreting the Story

Working with a partner, in a small group, or with the whole class, share in some or all of the following activities. You can decide the order in which to cover the material and the amount of time to spend on each activity. Allow for different reactions to and interpretations of the various aspects of the story.

1. Share your initial reaction to the story (for example, you may share the responses you have recorded in your reading log entry). Raise any questions you may have.
2. Make sure that everyone understands what happens in the story.
3. Define the term *man*. What does it take to become a man in society? Compare your definitions with Dave's.
4. Read aloud specific passages that reveal the place, time, and social environment of the story.
   a. Examine the clues that reveal where and over what period of time the story takes place.
   b. Examine the clues that reveal the manners, customs, rules, and/ or moral codes of the society in which the story is set.
5. Read aloud the first paragraph of the story. Characterize Dave based on his thoughts at this time.
   a. Examine his treatment by others.
   b. Examine his conflicts (internal and external).
   c. Examine his choices.
   d. Examine his values.
6. Read aloud the scene that takes place in Joe's store (pp. 103–04). One student can read the narration, one can read the part of Joe, and one can read the part of Dave. Characterize the relationship between Dave and Joe.
7. Read aloud the first scene between Dave and his mother (pp. 104–05). One student can read the narration, one can read the part of the mother, and one can read the part of Dave. Characterize the relationship between Dave and his mother.
8. Read aloud the first scene between Dave and his father (p. 105). One student can read the narration, one can read the part of the

father, and one can read the part of Dave. Characterize the relationship between Dave and his father.

9. Read aloud the second scene between Dave and his mother (pp. 106–07). One student can read the narration, one can read the part of the mother, and one can read the part of Dave.
   a. Characterize the relationship between Dave and his mother at this point.
   b. What significant information about their lives is revealed in this section? Remember that each reader may focus on different significant details.

10. Discuss what the gun means to Dave.
    a. Refer to specific passages in the story, focusing on the images.
    b. Compare his view with your own view of guns. In what ways are your views different or similar?

11. Characterize Dave in the scene with the mule (pp. 108–09). Observe negative and/or positive qualities.

12. Read aloud the scene of Dave, his parents, Mister Hawkins, and the crowd (pp. 109–11). One student can read the narration and others can take the parts of Jim Hawkins, Dave's mother, Dave's father, Dave, and two or three men in the crowd.
    a. Characterize the relationship between Dave and the others.
    b. Examine Dave's reaction to what happens.

13. Discuss the implications of Dave's final decision at the end of the story. If you were Dave, what would you have done?

14. Read the poem by Langston Hughes on page 205. Discuss its meaning. Discuss the ways in which it is similar to and different from "The Man Who Was Almost a Man."

15. Compare the process of growing up as explored in this story with the exploration of this subject in one or more other stories (for example, "Two Portraits," "A Trifle from Real Life," "Araby," "A Handful of Dates," "The Plane Reservation," "Girl").
    a. Examine the similarities and differences.
    b. Examine the authors' attitudes toward the process of growing up.

16. Compare the role of work in this story with the role of work in one or more other stories (for example, "The Necklace," "The Egg," "Dead Men's Path," "A Handful of Dates," "A Woman Like Me," "The Grass-Eaters").
    a. Examine similarities and differences.
    b. Examine the authors' attitudes toward work.   ●

Suggested Literary Journal Topic

What sort of future for Dave is implied in the last few paragraphs? Use at least one quotation in your response; include the page number within parentheses.   ●

Harlem
Langston Hughes   United States, 1951

ABOUT THE AUTHOR

Langston Hughes (1902–1967) was born in Missouri. A poet, playwright, fiction writer, and newspaper columnist, he was a member of a group of writers who helped form the Harlem Renaissance, a group that emphasized topics related to the African-American experience.

THE TITLE OF THE POEM

The title, "Harlem," refers to a section of New York City that became one of the largest African-American communities in the United States. A center of art and literature in the 1920s, Harlem deteriorated rapidly after World War II and the area became depressed economically.

What happens to a dream deferred?

Does it dry up like a raisin in the sun?
Or fester like a sore—
And then run?
Does it stink like rotten meat?
Or crust and sugar over—
like a syrupy sweet?

Maybe it just sags
like a heavy load.

Or does it explode?

Discussion Activities: "Dead Men's Path" by Chinua Achebe (pp. 113–15)

Write after You Read

Explore your response to "Dead Men's Path" by recording your reactions in your reading log, following the guidelines on page 12.   •

Responding to, Analyzing, and Interpreting the Story

Working with a partner, in a small group, or with the whole class, share in some or all of the following activities. You can decide the order in which to cover the material and the amount of time to spend on each activity. Allow for different reactions to and interpretations of the various aspects of the story.

1. Share your initial reaction to the story (for example, you may share the responses you have recorded in your reading log entry). Raise any questions you may have.
2. Make sure that everyone understands what happens in the story.
3. Discuss what you think should be the goal of a school. Compare your goal with Michael Obi's.
4. Read aloud specific passages that reveal the place, time, and social environment of the story.
   a. Examine the clues that reveal where and over what period of time the story takes place.
   b. Examine the clues that reveal the manners, customs, rules, and/ or moral codes of the society in which the story is set.
5. Referring to specific passages, analyze the character of Michael.
   a. Examine the details that reveal his outward appearance and behavior.
   b. Examine the details that reveal his inner emotional and moral qualities.
   • Explore his positive and negative characteristics.
   • Explore his values.
   • Explore his conflicts (internal or external).
   • Explore his choices.
   • Explore his changes.
6. Characterize Nancy, using the guidelines in activity 5 above.
7. If you were to choose one or two words to describe your impression of the tone of the story as a whole, what might the word(s) be?
8. If you were to choose one or two words to describe the author's attitude toward each of the characters, what might the words be?
9. Compare the exploration of cultural identity in this story with the exploration of cultural identity in one or more other stories (for example, "The Americanization of Shadrach Cohen," "Six Feet of the Country," "Swaddling Clothes," "The Plane Reservation," "Las papas," "Village").
   a. Examine similarities and differences.
   b. Examine the authors' attitudes toward cultural identity.
10. Compare the desire for success as explored in this story with the exploration of this subject in one or more other stories (for example, "The Necklace," "The Americanization of Shadrach Cohen," "The Egg," "Babylon Revisited," "Like a Bad Dream").
    a. Examine similarities and differences.
    b. Explore the authors' attitudes toward success.

Suggested Literary Journal Topic

On page 115, the priest says, "let the hawk perch and let the eagle perch." Discuss what you think he means and what this saying reveals about him.

Discussion Activities: "Six Feet of the Country" by Nadine Gordimer (pp. 116–25)

Write after You Read

Explore your response to "Six Feet of the Country" by recording your reactions in your reading log, following the guidelines on page 12.   ●

Responding to, Analyzing, and Interpreting the Story

Working with a partner, in a small group, or with the whole class, share in some or all of the following activities. You can decide the order in which to cover the material and the amount of time to spend on each activity. Allow for different reactions to and interpretations of the various aspects of the story.

1. Share your initial reaction to the story (for example, you may share the responses you have recorded in your reading log entry). Raise any questions you may have.
2. Make sure that everyone understands what happens in the story.
3. Share information about the funeral practices of your particular religion or culture. Compare them with the practices described in the story.
4. Without looking at the story, try to remember and describe one scene that stands out in your mind. Take turns describing the scenes you remember. Then, looking at the text, read the scenes aloud and analyze why each scene is particularly memorable. Ask questions such as these:
   a. Is the scene memorable because you can identify with it? If so, what similar experience have you had?
   b. Is the scene memorable because it is so different from your own experience? If so, how has the author succeeded in capturing your attention?
   c. Is this scene memorable because of your positive reaction to it? If so, which images account for your positive reaction?
   d. Is this scene memorable because of your negative reaction to it? If so, which images account for your negative reaction?
5. Read aloud specific passages that reveal the place, time, and social environment of the story.
   a. Examine the details that reveal where and over what period of time the story takes place.
   b. Examine the details that reveal the manners, customs, rules, and/or moral codes of the society in which the story is set.
6. Referring to specific passages, analyze the character of Lerice.

a. Examine her outward appearance and behavior.
b. Examine her inner emotional and moral qualities.
  - Explore her positive and negative characteristics.
  - Explore her values.
  - Explore her conflicts (internal or external).
  - Explore her choices.
  - Explore her changes.
7. Characterize Petrus.
   a. Analyze the way he speaks to his boss.
   b. Analyze his reactions to the body.
8. Referring to specific passages, analyze the character of the narrator, looking for some or all of the following clues.
   a. Examine the clues about the narrator's background.
   b. Evaluate his attitude toward his wife.
   c. Evaluate his attitude toward the workers.
   c. Evaluate the way he presents information and determine what that suggests about his character.
   d. Discuss his positive and negative qualities and values.
   e. Discuss his conflicts (internal and external).
   f. Discuss his changes.
9. Why do you think the author has chosen to tell the story from this man's point of view? How would the story be different if it were told from another point of view?
10. If you were to choose one or two words to describe your impression of the tone of the story as a whole, what might the word(s) be?
11. If you were to choose one or two words to describe the author's attitude toward each of the characters, what might those words be?
12. Compare the marriage of the narrator and Lerice with the marriage of another couple in one or more stories (for example, "The Story of an Hour," "The Necklace," "Babylon Revisited," "Like a Bad Dream," "Swaddling Clothes").
    a. Examine similarities and differences.
    b. Explore the authors' attitudes toward marriage.
13. Compare racial attitudes in this story with racial attitudes in another story (for example, "The Man Who Was Almost a Man," "Village").
    a. Examine similarities and differences.
    b. Explore the authors' attitudes toward racial attitudes.

Suggested Literary Journal Topic

Write an editorial for a newspaper or magazine published in a democracy. Explain the incident described in "Six Feet of the Country" as though it were a true story, and offer your opinion about what happened.

Discussion Activities: "Like a Bad Dream" by Heinrich Böll (pp. 126–31)

Write after You Read

Explore your response to "Like a Bad Dream" by recording your reactions in your reading log, following the guidelines on p. 12. •

Responding to, Analyzing, and Interpreting the Story

Working with a partner, in a small group, or with the whole class, share in some or all of the following activities. You can decide the order in which to cover the material and the amount of time to spend on each activity. Allow for different reactions to and interpretations of the various aspects of the story.

1. Share your initial reaction to the story (for example, you may share the responses you have recorded in your reading log entry). Raise any questions you may have.
2. Make sure that everyone understands what happens in the story. You may want to outline the deal on the blackboard.
3. Bertha says, "Life . . . consists of making compromises and concessions" (p. 129). Discuss the extent to which you agree with her. As you discuss this issue, you may want to answer questions such as these:
   a. If you have ever made compromises and concessions, what were they?
      - What process did you undergo in deciding to make them (for example, did someone influence your decision or did you make it on your own)?
      - Were you pleased or disturbed by the outcome?
   b. What compromises and concessions are made in this story?
      - In what ways are they similar to your own compromises and concessions?
      - Would you make the same compromises and concessions the characters do?
4. Read aloud specific passages that reveal the place, time, social environment, and physical environment of the story.
   a. Examine the details that reveal where and over what period of time the story takes place.
   b. Examine the details that reveal the manners, customs, rules, and/or moral codes of the society in which the story is set.
   c. Examine the details of physical objects and discuss the connection between the objects and the emotional or moral state of the characters.

5. Referring to specific passages, analyze the character of Bertha.
   a. Examine her outward appearance and behavior.
   b. Examine her inner emotional and moral qualities.
      • Explore her positive and negative qualities and values.
      • Explore her conflicts (internal or external).
      • Explore her choices.
      • Explore her changes.
6. Characterize Mr. and Mrs. Zumpen. Use the guidelines in activity 5, above.
7. Analyze the character of the narrator. You might want to make separate lists of his positive and negative qualities. This can be done in two groups, with one group gathering evidence on his positive qualities and the other group gathering evidence on his negative qualities; the two groups can then debate.
8. Read the following passage from page 130 and discuss what you think the Madonna might symbolize.

   I was wondering about something. I got up, went into the bedroom, and looked at the baroque Madonna, but even there I couldn't put my finger on the thing I was wondering about.

9. Assume that the local newspaper has found out about what the characters did and assigns you the task of covering the story. Write a newspaper article describing the incident, including quotations from the story—perhaps in the form of interviews with the characters. You can divide into three groups to write three different articles.
   a. One group can write an article for a newspaper that sensationalizes its stories.
   b. Another group can write an article for a newspaper that gives the personal angle of a story.
   c. The third group can write an article for a newspaper that provides straightforward coverage of its stories.
   Each group should create a headline for the article, and then share the article with the rest of the class. Compare the articles.
   a. Which details of the story are emphasized in each article? Why?
   b. Which article most helps you to understand the story?
10. Compare the marriage of Bertha and the narrator with the marriage of another couple in one or more stories (for example, "The Story of an Hour," "The Necklace," "Babylon Revisited," "Swaddling Clothes").
    a. Examine similarities and differences.
    b. Explore the authors' attitudes toward marriage.
11. Compare the ethical dilemma of the narrator with the dilemma of a character in one or more other stories (for example, "Dead Men's Path," "Six Feet of the Country," "Swaddling Clothes," "A Woman Like Me," "Village").

a. Examine similarities and differences.
b. Examine the authors' attitudes toward the ethical dilemmas.   ●

Suggested Literary Journal Topic

Imagine that you are the narrator's psychiatrist and that the narrator has just told you the whole story ("Like a Bad Dream"). He has left your office, and it is time for you to assess what you have just heard. His last words, which you cannot get out of your mind, were: "It is beyond understanding." You decide to write in your notebook in an attempt to analyze what "It" refers to. As you write, you include whatever details and quotations from the story seem to be relevant.   ●

Discussion Activities: "Swaddling Clothes" by Mishima Yukio (pp. 132–36)

Write after You Read

Explore your response to "Swaddling Clothes" by recording your reactions in your reading log, following the guidelines on page 12.   ●

Responding to, Analyzing, and Interpreting a Story

Working with a partner, in a small group, or with the whole class, share in some or all of the following activities. You can decide the order in which to cover the material and the amount of time to spend on each activity. Allow for different reactions to and interpretations of the various aspects of the story.

1. Share your initial reaction to the story (for example, you may share the responses you have recorded in your reading log entry). Raise any questions you may have.
2. Make sure that everyone understands what happens in the story.
3. Discuss attitudes in your community or culture (or your own attitude) toward children born outside of marriage. Compare those attitudes with the attitudes revealed in the story.
4. Without looking at the story, try to remember and describe one scene that stands out in your mind. Take turns describing the scenes you remember. Then, looking at the text, read the scenes aloud and analyze why each scene is particularly memorable. Ask questions such as these:

     a. Is the scene memorable because you can identify with it? If so, what similar experience have you had?

     b. Is the scene memorable because it is so different from your own experience? If so, how has the author succeeded in capturing your attention?

     c. Is this scene memorable because of your negative reaction to it? If so, which images account for your negative reaction?

     d. Is this scene memorable because of your positive reaction to it? If so, which images account for your positive reaction?

5. Referring to specific passages, analyze the character of Toshiko's husband.

     a. Examine his outer appearance.

     b. Examine his behavior and his reaction to the events that take place in the story.

     c. Analyze his choice of friends.

6. Referring to specific passages, analyze the character of Toshiko.

     a. Examine her outward appearance and behavior.

     b. Examine her inner emotional and moral qualities.

        • Explore her positive and negative characteristics.

        • Explore her values.

        • Explore her conflicts (internal or external).

        • Explore her choices.

        • Explore her changes.

7. Read aloud specific passages in the story that reveal the place, time, social environment, and physical environment of the story.

     a. Examine the details that reveal where and over what period of time the story takes place.

     b. Examine the details that reveal the manners, customs, rules, and/or moral codes of the society in which the story is set.

     c. Examine the physical details that reveal the emotional or moral state of the characters.

8. Toshiko sees the newspapers as a "symbol" (p. 134). Explore this idea.

     a. What might the newspapers symbolize?

     b. Discuss any other objects or events in the story that appear to act as symbols. What might they symbolize?

9. If you were to choose one or two words to describe your impression of the story as a whole, what might the word(s) be?

10. What is your attitude toward Toshiko? toward her husband? toward the baby?

     a. What has the author done to make you feel this way? In other words, which passages affect or control your attitudes?

     b. If you were to choose one or two words to describe the author's attitude toward each of the characters, what might those words be?

11. Compare the attitude toward fate in this story with the attitude toward fate in one or more stories (for example, "The Egg," "A Woman Like Me," "The Grass-Eaters").
    a. Examine similarities and differences.
    b. Examine the authors' attitudes toward fate.
12. Compare the exploration of the role and identity of the woman in this story with the exploration of the role and identity of women in one or more stories (for example, "The Story of an Hour," "The Necklace," "Two Portraits," "Girl," "A Woman Like Me").
    a. Examine similarities and differences.
    b. Examine the authors' attitudes toward the role and identity of women.   •

Suggested Literary Journal Topic

Are Toshiko's reactions normal? Use at least one quotation in your answer; include the page number within parentheses.   •

Discussion Activities: "A Handful of Dates" by Tayeb Salih (pp. 137–40)

Write after You Read

Explore your response to "A Handful of Dates" by recording your reactions in your reading log, following the guidelines on page 12.   •

Responding to, Analyzing, and Interpreting the Story

Working with a partner, in a small group, or with the whole class, share in some or all of the following activities. You can decide the order in which to cover the material and the amount of time to spend on each activity. Allow for different reactions to and interpretations of the various aspects of the story.

1. Share your initial reaction to the story (for example, you may share the responses you have recorded in your reading log entry). Raise any questions you may have.
2. Make sure that everyone understands what happens in the story.
3. If you have had a special relationship with a grandparent or other older person, describe your relationship. Compare and contrast your relationship with the boy's relationship with his grandfather.
4. If you have had religious instruction, explain how and what you were taught. In what ways is your experience similar to or different from the boy's experience with religious instruction?

5. Read aloud specific passages in the story that reveal the place, time, social environment, and physical environment of the story, beginning with the first paragraph.

   a. Determine where and over what period of time the story takes place.

   b. Examine the manners, customs, rules, and/or moral codes of the society in which the story is set.

   c. Examine the physical details that reveal the emotional or moral state of the characters.

6. The point of view of the story (the perspective through which the story is told) is that of an adult narrator looking back on his earlier life. With this dual point of view, there are two characters to analyze: the boy and the adult.

   a. Using clues from the story, determine the approximate age of the boy. What do you know about boys of that age that might help you understand this story?

   b. Is there anything unique or special about the way the adult narrator presents the information that suggests something about the narrator's character? Can you tell what kind of man the boy turned out to be?

   c. Why do you think the author has chosen this point of view? How would the story be different if it were told from another point of view?

7. Referring to specific passages, analyze the characters of the boy, the grandfather, and Masood. This activity can be done with the whole class, or the class can be divided into three groups, with each group analyzing one character. The three groups can then share their discoveries.

   a. Examine his outward appearance and behavior.

   b. Examine his inner emotional and moral qualities.

   - Explore his positive and negative characteristics.
   - Explore his values.
   - Explore whether he has choices.
   - Explore whether he is undergoing a conflict (internal or external).
   - Explore whether he changes.

   Then analyze the relationships among the three characters and their attitudes toward one another.

8. If you were to choose one or two words to describe your impression of the tone of the story as a whole, what might the word(s) be?

9. What is your attitude toward the grandfather? the boy? Masood?

   a. What has the author done to make you feel this way? In other words, which passages affect or control your attitudes?

   b. If you were to choose one or two words to describe the author's attitude toward each of the characters, what might those words be?

10. Discuss the author's attitude toward religion and toward business.
11. Select different aspects of nature referred to in the story (for example, land, trees, dates) and discuss how they might act as symbols to suggest a meaning other than their literal (dictionary) meaning.
12. Compare the role of religion in this story with the role of religion in one or more stories (for example, "Two Portraits," "The Americanization of Shadrach Cohen," "Araby," "Dead Men's Path," "Like a Bad Dream").
    a. Examine similarities and differences.
    b. Examine the authors' attitudes toward religion.
13. Compare the experience of growing up in this story with the experience of growing up in one or more other stories (for example, "A Trifle from Real Life," "Araby," "The Man Who Was Almost a Man," "The Plane Reservation," "Girl," "Las papas").
    a. Examine similarities and differences.
    b. Examine the authors' attitudes toward the experience of growing up.   •

Suggested Literary Journal Topic

Imagine that you are the narrator, now a grown man. You have just learned that Masood has become gravely ill. Write him a letter to tell him what you remember about him, to explain how you felt on the day you saw the men dividing up the sacks between them, and to share what you now think about what happened.   •

Discussion Activities: "The Plane Reservation" by Massud Farzan (pp. 141–46)

Write after You Read

Explore your response to "The Plane Reservation" by recording your reactions in your reading log, following the guidelines on page 12.   •

Responding to, Analyzing, and Interpreting the Story

Working with a partner, in a small group, or with the whole class, share in some or all of the following activities. You can decide the order in which to cover the material and the amount of time to spend on each activity. Allow for different reactions to and interpretations of the various aspects of the story.

1. Share your initial reaction to the story (for example, you may share the responses you have recorded in your reading log entry). Raise any questions you may have.
2. Make sure that everyone understands what happens in the story.
3. If you have returned home (or to any place where you spent a great deal of time in your past) after a long absence, describe what you discovered. You may want to answer questions such as these:
   a. Was everything the same as when you left?
   b. Had anything changed?
   c. Were you disturbed or happy at what you found? Compare your reactions to those of Morad.
4. Read aloud specific passages in the story that reveal the place, time, social environment, and physical environment of the story, beginning with the first paragraph.
   a. Examine the details that reveal where and over what period of time the story takes place.
   b. Examine the details that reveal the manners, customs, rules, and/or moral codes of the society in which the story is set.
   c. Examine any physical details that reveal the characters' emotional or moral state.
5. Analyze the character of the mother.
   a. Explore the significance of her reaction to Morad.
   b. Explore the significance of her reactions to her husband.
6. Analyze the character of the father.
   a. Explore the significance of his reaction to Morad.
   b. Explore the significance of his reaction to his wife.
   c. Examine the way he spends his time.
7. Referring to specific passages, analyze the character of Morad.
   a. Examine his outward appearance and behavior.
   b. Analyze his inner emotional and moral qualities.
      - Explore his positive and negative qualities.
      - Explore his values.
      - Explore his conflicts (internal or external).
      - Explore his choices.
      - Explore his changes.
8. Analyze Morad's reliability as a narrator.
   a. Evaluate the level of his emotional involvement in the situation.
   b. Speculate on whether he might be withholding information or ignoring significant facts.
   c. Why do you think the author has chosen this point of view? How would the story be different if it were told from another point of view, for example, from the point of view of his mother? his father? the laundress?
9. If you were to choose one or two words to describe your impression of the tone of the story as a whole, what might the word(s) be?

10. If you were to choose one or two words to describe the author's attitude toward each of the characters, what might those words be?
11. Discuss the author's attitude toward parent-child relationships.
12. Discuss the author's attitude toward cultural differences.
13. Compare the parent-child relationships in this story with the (grand)parent-child relationships in one or more other stories (for example, "A Trifle from Real Life," "The Egg," "Babylon Revisited," "War," "A Handful of Dates," "Girl").
    a. Examine similarities and differences.
    b. Examine the authors' attitudes toward parent-child relationships.
14. Compare the exploration of cultural identity in this story with the exploration of cultural identity in one or more other stories (for example, "The Americanization of Shadrach Cohen," "Dead Men's Path," "Six Feet of the Country," "Swaddling Clothes," "Las papas," "Village").
    a. Examine similarities and differences.
    b. Examine the authors' attitudes toward cultural identity. ●

Suggested Literary Journal Topic

Imagine that Morad has a close friend in America to whom he confides his deepest feelings. Write the letter that you think Morad would write to explain what has happened during his visit and how he feels about what has taken place. Make the letter vivid by quoting conversations and using other specific details. ●

Discussion Activities: "The Verb *to Kill*" by Luisa Valenzuela (pp. 147–49)

Write after You Read

Explore your response to "The Verb *to Kill*" by recording your reactions in your reading log, following the guidelines on page 12. ●

Responding to, Analyzing, and Interpreting the Story

Working with a partner, in a small group, or with the whole class, share in some or all of the following activities. You can decide the order in which to cover the material and the amount of time to spend on each activity. Allow for different reactions to and interpretations of the various aspects of the story.

1. Share your initial reaction to the story (for example, you may share the responses you have recorded in your reading log entry). Raise any questions you may have.

2. Make sure that everyone understands what happens in the story. (There may be some disagreement about this. If so, you might want to have a debate about what actually happens.)

3. On page 148, the narrator reports, "We spend hours talking about the things that he does to his victims before killing them just for fun. The papers often talk about degenerates like him." Find newspaper articles that "talk about degenerates" and bring them to class.
   a. Discuss the way in which the articles are written (for example, are they sensationalist or straightforward?).
   b. Then discuss the effect the articles have on you as a reader.

4. Gather details from the story to characterize the man. Use the following suggestions as you search for clues, and then put the clues together to form a character sketch.
   a. Gather details about his appearance.
   b. Gather details about what he does.
   c. Examine what others say about him.
   d. Examine how others react to him.

5. Referring to specific passages, analyze the narrator of the story.
   a. What is the narrator's approximate age?
   b. What do you know about the narrator's background?
   c. What is the narrator's relationship to the other characters?
   d. How did the narrator acquire the information that is presented? Are the sources reliable?
   e. Is there anything unique or special about the way the narrator presents the information that suggests something about the narrator's character?
   f. Does the narrator seem to be withholding information or ignoring significant facts?
   g. Does the narrator reveal any prejudice toward any of the characters?
   h. Does the narrator ever seem confused?
   i. Are the narrator's comments about the other characters valid?
   j. Does the narrator undergo any changes that affect the information?
   k. What is your overall impression of the narrator?

6. Why do you think the author has chosen to tell the story from the point of view of this narrator? How would the story be different if it were told from another point of view, for example, from the point of view of the narrator's mother? a narrator who is not a character in the story?

7. Go through different scenes of the story to find incongruities between what seems to be true or real and what is actually true or real. You might want to ask questions such as these:

      a. Does anything happen that is unexpected or different from what is expected or hoped for?

      b. Does a character think or believe something that is different from the truth?

      c. Does a character say something that, either intentionally or unintentionally, means the opposite of what it seems to say?

  8. If you were to choose one or two words to describe your impression of the tone of the story as a whole, what might the word(s) be?

  9. If you were to choose one or two words to describe the author's attitude toward each of the characters, what might those words be?

10. Compare the experience of growing up in this story with the experience of growing up in other stories (for example, "Two Portraits," "Araby," "The Egg," "A Handful of Dates," "Girl").

      a. Examine similarities and differences.

      b. Examine the authors' attitudes toward young people.

11. Compare the female experience explored in the story with the female experience explored in one or more other stories (for example, "The Necklace," "The Story of an Hour," "Two Portraits," "Girl," "A Woman Like Me").

      a. Examine similarities and differences.

      b. Examine the authors' attitudes toward the female experience. ●

Suggested Literary Journal Topic

Write an interior monologue (conversation with himself) for the man in the story, providing what you think are his thoughts at different stages of this entire experience. ●

Discussion Activities: "Girl" by Jamaica Kincaid (pp. 150–51)

Write after You Read

Explore your response to "Girl" by recording your reactions in your reading log, following the guidelines on page 12. ●

Responding to, Analzying, and Interpreting the Story

Working with a partner, in a small group, or with the whole class, share in some or all of the following activities. You can decide the order in which to cover the material and the amount of time to spend on each activity. Allow for different reactions to and interpretations of the various aspects of the story.

1. Share your initial reaction to the story (for example, you may share the responses you have recorded in your reading log entry). Raise any questions you may have.
2. Make sure that everyone understands what is happening in the story.
3. How would you feel if you were the "girl" of the story?
4. Read aloud specific passages in the story that reveal the place, time, and social environment.
   a. Examine the clues that reveal where and over what period of time the story takes place.
   b. Examine the manners, customs, rules, and/or moral codes of the society in which the story is set.
5. Examine the images in the story.
   a. Do any words or phrases enable you to create mental pictures of people or scenes?
   b. Does one type of image predominate?
   c. If there is a change from one type of image to another, what might this reveal about the story's meaning?
   d. Examine any concrete details that might be connected to the characters' emotional or moral state.
6. Referring to specific lines, analyze the characters in the story.
   a. Examine any details that might give clues to outward appearance and behavior.
   b. Examine inner emotional and moral qualities.
      - Explore their positive and negative characteristics.
      - Explore their values.
      - Explore their choices.
      - Explore their conflicts (internal or external).
      - Explore their changes.
   Then analyze the relationships between the characters and their attitudes toward one another.
7. If you were to choose one or two words to describe your impression of the tone of the story as a whole, what might the word(s) be?
8. If you were to choose one or two words to describe the author's attitude toward each of the characters, what might those words be? Discuss the author's attitude toward the relationship among the characters.
9. Read the quotations about parents and children on page 191. Discuss the quotations to uncover their meaning or significance. Substituting the word "mother" for "father," apply the quotations to the story, where appropriate.
10. Compare the experience of growing up in this story with the experience of growing up in one or more other stories (for example, "A Trifle from Real Life," "Araby," "The Egg," "The Man Who Was Almost a Man," "The Plane Reservation," "The Verb *to Kill*," "Las papas").

    a. Examine similarities and differences.

    b. Examine the authors' attitudes toward the experience of growing up.

11. Compare the exploration of female experience in this story with the exploration of the female experience in one or more stories (for example, "The Necklace," "The Story of an Hour," "Two Portraits," "Swaddling Clothes," "A Woman Like Me," "The Verb *to Kill*").

    a. Examine similarities and differences.

    b. Examine the authors' attitudes toward the female experience. ●

Suggested Literary Journal Topic

What do you think is the most significant word in this story? Explain your choice. ●

Discussion Activities: "A Woman Like Me" by Xi Xi (pp. 152–62)

Write after You Read

Explore your response to "A Woman Like Me" by recording your reactions in your reading log, following the guidelines on page 12. ●

Responding to, Analyzing, and Interpreting the Story

Working with a partner, in a small group, or with the whole class, share in some or all of the following activities. You can decide the order in which to cover the material and the amount of time to spend on each activity. Allow for different reactions to and interpretations of the various aspects of the story.

1. Share your initial reaction to the story (for example, you may share the responses you have recorded in your reading log entry). Raise any questions you may have.

2. Make sure that everyone understands what happens in the story.

3. Do you believe in Fate? Explain. Compare your beliefs and attitudes with those of the narrator in the story.

4. Without looking at the story, try to remember and describe one scene that stands out in your mind. Take turns describing the scenes you remember. Then, looking at the text, read the scenes aloud and analyze why each scene is particularly memorable. Ask questions such as these:

    a. Is the scene memorable because you can identify with it? If so, what similar experience have you had?

    b. Is the scene memorable because it is so different from your own experience? If so, how has the author succeeded in capturing your attention?

    c. Is this scene memorable because of your positive reaction to it? If so, which images account for your positive reaction?

    d. Is this scene memorable because of your negative reaction to it? If so, which images account for your negative reaction?

5. Read aloud specific passages that reveal the place, time, and social environment of the story.

    a. Determine where and over what period of time the story takes place.

    b. Examine the manners, customs, rules, and/or moral codes of the society in which the story is set.

6. Examine the roles and identity of women in this society. For example, you might want to explore these questions:

    a. What jobs are acceptable?

    b. What jobs are unacceptable?

7. Referring to specific passages, characterize Aunt Yifen.

    a. Explore the significance of her life experience.

    b. Explore the significance of her relationship with the narrator.

    c. Examine her positive and negative qualities.

8. Referring to specific passages, analyze the character of the narrator.

    a. Examine her outward appearance and behavior.

    b. Explore her inner emotional and moral qualities.

      • Explore her positive and negative characteristics.

      • Explore her values.

      • Explore her conflicts (internal and external).

      • Explore her choices.

      • Explore her changes.

9. Characterize Xia, the narrator's boyfriend.

    a. Gather details from the story that reveal what he is like.

    b. Speculate on what you think he might do when he finds out what the narrator does for a living.

10. Choose one or more of the following subjects (or another subject) mentioned by the narrator and explore its importance in the story: fate, fear, courage, death, suicide, love, the meaninglessness of life. The class can divide into groups to explore different subjects and then regroup to share discoveries.

11. If you were to choose one or two words to describe your impression of the story as a whole, what might the word(s) be?

12. If you were to choose one or two words to describe the author's attitude toward the narrator, what might the word(s) be?

13. Compare the attitude toward fate in this story with the attitude toward fate in one or more other stories (for example, "The Egg," "Swaddling Clothes," or "The Grass-Eaters").

    a. Examine similarities and differences.

   b. Examine the authors' attitudes toward acceptance of fate.
14. Compare the exploration of the role and identity of the woman in
    this story with the exploration of the role and identity of women in
    one or more other stories (for example, "The Necklace," "The
    Story of an Hour," "Two Portraits," "Swaddling Clothes," "Girl").
    a. Examine similarities and differences.
    b. Examine the authors' attitudes toward the role and identity of
       women.   ●

Suggested Literary Journal Topic

   Is the narrator "unsuitable for any man's love" (p. 152)? Use at least
two quotations in your response; include page numbers within parentheses. ●

Discussion Activities: "The Street-Sweeping Show" by Feng Jicai (pp. 163–66)

Write after You Read

   Explore your response to "The Street-Sweeping Show" by recording
your reactions in your reading log, following the guidelines on page 12. ●

Responding to, Analyzing, and Interpreting the Story

   Working with a partner, in a small group, or with the whole class, share
in some or all of the following activities. You can decide the order in which
to cover the material and the amount of time to spend on each activity.
Allow for different reactions to and interpretations of the various aspects of
the story.

   1. Share your initial reaction to the story (for example, you may share
      the responses you have recorded in your reading log). Raise any
      questions you may have.
   2. Make sure that everyone understands what happens in the story.
   3. Discuss what you know about how the government works in your
      own community. Compare it with the government portrayed in the
      story.
   4. Read aloud specific passages in the story that reveal the place, time,
      social environment, and physical environment of the story.
      a. Examine the details that reveal where and over what period of
         time the story takes place.
      b. Examine the manners, customs, rules, and/or moral codes of the
         society in which the story is set.

    c. Examine the physical details that reveal the emotional or moral state of the characters.

5. Characterize Secretary Zhao.
    a. Explore the significance of his appearance.
    b. Explore the significance of the way he reacts to the mayor.

6. Referring to specific passages, analyze the character of the mayor.
    a. Examine his outward appearance and behavior.
    b. Examine his inner emotional and moral qualities.
       • Explore his positive and negative characteristics.
       • Explore his conflicts (internal or external).
       • Explore his choices.
       • Explore his values.
       • Explore his changes.

7. If you were to choose one or two words to describe your impression of the tone of the story as a whole, what might the word(s) be?

8. If you were to choose one or two words to describe the author's attitude toward each of the characters, what might those words be?

9. Examine the author's attitude toward National Cleanup Week.

10. Examine the author's attitude toward the political system of the city.

11. Compare the role of work in this story with the role of work in one or more other stories (for example, "The Necklace," "The Egg," "The Man Who Was Almost a Man," "Dead Men's Path," "Like a Bad Dream," "A Handful of Dates," "A Woman Like Me," "The Grass-Eaters").
    a. Examine similarities and differences.
    b. Examine the authors' attitudes toward work.

12. Compare the relationship between citizens and their country or government in this story with similar relationships in one or more other stories (for example, "War," "Six Feet of the Country," "Village").
    a. Examine similarities and differences.
    b. Examine the authors' attitudes toward the relationship between citizens and their country or government.   •

Suggested Literary Journal Topic

Write a one-paragraph version of the story that you think was told on television about the street sweeping. Then write a one-paragraph version of the truth behind the story. Use at least two quotations; put the page number within parentheses.   •

Discussion Activities: "The Grass-Eaters" by Krishnan Varma (pp. 167–70)

Write after You Read

Explore your response to "The Grass-Eaters" by recording your reactions in your reading log, following the guidelines on page 12.   •

Responding to, Analyzing, and Interpreting the Story

Working with a partner, in a small group, or with the whole class, share in some or all of the following activities. You can decide the order in which to cover the material and the amount of time to spend on each activity. Allow for different reactions to and interpretations of the various aspects of the story.

1. Share your initial reaction to the story (for example, you may share the responses you have recorded in your reading log entry). Raise any questions you may have.
2. Make sure that everyone understands what happens in the story. Take care to determine the chronology of the story: the order in which events have taken place in the characters' lives. You might want to make a time line of the key events.
3. Compare your own life-style with the lives of the characters in the story.
4. If you were to create a filmed advertisement (a "trailer") for a movie based on "The Grass-Eaters," which scene would you select?
   a. Why?
   b. Discuss ways in which you might film the scene.
5. Read aloud specific passages that reveal the time, physical environment, and social environment of the story.
   a. Determine over what period of time the story takes place.
   b. Gather together details about the city. What pattern emerges to describe the place?
   c. Examine the manners, customs, rules, and/or moral codes of the society in which the story is set.
   d. Examine the physical details that reveal the emotional and moral state of the characters.
6. Analyze Swapna's values by examining her reactions in paragraph 5 and her reactions to the freight wagon and to her husband. Compare her values with her husband's.
7. Referring to specific passages, analyze the character of Ajit Babu.
   a. Examine his outward appearance and behavior.
   b. Examine his inner emotional and moral qualities.
     • Explore his positive and negative characteristics.

- Explore his values.
- Explore his conflicts (internal or external).
- Explore his choices.
- Explore his changes.

8. If you were to choose one or two words to describe your impression of the tone of the story as a whole, what might the word(s) be?

9. If you were to choose one or two words to describe the author's attitude toward each of the characters (Misrilal, Swapna, and Ajit Babu) what might those words be?

10. Examine the author's attitude toward the situation in Calcutta.

11. Why do you think the author has chosen to tell the story from Ajit Babu's point of view? How would the story be different if it were told from another point of view, for example, from the point of view of his wife? a Westerner?

12. If you were in Ajit Babu's place, how would you have reacted?

13. Compare the marital relationship in this story with the marital relationship in one or more other stories (for example, "The Story of an Hour," "The Necklace," "The Egg," "Babylon Revisited," "Six Feet of the Country," "Like a Bad Dream," "Swaddling Clothes," "The Plane Reservation").
    a. Examine similarities and differences.
    b. Examine the authors' attitudes toward marriage.

14. Compare the role of work in this story with the role of work in one or more other stories (for example, "The Necklace," "The Egg," "Babylon Revisited," "The Man Who Was Almost a Man," "Like a Bad Dream," "A Handful of Dates," "A Woman Like Me," "The Street-Sweeping Show").
    a. Examine similarities and differences.
    b. Examine the authors' attitudes toward work.

Suggested Literary Journal Topic

Select one passage (from one sentence up to one paragraph) that you find meaningful in some way. For example, you may choose a passage that you like or one that you think best illustrates an idea. Copy the passage (noting the page number in parentheses), and then discuss what you perceive to be its meaning or significance.

Discussion Activities: "Las papas" by Julio Ortega (pp. 171–75)

Write after You Read

Explore your response to "Las papas" by recording your reactions in your reading log, following the guidelines on page 12.

Responding to, Analyzing, and Interpreting the Story

Working with a partner, in a small group, or with the whole class, share in some or all of the following activities. Allow for different reactions to and interpretations of the various aspects of the story.

1. Share your initial reaction to the story (for example, you may share the responses you have recorded in your reading log entry). Raise any questions you may have.
2. Establish the facts: make sure that everyone understands what happens in the story.
3. Share your associations with special foods that are connected to your culture, religion, country of origin, and/or family. Compare your associations to the narrator's associations with potatoes.
4. Read aloud specific passages that reveal the place, time, social environment, and physical environment of the story.
    a. Examine the details that reveal where and over what period of time the story takes place.
    b. Examine any concrete details that reveal the characters' emotional or moral state.
    c. Examine the manners, customs, rules, and/or moral codes of the society or community in which the story is set.
5. Examine the images and ideas connected to potatoes.
    a. Do any words or phrases appeal to your sense of sight? sound? taste? smell? touch?
    b. Does one type of image predominate?
    c. Examine any concrete details that reveal the characters' emotional or moral state.
6. Referring to specific passages, analyze the character of the man.
    a. Examine the details that reveal his age and background.
    b. Examine his inner emotional and moral qualities.
        • Explore his positive and negative characteristics.
        • Explore his values.
        • Explore his conflicts (internal or external).
        • Explore his choices.
        • Explore his changes.
7. Characterize the boy.
    a. Examine his reaction to what the man is doing.
    b. Examine his relationship with the man.
8. If you were to choose one or two words to describe your impression of the tone of the story as a whole, what might the word(s) be?
9. What is your attitude toward each of the characters?
    a. What has the author done to make you feel this way? In other words, which passages affect or control your attitudes?
    b. If you were to choose one or two words to describe the author's

attitude toward each of the characters, what might those words be?

10. Go through different scenes of the story to find incongruities between what seems to be true or real and what is actually true or real. You might want to ask questions such as these:
    a. Does anything happen that is unexpected or different from what is expected or hoped for?
    b. Does a character think or believe something that is different from the truth?
    c. Does a character say something that, either intentionally or unintentionally, means the opposite of what it seems to say?

11. Read the quotations about parents and children on pages 173–74. Discuss the quotations to uncover their meaning or significance. Apply the quotations to the story, where appropriate.

12. Compare the experience of growing up in this story with the experience of growing up in one or more other stories (for example, "A Trifle from Real Life," "Araby," "The Man Who Was Almost a Man," "A Handful of Dates," "The Plane Reservation," "Girl").
    a. Examine similarities and differences.
    b. Examine the authors' attitudes toward the experience of growing up.

13. Compare the exploration of cultural identity in this story with the exploration of cultural identity in one or more other stories (for example, "The Americanization of Shadrach Cohen," "Dead Men's Path," "Six Feet of the Country," "Swaddling Clothes," "The Plane Reservation," "Village").
    a. Examine similarities and differences.
    b. Examine the authors' attitudes toward cultural identity.   •

Suggested Literary Journal Topic

Read the following passage from page 172. Then write your response, explaining what you think the character means and whether you agree with him.

> Some people say, and it's probably true, that the loss of even one domesticated plant makes the world a little poorer, as does the destruction of a work of art in a city plundered by invaders.   •

Discussion Activities: "Village" by Estela Portillo Trambley (pp. 176–82)

Write after You Read

Explore your response to "Village" by recording your reactions in your reading log, following the guidelines on page 12.   •

Responding to, Analyzing, and Interpreting the Story

Working with a partner, in a small group, or with the whole class, share in some or all of the following activities. You can decide the order in which to cover the material and the amount of time to spend on each activity. Allow for different reactions to and interpretations of the various aspects of the story.

1. Share your initial reaction to the story (for example, you may share the responses you have recorded in your reading log entry). Raise any questions you may have.
2. Make sure that everyone understands what happens in the story.
3. If you were drafted by your country to fight in a war, would you do so? Why, or why not?
4. If you were to write a newspaper article about this incident, what would the headline be?
   a. Write down several possible headlines, alone or with a partner.
   b. Then share your headlines with the rest of the class.
   c. Discuss the different effects the headlines might have on the readers of the newspaper.
5. Read aloud specific passages that reveal the place, time, social environment, and physical environment of the story.
   a. Examine the details that reveal where and over what period of time the story takes place.
   b. Examine the manners, customs, rules, and/or moral codes of the society or community in which the story is set.
6. Examine the images connected to war.
   a. Do any words or phrases appeal to your sense of sight? sound? taste? smell? touch?
   b. Does one type of image predominate?
   c. Examine any concrete details that reveal the characters' emotional or moral state.
7. Characterize Sergeant Keever.
   a. Explore the significance of his reaction to the communique.
   b. Explore the significance of his reaction to Rico.
   c. Explore the significance of his use of language.
8. Referring to specific passages, analyze the character of Rico.
   a. Examine his outward appearance and behavior.
   b. Explore his inner emotional and moral qualities.
      • Examine his positive and negative characteristics.
      • Examine his conflicts (internal and external).
      • Examine his choices.
      • Examine his changes.
9. If you were to choose one or two words to describe your impression of the tone of the story as a whole, what might the word(s) be?
10. What is your attitude toward each of the characters?

    a. What has the author done to make you feel this way? In other words, which passages affect or control your attitudes?

    b. If you were to choose one or two words to describe the author's attitude toward each of the characters, what might those words be?

11. Examine the author's attitude toward Rico's action.

12. Go through different scenes of the story to find incongruities between what seems to be true or real and what is actually true or real. You might want to ask questions such as these:

    a. Does anything happen that is unexpected or different from what is expected or hoped for?

    b. Does a character think or believe something that is different from the truth?

    c. Does a character say something that, either intentionally or unintentionally, means the opposite of what it seems to say?

13. Create opposing teams to research the issue of whether a soldier should always follow his superior's orders.

    a. Each team should gather evidence from the story and, if possible, from other sources to prove that its side is correct.

    b. Teams should then take turns debating the issue.

14. If you had been in Rico's place, what would you have done?

15. Read the quotations about war on page 196. Compare or contrast them to ideas in "Village."

16. Compare the exploration of war in this story with the exploration of war in the story "War" (74) and in the poem "Dulce et Decorum Est" (p. 197).

    a. Examine similarities and differences.

    b. Examine the authors' attitudes toward war.

17. Compare the exploration of cultural identity in this story with the exploration of cultural identity in one or more other stories (for example, "The Americanization of Shadrach Cohen," "Six Feet of the Country," "Swaddling Clothes," "The Plane Reservation," "Las papas").

    a. Examine similarities and differences.

    b. Examine the authors' attitudes toward cultural identity.   •

Suggested Literary Journal Topic

Is Rico unpatriotic? Use at least one quotation in your response; include the paragraph number within parentheses.   •

PART THREE

Writing an Essay

Part Three consists of four chapters that are designed to help you fulfill an assignment to analyze and interpret a work of fiction. Your instructor will determine the number of essays you will write and when they are due. You may be assigned to write an essay after you have read only one or two stories, or you may be assigned to write an essay after you have read several stories.

It is impossible to learn everything in Part Three before you begin to write an essay. There is too much to assimilate. Your instructor may work with certain chapters or sections in class at various points in the semester. At that time you can consult with the instructor and collaborate with classmates on planning and executing your essay. You may also refer to various sections on your own, just before or after you begin writing. Slowly, over the course of the semester, you can become familiar with the entire unit.

Chapter 5 provides guidelines for composing an essay: defining the audience, finding and developing a topic, drafting and organizing, giving and responding to feedback on work in progress, and revising and completing the essay. These guidelines are illustrated with examples of a student writer at work. You can refer to Chapter 5 as you are working on various stages of composing.

Chapter 6 provides guidelines for selecting evidence from a story to analyze character, setting, point of view, imagery, symbolism, tone, and abstract ideas. These guidelines are illustrated with sample analyses. You can refer to Chapter 6 when you are discussing the stories and when you are planning an essay.

Chapter 7 provides guidelines for selecting and incorporating quotations into your own writing and properly documenting your sources. These guidelines are illustrated with excerpts from student writing. You can refer to Chapter 7 when you are writing an essay.

Chapter 8 provides guidelines for proofreading and editing your essay and for preparing a final copy to present for evaluation. You can refer to Chapter 8 when you are ready to hand in a draft or completed essay.

Together, the chapters will enable you to develop many of the analytical and argumentative skills you need for effective academic writing.

Writing an Interpretive Essay

Chapter 5 provides guidelines for fulfilling an assignment to analyze and interpret one or more works of fiction in an essay.

When you analyze a short story, you break it down into parts to examine its elements closely. To interpret the story, you piece the parts together to discover a pattern that reveals a theme, a larger, implied meaning of the story.

In writing an essay about fiction, remember that you should not merely summarize. Instead, use the details of the story as evidence to substantiate claims you make about the story's underlying significance or meaning.

SUGGESTED ESSAY ASSIGNMENTS

The following assignments suggest three general ways to write about literary works.

Essay Assignment: Writing about One Story

Write an essay in which you analyze and interpret one story. Use details and quotations from the story to support your ideas.

Essay Assignment: Comparing and Contrasting Two Stories

Write an essay in which you compare and contrast two stories that have similar elements or themes. Use details and quotations from both stories to support your ideas.

Essay Assignment: Writing about Several Stories

Write an essay in which you explore a theme or subject that is common to several stories. Use details and quotations from each story to support your ideas.

DEFINING THE AUDIENCE

Being aware of the audience—your reader(s)—as you plan an essay can help you shape your thoughts. Though in this course some or all of your classmates may become reviewers of your work in progress, ultimately it is your instructor who does the final evaluation of your work. It is therefore important for you to understand this audience's needs and expectations.

ACTIVITY: *Defining your audience*

Although this activity can be done in small groups, it is a good idea to define your audience by communicating directly with the audience, your instructor. As a class, you can discuss some answers to these questions:

1. What does the instructor already know about the subject matter?
2. What does the instructor want to learn from you?
3. Why does the instructor expect you to repeat details from the story when the original material is available?
4. Why does the instructor want you to include quotations of passages that are well known to the instructor?

Raise any other questions that will help you define the audience.   ●

EXPLORING A TOPIC

To write an essay that interprets literature, you need to devise strategies that allow you to develop your ideas productively. The strategies suggested in this chapter are included to help you fulfill the assignment, but they are not meant to be taken as rigid instructions that you must follow.

The writing of one student, Rosa Gutierez, is included to show some of the strategies she used to write an essay that interprets Kate Chopin's "The Story of an Hour." Her final paper is reprinted on pp. 272–76; the story can be found on pp. 6–8. Since all writers differ, the approaches that worked well for Rosa may not work as well for you; and you may not write as much as Rosa does. Rosa's work was selected as an example of what can be done. Her final paper represents a lengthy and deep analysis of a story. Although you may not be required to write such a long paper, you can benefit from seeing how a writer's analysis of numerous details from a story can lead to a meaningful interpretation. Observing and practicing some of the strategies that Rosa employed may lead you to discover a successful way of approaching the writing of an interpretive essay.

Selecting a Story to Analyze

The first step in finding and developing a topic can be to reread all of the assigned stories to determine which one you want to analyze in depth. A more efficient approach is to review all of the writing you have done so far about the stories: your annotations, reading log, literary journal, and any notes you have taken during class discussions.

After reading what you have written, you may discover that one particular story affected you more than the others or find that there is one story that you want to explore further. If you still cannot decide, discuss the choices with a classmate or with your instructor.

A Student Writer at Work

After reviewing her writing, Rosa decided she would write about Kate Chopin's "The Story of an Hour." She was influenced in this choice not only by her admiration of the story but also by her instructor's positive comment on her journal entry.

Note: Rosa's journal entry (which follows) was originally handwritten; it has been typed so that you can read it easily. Otherwise it has been reprinted as it was written, with words crossed out and with errors. The journal was written outside of class, after the class had begun discussing the story. The topic of the journal entry was assigned by Rosa's instructor.

The Journal Assignment

In "The Story of an Hour," by Kate Chopin, a woman reacts to the news of her husband's death. Using details from the story, analyze whether or not Mrs. Mallard can be considered a callous and hard woman.

Use at least one quotation to support your response; indicate the page number of the quotation in parentheses.

Rosa's Journal Entry on "The Story of an Hour"

According to the facts given in the story, in my opinion, Mrs. Mallard cannot be considered a callous and a hard woman. When her husband was alive, and even when she admits that she loved him sometimes, she respected him as every ~~wom~~ decent woman would. But this time was different, she was informed that Mr. Mallard died, and the part of herself, the one that she only knew, was replaced for a new one, that she didn't even knew that existed in herself. "She was beginning to recognize this thing that was approaching to possess her, and she was striving to beat it back with her will" (7). Mrs. Mallard didn't want to accept those thoughts that were coming to her mind about her husband. It was very hard for her to admit that her husband was an oppressor. This quotation gives a strong ~~enough~~ support to ~~say~~ confirm that she wasn't ~~call~~ a perverse wife.

At the time, Mrs. Mallard began ~~saying that~~ to refer to the freedom that she will have, it is stated in the story that "she abandoned herself" (7). So when she had those dreams about being happy, now that her husband was dead, it wasn't herself. It was a stronger feeling inside of her, that ~~she wa~~ the real herself wasn't aware of, that gave her the strenght to say what she really felt. It was an impulse . . . "the strongest impulse of her being!" (8). An impulse is a sudden inclination without time to meditate. If she had meditated about what she was thinking, she wouldn't have these "joyful" dreams.

Instructor's Comments

Good. You have chosen strong evidence to support your point that she is not callous—the fact that she was not *consciously* reaching for this freedom.

Rereading and Taking Notes on the Story

Reread the story you have selected. Knowing that you will be writing about this story, read carefully: you will need to be familiar with every scene and every word. One or more of these strategies may be helpful:

1. *Make additional annotations.* Mark or copy passages that contribute to your understanding of the story.
2. *Select significant quotations.* Copy down key quotations and note why you think they are important.
3. *Review the discussion activities connected to the story (Chapter 4).* Make lists of details from the story that correspond to questions or explorations that you find significant.
4. *Look up all unfamiliar words.* Use the Glossary and a dictionary. You may want to write the meaning above the word in the text, or keep a list of words and their meanings in your notebook or in a blank alphabetized address book.

A Student Writer at Work

Rosa xeroxed the story and made annotations on her xeroxed copy. She looked up and wrote the meanings of unfamiliar words in the margins. She underlined passages that she felt were important. She took notes on the story on notebook paper, listing some important quotations and then commenting on why she thought they were important. Some of those notes are included below.

Rosa's Notes on the Story (Quotations and Comments)

Quotation

"She abandoned herself . . . "

Comment

She is going to act in a different way than she would normally do.

Quotation

"new spring life"

Comment

She was experiencing a sensation of renewal, just as comes after the winter.

Quotation

"And she was striving to beat it back with her will"

Comment

She didn't want to accept these feelings.

Brainstorming Ideas to Find and Develop a Topic

To analyze a short story, you need to have a topic to focus on and ideas that reveal your own interpretation. If you have not yet chosen a topic, or if you have chosen one (such as the setting in "The Story of an Hour") but don't know what to say about it, you need some strategies for finding a focus. The strategies suggested here, known as *brainstorming*, can help stimulate your thinking. You may use the activities that you find effective or devise your own strategies.

Brainstorming activities represent a way of thinking on paper. Whenever you use them, you write primarily for yourself. Therefore, you should not be overly concerned with grammatical correctness at this stage.

MAKING A LIST

Making a list can be a valuable first step in writing. If it works for you, it can help you find a topic that you can write about in detail.

GUIDELINES

Guidelines for Making a List

1. Make a list of possible topics for an essay. If you have no topics in mind, you can select from the lists of topics suggested in Chapter 6 (for example, an analysis of a character; an analysis of the images; a discussion of the author's view on an abstract idea such as love, war, or childhood) or from the discussion activities in Chapter 4.
2. Take one of the listed topics and then make a list of details from the story that fit the topic. For example, if your topic is the setting in "The Story of an Hour," you can make a list of every detail in the story that relates to the setting.
3. Look for a pattern that can help you analyze these details.

A Student Writer at Work

Rosa had already decided to write her paper on "The Story of an Hour." She made a brief list of the topics she thought she might like to discuss in depth.

Rosa's List of Topics

the character of Mrs. Mallard
the setting
the role of women in society as revealed in the story
the idea of freedom

ACTIVITY: *Making a list*

Following the guidelines above, make a list of possible topics for an essay on a short story. Then make a list of details from the story that relate to one of the topics.   ●

FREEWRITING

Freewriting is a writing activity in which you write about a topic for several minutes without stopping. You write whatever comes into your mind about your topic, without trying to write the perfect essay. In other words, you talk to yourself on paper. This technique is one way to get started on your paper and to find something to say about a topic. If it works for you, it can help you find out what you think is important about the story.

GUIDELINES

Guidelines for Freewriting

1. Write a topic or the title of a story at the top of a blank page.
2. Write for approximately ten minutes on the topic or title. Try to keep your pen moving without stopping.
3. Write whatever comes into your mind about the topic or title.
4. Don't focus on grammar, punctuation, or spelling.

A Student Writer at Work

Rosa decided to freewrite on the topic of *the role of women in society* as revealed in "The Story of an Hour." She began writing whatever came into her mind about this topic to see what ideas would emerge. By writing just for herself, Rosa discovered that the issue of women's limited rights as revealed in the story was what she found most compelling.

Note: The words within parentheses indicate when Rosa was making editorial comments to herself on paper.

Excerpt from Rosa's Freewriting

"Free, free, free!" were the first words said by Louise when she abandoned herself. (*not for the introduction*)
   In 1890's . . . (*If I do this, then I'm not going to be speaking about character.*)
   To be a woman in the 1890s wasn't easy. Kate Chopin challenged what people of her epoch said. The society of that time was very conservative. Women didn't have any kind of rights. At

this time of the American society, Kate Chopin, under these circumstances, dared to write "The Story of an Hour." . . .

ACTIVITY: *Freewriting*

Freewrite for five to ten minutes to explore a topic for your essay. Remember that you are not trying to write a perfect composition; you don't even have to write in complete sentences. Just talk to yourself on paper to find out what you are thinking. If you cannot find anything significant to say about a chosen topic, try freewriting about another topic.   ●

LOOPING

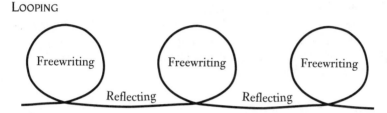

Looping[1] is a writing activity in which you loop (join together) two or more freewriting exercises and reflect on what you have written. If this technique works for you, it can help you explore a topic in some depth.

GUIDELINES   ## Guidelines for Looping

1. Freewrite on a topic for several minutes.
2. Stop.
3. Read what you have just written.
4. Find an idea in your freewriting that you want to pursue.
5. Write that idea in a new sentence.
6. Freewrite on that idea.
7. Repeat steps 2 through 6 once or twice.

ACTIVITY: *Looping*

Follow the guidelines for looping to explore a topic for your essay. Share your writing with classmates to discuss the ideas that have emerged.   ●

---

[1] Based on the work of Peter Elbow.

CUBING

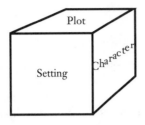
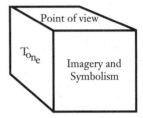

Cubing is a writing activity that allows you to explore a story quickly from six different perspectives. Imagine that your story is inside a cube and that you are looking at it through each of the six sides. Move quickly from one set of questions to another, writing down whatever each perspective suggests to you about the story. If this technique works for you, it can help you find a topic for your essay.

GUIDELINES

Guidelines for Cubing

Explore a story through these six perspectives:

1. Plot: What is happening? What is the main conflict?
2. Setting: Where does the story take place? when? over what period of time? What do the concrete details reveal about the society and/or the characters?
3. Character: Who is the story about? Does the character have choices or undergo changes?
4. Point of View: Who is narrating the story? How would the story be different if the narrator were different?
5. Imagery and Symbolism: What are the dominant images? Are they connected to any feelings or states of mind? Might any events or objects represent abstract ideas?
6. Tone: Which words or expressions reveal the author's attitude toward character, narrator, event, or subject matter?

ACTIVITY: Cubing

Follow the guidelines for cubing to explore a story from several perspectives. Spend only a few minutes on each perspective. After you have covered all six categories, read over your writing. Mark any sections that you think might lead you to writing an essay.   ●

CLUSTERING

Clustering is a technique that enables you to create a visual pattern of ideas and details. If it works for you, it can help you focus on a topic and see significant relationships among abstract ideas and concrete details.

GUIDELINES

Guidelines for Clustering

1. Choose a word or expression that is significant to a story or that might become the central topic of your essay.
2. Write the word or expression in the center of a blank page and circle it.
3. Write down any word or expression from the story or your own mind that is associated with the topic. The word or expression may be an image, an action, an abstract idea, a quotation, a detail, and so on.
4. Circle the words you have written, draw lines and/or arrows from the central word to each of the new words, and draw lines and/or arrows between words that seem to connect.
5. If something new occurs to you, add the word, circle it, and connect it to relevant words.

In the following example, the central word is *freedom;* all of the other words are taken from Kate Chopin's "The Story of an Hour" (pp. 6–8).

ACTIVITY: *Clustering*

Following the guidelines for clustering, choose a word or expression that might represent the central topic for an essay on a short story. The words in your cluster may be taken directly from the story and/or may come from your own ideas related to the topic. ●

WRITING A TRIAL DRAFT

When you take notes and brainstorm, you generate ideas to explore your own understanding of the story. When you write an essay, you share your understanding with others, bringing your thoughts into focus for your readers.

Since each writer approaches writing differently, it is not possible to tell you exactly how to compose your essay. You may prefer to write an essay just as you freewrite, or you may prefer to plan an essay first.

This section provides guidelines for moving toward the essay-writing stage by writing a *trial draft*. *Trial* refers to the process of testing or trying. A *draft* is a preliminary essay. When you write a trial draft, you test out the ideas you have generated while brainstorming to see how they will work together. The draft is not the final paper that your instructor will evaluate.

A trial draft may be written for yourself only, or your instructor may provide class time for you to share this draft with another student or in a small group. If so, class members can share their reactions to your writing and give you ideas for proceeding.

GUIDELINES

Guidelines for Writing a Trial Draft

1. Sit down and write.
2. Remember that a trial draft is a first try.
   a. Don't try to write the perfect paper now.
   b. Focus on the development of ideas rather than on grammar, spelling, or punctuation.
   c. If you can't think of a beginning, start in the middle.
   d. If you can't think of an ending, just stop.

If you are a writer who needs a more structured approach to writing, refer to the next section for guidelines on organizing an essay.

A Student Writer at Work

Rosa wrote a trial draft that she brought to class to share with a small group of classmates. Her readers helped her decide how to proceed. Part of her trial draft is included in the next section on organizing an essay.

ORGANIZING THE ESSAY

Your essay should be well organized, because structure enables you to communicate your ideas accurately and effectively to your readers. At some stage in the writing process, then, you need to focus your attention on the format of your essay. When that stage occurs is dependent on several factors, for example, your own approach to writing and the topic you are writing about. You may need to plan the organization of your essay before you write a draft. Or you may find that you cannot determine the most effective organizational pattern for your essay until you begin or have written a trial draft. When you are ready to structure your writing, you may follow these general guidelines.

An essay in which you analyze and interpret a work of fiction needs a carefully constructed arrangement: a beginning, a middle, and an ending. These sections of an academic essay are known as the *introduction, body,* and *conclusion.*

The following chart provides an overall view of how such an interpretive essay can be developed (although it by no means represents a rigid formula). The various parts of this chart are discussed at length in the sections that follow on the introduction, body, and conclusion of an essay.

Introduction

Focus on a particular topic: Make a point or ask a question about the topic.

Body

Provide evidence to prove or support the point or to answer the question about the topic.

Supporting points
    details
    examples
    quotations

Conclusion

Relate the point you make about the topic to a larger meaning of the story.

A student example of this format for an interpretive essay is provided on pages 272–75.

With your instructor's permission, you might want to experiment with alternative formats. Several possibilities are listed here.

- a letter from you to the author or to one of the characters
- a letter from one character to another, either within a story or between stories
- a letter from a character in a story to someone who is *not* in the story (for example, the author, a friend)
- a court scene in which lawyers debate an issue raised in a story
- a psychiatrist's case study of a patient (character)
- an editorial in which you present your opinion on an issue raised in a story

Even if you use an imaginative approach, your essay should be carefully organized. And the essay should still fulfill the assignment to analyze and interpret by providing evidence (details and quotations) to support ideas.

The Introduction

The purpose of the introduction is to focus on the topic: to tell readers what the essay is about. The introduction serves to involve readers in your interpretation of the story and to supply the information they need to understand the direction your essay will take. This is usually accomplished in one or two paragraphs.

FULFILLING A READER'S EXPECTATIONS

The following features are those that your readers will usually need and expect in the opening paragraphs of an essay that analyzes a work of fiction. If these guidelines do not suit your essay, discuss alternatives with your instructor.

COMMON FEATURES OF THE INTRODUCTION

The introduction to an interpretive essay will usually accomplish these things, *though not necessarily in this order and not necessarily in separate sentences:*

1. Identify the reading by *title* (within quotation marks) and *author* (full name).
2. Focus on a particular *topic* (for example, a character, the setting, an abstract idea such as love) *either* by
   a. stating directly what point(s) you will support or prove about the topic, *or*
   b. raising a question or questions about the topic.

Although there are certain features your readers will need and expect, the introduction is flexible. Its content and form are dependent on your subject matter and individual writing style. The following guidelines are designed to help you make decisions about how to compose an introduction.

DRAFTING AN INTRODUCTION

It can be difficult to write a fully developed introduction in an early draft. You can spend hours trying to write the "perfect" introduction before you even get started on the body of the essay. To save yourself valuable time, you might want to follow this advice: in the trial draft of your introduction, simply (1) identify the story by title and author, (2) indicate what topic you will discuss in the paper (for example, a certain character, the setting, a relationship, an abstract idea such as love or war). At this stage, since you are writing primarily for yourself, it is acceptable to write simply, "I am going to discuss Louise Mallard's character in 'The Story of an Hour.'" The student examples in this book can help you find a more subtle way to introduce your subject, and you can then revise your draft.

If you do not know yet how best to focus your ideas, you can read the guidelines below for developing a focus. Or you can start writing the body of your paper (see pp. 255–60) in order to develop a focus. You can later revise your draft by writing an introduction that includes a focal point.

DEVELOPING A FOCAL POINT

When you focus on a specific topic, you set up an expectation that your essay will support or prove a point about or answer a question about that topic. Then, in the body of the essay, you provide evidence from the story to fulfill that expectation. Your goal is to enable your readers to understand or accept the validity of your ideas (readers do not necessarily have to agree with your interpretation).

Each story allows for many possible focal points. The area you focus on depends upon what you find to be significant in the story. If you want to focus on a certain character, for example, you need to decide what point(s) you want to make about the character or what question(s) you want to answer about the character. Your focal point should be something that you can discuss at length by providing details, examples, and quotations from the story. The support you provide should be consistent: the details and events should reveal a pattern related to the character.

The focal point for your essay will probably emerge out of your annotations, reading log entries, class discussions, literary journal entries, notes, and/or brainstorming activities. Here is one possible approach to making sense of this material:

- *Review all that you have written.* Read over your annotations, notes, journal entries, and so on.
- *Decide what topic you would like to focus on.* This may be a subject that

you repeatedly referred to in your writing or a subject that you didn't focus on at first but now would like to explore further.

- *Reread the story to find material related to your topic.* Underline or list relevant details from the story.
- *Group the details under specific categories.* For example, if you are writing about setting, you can make separate lists for animate scenes (for example, scenes of nature) and inanimate objects (for example, furniture, clothing).
- *Look for a pattern in the details and events of the story.* This search for a pattern may lead you to a fuller understanding of your chosen topic. For example, if you are writing about setting, determine whether the details have something in common, such as hidden references to rebirth, love, freedom, or lack of communication.
- *Analyze those details to discover their deeper meaning.* Think about how those references are connected to what happens in the story. For example, if the physical details (doors, walls, and so on) hint at a lack of communication and the characters in the story have trouble communicating, you can focus on the connection between the setting and the problem of communication.
- *Express in one or two sentences what you find to be the most significant point(s) to make or question(s) to raise about your chosen topic.*

   For example, one student found a significant relationship between the natural setting and the main character's situation in "The Story of an Hour." The idea she wanted to prove was: "Through nature, Mrs. Mallard discovers her own need for liberty." By including this sentence in her introduction, she set up an expectation for readers: that the body of the essay would support or prove this idea. The student writer's responsibility was to (1) explain the relationship between nature and the idea of liberty and (2) show how Mrs. Mallard comes to understand her own need for liberty as she is exposed to nature.

   Another student asked, "Did Louise Mallard achieve freedom?" By including this sentence in his introduction, he set up an expectation for readers: that the rest of the essay would provide his answer to the question.

If you have difficulty developing a focal point, you may want to reread the story, take more notes, and/or do more brainstorming. Looping (see p. 241) can be an especially useful activity because it can help you discover important ideas within your own writing. If you find that working alone is not productive, you should discuss the story with a classmate or your instructor to discover what is important to you about the story.

Whatever process you undergo to develop a focal point, remember that at this stage, your point(s) or question(s) are tentative. As you move through several stages of writing, your thinking may undergo several changes. The introduction can be revised many times, until you are satisfied that it is well matched with the evidence provided in the rest of the essay. Conversely, the body can be revised so that it is well matched with the introduction.

Student Writers at Work

Below are excerpts from introductions to student essays about Kate Chopin's "The Story of an Hour." Each excerpt focuses on a particular topic through statements or a question that the student will support or answer in the rest of the essay.

1. Through nature, Mrs. Mallard discovers her own need for liberty.

    B.L.

2. Louise Mallard is extremely childlike in her thinking, attempts to hide her feelings from all those around her, and withdraws into a fantasy world to avoid her responsibilities.

    A.D.

3. Louise Mallard is unable to accept reality.

    T.A.

4. Chopin presents Mrs. Mallard's dream as a symbol of women's demand and wish for power in the family and in society. Through Mrs. Mallard's fantasy, Chopin suggests that the role of women should be changed. However, Chopin also accepts the fact that there are limits to these changes.

    N.N.

5. Does Louise Mallard achieve freedom?

    G.T.

6. Why does Louise Mallard die?

ACTIVITY: *Finding evidence to support a focal point*

Read the above student statements and questions. Pick out details and events from "The Story of an Hour" (pp. 6–8) that you think can be used to support each point or answer each question.   ●

PROVIDING GENERAL BACKGROUND INFORMATION

You can choose from a variety of approaches to open your essay. Many of these choices move readers from the *general* to the *specific*. In other words, you can begin with general background information and then reveal the connection between that information and the specific topic you are focusing on in your essay. For example, if you open the essay with a general definition, you should link the definition with a specific aspect of the story. In the following example, a general comment about women in the nineteenth century is connected to details of a particular woman's story.

General

Specific

> "The Story of an Hour" by Kate Chopin reveals a great deal about the status and function of women in the American society during the second half of the nineteenth century. In her story, Chopin achieves this by giving the reader an intense insight into Mrs. Mallard's character through her feelings, acts, and thoughts. When Mrs. Mallard first learns about her husband's death, she feels depressed. However, as she sits alone in front of a window, she realizes that there are unfamiliar but positive feelings that she has never experienced before, seizing her body and soul.

To provide general background information, you may want to use one or more of the following approaches. The opening lines of student essays analyzing "The Story of an Hour" (pp. 6–8) are provided as examples.

LIFE EXPERIENCES

You can begin your paper by discussing some general human experience (such as love and marriage) before you focus on the specific example (of love and marriage) that is described in the story.

EXAMPLE

Human emotions are complex and sometimes inexplicable, as are our behaviors. It is hard to understand why people often try to impose themselves on others, taking others' freedom, as the husband does in "The Story of an Hour."

PHILOSOPHICAL CONCEPTS

You can begin by discussing some general philosophical concept such as fate, time, death, or good vs. evil before you focus on that concept as it is revealed in the story.

EXAMPLE

It is in human nature to seek freedom. And we have no control over the fact that we are born to be free. That is what Louise Mallard realizes in "The Story of an Hour."

BIOGRAPHICAL INFORMATION

If background information on the author or the work itself is applicable to the development of the story and to the focus of your essay, you may include that information in the introduction. If information is gleaned from sources other than those used in class, you should cite and document the information according to specific guidelines (see "Citing Outside Material," pp. 328–33).

EXAMPLE

Kate Chopin was a young widow. And so she was able to understand the many emotions of a woman who learns that her husband has died unexpectedly.

HISTORICAL BACKGROUND

If a discussion of the historical period in which the story is set would shed light on the meaning of the story, you may include relevant material taken from a class lecture, a textbook, or a library book or article. If you include material from outside sources that is not common knowledge, you should cite and document the information (see "Citing Outside Material," pp. 328–33).

EXAMPLE

In "The Story of an Hour," Kate Chopin presents the role and the feeling of women in the nineteenth century. As Chopin suggests, women at the time had very few rights.

A QUOTATION

You can begin with a quotation from the story that relates to the topic of your essay. You may also choose a quotation from outside the story, most likely one that is a famous saying or one that directly relates to the meaning of the story. If you use a quotation that is not in the story, you should cite the source (see "Citing Outside Material," pp. 328–33).

EXAMPLE

"Free! Body and soul free!" (8). Every human being is born free, according to Kate Chopin.

A DEFINITION

You can define a term that is important to achieve an understanding of the story. For example, the word *pride*, which can be used to analyze a character's behavior, has many meanings. You may want to discuss one or more of those meanings to relate the definition to the characterization that you will discuss in the paper.

EXAMPLE

What is freedom? According to *The American Heritage Dictionary*, freedom is "the capacity to exercise choice." In "The Story of an Hour," Kate Chopin presents Louise Mallard as a woman without freedom, one who could not make her own choices in life.

A PLOT SUMMARY

You might want to give an overview of the story before you narrow your discussion down to a specific aspect. If you do so, you should include only what you consider to be the most important details. (See p. 23 on summarizing a plot.)

EXAMPLE

"The Story of an Hour" by Kate Chopin shows us the unexpected reaction of Louise Mallard after she loses her husband. She grieves at
first, then surprisingly becomes cheerful at the thought of her husband
being around no longer.

AN ELEMENT OF FICTION

If you are examining how a specific element of fiction functions in the
story, you may want to begin by explaining that element (see "Examining
Elements within a Story," pp. 23–37). For example, you can discuss *setting*
in general before you focus on the setting of the story in particular.

EXAMPLE

Spring is the time of year when nature becomes vivid again after long
months of cold, gray, sad weather. In "The Story of an Hour," the
spring scene offers a parallel to a personal situation.

A Student Writer at Work

After rereading and taking notes on "The Story of an Hour" and after
brainstorming ideas (see pp. 239–44), Rosa wrote a trial draft of an essay
analyzing the story. The introduction of the draft is reprinted here. It has
been typed so that it is easy to read, but errors have not been corrected and
Rosa's cross-outs are included. As you will see, Rosa had several false starts
until she found a first sentence she was comfortable with. Her paper opens
with some background information (not necessarily accurate) about America
in the 1890s.

Introduction to Rosa's Trial Draft (First Version)

1890's
The American of the 1890's was
The role of a woman in the American society of 1890's

historical back-
ground

The life of a woman in the American society of the 1890's must not
have been a very easy one. Women played a very ~~unjust~~ unfair role.
~~They didn't have any kind of rights.~~ It was believed that ~~men were~~
~~superior~~ males were superior, therefore they were ~~supposed~~ expected to
be submissive to them. ~~They didn't enjoy any kind of rights.~~ Neither
could they vote as any other citizen ~~and neither~~ nor could they ~~de~~ dis-
aprove what their husbands said. They were not considered for any type
of decision. Despite the conceptions of those days ~~a brave woman by~~

author's name
title

~~the named Kate Chopin wrote a short story, "The Story~~ a woman
named Kate Chopin was brave enough to challange the society in which
she lived. Her story "The Story of an Hour" seeked to raise awareness

plot summary

of the ~~life woman had kind of unjust~~ unreasonable life women were
having. In this story Josephine, an oppressed wife, finds out that her
husband died. Instead of feeling sad, she rejoyced at the announcement.

But she had her reasons. ~~For Kate Chopin, after experiencing having experienced the death of her husband and after experiencing life with freedom, since her husband w had died, was able to write this story. She felt committed to open the eyes of other women who were still being oppressed by men. The It was~~ Kate Chopin was able to write this story since she had experienced the freedom that many other women didn't have, ~~since~~ because her husband had died.   biographical information

After Rosa read her draft to classmates and discussed it with her instructor, she decided that the introduction did not have a clear enough focus. She rewrote the introduction two or three times until she was satisfied with the result.

Her final introduction is reprinted below, edited for publication in this book. The introduction moves from general historical and biographical background information to a focus on the motivation of the main character of the story.

Introduction to Rosa's Final Paper

The life of a woman in the American society of the 1890s was not an easy one. Women played a very insignificant and unfair role. It was believed that males were superior; therefore women were expected to be submissive to them. Women were unable to enjoy many rights. They could not vote in elections; some women could not disagree with what their husbands said. They were not considered for many decisions.   historical background

Despite the conceptions of those days, a woman named Kate Chopin was brave enough to challenge the society in which she lived. Her story "The Story of an Hour" seeks to raise awareness of the unreasonable life women were having. She was capable of writing this story since she had herself experienced the freedom that many other women did not have, because her husband had died. She felt committed to open the eyes of other women. In the story Mrs. Mallard, who had been an oppressed wife, finds out that her husband has just died. Instead of feeling sad, she rejoices at the announcement. But she has her reasons. Even though Mrs. Mallard rejoices at her husband's death, she should not be considered a hard or callous woman.   author's name

title
biographical information

plot summary

focal point

Rosa's responsibility to her readers is to provide evidence to support her idea that Louise Mallard should not be considered a callous woman.

Rosa's entire final paper (edited for publication in this book) is reprinted on pages 272–76. You can decide for yourself whether she has fulfilled her responsibility to provide valid evidence to prove her point.

ACTIVITY: *Evaluating introductions*

The following passages are introductions to drafts of student essays analyzing "The Story of an Hour" by Kate Chopin. All have been edited for errors. Working with the whole class or in a small group, evaluate each introduction.

Read the introduction in two ways:

1. Look for the common features of an introduction:
   a. *Identification of the reading:* Has the writer included the full name of the author and the title of the story being discussed?
   b. *A focus:* Can you tell from the introduction what topic the writer will explore in the essay?
2. Examine your overall impression of the introduction. Allow for differences of opinion in the group.
   a. Ask questions such as these and explain your response:
      - Is the introduction too long? too short? Is it too detailed? not detailed enough?
      - If a point is made about the topic, does it arouse interest in the writer's interpretation of the story? Or does the statement diminish interest by telling too much?
      - Is the organization of the sentences logical?
      - Is the writing style pleasing?
   b. If you think the introduction should be revised, what suggestions would you have for the writer?

A

In "The Story of an Hour," Kate Chopin portrays a woman who receives the news of her husband's death and who, after having overcome her reflexive reaction of grief, looks forward to her new freedom. However, the supposedly dead husband reappears quite unexpectedly, horrifying the woman to death. In this paper, the setting of the story will be analyzed in its relation to the character development of the woman, Louise Mallard. The conclusions will then be generalized and transferred to the more fundamental relation between human beings, nature, and freedom.

T.C.

B

"The Story of an Hour" reveals the values of the society in which it is set (1894). It describes the feelings of freedom of a woman who just found out that her husband died. But her joy is suddenly ended by the husband walking through the front door without a sign of being injured or sick. His wife, who had heart problems, dies from a heart attack when she sees him walking through the door. She suddenly realizes that she is not free anymore and the thought of losing her independence again kills her.

B.L.

C

In Kate Chopin's "The Story of an Hour," the main character, Mrs. Mallard, is informed of her husband's tragic death through her sister and a close friend, Richards. Mrs. Mallard's first reaction is normal for any loving wife: "She wept at once, with sudden wild abandonment, in her sister's arms" (7). After spending a short amount of time by herself, Mrs. Mallard's grief turns into a feeling of relief. She no longer has to deal with the restrictions within a marriage. She is looking forward to a new life of freedom. Just as she begins to enjoy this feeling of freedom, the doorbell rings. It is her supposedly dead husband who is not even aware that an accident has occurred. Unable to accept reality, she suffers a heart attack, which leads to her immediate death. In this story, Chopin shows that life is a series of unexpected events, both positive and negative, depending on how you view them.

T.A.

D

"The Story of an Hour" by Kate Chopin is a short story about a woman, Mrs. Mallard, who is told that her husband has died in an accident. Her first reaction is that of sadness, which later becomes one of euphoria at the thought of being free at last. However, her husband later comes home and his wife learns that he had not even been near the accident. Mrs. Mallard dies of "joy that kills" (8). Thus, Chopin suggests that the only way that women can achieve freedom, which is acquiring self-assertion, is through death.

W.J.
●

ACTIVITY: *Examining your own introduction*

To determine whether you have an effective introduction to your paper, you can subject it to intense scrutiny. Your examination of the introduction can be likened to an X-ray, which can pass through an object and reveal its structural weaknesses. Use the form on page 256 to help you evaluate your own work. You may write down the answers or just use the form as a mental guide to help you evaluate your work.   ●

The Body

The body of the paper is its longest section. In several paragraphs, you supply evidence to develop your focus. Each paragraph or set of paragraphs provides at least one supporting point that relates to and expands on the topic that you focused on in the introduction. Within each paragraph are

X-Ray Form for an Introduction

Read your introduction and answer the following questions.

1. Does it identify the work by providing the author's full name and the title (within quotation marks)?

   yes____   no____

   If not, what's missing? _____

   _____

2. Does it focus on a particular topic and indicate the point(s) you will prove or the question(s) you will answer?

   yes____   no____

   If so, underline the sentence(s) or write the sentence(s) here, as they appear in

   your paper. _____

   _____

   _____

   _____

   If not, reflect on what topic you want to focus on. If you are not sure how to develop a focal point, discuss a possible idea or question with a classmate or with your instructor. Then create a sentence or sentences to reveal your focus. When you revise the introduction, you can add this material.

   _____

   _____

   _____

   _____

details, examples, and quotations that act as evidence to substantiate the supporting point. Each quotation is further explained through interpretive comments (see "Quoting," pp. 316–27).

Note: It is not always necessary or even preferable to analyze every scene or detail of a story.

STRUCTURING THE BODY

There are many ways to organize the body of an essay. None of the patterns suggested below represents a rigid formula. You may try variations on these structures or devise another structure that is better suited to your topic. You can use the drafting process to experiment with organization; these first attempts can later be revised.

Note: For specific guidelines on selecting evidence to include in the body of a paper, see Chapter 6.

1. Explore a topic by providing relevant evidence from different scenes *chronologically* (in the order in which the scenes occur in the story).

    Begin at the beginning of the story and provide evidence to support any points that you make about a topic (for example, about a character or the setting or an abstract idea such as manhood). Then move through the story, examining one scene at a time. In other words, make a new point about your topic and provide evidence from each relevant scene, until you reach the end of the story.

    With such an organizational pattern, each paragraph or set of paragraphs usually examines a different scene in the story. For example, if you were writing an essay about "The Story of an Hour" (pp. 6–8), the body of your paper might first make a point about and analyze the first scene in the story, when Louise Mallard learns of her husband's death. The next paragraph(s) could make a point about and analyze the next scene, when she sits alone and motionless by an open window. The next paragraph(s) could make a point about and analyze the scene in which she abandons herself, and so on.

2. Explore a topic by providing relevant evidence from different scenes *in order of importance* (according to your view of what is important), not necessarily following the exact chronology of the story.

    You can begin at the end of the story and move backward, or you can begin in the middle and move forward to the end or backward to the beginning. You may want to begin with what you think is the least important scene and end with the most important, so that your argument gets stronger.

    With such an organizational pattern, each paragraph or set of paragraphs examines and makes a point about a different event or detail of the story in whatever order makes most sense. For example, if you were writing an essay about "The Story of an Hour" (pp. 6–8) to analyze the behavior of Louise Mallard, you could begin with the scene in which she abandons herself, and then you could move backward to the scene outside her window. Then you could jump forward to examine what she reveals about her past relationship with her husband. And so on.

3. Explore a topic by providing relevant evidence according to a set of *categories* that you determine.

   You can determine a set of categories according to which you will analyze details of a story. With such an organizational pattern, each paragraph or set of paragraphs usually examines and makes a point about a different category. For example, you might divide a discussion of "The Story of an Hour" (pp. 6–8) into categories such as women/marriage/love or nature/freedom/death, and so on. The body of your paper might first discuss the details related to nature, then the details related to freedom, then the details related to death. Such an essay would make sense, however, only if all of the categories are in some way linked and if you show how the different areas are connected or follow logically from one another.

4. Explore a topic by *comparing and contrasting* two or more stories, by providing relevant evidence from different scenes chronologically (in the order in which they occur in the stories) *or* in order of importance, *or* by creating categories as a basis of comparison.

   Focus on the same or a similar topic in the different stories. In this way you can reveal through a parallel structure the stories' similarities and differences. Here are some organizational possibilities:

   a. Discuss and make points about one story at a time, dividing the body into two sets of paragraphs, one set for each story. The second set of paragraphs can cover the same or similar points covered in the first set; you can show how the stories compare on each point.

   b. Discuss one point about the topic at a time, providing evidence from both stories within each paragraph, paragraph by paragraph.

   c. Discuss similarities first, and then differences (or vice versa).

A Student Writer at Work

The eighth and ninth paragraphs of Rosa's essay are reprinted below. In each paragraph, Rosa discusses a different aspect of her topic and supports each new point with details and quotations from the story. Note that each time Rosa presents a quotation, she explains or interprets it (see "Quoting," pp. 316–27).

Paragraphs 8 and 9 of Rosa's Final Essay

point of paragraph 8: Mrs. Mallard properly resists the new feelings

It can be proved that Mrs. Mallard doesn't want to accept this new feeling by these words: "she was striving to beat it back with her will" (7). Mrs. Mallard, being the respectful and good woman that she knows

Quotation

Interpretation

she is, initially cannot accept these strange feelings that are trying to possess her.

point of paragraph 9: The new feelings take control of Mrs. Mallard and she finally accepts freedom

That "she abandoned herself" (7) clearly shows that she is going to act in a different way from the way she normally does. When these feelings totally take control of her, she begins to realize the freedom that she will be able to have. "[F]ree, free, free" (7) is the cry when Mrs. Mallard realizes that she finally can have the opportunity to act as she wishes to. These are the first words this woman proclaims when she is under the rule of these new feelings. Feelings are emotions that take possession of a person and are difficult to control. It is under these circumstances that Mrs. Mallard finally lets go of what she apparently has been keeping inside of her for a long time: "Her pulses beat fast, and the coursing blood warmed and relaxed every inch of her body" (7). As her body shows, it is not easy for her to express these random feelings. After this, she feels relaxed, a sensation that is felt when someone discharges a strong emotion.

Quotation
Interpretation

Quotation
Interpretation

Quotation

Interpretation

ACTIVITY: *Connecting quotation and interpretation*

Read the two paragraphs above, and discuss Rosa's interpretations to determine whether they help you understand the significance or meaning of the quotations she uses.   ●

ACTIVITY: *Analyzing the body of an essay*

Rosa's final essay analyzing Kate Chopin's "The Story of an Hour" is reprinted on pages 272–76. The organizational pattern that worked best for her was similar to the "order of importance" scheme described on pages 257–58: she explored her topic by providing relevant evidence from different scenes in an order that she found significant, without following the exact chronology of the story.

Examine the body of Rosa's essay to discover which scenes she analyzes and to analyze how she pieces together evidence to substantiate her claim that Louise Mallard should not be considered a callous woman.   ●

LINKING INDIVIDUAL PARAGRAPHS

The body paragraphs of an essay can have different purposes. They can be created to make a new point, or they can be created simply to expand on a point already made. For example, one paragraph might provide an extended example or more details to illustrate or clarify a point made in the preceding paragraph.

A body paragraph can also act as a transition from one paragraph to another; such a paragraph can even be a single sentence. For example, a transitional paragraph might consist of a question such as "Then why does Louise Mallard die?" This question could act as a bridge between one paragraph that discusses the character's happiness and another paragraph that discusses her sudden death.

Paragraphing is an important signaling system. The sight of a newly indented paragraph sends a message to a reader that the writer is introducing a new aspect of the topic or is shifting emphasis. The initial sentence(s) of a new paragraph usually act as a transition, helping readers connect what they have just read with what they are about to read.

In your own essays, the functions that your sentences and paragraphs serve will be determined by your content and purpose. As you revise your paper (see "Revising," pp. 268–72), ask yourself why you have created each paragraph. If you yourself understand why your paragraphs exist and why they are linked as they are, you are more likely to create an essay that makes sense to your readers.

ACTIVITY: *Analyzing a link between paragraphs*

Read the eighth and ninth paragraphs of Rosa's essay (reprinted on pp. 272–76). Discuss whether the first sentence(s) of the ninth paragraph help(s) you connect what you have just read (in the eighth paragraph) with what you are about to read.   ●

ACTIVITY: *Organizing the body of an essay*

To plan the organization of the body of your essay, you might find it helpful to make a list of the details, examples, and quotations that you think you will use as evidence to support your focal point. You may choose to list these items in the order in which they occur in the story. Or you may want to list them in order of importance. Or you may create categories (for example, nature, fear, freedom) and place items within the appropriate category on the list. Then consider how each of the items or categories follows a pattern that can help you develop supporting points to prove a point or answer a question.   ●

The Conclusion

The conclusion, usually one to two paragraphs, grows out of the rest of the essay. Having introduced and provided evidence about a topic, now you can discuss the implications of what you have written. The way your essay begins will to some extent determine how it ends. If you state directly what point you will support or prove about a topic, now you can expand on that point. If you raise a question about a topic, now you can answer the question. In each case, you can reveal a larger meaning of the story by relating the topic to a *theme*, a truth the author reveals (see "Discovering Themes," pp. 38–39). In other words, you can explain what you think the author thinks.

Occasionally you may disagree with what the author thinks or with how the author transmits an idea. For example, the author may have a view about women or success that you do not accept. In such a case, you may end your essay with your own opinion on the subject. But first you should establish the author's view. Then you can measure your own values against the author's.

There are many ways to bring your essay to its end. The approaches that you can use to provide general information for an introduction also can be useful for a conclusion. For example, you can include a quotation, a definition, historical details, and so on (see pp. 246–52). Which approach you choose will depend on your topic and purpose.

CONCLUDING THE ESSAY

In concluding your essay interpreting a work of fiction, you can use one or more of these strategies. In each case, you generalize about what happens in the story to give it a more universal meaning. You share your interpretation of what the author says or thinks in the story.

1. Discuss the connection between what happens in the story and the author's view of society.
2. Discuss the connection between the story and the author's view of human behavior.
3. Discuss the connection between the story and the historical period in which it is set.
4. Discuss the connection between the story and a philosophical or ethical concept.
5. Discuss the connection between what happens in the story and what happens in the real world today.

If none of the suggestions above suits your topic and purpose, discuss alternatives with your instructor. You may find, for example, that your essay raises more questions than it answers. In that case, perhaps your conclusion should be primarily a series of questions. Or you may feel that there are multiple interpretations. In that case, your conclusion could discuss the alternative interpretations.

Even though the conclusion is a natural outgrowth of the rest of the essay, it can be difficult to write. You may need several tries before you are satisfied. At first, you can write just one sentence to show that your paper has come to an end. Later you can revise your work.

A Student Writer at Work

Unlike many student writers, Rosa did not have trouble writing her conclusion. In fact, she had her conclusion in mind before she even knew how she was going to develop the body of her paper.

As you can see, in her conclusion she reviews some of the key facts of the story, and she emphasizes and expands on her main point. She also reveals a larger meaning of the story by connecting the characterization of Louise Mallard to the author's view of the society in which she lives.

Conclusion of Rosa's final essay

main point

larger meaning

Throughout the story, we see how a wife discovers that her husband's death brings her satisfaction. Although this may seem cruel or immoral, she cannot be considered a hard or callous woman. The facts in the story declare so. When her husband was alive, and even though she admits that she loved him only "sometimes" (8), she respected him as any decent woman would. But this time is different; a set of emotions constrains her to act in a different way from how she would normally. Without any kind of intention, she is reaching for freedom, the freedom that her life had always lacked. Mrs. Mallard is a victim of the society of her days, a society in which women were seen just as objects of possession. This story was written in order to create consciousness in other women about the issue of oppression.

ACTIVITY: *Organizing an essay*

If you find it useful, you can use the chart on page 245 to plan the organization of your essay before you write, or to examine the organization of a draft after you have written. You may write down the information or just use the chart as a mental guide to help you shape or evaluate your work. Remember that this is not a formula you must follow. •

WRITING AND EVALUATING AN INTERIM DRAFT

For many writers, composing an essay involves going through a drafting process, that is, writing more than one version of the essay. Some of the writing can be done just for yourself. But, eventually, you will be asked to prepare an essay for someone else to read.

This section provides advice for writing an interim draft: a draft that is written between the first and final stages of composing. Although others may read this draft, it is still considered work in progress.

A Student Writer at Work

Writing the interim draft was a long process for Rosa, as she is a careful writer who uses many words to transmit her ideas. In the interim draft, she worked hard on her introduction, rewriting it two or three times (see p. 253), and then slowly built up evidence to support the main point she wanted to make. She kept returning to the story to find quotations to substantiate her claims about the main character. Part of her interim draft is included in the section "Revising" (pp. 268–72).

ACTIVITY: *Preparing an interim draft*

Following the guidelines on page 263, prepare an interim draft to be read by your classmates and/or instructor. •

GUIDELINES

Guidelines for Writing an Interim Draft

1. Reflect on the purpose of the assignment.
2. Reread your trial draft, if you have written one.
3. Devise a tentative organizational plan for the essay, either in your head, in outline form, or in a chart.
4. Set aside some uninterrupted time and start to write. You may have to force yourself to begin. But once you get started, your writing will probably begin to flow.
5. Structure your writing so that it has an introduction, body, and conclusion. Try to follow the organizational pattern that you have planned, but be flexible in your approach. If the plan doesn't work, allow another organizational pattern to emerge from your material.
6. Provide evidence (supporting points, details, examples, quotations) to substantiate points you are making about your topic.
7. Understand that writing a draft may be a messy process, with cross-outs, additions, and so on. You may pause to read, rethink, and rewrite certain sections before you reach the end.
8. Prepare a legible copy of the essay, if it is to be shared with your classmates or instructor.

Before you bring your interim draft to class for evaluation, use the following checklist for content.

Checklist for Content: Self-Evaluation

Does my essay provide

- the title of the story and the full name of the author?
- a focus on a particular topic?
- sufficient evidence from the story to support or prove a point or answer a question about the topic (supporting points, details, examples, quotations)?
- a discussion that reveals a larger meaning of the story?

If the answer to any of the questions is no, either add the missing material to your draft or make a note (mental or written) of what you will include in the final essay. If you are not sure what to include, ask for advice.

RECEIVING FEEDBACK ON A DRAFT

By sharing your work in progress with others, you can become aware of how readers (your classmates and/or instructor) react to your writing. Then you can plan ways to improve it. The feedback you receive may be provided through written and/or oral comments.

The following guidelines can help you and your classmates learn how to give and receive helpful feedback in a comfortable and supportive environment.

Peer Review

Peer review is a collaborative process in which you work with a group of student writers (your peers) to discuss work in progress. Peer reviewing can be valuable in training you to internalize criteria for evaluating written work. By asking other writers questions about their drafts and by having readers ask you questions about your draft, you can learn to ask questions of yourself about your own writing. This process can lead you to become a critical reader of your own writing.

Peer review groups ideally provide a place for exploration and discovery of ideas. Since one's own writing can be a sensitive topic, it is important to keep the discussion focused in a positive way. In addition to talking about your essays, you can talk about the stories themselves to clarify and expand on your ideas. When you are confused, you can ask questions. When you disagree, you can debate (not argue!). When you have suggestions, you can offer them.

ACTIVITY: Discussing guidelines for giving and accepting feedback

To prepare for peer review, read the recommendations on page 265 for giving and accepting criticism. The recommendations are reprinted from a book on problem solving titled *The Revised All New Universal Traveler*. To get their points across, the authors of the book humorously refer to problem solving as a journey, and they give advice in the form of tips for travelers.

Use this opportunity to express your concerns and to ask questions about peer review.   •

The peer review form on page 266 is based on the recommendations on page 265 and can act as a guide as you respond to someone else's paper.

HOW TO CRITICIZE PAINLESSLY

The need for assertive criticism often emerges in the realm of conscious problem-solving.

Here is a fool-proof method for telling yourself or someone else that something is wrong without fear of losing a friendship or of starting a battle.

The trick is to place the criticism within a context of positive reinforcements ... just simple diplomacy.

1. BEGIN WITH TWO POSITIVE REINFORCEMENTS
   "You really are a well-seasoned traveler."
   "You have all of the best gear for hiking."
2. INSERT YOUR CRITICISM
   "I wish we could stay in step when we hike together."
3. ADD ONE MORE POSITIVE REINFORCEMENT
   "I notice that you can adapt easily to most things."
4. FINISH WITH A RAY OF HOPE
   "If we work on this together, I'm sure we'll be able to get harmony into our stride."

Now you try it!

HOW TO ACCEPT CRITICISM

It is easier to feel a discontent than it is to accept the challenge of constructively improving the situation. And it is also easier, as the old saying goes, "to give criticism than it is to receive it." Being "defensive" of our position, which we imagine to be under attack from outside, is wasted motion. But it is also far more normal than an outlook of receptive self-improvement.

Be *abnormal.* Instead of wasting time with defenses and soothing self-inflicted, imaginary hurts, get procedural. *Accept* the comments for further *ANALYSIS and DEFINITION.* If the criticism then seems appropriate, "try it on for size." If not, discard it as irrelevant and the matter is finished.

Peer Review Form

Writer's name _____ Reviewer's Name _____

Directions: Read the writer's draft and then fill in your responses. Your goal in reviewing a paper is to help the writer. Unless errors interfere with your ability to understand what the writer is saying, read for meaning only.

1. *Begin with positive reinforcement.* Tell the writer what you like about the paper and what you think should not be changed.

2. *Insert your criticism.* Tell the writer what confused you, bothered you, or left you wanting more. Be specific.

3. *Finish with a ray of hope.* Give the writer helpful suggestions. Be specific. If you were the writer of this paper, what would you do to strengthen it?

Guidelines for Peer Reviewing

1. Form pairs or small groups of students.
2. Exchange drafts and read silently, or take turns reading your own drafts aloud.
3. Use the peer review form on page 266 and/or the questions below as a guide for discussion. Your instructor will help you decide whether to provide written and/or oral feedback.
4. Discuss the responses to the drafts, helping the writer understand what is effective in the paper and what might be done to make it better.
5. After the discussions, write a note to yourself or to your instructor, explaining what you may do to improve the paper.

ACTIVITY: *Peer reviewing*

Bring your draft to class and exchange papers with one or more students. Evaluate each other's papers by examining (1) what you like about the paper and (2) what you think can be done to strengthen it. You may use the peer review form on page 266 and/or the following suggestions to guide your discussion.

1. The opening paragraphs should present a clearly focused topic.
   - Summarize what the student writer focuses on.
2. The evidence in the body of the essay should accurately and adequately develop the topic focused on in the introduction.
   - Discuss which evidence you find most effective.
   - Discuss other details or quotations from the story that might enrich or strengthen the essay.
   - Discuss any other arguments that might support or prove the essay's points.
   - Discuss any section that needs clarification.
   - Discuss any material that might seem extraneous.
3. The material should be logically developed.
   - Discuss which section of the paper most logically presents evidence to support ideas.
   - Discuss why and how certain sentences or paragraphs, if any, could benefit from rearrangement.
4. The conclusion should grow logically out of the other parts of the essay.
   - Discuss the student writer's overall interpretation of the story. ●

Instructor's Comments

Your instructor may read your work in progress and give you *written feedback* on your interim draft, perhaps pointing out strengths as well as weaknesses in your writing and providing suggestions for revision. If you don't understand any of the written comments, ask questions so that you know how to proceed.

You may receive *oral feedback* on a draft through a conference with your instructor. If so, you will probably find the conference most useful if you do most of the talking. You can ask questions about any oral or written feedback you received earlier and you can respond to any questions your instructor may have about your writing. As you discuss the story or stories you have analyzed, you may discover ideas that you can include in the next draft. Write down the ideas in a notebook or on a sheet of paper before or just after you leave the conference so that you don't forget what you want to say.

A Student Writer at Work

Rosa received feedback on her interim draft from both her classmates and her instructor. Some of the comments and her revisions are included in the next section, "Revising."

REVISING

By now, one or more students and/or your instructor may have commented on your paper. If you have followed the recommendations for accepting criticism (p. 265), you have accepted the comments for further analysis. Now is the time to analyze. You need to determine which comments are most helpful and how to revise the paper to meet your own goals and your readers' needs and expectations.

Revising entails more than just rewriting a paper. It means making decisions about what to keep, what to add, what to delete, what to change,

---

GUIDELINES

Guidelines for Revising

Revise your paper by asking questions such as these:
- What should I keep?
- What should I add?
- What should I delete?
- What should I change?
- What should I rearrange?
- What should I rethink?

what to rearrange, and what to rethink. Like drafting, revising allows you to think about your thinking, to take a new look, to reshape and refine your thoughts.

There can be no hard and fast rules for revision, of course, because each writer has a different paper and different reviewer responses. But the following questions may help you sift through the criticism you have received.

What Should I Keep?

Reread your reviewers' comments and/or your own notes to remember what your readers liked about your paper. Though it may not be possible to save everything that appealed to them, you should keep their positive impressions in your mind as you rewrite.

What Should I Add?

Reread the comments and/or notes to discover whether any of your readers needed more general background information to understand your subject. If so, determine from your reviewers' comments where you need more information. This might mean adding only a brief phrase or a few explanatory sentences.

Reread the comments and/or notes to discover whether more details, quotations, or other evidence are needed to illustrate or support points you have made. If so, make note of the spots where your readers want to know more. Brainstorming activities can be useful in helping you generate new ideas or examples (see pp. 239–44).

What Should I Delete?

It is possible that one of your readers suggested that you used too much detail or included too much information. This is especially difficult criticism to hear because this reviewer may be recommending deletion of some of your favorite parts. Before you take anything out, remember that this is one reader's reaction. As with all criticism, you might determine that the suggestion is not appropriate and decide to retain the material in your revision. However, if another reader made the same comment, this is probably advice worth taking.

What Should I Change?

If any of your readers expressed confusion, make note of the section or sections of your draft that caused the problem. If you have discussed the draft with your readers, you probably know why the confusion exists. In fact, you may have solved the problem already just by explaining to your reviewers what you meant to say. Now you need to rewrite the confusing section. You may want to experiment with one or two versions. Then read them aloud to yourself or show them to a classmate or your instructor. They can help you determine which version is clearer.

What Should I Rearrange?

If you have been told that your paper needs a more logical development, it might be a good idea to outline your draft briefly, paragraph by paragraph, summarizing each paragraph. Then look at your outline to see where the logic of the organization breaks down. Revise the outline to reflect a better organization. Then rearrange the material in your draft. A similar process can be applied to individual paragraphs.

What Should I Rethink?

It is possible that, in spite all of your efforts, you may not have proved a point or answered a question about your topic. It is also possible that you have not done so because you yourself don't really know what you want to say. Since that might be true, you will have to reconsider what you have written. Try a brainstorming strategy such as looping on your topic (see p. 241), or discuss your topic with a classmate or your instructor to find what is important to you about this topic.

Once you have come to an understanding of the discovery you want to share, you need to find a way to transmit your thoughts within the paper. In some cases that will involve rewriting the beginning. In some cases, that will mean rewriting the ending. In any case, your goal should be to allow readers to understand or accept your point of view.

A Student Writer at Work

Rosa received feedback on her interim draft from both her classmates and her instructor. She first told them where she thought she needed help. She then presented the paper orally to the class. When she finished, they told her what they liked about the paper and how they thought it could be improved. She also received written feedback from her instructor. She then met with her instructor to decide how to proceed.

After consulting with her instructor, Rosa revised portions of her paper, refocusing her introduction (see p. 273), expanding on several paragraphs by adding new points and quotations, and incorporating two new paragraphs. Two of the comments Rosa received and the changes she made are reprinted here.

Instructor's Comment

This is a very good interim draft. You show compassion toward the character and her situation. Your analysis of her acceptance of freedom is quite well done, showing that she is driven by instinct and emotion.

When you revise the paper, you could develop further the paragraph on nature. This scene in the story is crucial to your argument that Louise is not a hard woman. Go through the details—inside and outside her room. Then take your readers through an interpretation of those details. Why does Chopin emphasize nature?

Rosa's Paragraph on Nature in Her Interim Draft

Other important details presented in the story before her thoughts, are the ones related with nature. As she is alone and she sits facing a window, symbols of a rebirth begin to appear. The "new spring life" represents a total beginning of things. The blue sky that could be seen even when there are clouds, means that there is the hope of starting a new life again. Having this in mind, we begin to appreciate that there is going to be something different about this announcement of death.

Rosa's Revision of the Paragraph on Nature

Other important details presented in the story, before we learn her thoughts, are the ones related to nature. As she is alone and sits looking outside, symbols of a rebirth begin to appear. That she sits "facing the open window" (7) means that there is going to be a new chapter in her life or a way out from her past life. The "new spring life" represents a total commencement of things. The color green can mean hope, and that is what Mrs. Mallard sees in the trees. In the air is "the delicious breath of rain" (7). Water is something that brings freshness, and freshness is synonymous with recent, newborn things. And if this freshness is in the air, then Mrs. Mallard is breathing this air full of vigor. She also sees "patches of blue sky showing here and there through the clouds that had met and piled one above the other in the west facing her window" (7). Even when there are clouds in the sky— her husband's death—there is also the desire of making a new present. The combination of all these details that describe nature have a major significance. Just as the change of seasons happens in a natural way, people also change, and that is natural. The change that Louise experiences is something natural, something that could have happened to anyone.

Peer Reviewer's Comment

You do a good job of analyzing the character and showing why she thinks the way she does. But you haven't really analyzed what finally happens to her. It may not be absolutely necessary, but I think you should write more about the ending. Why do you think Louise dies? What do you think Chopin means by that ending?

Rosa's Revision (An Additional Paragraph)

At the end of the story, Louise learns that her husband has not died, and she suddenly dies. And "[w]hen the doctors came, they said she had died of heart disease—of joy that kills" (8).

With the discovery that her husband is not really dead, Mrs. Mallard receives a big shock. Now that she knows what freedom is, it is impossible for her to live without it. Ironically, "joy" means something different to her from what the doctors mean. For her, joy means to be free, and she will fight for it, even if she needs to die. She is dead and free rather than alive and repressed.

After making these and other changes (such as dividing her introduction into two paragraphs), Rosa corrected the grammatical errors that her instructor had underlined. Her final, edited composition is reprinted on pages 272–76.

ACTIVITY: *Revising your essay*

Follow the guidelines on pages 268–70 for revising your interim draft. If you need help, consult a classmate or your instructor.   ●

COMPLETING THE ESSAY

Once you have revised your draft, there are at least three more steps you can take to complete the final essay.

GUIDELINES

Guidelines for Completing the Essay

1. *Evaluate the essay as a whole.* Concentrate on pulling everything together into a whole essay in which every part fits well. Your introduction, body, and conclusion should be well matched. The essay should introduce a topic, prove a point or answer a question about the topic, and discuss the larger implications of the story as revealed through the analysis of the topic.
2. *Proofread and edit the essay.* Turn your attention to grammar, punctuation, spelling, and mechanics. Give your essay a final check to catch any errors you might have made. (See "The Editing Process," pp. 339–44).
3. *Follow the guidelines for preparing a final manuscript.* (See pp. 343–44.)

The Character of Louise Mallard
Rosa Gutierrez

Rosa Gutierrez wrote "The Character of Louise Mallard" to fulfill a writing assignment for a literature and composition course. Born in

Puerto Rico, Rosa studied English for several years before entering college in the United States. Of her experience in the course, Rosa said:

> *At first my reason to take this course was to fulfill my English requirement. But now I see it in a different way. I am really learning to write, and I know that at the beginning I wasn't able to do so effectively. I'm sure I've gained a lot from this experience since I've had the opportunity to deal with people with different values, cultures, religions, and beliefs. This is what made the experience unique. It is so interesting because I can tell what are going to be the interpretations of the stories of other members of the class according to where they come from! I know I am seeing things from a completely different perspective.*

Note: The essay you are about to read is a finished composition, which has been carefully edited for publication in this book. In earlier sections of this chapter, you can see how Rosa got started on this assignment and can trace the various stages of thinking and writing and rewriting she went through to produce her essay.

The life of a woman in the American society of the 1890s was not an easy one. Women played a very insignificant and unfair role. It was believed that males were superior; therefore women were expected to be submissive to them. Women were unable to enjoy many rights. They could not vote in elections; some women could not disagree with what their husbands said. They were not considered for many decisions.

Despite the conceptions of those days, a woman named Kate Chopin was brave enough to challenge the society in which she lived. Her story "The Story of an Hour" seeks to raise awareness of the unreasonable life women were having. She was capable of writing this story since she had herself experienced the freedom that many other women did not have, because her husband had died. She felt committed to open the eyes of other women. In the story Mrs. Mallard, who had been an oppressed wife, finds out that her husband has just died. Instead of feeling sad, she rejoices at the announcement. But she has her reasons. Even though Mrs. Mallard rejoices at her husband's death, she should not be considered a hard or callous woman.

At the beginning of the story Mrs. Mallard is presented as a normal wife who could be deeply affected after learning that her husband is dead, since she suffers from heart problems: "Knowing that Mrs. Mallard was afflicted with a heart trouble, great care was taken to break to her as gently as possible the news of her husband's death" (6). The ones responsible for making the announcement think they know her very well. They are sure of how Mrs. Mallard is going to react: as any normal wife that finds out about her husband's death. They believe that she will react in an inconsolable way, because she always seemed loyal and faithful to her husband. But her first reactions seem different from how other women would have taken it: "She did not hear the story as many women have heard the same" (7). This is something that the author wants us to know, but the characters in the story are not aware of the implications of her actions. She accepts her husband's death without doubts—there is no "paralyzed inability to accept" it (7)—and wants to be alone. These details reveal to us for the first time that there is going to be something different about Mrs. Mallard. If someone is notified about a death, a normal reaction would be not to believe it and to be near people, the opposite of what Mrs. Mallard does.

Louise Mallard is a repressed woman. The narrator describes her with these words: "She was young, with a fair, calm face, whose lines bespoke repression" (7). The lines of her face are the physical evidence of the oppression that she was living under. Her repression is also revealed when a strange impulse takes control of her and she thinks:

> There would be no one to live for her during those coming years: she would live for herself. There would be no powerful will bending hers in that blind persistence with which men and woman believe they have a right to impose a private will upon a fellow-creature. (8).

This statement confirms that she is a dominated wife. Living with her husband means always doing his will, even things that she does not want to do. It is important to note that Chopin clearly states that this imposing of will is done by women as well as by men. But in this particular case, a man is imposing his wish. Because of this, Mrs. Mallard must have lacked the opportunity to express her thoughts and opinions. But now it is different; she has the fortuity to live her own life as she wishes. There is not going to be anyone telling her what to do or what she cannot do.

Other important details presented in the story, before we learn her thoughts, are the ones related to nature. As she is alone and sits looking outside, symbols of a rebirth begin to appear. That she sits "facing the open window" (7) means that there is going to be a new chapter in her life, or a way out from her past life. The "new spring life" represents a total commencement of things. The color green can mean hope, and that is what Mrs. Mallard sees in the trees. In the air is "the delicious breath of rain" (7). Water is something that brings freshness, and freshness is synonymous with recent, newborn things. And if this freshness is in the air, then Mrs. Mallard is breathing this air full of vigor. She also sees "patches of blue sky showing here and there through the clouds that had met and piled one above the other in the west facing her window" (7). Even when there are clouds in the sky—her husband's death—there is also the desire of making a new present. The combination of all these details that describe nature have a major significance. Just as the change of seasons happens in a natural way, people also change, and that is natural. The change that Louise experiences is something natural, something that could have happened to anyone.

Mrs. Mallard feels that something is approaching her, and she is afraid of it. "But she felt it, creeping out of the sky" (7), suggesting the sensation of renewal that she is experiencing, just as the "new spring life" comes after the winter. The sensation of renewal includes feelings of hope and faith for the future. She is scared because she does not know what they are about.

A change is going on inside of her and she is aware of it: "She was beginning to recognize this thing that was approaching to possess her" (7). The part of herself that she is aware existed within her is gently replaced by one that she had never perceived.

It can be proved that Mrs. Mallard does not want to accept this new feeling by these words: "she was striving to beat it back with her will" (7). Mrs. Mallard, being the respectful and good woman that she knows she is, initially cannot accept these strange feelings that are trying to possess her.

That "she abandoned herself" (7) clearly reveals that she is going to act in a different way from the way she normally does. When these feelings totally take control of her, she begins to realize the freedom that she will be able to have. "[F]ree, free, free" (7) is the cry when Mrs. Mallard realizes that she finally can have the opportunity to act as she wishes to. These are the first words this woman proclaims when she is under the rule of these new feelings. Feelings are emotions that take possession of a person and are difficult to control. It is under these circumstances that Mrs. Mallard finally lets go of what she apparently has been keeping inside of her for a long time: "Her pulses beat fast, and the coursing blood warmed and relaxed every inch of her body" (7). As her body shows, it is not easy for her to express these random feelings. After this, she feels relaxed, a sensation that is felt when someone discharges a strong emotion.

These feelings that take control of Mrs. Mallard make her see the death of her husband as a good thing for her. Now the lines of her face that were described as ones that "bespoke repression" will not have to suffer anymore. No one can restrain her, and she can have the opportunity to start a new life again.

Rejoicing at the death of a husband is something that many people consider evil, because it is against the moral standards of a society. Although many readers would interpret this happiness as an evil thing, it must be understood that she feels it because a stronger feeling inside of her drives her to this. It is an impulse, "the strongest impulse of her being!" (8). An impulse is a sudden inclination without time to meditate. The passive woman that everyone knows is incapable of thinking like this. There is no "reflection, but rather . . . a suspension of intelligent thought" (7). If she had meditated about what she is thinking, she would not have had these joyful dreams.

At the end of the story, Louise learns that her husband has not died, and she suddenly dies. And "[w]hen the doctors came, they said she had died of heart disease—of joy that kills" (8). With the discovery that her husband is not really dead, Mrs. Mallard receives a big shock. Now that she knows what freedom is, it is impossible for her to live without it. Ironically, "joy" means something different to her from what the doctors mean. For her, joy means to be free, and she will fight for it, even if she needs to die. She is dead and free rather than alive and oppressed.

Throughout the story, we see how a wife discovers that her husband's death brings her satisfaction. Although this may seem cruel or immoral, she cannot be considered a hard or callous woman. The facts in the story declare so. When her husband was alive, and even though she admits that she loved him only "sometimes" (8), she respected him as any decent woman would. But this time is different; a set of emotions constrains her to act in a different way from how she would normally. Without any kind of intention, she is reaching for freedom, the freedom that her life had always lacked. Mrs. Mallard is a victim of the society of her days, a society in which women were seen just as objects of possession. This story was written in order to create consciousness in other women about the issue of oppression.

Work Cited

Chopin, Kate. "The Story of an Hour." 1894. Rpt. in *The International Story: An Anthology with Guidelines for Reading and Writing about Fiction*. Ruth Spack. New York: St. Martin's, 1994. 6–8.

Selecting Evidence for Critical Analysis of a Story

Chapter 6 is designed to help you select evidence from a short story to analyze and interpret the story. Guidelines are provided for inferring meaning from evidence and for using evidence to support a point or to answer a question.

The chapter is subdivided into sections that focus on different *elements of fiction* (character, setting, point of view, imagery, symbolism, tone) and on the development of an *abstract idea* or issue. In some stories, one element may stand out as the major device through which the meaning of the story is expressed. In other stories, the elements may be so closely connected that they are inseparable. In your essay, you may focus on one element or combine a study of two or more elements. For example, you might examine primarily one character, or you might examine the relationship between character and setting. Or your essay may focus on an abstract idea, and you might examine several elements of fiction to reveal how the idea is developed in the story.

Whatever your chosen topic, your goal is to select pertinent details from a story to support the points you are making about the topic. Although presentation of details is selective (you cannot present every detail of a story in your essay), you should be careful not to deliberately ignore details because they contradict your points. If there is a contradiction, you can adjust your focus to reflect the details. By the same token, you should be careful not to create details that do not appear in the story. Although you are interpreting—reading between the lines—you should analyze only the lines that the author provides.

SELECTING EVIDENCE ABOUT CHARACTER

Characters are the people in stories, or the animals or objects that have human traits.

Character *is a term that refers to*
- outward appearance and behavior
- inner emotional, intellectual, and moral qualities

Character *is revealed in a story by*
- how a person is described

277

- what a person does, says, and thinks
- what others in the story say and think about the person
- how others in the story react to the person

Character *is also revealed by*
- the choices the person makes
- the changes the person undergoes

Character *is often shaped by a struggle between opposing forces, involving*
- internal conflict: person vs. self
- external conflict: person vs. person
  person vs. nature
  person vs. society
  person vs. fate

When you undergo the process of analyzing a character, you should examine any of the aspects of character listed above that are applicable to the story.

Most stories have at least one *main* or *major character* (sometimes called the *hero* or *heroine* or *protagonist*), the person around whom the story revolves. Most stories also have at least one *minor character*, a character who is not the focus of the story but who still plays an important role. Often these characters provide contrasts with one another. Examining each character and the relationships between and among characters can help you interpret a story.

Analyzing Key Words and Phrases Related to Character

Since characters are created out of words, it is a good idea to look closely at the words used by the author to develop a character. A short story writer rarely tells readers directly what a character is like. Instead, the writer *suggests* what the character is like. By studying suggestive words carefully, you may be able to find a pattern that reveals (1) the significance of a character's outer appearance and (2) the character's inner emotional, intellectual, and/or moral qualities.

ANALYZING OUTER APPEARANCE

The following passage is taken from Heinrich Böll's "Like a Bad Dream" (pp. 126–31), originally published in Germany in 1966. The italicized words refer to the narrator's outer appearance.

> Bertha had decided what I was to wear: *a dark jacket, trousers a shade lighter*, and *a conservative tie*. That's the kind of thing she learned at home, and at boarding school from the nuns. Also what to offer guests: when to pass the cognac, and when the vermouth, how to arrange dessert. It is comforting to have a wife who knows all about such things.

In the preceding paragraph, the narrator tells how he is dressed. There are many ways to interpret this information. The description suggests that he is dressed appropriately, since some care has been taken to assure that his trousers are "a shade lighter" than his "dark" jacket. That his tie is "conservative" might reflect his own conservative attitude—or the attempt to appear conservative. Of course, a consistent interpretation of these details can be achieved only when the information provided in this paragraph is compared with information provided in the rest of the story. In that way, the full significance of the narrator's outer appearance can be revealed.

ANALYZING INNER QUALITIES

Another look at the paragraph reveals other significant information about the narrator. While each reader might focus on different details, the italicized words refer to one reader's discovery of clues to the narrator's inner qualities.

> *Bertha had decided* what I was to wear: a dark jacket, trousers a shade lighter, and a conservative tie. That's the kind of thing she learned at home, and at boarding school from the nuns. Also what to offer guests: when to pass the cognac, and when the vermouth, how to arrange dessert. *It is comforting to have a wife who knows all about such things.*

The italicized details reveal something about the narrator's relationship with his wife. He allows her to make decisions about such basic things as his clothing ("Bertha had decided what I was to wear"). It also appears that his wife makes many other decisions about how they live ("Also what to offer guests . . ."). A clue to the narrator's feeling about this relationship can be found in the last sentence: he finds it "comforting." There are many ways to interpret this information: the main character may be indecisive, dominated, insecure, and/or in love. It is even possible that he is being sarcastic. A consistent interpretation can be accomplished only by looking at this passage in the context of the whole story, to see how these details fit a pattern of behavior and thinking that reveals what this man is really like.

ACTIVITY: *Analyzing key words and phrases related to a character*

Read the following passage, the first paragraph of Mishima Yukio's story, "Swaddling Clothes" (pp. 132–36), originally published in Japan in 1966.

1. Underline or in some way identify words or phrases that refer to the husband's outer appearance. Analyze those words or phrases to discover the possible significance of the description.
2. Then underline or in some way identify words or phrases that you

think refer to the husband's inner qualities. Analyze those words or phrases to discover clues to what the character is really like.

> He was always busy, Toshiko's husband. Even tonight he had to dash off to an appointment, leaving her to go home alone by taxi. But what else could a woman expect when she married an actor—an attractive one? No doubt she had been foolish to hope that he would spend the evening with her. And yet he must have known how she dreaded going back to their house, unhomely with its Western-style furniture and with the bloodstains still showing on the floor.   ●

Developing a Vocabulary for Discussing Character

When you analyze a character, you re-create that character by using primarily your own words to reveal what a character is really like.

As you analyze key words and phrases about character (see the section above), you need to describe and interpret the character's appearance and behavior. While you already have some vocabulary to achieve this goal, it is useful to expand that vocabulary to make your writing more vivid and precise.

The following adjectives represent only a small number of possible adjectives that can be applied to various characters in fiction. Within each group of synonyms, each word has a slightly different meaning or emphasis. Some words have a strongly positive connotation, others have a strongly negative connotation, and others may be weakly positive or negative. The activity that follows the list can help you discover the subtle differences in meaning.

1. evil, wicked, sinful, corrupt, unprincipled
2. kind, tender, mild, gracious, indulgent
3. beautiful, handsome, graceful, elegant, delicate
4. foolish, silly, simple, unwise, indiscreet
5. insensitive, indifferent, dull, frigid, cold-hearted
6. impotent, powerless, weak, helpless, incompetent
7. submissive, obedient, passive, humble, resigned
8. strong, energetic, tough, forceful, powerful
9. strict, religious, harsh, rigid, scrupulous
10. sincere, frank, honest, open, artless
11. shy, fearful, modest, timid, wary
12. dishonest, false, crooked, deceptive, dishonorable
13. proud, arrogant, haughty, dignified, majestic
14. successful, prosperous, fortunate, victorious, unbeaten
15. discontent, depressed, regretful, displeased, morose
16. honest, candid, genuine, upright, ingenuous

ACTIVITY: *Developing a vocabulary for discussing character*

Working in pairs or a small group, select one set of words from the list above.

1. Using a dictionary, discover a precise meaning of each word in the set.
2. Using the precise meaning that you have discovered, create a character (either orally or in writing) who fits the definition of one of the words. Describe a circumstance in which the chosen trait is revealed.
3. Either orally or by reading what you have written, share the circumstance you have created with the rest of the class. Your classmates can try to guess the character trait that you are illustrating. •

ACTIVITY: *Identifying character traits*

Read the following passage, the first paragraph of Mishima Yukio's story, "Swaddling Clothes" (pp. 132–36), originally published in Japan in 1966. Identify one or two of Toshiko's character traits, as revealed in this passage. (You may want to consult the list of adjectives on p. 280.) Explain which details led you to characterize her in this way.

> He was always busy, Toshiko's husband. Even tonight he had to dash off to an appointment, leaving her to go home alone by taxi. But what else could a woman expect when she married an actor—an attractive one? No doubt she had been foolish to hope that he would spend the evening with her. And yet he must have known how she dreaded going back to their house, unhomely with its Western-style furniture and with the bloodstains still showing on the floor. •

Asking Questions about Character

One of the best ways to achieve an understanding of characters can be to ask yourself a series of questions. By answering some or all of the following questions about the characters in a story, you may discover an aspect of the story that you would like to analyze.

Note: Not all of the questions will apply to every story you read.

Main character(s)
1. Who is the main character? (or main characters, if there is more than one)
   a. What is significant about how the main character is described?
   b. What are the main character's significant actions? What motivates the character to behave in this way?
   c. What are the main character's significant spoken words? Why are they significant?
   d. What are the main character's inner thoughts and feelings?

Choices
2. Does the main character have choices?
   a. If so, how do the choices help you understand the story?
   b. If not, what is the significance of the lack of choice?

Conflicts
3. Is there an internal conflict, for example, is the character struggling with inner impulses that are difficult to control? with a guilty conscience?
4. Is there an external conflict, for example, is the character struggling against another character? against nature? against society? against fate?

Changes
5. Does the main character undergo changes?
   a. If so, how do the changes help you understand the story?
   b. If not, what is the significance of the lack of change?

Minor character(s)
6. Who are the minor characters?
   a. What is significant about how they react to the main character?
   b. What is significant about how the main character reacts to the minor characters?
   c. What is significant about what the minor characters say to or think about the main character?

ACTIVITY: *Asking questions about character*

All of the short stories in this book have characters worthy of analysis. Select one of the stories and apply some or all of the above questions to the characters. Record any ideas you discover that you might want to write about in an interpretive essay.   ●

Focusing on a Topic for an Essay on Character

When you write an essay about characters, your primary goal is to explore the significance of, prove a point about, or answer a question about the character(s). Another goal is to show the connection between the character(s) and the work as a whole by discussing a larger meaning of the story.

There are numerous ways to examine fictional characters. The following topics may give you an idea of how to approach the writing of the essay. You can select one of the topics, combine topics, or design your own topic, with your instructor's approval.

1. Analyze the character's major traits, one by one.
2. Analyze the character's growth or change.
3. Analyze the central events in the character's life, one by one.
4. Analyze the character's inner conflict.

5. Analyze the conflict between or among characters.
6. Analyze the relationship between character and another element of fiction, such as setting.
7. Compare and analyze characters from different stories.

You may also select a topic from the activities related to character in Chapter 4, "Discussion Activities." For example, a suggested topic for a literary journal entry may become the focus for an essay. Your instructor may provide other specific suggestions for writing about a particular story.

SELECTING EVIDENCE ABOUT SETTING

The term *setting* refers to a story's place, time, social environment, and physical environment. The setting is often connected to character development and/or to the values of the society in which a story is set. Setting can even have a direct effect on characters and action. Characters' attitude and behavior may be influenced by the time and place in which they live. Characters' emotional states can be affected by the physical environment.

Setting is created primarily through images. Often an aspect of the setting is actually a symbol representing something else. For example, a wall can symbolize a barrier of communication between two people. Therefore when you discuss setting you often discuss imagery and symbolism (see pp. 294–305).

In some short stories, the setting is central. Other stories have few or no references to setting. When details of setting are provided, they can give clues to a story's meanings or significance.

Details related to **place** *may provide information about*
- the geographical location (for example, the country or city)
- the size and type of location (for example, a large city or a small village)
- the site of the action (for example, indoors or outdoors, a room or a street)

Details related to **time** *may provide information about*
- the length of time during which the action occurs (for example, several years or only an hour)
- the time of day (for example, through actual clock time or through descriptions of light, darkness, and shadows, or through activities such as eating supper)
- time of year (for example, through references to the seasons)
- the year (for example, 1931)
- the period of history (for example, World War I)

Details related to **social environment** *may provide information about*
- social and economic class or level
- manners

- customs
- rules
- religious rites
- moral codes

A story's **physical environment** *may be revealed through references to or descriptions of*
- nature
- objects
- clothing
- physical appearance
- buildings and rooms
- climate and weather
- sounds, smells

These details often
- indicate the emotional or moral state of the characters
- indicate the relationship between and among characters

Analyzing Key Words and Phrases Related to Setting

Writers of fiction create imaginary worlds using real-life words and images. They select whatever suits their purpose: location, time, social environment, and so on. Often the setting reflects a character's inner thoughts or a whole society's set of values. By examining closely the real-life words and images related to the setting of the story, you can uncover something significant.

The following passage is the sixth paragraph of Joyce Carol Oates's story, "Where Are You Going, Where Have You Been?" (United States, 1970), which can be found in its entirety in Oates's short story collection, *Wheel of Love.* "Where Are You Going, Where Have You Been?" is the story of a fifteen-year-old girl who spends much of her time hanging out at a shopping mall with her friends. The girl is ultimately attracted to a man who turns out to be dangerous. The italicized words in the passage refer to an aspect of the setting—a restaurant—that holds clues to the story's meaning.

> Sometimes they [fifteen-year-old girls] did go shopping or to a movie, but sometimes they went across the highway, ducking fast across the busy road, to *a drive-in restaurant* where older kids hung out. *The restaurant was shaped like a big bottle, though squatter than a real bottle, and on its cap was a revolving figure of a grinning boy who held a hamburger aloft.* One night in mid-summer they ran across, breathless with daring, and right away someone leaned out a car window and invited them over, but it was just a boy from high school they didn't like. It made them feel good to be able to ignore him. They went up through the maze of parked and cruising cars to *the bright-lit, fly-infested restaurant,* their faces pleased and expectant as if they were entering a sacred building that

loomed out of the night to give them what haven and what blessing they yearned for. They sat at *the counter* and crossed their legs
at the ankles, their thin shoulders rigid with excitement and listened to the music that made everything so good: the *music was
always in the background* like music at a church service, it was
something to depend on.

In the above paragraph, the narrator reveals that the restaurant the girls go
to is a "drive-in." A drive-in restaurant is usually one which has no indoor
seating. There is a "counter" at which people can sit on high stools to order
their food. But the food is often eaten in cars in the parking lot of the
restaurant. Why does Oates set this scene in a drive-in restaurant? There
are many possible reasons for this. Perhaps she wants to suggest a world
that lacks comfortable intimacy, for there is no opportunity here for people
to sit together indoors. Perhaps she wants to suggest something about some
American teenagers' tendency to hang out outdoors, like hunters and
hunted. You can speculate on other reasons.

This particular drive-in restaurant "was shaped like a bottle" on top of
which was "a revolving figure of a grinning boy who held a hamburger."
Such restaurants with plastic figures do exist in the United States. It is
possible that Oates is simply describing one such restaurant. But perhaps
there is a deeper reason for this choice. Perhaps the emphasis is on the
hamburger: a food product that tastes good but that has negative nutritional
value. Does this reflect the values of the teenagers (for example, physical
pleasure is more important than health)? What other interpretations are
possible?

That the restaurant is "bright-lit" and "fly-infested," with "music always in the background," can lead to further interpretation of the values of
these young people and also of the people who own and run such establish-
ments.

A further look at the same paragraph reveals other significant information. While each reader may focus on different details, the italicized words
refer to one reader's discovery of clues to the values of the teenagers.

Sometimes they [fifteen-year-old girls] did go shopping or to
a movie, but sometimes they went across the highway, ducking
fast across the busy road, to a drive-in restaurant where older kids
hung out. The restaurant was shaped like a big bottle, though
squatter than a real bottle, and on its cap was a revolving figure of
a grinning boy who held a hamburger aloft. One night in midsummer they ran across, breathless with daring, and right away
someone leaned out a car window and invited them over, but it
was just a boy from high school they didn't like. It made them
feel good to be able to ignore him. They went up through the
maze of parked and cruising cars to the bright-lit, fly-infested restaurant, *their faces pleased and expectant as if they were entering a sacred building that loomed out of the night to give them what haven and
what blessing they yearned for.* They sat at the counter and crossed

their legs at the ankles, their thin shoulders rigid with excitement and *listened to the music that made everything so good:* the music was always in the background *like music at a church service, it was something to depend on.*

The narrator tells us that this restaurant is "shaped like a big bottle" and is "fly-infested." Yet to the girls it is a "sacred building" that gives them "haven" and a "blessing." Furthermore, to them, the music—which we may assume is loud rock music that teenagers enjoy—is "like music at a church service." What is the author suggesting? Perhaps conventional religion, the kind that provides ethical and moral values, has been replaced in this modern society by something more superficial, more plastic, more pleasurable. You can speculate on other interpretations that might explain this passage. Of course, a consistent interpretation can be accomplished only by looking at this passage in the context of the whole story, to see how these details fit into an overall pattern that reveals the significance of this environment.

ACTIVITY: *Analyzing key words and phrases related to setting*

Read the following passage, the first paragraph of Tayeb Salih's story, "A Handful of Dates" (pp. 137–40), originally published in Sudan in 1968. (*Note:* The *Koran* is the sacred text of the religion of Islam; a *mosque* is a Moslem house of worship.)

1. Underline or in some way identify phrases that refer to a specific place or time.
2. Then underline or in some way identify words or phrases in the passage that indicate the significance of the place or time.

> I must have been very young at the time. While I don't remember exactly how old I was, I do remember that when people saw me with my grandfather they would pat me on the head and give my cheek a pinch—things they didn't do to my grandfather. The strange thing was that I never used to go out with my father, rather it was my grandfather who would take me with him wherever he went, except for the mornings when I would go to the mosque to learn the Koran. The mosque, the river, and the fields—these were the landmarks in our life. While most of the children of my age grumbled at having to go to the mosque to learn the Koran, I used to love it. The reason was, no doubt, that I was quick at learning by heart and the Sheikh always asked me to stand up and recite the *Chapter of the Merciful* whenever we had visitors, who would pat me on my head and cheek just as people did when they saw me with my grandfather.   ●

Developing a Vocabulary for Discussing Setting

When you analyze a story's setting, you re-create that setting in your own words. While you already have some vocabulary to achieve this goal, it is useful to expand that vocabulary to make your writing more vivid and precise.

The following adjectives represent only a small number of possible adjectives that can be applied to various settings in fiction. Within each group of synonymns, each word has a slightly different meaning or emphasis. The activity that follows the list can help you discover the subtle differences in meaning.

1. clean, tidy, spotless, orderly
2. dirty, murky, filthy, polluted
3. spacious, expansive, boundless, ample
4. dark, gloomy, evil, threatening
5. peaceful, quiet, harmonious, placid
6. romantic, idealistic, sentimental, fanciful
7. dangerous, threatening, hazardous, unprotected
8. dilapidated, decayed, ruined, crumbling
9. dismal, gloomy, depressing, somber
10. elegant, tasteful, cultured, luxurious
11. mysterious, secret, mystical, obscure
12. nasty, unpleasant, offensive, foul
13. natural, real, typical, authentic
14. warm, friendly, congenial, intimate
15. spiritual, religious, sacred, supernatural
16. pleasant, appealing, enchanting, captivating

ACTIVITY: *Developing a vocabulary for discussing setting*

Working in pairs or in a small group, select one set of words from the list above.

1. Using a dictionary, discover the precise meaning of each word in the set and the subtle differences of meaning or emphasis among them.
2. Using the precise meaning that you have discovered, create a scene (either orally or in writing) whose setting fits the definition of one of these words.
3. Either orally or by reading what you have written, share the scene you have created with the rest of the class. Your classmates can try to identify the descriptive adjective that you are illustrating.   ●

ACTIVITY: *Generalizing from details*

Read the first paragraph of Tayeb Salih's "A Handful of Dates," reprinted on page 286. Then describe the scene by using one or more adjectives listed above.   ●

Asking Questions about Setting

One effective way to generate ideas about a story's setting can be to ask yourself a series of questions. By answering some or all of the following questions about the setting in a story, you may discover an aspect of the story that you would like to analyze.

Note: Not all of the questions will apply to every story you read.

Place

1. What is significant about where the story takes place?

Time

2. How long does it take for the action to occur? Is there anything signficant about the length of time it takes for the sequence of events/thoughts to occur?
3. What is significant about the time of day in which the story takes place?
4. What is significant about the time of year in which the story takes place?
5. What is significant about the year(s) or the historical period in which the story takes place?

Social environment

6. What is significant about the manners, customs, rules, and/or moral codes of the society in which the story takes place?

Physical environment

7. Which physical details reveal the emotional or moral state(s) of the character(s)? (Examine references to nature, objects, buildings and rooms, clothing, climate and weather, sounds, smells, and so on.)
8. Which physical details reveal the nature of the relationship between or among characters?

ACTIVITY: *Asking questions about setting*

Select a story from this book, and apply some or all of the above questions to the details related to setting. Record any ideas you discover that you may want to write about in an interpretive essay.   ●

Focusing on a Topic for an Essay on Setting

When you write an essay about setting, your primary goal is to explore the significance of, prove a point about, or answer a question about the setting. Another goal is to show the connection between the setting and the work as a whole, by discussing a larger meaning of the story.

There are numerous ways to examine setting. The following topics may give you an idea of how to approach the writing of the essay. You can select one of the topics, combine topics, or design your own topic, with your instructor's approval.

1. Begin at the beginning of the story, and analyze each different place in which the action of the story occurs.
2. Select one image, such as a door or wall, and then analyze each scene in which the door or wall is significant.
3. Analyze one key scene, for example a scene of nature or a scene in a restaurant, and then analyze the relationship between that scene and the main character's inner thoughts, growth, or change, or between that scene and the society's values.
4. Analyze the indoor scenes, then analyze the outdoor scenes.
5. Compare and analyze settings from different stories.

You may also select a topic from the activities related to setting in Chapter 4, "Discussion Activities." For example, a suggested topic for a literary journal entry may become the focus for an essay. Your instructor may provide other specific suggestions for writing about a particular story.

SELECTING EVIDENCE ABOUT POINT OF VIEW

Point of view is a literary term that refers to the perspective from which a story is told. An author creates a *narrator* to tell the story, someone who may or may not be a character in the story. It is through the narrator's perspective (through the narrator's eyes and mind) that readers learn what happens in the story. Point of view is a technique and the narrator is a device that an author uses to influence the way a reader interprets a story.

The narrator who tells the story from a first-person perspective
- may be the main character
- may be a minor character
- may be an adult looking back on childhood (resulting in a "dual" or "double" point of view: the perspective of the child *and* the perspective of the adult narrator)

The narrator who tells the story from a third-person perspective
- may be all-knowing (omniscient): telling everything about all of the characters, including their inner thoughts
- may have limited knowledge of the characters: telling the inner thoughts of only one or two characters
- may be only an external observer: describing events objectively from the outside

The narrator
- is not the author
- may be unreliable
- does not necessarily hold or reflect the author's view

It is important to remember that even if the narrator knows almost everything about every character, the narrator is still limited in some way (since all human beings are limited in some way). It is only by piecing together several or all of the elements of fiction that you can move toward an understanding of the author's view.

Analyzing Key Words and Phrases Related to Point of View

When you analyze the point of view of a story, your primary purpose usually is to show how the point of view shapes a theme. You need to examine the author's technique to understand why the point of view the author has chosen helps lead readers to an understanding of the story.

The following passage is the first paragraph of John Updike's story, "A&P" (United States, 1962), which can be found in its entirety in Updike's short-story collection *Pigeon Feathers and Other Stories*. "A&P" is the name of a grocery store, which is where the story is set. The italicized words in the passage provide clues to the narrator's character and reliability.

> In *walks* these three girls in nothing but bathing suits. I'm in the third checkout slot, with my back to the door, so I don't see them until they're over by the bread. The one that caught my eye first was the one in the plaid green two-piece. She was a chunky kid, with a good tan and *a sweet broad soft-looking can with those two crescents of white just under it, where the sun never seems to hit*, at the top of the backs of her legs. I stood there with my hand on a box of HiHo crackers trying to remember if I rang it up or not. I ring it up again and *the customer starts giving me hell*. She's *one of these cash-register-watchers, a witch about fifty* with rouge on her cheekbones and no eyebrows, and I know *it made her day to trip me up*. She'd been watching cash registers for fifty years and probably never seen a mistake before.

IDENTIFYING THE NARRATOR

Since this is only the first paragraph of a story, it would be too early to determine whether this first-person narrator is the main character. But there are clues as to this narrator's gender and age. It is probably safe to assume that anyone so focused on three girls in bathing suits is male. His use of language provide clues as to his age and perhaps his educational background. His nonstandard grammar—he uses "walks" instead of "walk"—may suggest that he is not yet an adult, either because he has not yet gained mastery of the English language or because he chooses not to speak English well. What else might this detail reflect?

Other uses of language may suggest his adolescence: it is not uncommon for a young man to be sexually aroused by "a sweet broad soft-looking can [buttocks]." His adolescence is further emphasized in his use of the slang expression "giving me hell" and in his disdain of a woman who is "about fifty" and whom he refers to as "a witch." What other details might suggest his age?

DETERMINING THE NARRATOR'S RELIABILITY

How reliable is this narrator? To some extent, the answer to that question depends upon who the reader is. For example, certain male adolescents reading the story might identify with the narrator and thus accept his story as valid. Certain older adult readers might be more skeptical. Such readers might focus on the narrator's possible poor education, might interpret the narrator's attitude toward females as immature, might see the narrator as too emotionally involved with or too prejudiced toward the other characters. Any of these reactions could cause readers to question the reliability of the narrator.

A fuller understanding of why the author chose to tell this story from the point of view of a male adolescent can be achieved only by studying this passage in the context of the whole story. Only then will it become clear how this point of view helps to shape the meanings or significance of the story.

ACTIVITY: *Analyzing key words and phrases related to point of view*

Read the following passage, the first paragraph of Massud Farzan's 1969 story, "The Plane Reservation" (pp. 141–46), which is set in Iran. Underline or copy words or phrases that provide clues to the background, character and/or reliability of the narrator. Analyze those words or phrases.

> We lived on 23 Sadness Street. But it was a narrow street—cars couldn't enter—so I asked the cabdriver to drop me on the corner of Sadness and Pomegranate Blossoms. I paid the fare we had settled at the airport, plus a generous tip. The driver asked for more, speaking slowly and with funny gestures. I said no, and why do you speak like that, I am not a foreigner; I am just a Persian like yourself. He became embarrassed and I paid him a little more. He then helped me carry the heavy suitcase as far as 23 Sadness Street. ●

Developing a Vocabulary for Discussing Point of View

Much of the vocabulary you use to analyze point of view has been presented: first-person narrator, dual point of view, unreliable, objective, limited, omniscient, and so on.

In addition to using some of these words, you will also need to know how to refer to the narrator. If the narrator has a name, of course you can use the name. But often the narrator's name is not given. If the unnamed narrator is telling the story in the first person, you can refer to the narrator as "the narrator" or "the speaker." If the narrator's profession or some other identification is provided, you can refer to "the lawyer" or to "the husband." For variety, you may use a term such as "the lawyer-narrator." Remember not to refer to the narrator as "the author."

The verb tense to use when writing about the narrator is primarily the present tense (see p. 342). For example, you can write:

"The narrator reveals . . ."
"The narrator discloses . . ."
"The narrator brings to light . . ."

"The narrator recognizes . . ."
"The narrator learns . . ."
"The narrator discovers . . ."

"The narrator thinks . . ."
"The narrator perceives . . ."
"The narrator imagines . . ."

"Through the narrator we learn . . ."
"According to the narrator, the main character is . . ."
"Using the first-person point of view, the author creates a narrator who . . ."

ACTIVITY: *Analyzing point of view*

Read the paragraph on p. 290 taken from John Updike's story "A&P." Using the present tense, describe the narrator, providing details from the paragraph to support your description. ●

Asking Questions about Point of View

One effective way to generate ideas about point of view can be to ask yourself a series of questions. By answering some or all of the following questions about the point of view of a story, you may discover an aspect of the story that you would like to analyze.

Note: Not all of the questions will apply to every story you read.

Identifying point of view

1. Is the story told from a first-person point of view or from a third-person point of view?
2. Is the narrator a major character, a minor character, or a nonparticipant?
3. If the narrator is the main character,
   a. Is the story told from the perspective of an adult, an adolescent, or a child?
   b. Is the story told from a dual point of view (for example, through the perspective of the adult narrator *and* the child that the narrator used to be)?
4. How much does the narrator know about the main character?
5. How much does the narrator know about the minor characters?
6. Does the narrator analyze or comment on the action and/or characters? Or is the narrator simply an objective observer?

Analyzing point of view

7. How reliable is the narrator?
   a. What is the narrator's background?
   b. What is the narrator's relationship to the other characters?
   c. How did the narrator acquire the information that is presented? Are the sources reliable?
   d. Is there anything unique or special about the way the narrator presents the information that suggests something about the narrator's character?
   e. Does the narrator seem to be withholding information or ignoring significant facts?
   f. Is the narrator emotionally involved in any of the situations?
   g. Does the narrator reveal any prejudice toward any of the characters?
   h. Does the narrator ever seem confused?
   i. If the narrator comments on the characters or action, are the comments valid?
   j. Does the narrator undergo any changes that affect the information?
   k. What is your overall impression of the narrator?
8. Why do you think the author has chosen this point of view? How would the story be different if it were told from another point of view?

ACTIVITY: *Asking questions about point of view*

Select a short story from this book, and apply the relevant questions (above) to determine and analyze point of view. Record any ideas you discover that you may want to write about in an interpretive essay.   ●

Focusing on a Topic for an Essay on Point of View

When you write an essay about point of view, your primary goal is to explore the significance of, prove a point about, or answer a question about point of view. Another goal is to show the connection between point of view and the work as a whole, by discussing a larger meaning of the story.

There are numerous ways to examine point of view. The following topics may give you an idea of how to approach the writing of the essay. You can select one of the topics, combine topics, or design your own topic, with your instructor's approval.

1. Analyze the reliability of the narrator.
2. Analyze the changes the narrator undergoes, and relate those changes to the events of the story.
3. Analyze why this particular perspective is effective for telling the story.
4. If there is a double perspective, compare, contrast, and analyze the

different perspectives (for example, the perspective of the child and the perspective of the adult that the child has become).

5. Analyze the relationship between point of view and another element of fiction, such as setting.
6. Compare and analyze points of view in different stories.

You may also select a topic from the activites related to point of view in Chapter 4, "Discussion Activities." For example, a suggested topic for a literary journal entry may become the focus for an essay. Your instructor may provide other specific suggestions for writing about a particular story.

SELECTING EVIDENCE ABOUT IMAGERY

Writers of fiction use everyday language in unique ways to go beyond physical description in order to express feelings and states of mind. This unique use of language is known as *figurative language:* words that carry suggestive or symbolic meaning in addition to their literal (primary, factual) meaning. Most figurative language is created through *images:* mental pictures that tap into readers' past experiences and memories and, through association, allow them to imagine, visualize, and re-create physical scenes and sensations.

Writers use images in various ways to bring the world of the story alive and to give it deeper meaning; some of those ways are illustrated below. (*Note:* Examples are taken from Ray Bradbury's 1950 story, "There Will Come Soft Rains," which can be found in his collection, *The Martian Chronicles.* "There Will Come Soft Rains" is the story of a house that survives a nuclear attack.)

1. A writer uses imagery (a collection of images) to appeal to readers' senses of
   - *sight:* "The house stood alone in a city of rubble and ashes."
   - *sound:* "In the living room the voice-clock sang, '*Tick-tock, seven o'clock, time to get up, time to get up, seven o'clock!*' as if it were afraid that nobody would."
   - *taste:* "two cool glasses of milk"
   - *smell:* "Behind the door, the stove was making pancakes which filled the house with a rich baked odor and the scent of maple syrup."
   - *touch:* "hands raised to catch a ball"
2. A writer uses *figures of speech* to make unusual, unpredictable comparisons that give images rich associations or deeper meaning:
   - *simile:* an explicit comparison between two things of a different kind or quality, usually introduced by *like* (with nouns) or *as*
     "Heat snapped mirrors like the first brittle winter ice."
     "the regiments of mice hummed out as softly as blown gray leaves in an electrical wind"

- *metaphor:* an implied comparison (not introduced by *like* or *as*) between two things of a different kind of quality
"The house was an altar."
- *personification:* human or lifelike qualities given to something non-human or lifeless.
"the fire was clever"

3. A writer sometimes creates concrete images as *symbols* that stand for something abstract or invisible. (For a fuller discussion of symbols, see "Selecting Evidence about Symbolism," pp. 299–305.)

Analyzing Key Words and Phrases Related to Imagery

When you analyze a story's imagery, your primary purpose is to un-cover the author's purpose in creating certain images and patterns of images and to reveal the connection between that purpose and a larger meaning of the story.

The following passage is taken from James Joyce's 1914 story, "Araby" (pp. 69–73). The narrator of the story is describing the evening play of a group of boys. Though the passage is full of images, only a few have been selected and italicized to show how image patterns can be interpreted.

> When the short days of winter came dusk fell before we [boys] had well eaten our dinners. When we met in the street the houses had grown sombre. The space of the sky above us was the colour of ever-changing violet and towards it the lamps of the street lifted their feeble lanterns. The cold air stung us and we played till our bodies glowed. Our shouts echoed in the silent street. The career of our play brought us through the *dark muddy lanes* behind the houses where we ran the gauntlet of the rough tribes from the cottages, to the back doors of the *dark dripping gardens* where odours arose from the ashpits, to the *dark odorous stables* where a coachman smoothed and combed the horse or shook music from the buckled harness. When we returned to the street light from the kitchen windows had filled the areas.

In this passage, the narrator reveals that the area where the boys play has "dark muddy lanes," "dark dripping gardens," and "dark odorous stables." The word *dark* is repeated three times, making it a dominant image. Why is this image significant? According to *The American Heritage Dictionary*, the primary meaning of *dark* is "with very little or no light." So, literally, the boys are playing in the dark, in the evening. But *dark* is a word that can have a negative connotation. Other definitions include "gloomy," "evil," "threatening," or "unenlightened." What might Joyce be suggesting by using the word *dark?*

Other words in the italicized phrases provide vivid images. "Lanes," "gardens," and "stables," in some contexts, can be connected to positive images. But the lanes are "muddy," the gardens are "dripping," and the stables are "odorous": all negative images in the context of this passage. By activating senses of sight (mud), sound (drip), and smell (odor), Joyce enables readers to visualize and imagine this scene. What could Joyce be implying by combining positive and negative images?

Why does Joyce place boys at play in such an environment? What do these images suggest about the environment in which the boys are growing up? What might the contrast between the ideal of boys at play (a positive image) and the actual scene of the play (a negative image) reveal?

Many interpretations are possible. Of course, a full interpretation of the images of this passage can be accomplished only by studying the passage in the context of the whole story. Only then will it become clear how images help to shape the story's meanings.

ACTIVITY: *Analyzing images*

Read the following passage, the first paragraph of Anton Chekhov's 1888 story, "A Trifle from Real Life" (pp. 53–57). Underline or in some way identify words or phrases or figures of speech that enable you to create mental pictures of what the author describes. Then analyze the images to discover the author's possible purpose in creating them.

> Nikolai Ilitch Belayeff was a young gentleman of St. Petersburg, aged thirty-two, rosy, well fed, and a patron of the race-tracks. Once, toward evening, he went to pay a call on Olga Ivanovna with whom, to use his own expression, he was dragging through a long and tedious love-affair. And the truth was that the first thrilling, inspiring pages of this romance had long since been read, and that the story was now dragging wearily on, presenting nothing that was either interesting or novel.

Developing a Vocabulary for Discussing Imagery

When you analyze a story's imagery, you need adjectives that allow you to make generalizations about the images (see lists of selected adjectives on pp. 280 and 287). You also need verbs that enable you to discuss the literal and suggestive meanings of the images.

The following verbs are among those commonly used to discuss imagery in fiction. They are provided with dictionary definitions and sample sentences. You can consult this list (and the lists on pp. 302–04 and 313) when you are writing your own paper.

delineate: to show by drawing or description; to portray; to outline

In "Araby," James Joyce *delineates* a life of confusion.

depict: to describe; to represent in words

Through images of darkness, Joyce *depicts* a secret world.

describe: to transmit a mental image with words

The narrator *describes* the house as "uninhabited" and "detached."

exemplify: to serve as an example of; to show by example

Araby *exemplifies* a world of romance.

express: to reveal; to represent by a sign or symbol

The "light from the kitchen windows" *expresses* warmth and homeyness.

illustrate: to make clear by using an example or comparison; to clarify by serving as an example or comparison

Through dark lanes, gardens, and stables, Joyce *illustrates* the gloomy atmosphere of the city.

personify: to give human or lifelike qualities to something nonhuman or lifeless

Joyce eerily *personifies* the street lamps, which "lifted their feeble lanterns."

portray: to describe in words; to create a picture of

Joyce *portrays* the boys' play as loud and energetic.

present: to offer for consideration

In the third paragraph of "Araby," Joyce *presents* a scene full of images of dark and light.

render: to represent in a verbal or artistic form

Joyce attempts to *render* what our participation in life is like.

reveal: to make known; to make known something that has been secret or hidden

Through the dark images, Joyce *reveals* that the life of the boys has a negative side.

show: to reveal; to indicate

By creating unpleasant images, Joyce *shows* the negative side of the boys' life.

sketch: to make an outline of; to indicate briefly

In just one or two paragraphs, Joyce *sketches* the life of the boys.

ACTIVITY: *Writing about images*

Read the first paragraph of Anton Chekhov's "A Trifle from Real Life," reprinted on page 296. Then, using the present tense, write a few lines in which you discuss the images that Chekhov creates.   ●

Asking Questions about Imagery

One of the best ways to generate ideas about imagery can be to ask yourself a series of questions. By answering some or all of the following questions about the images the author creates, you may discover an aspect of the story that you would like to discuss.

1. Which words appeal to the sense of sight? sound? taste? smell? touch?
2. Does one type of image predominate? For example, are most of the images related to sight, or to sound?
   a. If one sense predominates, how is this connected to the rest of the story?
      - Do the dominant sensory images reinforce a major idea or impression?
      - Do the dominant sensory images conflict with a major idea or impression?
   b. If there is a mixture of images, with no one sense predominating, how is this connected to the rest of the story?
      - Does the mixture of sensory images reinforce a major idea or impression?
      - Does the mixture of sensory images conflict with a major idea or impression?
   c. If there is a change from one type of image to another, how is this connected to the rest of the story?
      - Does the change reflect a change in a character or an idea?
      - Does the change parallel a development in the plot?
      - What does the change reveal about the story's meanings?
   d. If the images show a specific pattern (for example, images of color, or images of natural scenes), what is the significance of this pattern?
3. Do the images have positive or negative connotations? How are these positive or negative connotations connected to the story's meanings?

ACTIVITY: *Asking questions about imagery*

Select a short story from this a book, and apply some or all of the above questions to the images the author creates. Record any ideas you discover that you may want to write about in an interpretive essay.   ●

Focusing on a Topic for an Essay on Imagery

When you write an essay about imagery, your primary goal is to explore the significance of, prove a point about, or answer a question about the images. Another goal is to show the connection between imagery and the work as a whole, by discussing a larger meaning of the story.

There are numerous ways to examine imagery. The following topics may give you an idea of how to approach the writing of the essay. You can select one of the topics, combine topics, or design your own topic, with your instructor's approval.

1. Analyze a predominant image.
2. Analyze various images to show a pattern of references.
3. Analyze the relationship between imagery and another element of fiction, such as character.
4. Compare and analyze imagery in different stories.

You may also select a topic from the activities related to imagery in Chapter 4, "Discussion Activities." Your instructor may provide other specific suggestions for writing about a particular story.

SELECTING EVIDENCE ABOUT SYMBOLISM

A *symbol* is something that stands for something else. Often in a literary work, a symbol is a *concrete*, *physical* object (a thing, person, or place) or event that is used to represent something *abstract* or *invisible*, such as an emotion, an idea, or a value.

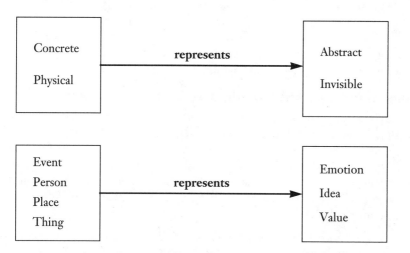

Not all objects or events in stories are symbols. Some objects or events are just what they are described or defined to be and have no hidden meaning. Some are simply images used to appeal to readers' senses (see "Selecting Evidence about Imagery," pp. 294–99).

Often if an author intends an object to be understood as symbolic, there will be some hint. For example, the description of the scenery surrounding characters is often connected to their actions or conversations (for example, foul-smelling air surrounding mean-spirited people). The repeated appearance or reference to an object (such as an egg or a crucifix) often suggests that the object holds a deeper meaning. A detailed description of the contents of a room or building may relate to the values or social status of the inhabitants or owners (for example, pictures of grandparents and children might represent the value of family life; expensive works of art might represent wealth). Likewise, the food characters eat, the clothes they wear, the books they read, the trips they take, the type of language they use, and so on, may hold clues as to their personalities, status, and values.

To determine whether these details are meant to be symbolic (that is, to actually represent something else) is to uncover the author's possible purpose in introducing them. Events and objects can have different kinds of meanings, depending on the author's intention and the reader's background. For example:

The meaning of an object or event can be

- *literal:* the object has a primary (factual) meaning, a dictionary definition
- *universal:* the object has a symbolic meaning that is understood in many countries around the world
- *cultural:* the object has a symbolic meaning that is understood only within a specific culture
- *contextual:* the object has a symbolic meaning that is understood only within the context of the story in which it appears

Determining an event's or object's literal and symbolic meanings can help you interpret a story (see also "Symbolism," pp. 31–32).

Analyzing Key Words and Phrases to Discover Symbolism

When you analyze a story's symbolism, your primary purpose is usually to show how the symbols lead to an understanding of the story's meanings.

The following passage is the first paragraph of James Joyce's 1914 "Araby" (pp. 69–73). Joyce's stories are full of symbolism. Although almost every image in "Araby" may have hidden meaning, only a few words in this passage have been selected and italicized to show how symbolic meaning can be inferred.

> North Richmond Street, being *blind*, was a quiet street except at the hour when the *Christian Brothers' School set the boys free.* An uninhabited house of two storeys stood at the *blind end*, detached from its neighbours in a square ground. The other houses of the street, conscious of decent lives within them, gazed at one another with brown imperturbable faces.

ANALYSIS OF LITERAL MEANING

The narrator is describing a street in Dublin, Ireland. The street is "blind." According to the *American Heritage Dictionary*, *blind* is an adjective that has thirteen meanings:

blind (blind) *adj.* **er, -est. 1.** Being without sight; sightless. **2.** Of, pertaining to, or for sightless persons. **3.** Performed by instruments and without the use of sight: *blind navigation.* **4.** Performed without preparation, forethought, or knowledge: *a blind attempt.* **5.** Unable or unwilling to perceive or understand: *blind to his faults.* **6.** Not based on reason or evidence: *blind faith.* **7.** *Slang.* Drunk. **8.** Independent of human control: *blind fate.* **9.a.** Difficult to comprehend or see; illegible: *blind writings.* **b.** Illegibly or incompletely addressed: *blind mail.* **10.a.** Hidden from sight: *a blind seam.* **b.** Screened from the view of an oncoming driver: *a blind intersection.* **11.** Closed at one end: *a blind socket.* **12.** Having no opening: *a blind wall.* **13.** *Bot.* Failing to flower.

The first stage of the process of understanding symbolism is to determine the literal meaning of a word as it is used in the story. In this story, the word *blind* is used to describe a street; the words that follow this description might reveal which of the thirteen dictionary definitions apply: "North Richmond street, being blind, was a quiet street." In other words, because the street is "blind," it is "quiet." That most logically leads to dictionary definition number 11: Closed at one end. If the street is closed at one end, there would be little or no traffic—and this would result in a "quiet" street. A later reference in the paragraph to the "blind end" of the street tells us that this is what is known as a dead-end street: a street with no exit.

ANALYSIS OF SYMBOLIC MEANING

After determining the literal meaning of the word *blind*, the next step can be to investigate its symbolic meaning. It is important to understand the use of the word in the context of the story. The first sentence states that the street is quiet except when the "Christian Brothers' School set the boys free." This suggests that the boys are not "free" until they leave school. What might Joyce be implying about this Christian school?

Once the boys leave school, the street is no longer quiet. This phenomenon is probably the result of the boys' noisily entering the street, perhaps to return home or to play. But this is a "blind" street, a street with no exit, a dead-end street. On a symbolic level, this could mean that, ironically, the boys are "set free" into an environment that has no exit, no way out. Given this meaning, what might the blind street symbolize?

Now, look back at the dictionary definitions to see if other meanings may apply.

Of course, a fuller understanding of the author's symbolic intentions can be achieved only by studying this passage in the context of the whole story. Only then will it become clear how symbols help to shape the meanings of the story.

ACTIVITY: Analyzing key words and phrases to discover symbolism

Read the following excerpt from the fifth paragraph of Sherwood Anderson's 1920 story, "The Egg" (pp. 78–85). Focus on an object or event that may suggest hidden meanings. Analyze the object or event for symbolic intent. (For best results, read at least the first four paragraphs of the story first.)

> One unversed in such matters [raising chickens on a farm] can have no notion of the many and tragic things that can happen to a chicken. It is born out of an egg, lives for a few weeks as a tiny fluffy thing such as you will see pictured on Easter cards, then becomes hideously naked, eats quantities of corn and meal bought by the sweat of your father's brow, gets diseases called pip, cholera, and other names, stands looking with stupid eyes at the sun, becomes sick and dies. A few hens and now and then a rooster, intended to serve God's mysterious ends, struggle through to maturity. The hens lay eggs out of which come other chickens and the dreadful cycle is thus made complete. It is all unbelievably complex.

Developing a Vocabulary for Discussing Symbolism

When you analyze a story's symbolism, you show what certain events and objects stand for. While you already have some vocabulary to achieve this goal, it is useful to expand that vocabulary to make your writing more vivid and precise.

The following verbs are among those commonly used to discuss symbolism in fiction. They are provided with dictionary definitions and sample sentences about James Joyce's "Araby" (pp. 69–73). You can consult this list when you are writing your own paper. (See also pp. 296–97 and 313.)

connote: to suggest or imply in addition to a literal meaning

> In the context of the story "Araby," the word "blind" *connotes* a world with no possibilities.

See usage note at *denote.*

convey: to transmit (an idea)

> Through the use of the word "blind," Joyce *conveys* the idea that the society in which the boys live is a dead-end world.

denote: to indicate; to refer to specifically; to mean explicitly

> In "Araby," the word "blind" *denotes* a place with a closed end.

Usage note: *Denote* is used to indicate the thing a word names, and *connote* to indicate our associations with that thing. Example: The word *home denotes* a place to live, but it *connotes* comfort and security.

embody: to represent in concrete form

> The "blind" street in "Araby" *embodies* the society in which the boys live.

evoke: to call to mind or memory

> The word "blind" itself *evokes* a sense of despair.

foreshadow: to indicate or suggest beforehand

> The "blind" street *foreshadows* the inner blindness of the main character.

hint (at): to convey an idea in an indirect fashion

> By setting his story in a "blind" street, Joyce *hints at* a world with a limited future.

imply: to express indirectly

> Joyce *implies* that the characters are as "blind" as the street.

infer: to conclude from evidence

> We can *infer* from the boy's later experience that the "blind" street is meant to suggest his inner blindness.

indicate: to serve as a sign (of)

> The use of the word "blind" twice in the same paragraph *indicates* that Joyce intends to call attention to it.

mirror: to reflect; to give back an image of

> The "blind" street *mirrors* the dead-end life of the boys.

prefigure: to foreshadow; to suggest, indicate or represent in advance

> The "blind" street *prefigures* the boy's inner blindness.

reflect: to give back an image of; to mirror

> The "blind end" of the street *reflects* a life of isolation.

represent: to stand for; to symbolize

> The "blind end" of the street *represents* the boys' limited possibilities.

signal: to make a sign that conveys information or initiates action; to make known a special characteristic

> The "blind" street *signals* the end of the boy's innocence.

signify: to have meaning; to serve as a sign of

> The "blind" street *signifies* the dead-end life of its inhabitants.

stand for: to represent; to symbolize

The "blind end" *stands for* the limitation of the boy's life.

suggest: to give a hint of; to call to mind by association

That the street is "blind" *suggests* that its inhabitants cannot see beyond their boundaries.

symbolize: to serve as a symbol of; to stand for; to represent

The "blind" street *symbolizes* the blindness of the society.

typify: to serve as a typical example of

The street described in the first paragraph of "Araby" *typifies* the streets in Dublin, Ireland.

ACTIVITY: *Writing about symbols*

Read the excerpt from Sherwood Anderson's "The Egg," reprinted on page 302. Then, using the present tense, write a few lines in which you discuss the possible symbolism in the paragraph.   ●

Asking Questions about Symbols

One of the best ways to generate ideas about symbols can be to ask yourself a series of questions. By answering some or all of the following questions about some of the events and objects in a story, you may discover some symbols that you would like to analyze.

Literal meaning
1. What is the dictionary definition of the object?
2. If there is more than one dictionary definition, which meaning applies to the story?
3. If more than one dictionary meaning applies to the story, might the author intend a double meaning? If so, what is the significance of the double meaning?

Universal meaning
4. Does the object have a symbolic meaning that is understood around the world?

Cultural meaning
5. Does the object have a symbolic meaning that is understood within the culture in which the story is set?

Contextual meaning
6. Does the object have a meaning that is symbolic only in the context of the story?

ACTIVITY: Asking questions to discover the symbolic meaning of events and objects

Select a short story from this book and apply the above questions to the objects and events in the story that you believe the author intends to be understood as symbolic. Record any ideas you discover that you may want to write about in an interpretive essay.   •

Focusing on a Topic for an Essay on Symbolism

When you write an essay about symbolism, your primary goal is to explore the significance of, prove a point about, or answer a question about the symbols. Another goal is to show the connection between symbolism and the work as a whole, by discussing a larger meaning of the story.

There are numerous ways to examine symbols. The following topics may give you an idea of how to approach the writing of the essay. You can select one of the topics, combine topics, or design your own topic, with your instructor's approval.

1. Analyze the meaning of a major symbol.
2. Analyze the meaning of and relationship among several symbols.
3. Analyze the relationship between symbolism and another element of fiction, such as character.
4. Compare and analyze symbolism in different stories.

You may also select a topic from the activities related to symbolism in Chapter 4, "Discussion Activities." For example, a suggested topic for a literary journal entry may become a focus for an essay. Your instructor may provide other specific suggestions for writing about a particular story.

SELECTING EVIDENCE ABOUT TONE

Tone is a literary term that refers to the feelings and attitudes generated by a story. Tone includes the emotional responses of the readers and the methods by which writers reveal their attitude or stance toward the characters, narrator, action, and subject of the story.

It is almost impossible to examine tone without examining *style:* a writer's *diction* (choice of words) and *sentence development* (arrangement of words). Tone is conveyed through the total effect created by the language an author uses, including *images* and *figures of speech* (pp. 30–31), *symbols* (pp. 31–32), and *irony* (pp. 33–34). Writers of fiction choose every word carefully to convey meaning.

Tone *is revealed through*
- the reader's reaction (for example, whether the reader feels sad, angry, afraid, delighted, and so on)
- the author's attitude
  a. toward the characters or narrator (for example, whether the au-

thor admires, is sympathetic toward, or is hostile toward the characters, and so on)

b. toward the action (for example, whether the author is bitter about, sarcastic toward, excited about, or shocked by what happens, and so on)

c. toward the subject matter (for example, whether the author is critical of, supportive of, or ambivalent about the subject, and so on)

When you begin the process of analyzing tone, you should examine your own reactions to the story as well as the language the author uses to produce those reactions and to convey the author's own attitudes.

Analyzing Key Words and Sentences Related to Tone

Since tone is conveyed primarily through the language an author uses, it is necessary to study the language of the story in order to discover its tone. Writers of fiction rarely, if ever, directly tell readers their attitudes toward the characters and ideas in their works. Instead, writers indirectly express their attitudes and feelings. By looking closely at diction, sentence structure, figures of speech, and so on, you can infer the tone and gain a deeper understanding of a story's meanings.

The following passage is the first paragraph of William Faulkner's "Dry September" (United States, 1931), which can be found in its entirety in *The Collected Stories of William Faulkner*. "Dry September" is the story of the lynching of an African-American man who is rumored to have raped a white woman. The opening passage describes a scene in a barber shop after the rumor has spread. Although several of the words and phrases in the passage give clues to the tone, only a few words have been italicized to show how an analysis of diction can provide clues to the author's attitude.

> Through the *bloody* September twilight, aftermath of sixty-two *rainless* days, it had gone like a fire in *dry* grass—the rumor, the story, whatever it was. Something about Miss Minnie Cooper and a Negro. Attacked, insulted, frightened: none of them, gathered in the barber shop on that Saturday evening where the fan stirred, without freshening it, the *vitiated* air, sending back upon them, in recurrent surges of *stale* pomade[1] and lotion, their own *stale* breath and odors, knew exactly what had happened.

ANALYSIS OF DICTION

The italicized words in this passage are all descriptive adjectives. Their primary (literal) definitions are provided along with some of their more suggestive dictionary definitions:

---

[1] **pomade:** perfumed hair ointment

WORD	LITERAL (DENOTATIVE) MEANING	SUGGESTIVE (CONNOTATIVE) MEANING
bloody	red (the color of blood)	cruel
rainless	without rain	arid (lacking feeling)
dry	lacking moisture	without tenderness
vitiated	spoiled	morally corrupt
stale	not fresh	impaired

The denotative definitions tell us what Faulkner literally describes. The suggestive meanings provide clues to Faulkner's attitude toward what he is describing.

Literally, the outdoor scene is *red* (probably because the twilight follows a red sunset) and it is *lacking moisture* because the town has been *without rain* for sixty-two days. The indoor scene, the barber shop, has air that is *spoiled* and *not fresh* (probably because of the heat and lack of moist air).

But Faulkner's choice of words suggests what he thinks about the town and its inhabitants. In this place where a rumor is spreading fast ("like a fire in dry grass") about something that happened between "Miss Minnie Cooper and a Negro," the atmosphere is *cruel* and the people *lack feeling and tenderness* and are *morally corrupt* and *impaired*. This, of course, is only one possible interpretation. A fuller understanding of the author's attitude toward the characters and ideas of the story can be achieved only by studying this passage in the context of the whole story.

ANALYSIS OF SENTENCE DEVELOPMENT

The passage on page 306, the first paragraph of "Dry September," consists of two sentences and a sentence fragment.

The first sentence consists of twenty-six words. The other sentence consists of forty-nine words. Both sentences require careful and repeated readings on the part of most readers, as they are long and their structure is not simple. It is possible that these difficult, complex sentences reflect Faulkner's sense that the situation of the story is troublesome and complicated. The unusual (and for some readers, confusing) order of the words, especially in the last sentence, may suggest the confusion of the situation.

The sentence fragment ("Something about Miss Minnie Cooper and a Negro"), which in grammatical terms is an incomplete sentence, may be structured deliberately to reflect the incomplete knowledge about the rumor ("none of them . . . knew exactly what had happened"). Faulkner may be implying that such incomplete knowledge, which reflects the ignorance of these people, can fragment a society.

ACTIVITY: Analyzing diction and sentence development

Read the following passage, the opening lines of Xi Xi's 1982 story, "A Woman Like Me," (pp. 152–62). Then answer these questions:

1. How do these opening lines make you feel?
   • Which words or phrases make you feel that way?
   • Does the length or structure or order of the sentences affect your response? If so, explain.
2. Based on your own impression of these opening lines, what do you think is the author's attitude toward the narrator?

> A woman like me is actually unsuitable for any man's love. So the fact that the emotional involvement between Xia and me has reached this point fills even me with wonder. I feel that the blame for my having fallen into this trap, from which there is no escape, rests solely with Fate, which has played a cruel trick on me. I am totally powerless to resist Fate. I've heard others say that when you truly like someone what may be nothing more than an innocent smile directed your way as you sit quietly in a corner can cause your very soul to take wing. That's exactly how I feel about Xia. So when he asked me: Do you like me? I expressed my feelings toward him without holding back a thing. I'm a person who has no concept of self-protection, and my words and deeds will always conspire to make me a laughing stock in the eyes of others. Sitting in the coffee shop with Xia, I had the appearance of a happy person, but my heart was filled with a hidden sorrow; I was so terribly unhappy because I knew where Fate was about to take me, and now the fault would be mine alone.   •

Developing a Vocabulary for Discussing Tone

When you analyze a story's tone, you need to use adjectives that allow you to make generalizations about the impression that the work gives and the attitudes that the author implies.

The following adjectives are among those commonly used to discuss tone in fiction, although they represent only a small number of possible choices. They are provided in pairs that present opposite or nearly opposite meanings. The first group of words refers to a reader's impression of a work as a whole. The second group refers to the author's attitude toward the material.

Reader's impression of the story as a whole

serene / nerve-racking
genial / frightening
comic / tragic
humorous / depressing
joyful / solemn
light / profound
lucid / obscure
playful / earnest
pleasant / horrifying
reassuring / ominous
heart-rending / insensitive

Author's attitude toward characters or ideas

admiring / condescending
amused / dismayed
approving / disapproving
assured / ambivalent
caring / hostile
complimentary / sarcastic
concerned / apathetic
confident / uncertain
hopeful / disillusioned
idealistic / cynical
impartial / biased
laudatory / mocking
optimistic / pessimistic
straightforward / ironic
sympathetic / unsympathetic
wistful / indifferent

ACTIVITY: *Developing a vocabulary for discussing tone*

Working alone, in pairs, or in a small group, select from the list of words categorized under "reader's impression" those words whose precise meanings you do not know.

1. Using a dictionary, find the meanings. (*Note:* These words are all adjectives. Some of them may be listed in the dictionary according to their noun or verb form.)
2. Using the precise meaning of one of the words, create in writing a scene whose tone fits the definition.
3. Reading what you have written, share the scene you have created with the rest of the class. Ask your classmates to identify the tone of the scene. •

ACTIVITY: *Manipulating tone*

Rewrite the scene you wrote in the above activity (or write a new scene) so that an incident is described in two or three different tones. For example, you can change a sympathetic tone to an unsympathetic tone, or a hopeful tone to a disillusioned tone. This can mean changing the diction or sentence structure, or both. •

ACTIVITY: *Determining tone*

Read the opening lines of "A Woman Like Me," by Xi Xi, reprinted on page 308. Then answer the following question:

How would you describe the tone of this selection in one or two words?   •

Asking Questions about Tone

One of the best ways to generate ideas about tone can be to ask yourself a series of questions. By answering some or all of the following questions about the tone of a story, you may discover an aspect of the story that you would like to analyze.

A reader's reaction
1. How does the story make you feel?
   - Do feel happy, sad, angry, fearful, confused, and so on?
   - Is the story humorous, sad, tragic, and/or frightening, and so on?
   - How has the author affected or controlled your response? In other words, which passages create the desired effect?

The author's attitude toward characters or narrator
2. What is the author's overall attitude toward the main character or narrator?
   - Is the author's attitude sympathetic, admiring, hostile, critical, or sentimental, or something else?
   - How is this attitude conveyed?
     a. Which words or groups of words suggest the author's stance?
     b. Does the length, structure, or word order of a sentence or group of sentences provide any clue to the development of the character?
3. What is the author's attitude toward the minor characters?
   - Is the author's attitude sympathetic, admiring, hostile, critical, or sentimental, or something else?
   - How are these attitudes conveyed?
     a. Which words or groups of words suggest the author's stance?
     b. Does the length, structure, or word order of a sentence or group of sentences provide any clue to the development of the characters?

The author's attitude toward action or events
4. What is the main conflict or key event of the story?
   - What is the author's attitude toward the conflict and/or events?
   - How is that attitude conveyed?

The author's attitude toward ideas or concepts
5. What ideas or concepts are presented in the story? (for example, ideas about subjects such as love, death, marriage, family, government, social class, money, religion, or war, and so on).
   - What is the author's attitude toward those ideas or concepts?
   - How is that attitude conveyed?

ACTIVITY: *Asking questions about tone*

Select a short story from this book, and apply some or all of the above questions to discover the tone of the story. Record any ideas that you may want to write about in an interpretive essay. ●

Focusing on a Topic for an Essay on Tone

When you write an essay about tone, your primary goal is to explore the significance of, prove a point about, or answer a question about tone. Another goal is to show the connection between tone and the work as a whole, by discussing a truth the author reveals, a larger meaning of the story.

There are numerous ways to examine tone. The following topics may give you an idea of how to approach the writing of the essay. You can select one of the topics, combine topics, or design your own topic, with your instructor's approval.

1. Analyze the diction (and sentence structure, if applicable) that reveals the author's attitude toward the main character and/or minor characters.
2. Analyze the diction (and sentence structure, if applicable) that reveals the author's attitude toward the action or events of the story.
3. Analyze the diction (and sentence structure, if applicable) that reveals the author's attitude toward ideas or concepts that are presented in the story.
4. Analyze changes of tone within the story.
5. Analyze the irony in the story (see "Irony," pp. 33–34).
6. Analyze the humor in the story.
7. Analyze the impression the story makes on you.
8. Analyze the relationship between tone and another element of fiction, such as point of view.
9. Compare and analyze tone in different stories.

You may also select a topic from the activities related to tone in Chapter 4, "Discussion Activities." Your instructor may provide other specific suggestions for writing about a particular story.

SELECTING EVIDENCE ABOUT AN ABSTRACT IDEA

One way to analyze and interpret a work of fiction is to focus on an *abstract idea* or issue that the story emphasizes or addresses repeatedly. For example, a story may deal with one or more of the following:

adolescence	betrayal
the American dream	childhood

class distinctions	materialism
corruption	money
cultural identity	oppression
death	the parent/child relationship
deceit	the past
discrimination	patriotism
an ethical dilemma	poverty
family	prejudice
fate	pride
fear	racism
good vs. evil	rebellion against authority
government	religion/religious teachings
growing up	search for identity
hypocrisy	success
illusion/disillusionment	time
love	trust
male or female roles	war
marriage	the work ethic

Once you know what idea or issue you want to focus on, you can trace the development of the idea or issue throughout the story. Through that process, you can come to a deeper understanding of the story.

Analyzing References to an Abstract Idea

Since an abstract idea may be developed through many elements of fiction, you can study several elements within an entire story in order to understand the author's purpose in bringing to light or emphasizing a certain idea or issue.

Kate Chopin's 1894 story, "The Story of an Hour" (pp. 6–8) is the story of an hour in the life of a woman whose husband has just died. In the story, Chopin deals with a number of ideas and issues, among them the concept of freedom.

Different readers will focus on different references. The following references are only a few that provide clues to Chopin's views on freedom.

- The first obvious reference to freedom is in the eleventh paragraph, when Louise says, "free, free, free!"
- In the thirteenth paragraph, Louise thinks of "years to come that would belong to her absolutely."
- In the fourteenth paragraph, Louise realizes that "there would be no powerful will bending hers."
- In the fourteenth paragraph, Louise refers to the imposition of "a private will upon a fellow-creature" as a "crime."
- In the fifteenth paragraph, Louise finds that "love" is less important than "this possession of self-assertion."
- In the last paragraph, Louise dies when her husband returns alive.

These selective references reveal the *main character's* attitude toward her new-found freedom. The reader/analyst can now consider the *author's* attitude toward freedom. Is depriving someone of freedom a "crime"? Does "self-assertion" count more than "love"? Is it better to die than to live without freedom?

To answer these or similar questions, it is useful to look back at the story, from the beginning, to look for clues. Many clues can be found, for example, in the setting, especially in the descriptions of nature outside the window in the "open square," where Louise views "the new spring life" (the fifth and sixth paragraphs, p. 7). It is possible to make a link between this scene of nature and Louise's new life: both represent a new, natural openness. In that sense, the author may not be criticizing Louise for enjoying her freedom even though she has been told that her husband is dead: Louise's desire for freedom is as natural as the trees, rain, and sky.

Of course, many more references can be examined, and elements of fiction other than setting can be brought to bear on the study of the concept of freedom in "The Story of an Hour."

ACTIVITY: *Identifying and analyzing references to an abstract idea*

Select one of the stories in this book, for example, "War," by Luigi Pirandello (pp. 74–77), and identify an idea or issue that is emphasized or referred to repeatedly. Make a list of some of the key references to that idea or issue. Then look for a pattern in the references that provide a clue to the author's stance toward the idea or issue. ●

Developing a Vocabulary for Discussing an Abstract Idea

When you focus on an abstract idea, you need precise verbs to discuss what you think the author believes. Some of the verbs already listed may be useful (see lists of selected verbs on pp. 296–97 and pp. 302–04). In addition, the following verbs, listed alphabetically, are among those commonly used to discuss an idea or issue. Consult a dictionary of usage, if necessary, to determine which verb or verb phrase to select.

THE AUTHOR . . .

brings to light	molds
concentrates on	opens up
creates	shapes
discloses	uncovers
emphasizes	underscores
exposes	underlines
focuses on	unmasks
idealizes	unveils
lays bare	voices

Asking Questions about an Abstract Idea

One of the best ways to generate ideas about an abstract idea can be to ask yourself a series of questions. You can approach the idea or issue by examining how it is expressed through various elements of fiction.

Note: Not all of the questions will apply to every story you read.

Character
1. Do the characters say anything about the idea or issue?
2. Are the characters' thoughts about the idea or issue revealed?
3. Is the characters' behavior connected to the idea or issue?

Setting
4. Does the geographical location influence your understanding of the idea or issue?
5. Does the year, the time of day or year, or the length of time over which the story takes place, influence your understanding of the idea or issue?
6. Does the social environment (manners, customs, rules, moral codes) influence your understanding of the idea or issue?
7. Does the story's physical environment (revealed through the clothing, weather, buildings, rooms, outdoor scenes, and so on) influence your understanding of the idea or issue?

Point of view
8. Does the perspective from which the story is told influence the way you perceive the idea or issue?
9. Does the narrator comment on the idea or issue?

Imagery
10. Do the images reveal the author's attitude toward the idea or issue?

Symbolism
11. Does the author's use of symbols reveal the author's attitude toward the idea or issue?

Tone
12. Does the diction (selection of words) reveal the author's attitude toward the idea or issue?
13. Does the sentence structure reveal the author's attitude toward the idea or issue?

ACTIVITY: Asking questions about an abstract idea

Select a short story from this book, and apply some or all of the above questions to an idea or issue the author addresses. Record any ideas you discover that you may want to write about in an interpretive essay.   ●

Focusing on a Topic for an Essay on an Abstract Idea

When you write an essay about an abstract idea, your primary goal is to explore the significance of, prove a point about, or answer a question about the idea. Another goal is to show the connection between the idea and the work as a whole, by discussing a truth the author reveals, a larger meaning of the story.

There are numerous ways to examine an abstract idea. The following topics may give you an idea of how to approach the writing of the essay. You can select one of the topics, combine topics, or design your own topic, with your instructor's approval.

1. Show how the idea or issue is revealed through various elements of fiction (for example, character, setting, point of view, imagery, symbolism, tone), one by one.
2. Select and analyze various references to a particular idea or issue.
3. Compare and analyze a similar idea or issue dealt with in different stories.

You may also select a topic from the activities related to abstract ideas in Chapter 4, "Discussion Activities." For example, a suggested topic for a literary journal entry may become the focus for an essay. Your instructor may provide other specific suggestions for writing about a particular story.

Quoting and Documenting Sources

Chapter 7 is designed to help you with two of the processes involved in incorporating material from a story or other source into your own essay: quoting and documenting. The chapter provides guidelines for selecting quotations and integrating them into your own writing. It also provides guidelines for identifying the sources you use to write your paper.

QUOTING

Sometimes in your writing, you may need to *quote* an author, that is, to repeat the author's exact words. Your reasons for quoting will be primarily to introduce or support a point you want to discuss. Quoting also enables you to enrich your writing by adding the author's distinctive language.

Selecting a Quotation

Although quotations serve an important purpose in an interpretive essay, you need to be careful not to use too many quotations. Too many quotations can break the flow of your discussion. Furthermore, you can become too dependent on the exact language of the story. When that happens, you may forget that your readers are interested primarily in learning how you interpret the material. Most of your essay will be written in your own words as you retell, analyze, and interpret a story. Use a quotation only when you think it is essential.

A Student Writer at Work

In her essay analyzing the character of Louise Mallard (pp. 272–76), Rosa selected several quotations from "The Story of an Hour" (pp. 6–8) to include in her own text. The quotations serve different purposes: to verify the facts of the story, to introduce an important concept, or to prove a point she has made. Note that, in most cases, she retells or explains the story in her own words.

Rosa began her fifth paragraph by generalizing about certain details:

> Other important details presented in the story, before we learn her thoughts, are the ones related to nature.

Rosa begins the next sentence by retelling a portion of the story, and then she interprets the scene:

> As she is alone and sits looking outside, symbols of a rebirth begin to appear.

In the next sentence she provides a quotation to verify the facts of the scene, and then she interprets the quotation:

> That she sits "facing the open window" (7) means that there is going to be a new chapter in her life or a way out from her past life.

Rosa places a quotation at the beginning of the next sentence to introduce a concept that she wants to comment on:

> The "new spring life" represents a total commencement of things (7). The color green can mean hope, and that is what Mrs. Mallard sees in the trees.

In the eighth paragraph, Rosa uses a quotation to prove a point she has just made:

> It can be proved that Mrs. Mallard does not want to accept this new feeling by these words: "she was striving to beat it back with her will" (7).

GUIDELINES | *Guidelines for Selecting a Quotation*

Before you decide to use a quotation, ask yourself this question: "Why am I quoting this passage?" If your answer is one of the following statements, then include the quotation in your essay:
1. Because I need to verify the facts of the story
2. Because I need it to introduce a concept I will comment on
3. Because I need to support or prove the point I just made

When you do decide to use an author's exact words, you must make it clear that the words are being reprinted from another source (see "Punctuating Quotations," pp. 324–27).

ACTIVITY: *Selecting a quotation*

Read the following statements written about "The Story of an Hour." Then search through the story (pp. 6–8) to find at least one quotation that can verify, introduce, or prove each statement.

1. Mrs. Mallard's husband adored her.
2. What Louise Mallard gains in her new life seems to outweigh what she loses.
3. Mrs. Mallard attempts to hide her feelings from all those around her.

4. There is a barrier between Mrs. Mallard and her sister Josephine.
5. Nature is connected with life and joy.
6. The description of Louise's appearance reveals her inner being.   ●

Incorporating Quotations into an Essay

Once you have decided to use a quotation, you need to incorporate it into your essay. And you need to do it in such a way that your essay doesn't have a choppy, unnatural rhythm. Otherwise, it may appear to your readers that the quotation has just been dropped into the essay for no reason.

GUIDELINES

Guidelines for Incorporating Quotations

When including quotations, you can use one or more of these strategies:
1. Introduce or in some way lead into the quotation so that readers know whose words are being quoted or can understand why the quotation is important.
2. Comment on the quotation after you have included it so that readers understand its connection to other points made in the paper.
3. Insert ellipses (spaced periods . . .) if you delete any words from the original quotation.
4. Use brackets [ ] to add words to or to substitute words for those in the original quotation.

INTRODUCING QUOTATIONS

There are a variety of ways to introduce a quotation, as demonstrated below. Whichever way you choose, you should place the quotation within a context. That is because a quotation takes on significance in relation to what surrounds it. A quotation can be confusing or meaningless unless the reader is reminded of whom it refers to, where it occurs in the story, or who said it.

Student Writers at Work

The following sentences are taken from student essays analyzing Kate Chopin's "The Story of an Hour." Note that the students combine quoted passages with paraphrases of the events and details of the story. In other words, they combine the author's exact words with their own words. In each example, it is possible to determine where or when the quotation occurs in the story, to whom it refers, or who said it.

Learning of her husband's death, she first reacts in a "storm of grief" (7).

T.C.

After grieving openly, she asks to be left alone in her bedroom, where she gazes through the open window; "She would have no one follow her" (7).

A.D.

At this point what she gains in her new life seems to outweigh what she loses, in this case her husband. This can be seen in the lines, "What could love, the unsolved mystery, count for in face of this possession of self-assertion which she suddenly recognized as the strongest impulse of her being" (8).

K.B.

Chopin describes a situation in which Louise's sister Josephine is "kneeling before the closed door with her lips to the keyhole, imploring for admission" (8).

T.C.

Josephine wants to get her sister back from her world to the real world and says, "open the door—you will make yourself ill" (8).

N.N.

COMMENTING ON QUOTATIONS

Obviously, what you say after you have included a quotation depends upon your purpose and subject matter. The important point to remember is that your readers will not understand why a quotation is included unless you tell them. In commenting, you can, for example:

1. Expand on the quotation: add details or facts or ideas that reveal its significance.
2. Explain what the quotation means.
3. Explain the connection between the quotation and what has been said earlier in the essay.
4. Refer to one important word or phrase in the quotation and explain its significance.

Student Writers at Work

The following examples taken from student essays show how students commented on the quotations introduced in the above examples.

Learning of her husband's death, she first reacts in a "storm of grief" (7) which exhausts her to the extent that she needs to rest.

T.C.

After grieving openly, she asks to be left alone in her bedroom, where she gazes through the open window; "She would have no one follow her" (7). By this act we can see that she is probably an extremely lonely person inside, unable to share her feelings with those around her.

A.D.

At this point what she gains in her new life seems to outweigh what she loses, in this case her husband. This can be seen in the lines, "What could love, the unsolved mystery, count for in face of this possession of self-assertion which she suddenly recognized as the strongest impulse of her being" (8). Here we can see that her values are starting to change as she discovers and realizes her own existence.

K.B.

Chopin describes a situation in which Louise's sister Josephine is "kneeling before the closed door with her lips to the keyhole, imploring for admission" (8), directing the reader's attention to the lack of communication and the alienation between the two sisters.

T.C.

Josephine wants to get her sister back from her world to the real world and says, "open the door—you will make yourself ill" (8). This door suggests the barrier between Josephine and her sister, Mrs. Mallard. It is the border of the real world (which is represented by Josephine) and the unreal one (which is viewed by Mrs. Mallard).

N.N.

USING ELLIPSES

Ellipses (spaced periods) can be helpful if you want to delete some words from the middle of a quotation, as long as you don't change the author's intended meaning. Use four spaced periods . . . . if the words omitted include a period at the end of a sentence. Otherwise, use three spaced periods (. . .).

There are primarily two reasons to use ellipsis:

1. Delete words to make a quotation fit logically into your own sentence.

   EXAMPLE
   Original: The delicious breath of rain was in the air.
   Altered: There is a "delicious breath of rain . . . in the air" (7).

2. Delete words from a quotation to make the quotation shorter or to select the part of the quotation that comes right to the point you want to emphasize.

EXAMPLE

Original: Into this she sank, pressed down by a physical exhaustion that
               haunted her body and seemed to reach into her soul.

Altered: She is so deeply affected by the news that "a physical exhaustion
               . . . seemed to reach into her soul" (7).

Note: Ellipsis is necessary only if you omit words from the middle of a
quotation you have selected. It is not necessary to use ellipsis if you
omit words from the beginning or from the end of the sentence containing the quotation you have selected.

EXAMPLE

Original: Into this she sank, pressed down by a physical exhaustion that
                haunted her body and seemed to reach into her soul.

Acceptable: She is so deeply affected by the news that she felt ". . . a physical
                exhaustion that haunted her body. . ." (7).

Preferable: She is so deeply affected by the news that she felt "a physical
                exhaustion that haunted her body" (7).

USING BRACKETS

If you need to add words to or substitute words in a quotation, put the
additional or changed word within brackets. *Note:* Use brackets [ ], not parentheses ( ), for this purpose.

1. Add words to help clarify a potentially confusing quotation.

   EXAMPLE

   Original: She wept at once, with sudden, wild abandonment, in her sister's
                  arms.

   Altered: "[Mrs. Mallard] wept at once, with sudden, wild abandonment, in
                  her sister's arms" (7).
                  or
                  "She [Mrs. Mallard] wept at once, with sudden, wild abandon-
                  ment, in her sister's arms" (7).

2. Substitute words to make a quotation fit smoothly into your own
   sentence, as long as you don't change the author's intended meaning.

   EXAMPLE

   Original: The delicious breath of rain was in the air.

   Altered: Mrs. Mallard can sense the "delicious breath of rain [that] was in
                  the air" (7).

   EXAMPLE

   Original: "Go away. I am not making myself ill."

   Altered: Louise tells her sister that she is "not making [herself] ill" (7).

Note: When you describe fictional events, use the present tense primarily (see "Guidelines for Using the Appropriate Verb Tense," p. 342).
You can use brackets to change a verb tense in the original story (for
example, past tense) to the present tense, to match the tense you are

using to write your essay. However, this is not necessary. Your instructor will tell you which approach is preferred.

EXAMPLE

Original: The delicious breath of rain was in the air.

Acceptable: As she faces the open window, a "delicious breath of rain [is] in the air" (7).

Acceptable: As she faces the open window, a "delicious breath of rain was in the air" (7).

Guidelines for punctuating quotations are on pp. 324–27.

ACTIVITY: *Integrating quotations*

To practice integrating quotations into a written text, select quotations from the source below (Passage 1) and insert them into the blank spaces in the paragraph taken from a student essay. Your goals are to:

1. Select an appropriate quotation.
2. Incorporate the source logically.
3. Punctuate correctly (see pp. 324–27).
4. Put the page number of the quotation within parentheses.

Work alone or with a partner.

PASSAGE 1

There stood, facing the open window, a comfortable, roomy armchair. Into this she sank, pressed down by a physical exhaustion that haunted her body and seemed to reach her soul.

She could see in the open square before her house the tops of trees that were all aquiver with the new spring life. The delicious breath of rain was in the air. In the street below a peddler was crying his wares. The notes of a distant song which some one was singing reached her faintly, and countless sparrows were twittering in the eaves.

There were patches of blue sky showing here and there through the clouds that had met and piled one above the other in the west facing her window.

She sat with her head thrown back upon the cushion of the chair, quite motionless, except when a sob came up into her throat and shook her, as a child who had cried itself to sleep continues to sob in its dreams.

from "The Story of an Hour" by Kate Chopin, page 7

PARAGRAPH FROM STUDENT ESSAY

As Louise Mallard recognizes her own need for freedom, hope for a better life arises in her. Images of hope also appear in the description of the setting. For instance, they are symbolized in the image of _____ ( ), where the clouds stand for sorrow and despair and the sky symbolizes the advent of a happier life. But Louise Mallard hopes for more than just a happier life; she hopes for a new life. Chopin provides two hints for this conclusion: the first, more obvious implication is given in the term, _____ ( ). The second, more subtle hint is symbolized in the haunting image of the woman sinking into a _____ ( ). We imagine the woman shrinking in a huge chair to the size of a little girl. Our imagination is even supported by Chopin, who compares Louise to a child who _____ ( ).

T.C.

Follow the same instructions for Passage 2 and the following paragraph from a student essay.

PASSAGE 2

Knowing that Mrs. Mallard was afflicted with a heart trouble, great care was taken to break to her as gently as possible the news of her husband's death.

It was her sister Josephine who told her, in broken sentences; veiled hints that revealed in half concealing. Her husband's friend Richards was there, too, near her. It was he who had been in the newspaper office when intelligence of the railroad disaster was received, with Brently Mallard's name leading the list of "killed." He had only taken the time to assure himself of its truth by a second telegram, and had hastened to forestall any less careful, less tender friend in bearing the sad message.

She did not hear the story as many women have heard the same, with a paralyzed inability to accept its significance. She wept at once, with sudden, wild abandonment, in her sister's arms. When the storm of grief had spent itself she went away to her room alone. She would have no one follow her.

from "The Story of an Hour," by Kate Chopin, page 7

PARAGRAPH FROM STUDENT ESSAY

At the beginning of the story we are told that Mrs. Mallard is _____ ( ). As the story proceeds, we can understand why this is so. She often exceeds her feelings, either in grief

or in joy. We view her exaggerated grief at the opening of the story, when she immediately cries uncontrollably at the news of her husband's death: _____ ( ). Other women would deny that their husbands were dead or would inquire more about their death. But Mrs. Mallard does not question the news: _____
_____ ( ).

A.D.
●

ACTIVITY: *Selecting and integrating a quotation*

After reading one of the short stories in Part Two, write a paragraph in which you examine a character or an aspect of the setting. Select at least one quotation that is relevant to the character or setting, and incorporate it into the paragraph, using the guidelines for incorporating quotations.   ●

Punctuating Quotations

Quotation marks are used to indicate the beginning and end of a quotation. In many of the following examples, the number within the parentheses refers to the page number from which the quotation is taken.

Double and single quotation marks

1. Use double quotation marks (" ") to enclose the title of a story.

   Kate Chopin wrote "The Story of an Hour" in 1894.

2. Use double quotation marks to enclose a direct quotation.

   The "new spring life" represents a total commencement (7).

3. Use single quotation marks (' ') to enclose a quotation within a quotation.

   When she finally realizes that she can have the opportunity to act as she wishes to, Mrs. Mallard says "over and over under her breath: 'free, free, free!'" (7).

   Note: Do not use quotation marks for words or phrases that do not appear in a story:

   Louise Mallard is a "liberated" woman. (*Note:* The word "liberated" does not appear in "The Story of an Hour.")

Periods

4. Place the period inside the end quotation mark.

   In the last line of the story, the doctors say that Louise Mallard died "of joy that kills."

5. Place the period after the page number, when the page number is included within parentheses at the end of a sentence.

   In the air is "the delicious breath of rain" (7).

COMMAS

6. Place commas *inside* the end quotation mark.

   "Go away," says Louise (8).

QUESTION MARKS AND EXCLAMATION POINTS

7. Place question marks (?) and exclamation points (!) *inside* the end quotation mark, if the quotation itself is a question or an exclamation.

   Mrs. Mallard keeps whispering, "Free! Body and soul free!" (8).

   Note: If the quotation ends with a question mark, exclamation point or dash, you do not need to add a comma before your own words:

   "What are you doing, Louise?" asks her sister Josephine (8).

8. Place question marks and exclamation points *outside* the end quotation mark, if your own sentence is a question or exclamation.

   Is Mrs. Mallard truly "free"?

SEMICOLONS, COLONS, AND DASHES

9. Place all semicolons (;) and colons (:) and dashes (--) *outside* the end quotation mark.

   After she recognizes that she is free, her blood "warmed and relaxed every inch of her body"; she is not only mentally but also physically changed by the realization (7).

INTRODUCING QUOTATIONS: COMMAS AND COLONS

10. Use a comma to introduce a short quotation with an expression such as "He says."

    Louise whispers, "Free! Body and soul free!" (8).

    Note: Do not use a comma if the quoted statement follows the subordinating conjunction *that:*

    The doctors say that "she had died of heart disease—of joy that kills" (8).

    Note: If commas are used to set off explanatory words, include an extra set of quotation marks:

    "Go away," responds Louise, "I am not making myself ill" (8).

Note: A comma is not necessary if the quotation is blended into your own sentence:

Louise Mallard walks down the stairs ∧"like a goddess of Victory" (8).

11. A colon can be used when a full sentence introduces a full-sentence quotation.

A change is going on inside of her and she is aware of it: "She was beginning to recognize this thing that was approaching to possess her" (7).

(See also item 12, below.)

LONG QUOTATIONS

12. Set off a lengthy quotation (more than four or five lines) with a colon, and with no quotation marks (unless the quotation includes dialogue), by indenting five spaces from the left margin. Double-space throughout.

> Her repression is also revealed when a strange impulse takes control of her and she thinks:
>
>> There would be no one to live for her during those coming years: she would live for herself. There would be no powerful will bending hers in that blind persistence with which men and women believe they have a right to impose a private will upon a fellow-creature. (8)
>
> This statement confirms that she is a dominated wife. Living with her husband means always doing his will, even things that she does not want to do.

LINES OF DIALOGUE

13. Quote multiple lines of dialogue between or among characters exactly as they appear on the page of the story, with different lines of dialogue on different lines of your text. Double-space throughout.

"Louise, open the door! I beg; open the door—you will make yourself ill. What are you doing, Louise? For heaven's sake, open the door."
    "Go away. I am not making myself ill" (8).

Note: If multiple lines of dialogue include narration, place double quotation marks at the beginning of each new paragraph but only at the end of the entire quotation. Use single quotation marks to enclose lines of dialogue.

"∧'Free! Body and soul free!'∧ she kept whispering.
    "∧Josephine was kneeling before the closed door with her lips to the keyhole, imploring for admission. ∧Louise, open the door! I

beg; open the door—you will make yourself ill. What are you do-ing, Louise? For heaven's sake open the door.'

"'Go away. I am not making myself ill.' No; she was drinking in a very elixir of life through that open window" (8).

ACTIVITY: *Punctuating quotations*

Exchange interim drafts with a classmate. Search for quotations within each other's papers. Using the guidelines for punctuating quotations, deter-mine whether the quotations are punctuated correctly. Discuss the correct forms with your partner. If you have questions, consult with your instructor. ●

CITING AND DOCUMENTING SOURCES

When you incorporate material from another source into your own text, for example through summary or quotation, you have an obligation to cite (mention) the source of that material. You must give credit to an author by documenting (accurately identifying) your source. Proper documentation legitimizes your use of the material.

This section provides guidelines for identifying the sources you use to write your essay. Your instructor may request that you use only assigned course materials to develop ideas for your essays. Outside sources should be consulted only with your instructor's permission. Documentation rules are presented in this book according to the style of the Modern Language Asso-ciation (MLA), a format used primarily in the humanities. In other courses, you may be expected to use other formats. Your instructors in those courses will provide the appropriate rules. *Note:* Although the formats are different, the underlying principles for documenting are the same or similar across disciplines.

Citing Course Material

Much of your college writing involves incorporating material from course reading into your own essays. That means, of course, that your readers are familiar with your sources. Nevertheless, you must mention the source (by author and/or title) if you refer to material other than your own.

INTRODUCING AND RETELLING A STORY

When you write an essay in which you analyze a short story, you should identify the author and title of the story in the opening paragraphs of your paper (see "Common Features of the Introduction," pp. 246–47).

EXAMPLES
Guy de Maupassant's "The Necklace" is the story of a clerk's wife who always dreams about being rich.

Mathilde Loisel, the main character in "The Necklace" by Guy de Maupassant, is a beautiful young woman who is married to a clerk.

INCORPORATING QUOTATIONS

Always include the page number(s) of a quotation taken from a story so that your reference can be found easily. Put the page number within parentheses after the quotation.

EXAMPLES

Mme. Loisel is not satisfied with her living conditions, as she feels she has been "born for all the delicacies and all the luxuries" (46).

Mathilde Loisel, "one of those pretty and charming girls who are sometimes, as if by a mistake of destiny, born in a family of clerks" (46), suffers enormously for living in what she calls poverty. [*Note:* The page number could instead be placed at the end of the sentence.]

LISTING SOURCE(S)

Your instructor may request that you include a separate list at the end of your essay, indicating which story or stories you interpreted. If so, use this form:

Chopin, Kate. "The Story of an Hour." 1894. Rpt. in The International Story: An Anthology with Guidelines for Reading and Writing about Fiction. Ruth Spack. New York: St. Martin's, 1994. 6–8.

(See also "Preparing the List of Works Cited," pp. 333–38.)

Citing Outside Material

Most of the essay writing you do for this course is based on a *primary source*, the short story you choose to analyze. Your instructor may ask you to draw on *secondary sources* as well, for example, critical or historical material that you can find in libraries or bookstores.

Your instructor and the reference librarian can guide you in your research to find secondary sources. Ask for help to learn how to use the library's card catalog or computer catalog to find books and articles related to your topic.

GIVING CREDIT TO SOURCES

In writing from researched sources, you support points that you make by citing facts and opinions from authorities in a given field. By including references to the words of these authorities, you reveal that you are aware of previous writing on your subject and that you are adding to that previous work. Your writing is building on a base of knowledge and thought on your subject.

When you use researched material in your own writing, careful documentation of sources is necessary. Documentation is an important convention of academic writing: Individuals who express ideas are entitled to receive credit for their ideas. Academic writers are therefore careful to give credit to all of their sources when they borrow ideas to use in their own writing.

Whenever you borrow words, ideas, or evidence from another writer, you need references in your text to alert your readers to the borrowed material. These references make it possible for readers to separate your ideas from someone else's and to find the source of the information you have referred to if they wish to do so.

DECIDING WHAT TO DOCUMENT

Once you understand why documenting is necessary, you need to decide what to document. The following list will help you make that decision. You should document the following borrowed material:

1. every quotation
2. every diagram, chart, or picture
3. any statistics
4. all ideas, opinions, facts, theories, and information that cannot be considered *common knowledge* to your audience. The term *common knowledge* refers to general information that is known by a large number of people within a community.

The items in point 4 are the most problematic, for it is sometimes difficult to decide what an audience's shared common knowledge is, especially if the audience represents a culture or community different from your own. Here are several guidelines for determining what is or might be common knowledge:

- If several of the sources you have consulted mention the same fact or idea without having documented it, you may assume that this fact or idea is common knowledge.
- If you yourself were aware of the fact or idea before reading the material, you may assume that this fact or idea is common knowledge. An exception to this guideline might be when the fact or idea is common knowledge to you because of your cultural background, in which case it might not be common knowledge to readers who have a different cultural background.
- If you are not sure whether something is common knowledge to the academic audience you are writing for, check with your instructor.

Another problem that you might have in documenting sources is that you may have some prior knowledge of your subject—from your own past reading or studying, for example—that you are unable to identify accurately because you no longer remember the exact source. If that is the case, it is wise to include a footnote in your essay explaining the general source of information. Then your instructor will understand why there is no formal documentation.

AVOIDING PLAGIARISM: QUOTING AND PARAPHRASING PROPERLY

To omit documentation of borrowed material is to commit *plagiarism*, the serious offense of presenting someone else's material as your own. Discovery of deliberate plagiarism can lead to severe penalties ranging from failure in a course to expulsion from school.

Students who do not understand the convention of documenting sources may unintentionally commit plagiarism. Teachers understand that unintentional plagiarism can occur. However, it is your responsibility to learn the conventions of academic writing to avoid plagiarism in the first place. You need to do your own work honestly, quote or paraphrase (restate an author's ideas in your own words) accurately, and document your sources properly. The following advice can help you.

GUIDELINES

Guidelines for Avoiding Plagiarism

Plagiarism is the act of using another person's ideas or expressions in your writing without acknowledging the source. Here are several ways to avoid plagiarism:

1. When you use the exact words of an author, make clear that the words are being reprinted from another source. Use quotation marks for short quotations, or set off a long quotation in the body of your text (see "Punctuating Quotations," pp. 324–27).
2. When you paraphrase an author's words (see guidelines on p. 331), identify the author.
3. Never hand in a paper written by someone else and present it as your own.
4. Never have anyone write any part of your paper.
5. Use proper formats for citing and documenting sources.

When you paraphrase a passage to include in your essay, your goal is to clarify its meaning for yourself and your readers. You take an example or idea from the reading to introduce or support an idea you want to discuss in your paper. Most often, you incorporate the paraphrased passage into your own sentence.

GUIDELINES ## Guidelines for Paraphrasing

After selecting a passage that you plan to refer to in your own essay, put the passage into your own words. In adjusting the author's words, you can rearrange word order, turn longer sentences into shorter ones, make two sentences out of one, or select only a key idea from a long sentence.

1. Look up the meaning of unfamiliar words.
2. Think about what the author really means.
3. Use one of these strategies to find your own words to rephrase the passage:
   a. Cover up the passage and write from memory.
   b. Take notes on the passage. Then cover up the passage and write the paraphrase from your notes.
   c. Go word by word, substituting synonyms. Then rewrite the substitute passage so that it makes sense.
4. Reread the original passage to make sure that you have preserved meaning and tone. Revise your paraphrase if necessary.
5. Integrate the paraphrase into your own sentence.

EXAMPLES OF PROPER CITATIONS

The following examples show three ways to borrow material *properly* from an outside source (in this case, an article written by Margaret Cully) and integrate it into an interpretive essay.

Original passage

"Kate Chopin was never a feminist or a suffragist; in fact, she was suspicious of any ideology."—Margaret Culley, from "The Context of *The Awakening*," page 117

Direct quotation

In her article, "The Context of *The Awakening*," Margaret Culley claims that Kate Chopin was "never a feminist or a suffragist" (117).

Paraphrase

According to Margaret Culley, Kate Chopin was uncomfortable with ideological movements such as feminism (117).

Paraphrase and quotation

According to Culley, Kate Chopin was "suspicious of any ideology" such as feminism (117).

EXAMPLES OF PLAGIARISM

The following examples show two ways of *improperly* borrowing material from an outside source (in this case, an article by Margaret Culley) and integrating it into an essay.

Original passage

"Kate Chopin was never a feminist or a suffragist; in fact, she was suspicious of any ideology."—Margaret Culley, from "The Context of *The Awakening,*" page 117

Plagiarism

It is clear from reading "The Story of an Hour" that Kate Chopin was suspicious about ideology.

This is plagiarism because there is no acknowledgment that the idea comes from another source that the student has read. The student writer should have included Margaret Culley's name and/or the title of the article, as well as the page number.

Plagiarism

Margaret Culley claims that Kate Chopin was suspicious of any ideology.

This is plagiarism because there are no quotation marks to identify the direct quotation, "suspicious of any ideology." Also, the page number is missing.

ACTIVITY: *Paraphrasing and quoting to avoid plagiarism*

Read the following passage. Then write (1) a paraphrase of the passage and (2) a sentence in which you quote from the passage. In each case, document the source by properly identifying the source.

Despite social and political advances, women in the 1890s still encountered disadvantages in almost every aspect of their lives, and a majority of the populace still believed that a woman's most sacred duty was to be "the angel in the house."—Margaret Culley, from "The Context of *The Awakening,*" page 119   •

CITING SOURCES

The following guidelines can help you properly cite sources in your paper, using the MLA format. The citations within your paper should be matched with a list of sources attached at the end of your essay (see "Preparing the List of Works Cited," pp. 333–38).

When you use the MLA format to cite outside sources, include the page number for a paraphase as well as for a quotation, and include the author's name.

1. If your sentence includes the author's name, place only the page number(s) of the source in parentheses.

   According to Matthew J. Bruccoli, the 1920s in America were a decade of optimism, prosperity, and rapid social change (219).

2. If your sentence does not contain the author's name, and if the context does not clearly identify the author, cite the author's last name, along with the page number(s) of the source, in parentheses.

   The 1920s in America were a decade of optimism, prosperity, and rapid social change (Bruccoli 219).

3. If your source has a corporate (agency, association) author or no author, place the corporate name (or title of the article, if there is no author) within parentheses along with the page number(s).

   There is no doubt that "the humanities are inescapably bound to literacy" (Commission on the Humanities 69).

   Or, include the name of the agency (or the title of the article, if there is no author) in your own sentence, and place the page number of the source within parentheses.

   The Commission on the Humanities has concluded that "the humanities are inescapably bound to literacy" (69).

GUIDELINES

General Guidelines for List of Works Cited

1. Put the list at the end of your essay. The list must be on a separate sheet.
2. Center the words Works Cited at the top of the page.
3. Double-space throughout.
4. Start the first line at the margin; indent the second line five spaces.
5. Put the author's last name first, followed by a comma and then the first name, followed by a period.
6. Put the list in alphabetical order, according to the last name of the author. If there is no author, alphabetize according to the first letter of the title. If the title begins with "A," "An," or "The," alphabetize according to the second word in the title.

Preparing the List of Works Cited *(Bibliography)*

A list of works cited, which includes the full bibliographic information of the sources used in your writing, should be placed at the end of an essay. (See the sample list on p. 334.) By glancing at the list, readers can see how recent, reliable, and thorough the material is. In addition, they can use the list as a resource if they wish to locate the sources themselves to investigate the same subject.

You are not expected to memorize the rules for documentation. Use the following guidelines as a reference when you are making your own list of sources. Carefully note the indentation, punctuation, and capitalization, as well as the order in which the publication information is given.

EXAMPLE

Works Cited

Ammons, Elizabeth. Conflicting Stories: American Women Writers at the Turn into the Twentieth Century. New York: Oxford UP, 1991.

Chopin, Kate. "The Story of an Hour." 1894. Rpt. in The International Story: An Anthology with Guidelines for Reading and Writing about Fiction. Ruth Spack. New York: St. Martin's, 1994. 6–8.

Culley, Margaret. "The Context of The Awakening." The Awakening: An Authoritative Text. Ed. Margaret Culley. New York: Norton, 1976. 117–19.

Ewell, Barbara E. Kate Chopin. New York: Ungar, 1986.

Gilbert, Sandra M., and Susan Gubar. The Madwoman in the Attic: The Woman Writer and the Nineteenth-Century Literary Imagination. New Haven: Yale UP, 1979.

Ziff, Larzer. The American 1890s: Life and Times of a Lost Generation. New York: Viking, 1966.

GUIDELINES

MLA *General Form*: *Books*

Bibliographic entries for books include, in this order:
- *author's name,* last name first. If there is more than one author, put first name first for second and third authors.
- *book title,* underlined. Capitalize all words, except prepositions, conjunctions, and articles (*exception:* capitalize an article—*a, an, the*—if it is the first word in the title or the first word after a colon).
- *city of publication* (and state, if city is not well known)
- *publisher,* shortened form. Use just the first surname of companies such as *Harcourt* for *Harcourt Brace Jovanovich, Inc.* or *Norton* for *W.W. Norton and Co., Inc.* Use just *UP* for *University Press,* such as *Oxford UP.*
- *year of publication*

Carefully follow the indentation, capitalization, and punctuation.

A book by one author

Ewell, Barbara C. Kate Chopin. New York: Ungar, 1986.

A book by two authors

Gilbert, Sandra M., and Susan Gubar. The Madwoman in the Attic:
    The Woman Writer and the Nineteenth-Century Literary
    Imagination. New Haven: Yale UP, 1979.

A book by three or more authors

Quirk, Randolph, Sidney Greenbaum, Geoffrey Leech, and Jan
    Svartvik. A Comprehensive Grammar of the English
    Language. London: Longman, 1985.

A book with an editor

Klein, Leonard S., ed. Latin American Literature in the 20th Century:
    A Guide. New York: Ungar, 1986.

A book with two or more editors

Hamalian, Leo, and John D. Yohannan, eds. New Writing from the
    Middle East. New York: Ungar, 1978.

A book other than the first edition

Rosenblatt, Louise M. Literature as Exploration. 4th ed. New York:
    MLA, 1983.

A book with a corporate (agency, association) author

Commission on the Humanities. The Humanities in American Life:
    Report of the Commission on the Humanities. Berkeley: U of
    California P, 1980.

A work in an anthology

Bruccoli, Matthew J. "On F. Scott Fitzgerald and 'Bernice Bobs Her
    Hair.'" The American Short Story. Vol. 1. Ed. Calvin
    Skaggs. New York: Dell, 1977.

A work that has been reprinted in a book

Chopin, Kate. "The Story of an Hour." 1894. Rpt. in The
    International Story: An Anthology with Guidelines for Reading
    and Writing about Fiction. Ruth Spack. New York: St. Martin's,
    1994. 6–8.

An introduction, preface, foreword, or afterword

Baxter, Charles. Introduction. Sudden Fiction International: Sixty
    Short-Short Stories. Ed. Robert Shapard and James
    Thomas. New York: Norton, 1989. 17–25.

A translation

Calvino, Italo.   The Uses of Literature.   Trans. Patrick Creagh.   San
     Diego: Harcourt, 1986.

A book in a language other than English

Schwarz-Bart, Andre.   Le Dernier des Justes [The Last of the
     Just].   Paris: Seuil, 1959.

A signed article in an encyclopedia or other reference book

Adams, Charles J.   "Islam."   World Book.   1992 ed.

An unsigned article in an encyclopedia or other reference book

"Kincaid, Jamaica."   Current Biography Yearbook.   1991 ed.

GUIDELINES

MLA *General Form*: *Articles in Periodicals*

Bibliographic entries for articles include, in this order:
- *author's name* (if there is one), last name first; for second and
  third authors, put first name first
- *title of the article,* within quotation marks
- *name of the periodical,* underlined
- *volume number* (for a scholarly journal)
- *date*—for weekly magazines and for newspapers give the full
  date (day, month, and year); for monthly magazines give the
  month or season and year; for scholarly journals give the volume number and the year (in parentheses)
- *page numbers* of the entire article. *Exception:* When the article
  is not printed on consecutive pages, write only the first page
  number and a plus sign (for example, 22 +).

FORMS FOR SPECIFIC TYPES OF PERIODICALS

Carefully follow the indentation, capitalization, and punctuation.

SCHOLARLY JOURNALS

Scholarly journals are periodicals that contain articles written by experts
and scholars in a field for other experts and scholars in the field. These
journals are available primarily in libraries and through subscription.

General form

Garrison, Joseph M.   "The Adult Consciousness of the Narrator in
     Joyce's 'Araby.'"   Studies in Short Fiction 10 (1973): 416–19.

A book review

Minami, Masahiko.   Rev. of <u>Acts of Meaning</u>, by Jerome
     Bruner.   <u>Journal of Narrative and Life History</u> 1 (1991): 253–54.

MAGAZINES

Most magazines are popular periodicals whose articles are written by
reporters or writers for the general public. Other magazines are periodicals
whose articles are written by experts and scholars for the general public.
These periodicals can be found in libraries and often at newsstands.

An article from a weekly magazine

Gordimer, Nadine.   "Three in a Bed: Fiction, Morals, and
     Politics."   <u>New Republic</u> 18 Nov. 1991: 36 + .

An article from a monthly magazine

Becker, Jillian.   "Nadine Gordimer's Politics."   <u>Commentary</u> Feb. 1992:
     51 + .

A signed editorial

Crane, Janet.   "The Changing Americas."   Editorial.   <u>Focus</u> Fall 1986:
     1.

An unsigned editorial

"Nationalities, Nations, and Nationalism."   Editorial.   <u>America</u> 28
     Apr. 1990: 419.

An interview—printed text

Kincaid, Jamaica.   "Jamaica Kincaid: Writes of Passage."   Interview.
     <u>Essence Magazine</u> May 1991: 86 + .

A public address—printed text

Morrison, Toni.   "Address to the American Writers Congress."   9 Oct.
     1981.   In <u>Nation</u> 24 Oct. 1981: 396–412.

NEWSPAPERS

An article from a newspaper

Gaines-Carter, Patrice.   "Looking North to a Better Life: Many D.C.
     Blacks Have Roots in the 'Great Migration.'"   <u>Washington Post</u> 16
     Feb. 1987: 1 + .

An editorial

"Odyssey through a New China."   Editorial.   <u>Boston Globe</u> 8 Jan.
     1993: 14.

A letter to the editor

Woods, Bob.   "Simple Justice."   Letter.   <u>Boston Globe</u> 13 Feb. 1993: 18.

A book review

Gladstone, Valerie.   Rev. of <u>Open Door</u>, by Luisa Valenzuela.   <u>New York Times Book Review</u> 30 Oct. 1988: 26.

FORMS FOR OTHER TYPES OF SOURCES

A personal interview

Sadow, Catherine.   Personal interview.   8 Jan. 1993.

A film, filmstrip, or videotape

<u>Bernice Bobs Her Hair</u>.   Dir. Joan Micklin Silver.   The American Short Story Series, Perspective Films, 1977.

CHAPTER EIGHT

The Editing Process

E rrors are expected and understood as a natural result of the language learning process, for both native and nonnative speakers of English. Most errors have logical causes, and you can learn from your mistakes by examining why you have made them. Since errors can shift a reader's attention away from your meaning, you want to remove from your writing any errors that prevent someone from understanding what you are saying.

The goal of *editing* is to produce a paper whose meaning is clear. Editing involves both proofreading (reading to look for mistakes) and the actual correcting of errors. Proofreading and correcting are slow and time-consuming processes, requiring that you closely read and reread your paper and refer to other sources, such as a grammar or usage handbook and a dictionary. Therefore, it is best to focus on these processes at a later stage in your writing, after you have developed and organized your ideas.

Though proofreading and correcting can be tedious, they are important procedures, for they help you prepare a clearly expressed and comprehensible paper to hand in for evaluation. A neat presentation that reveals an attempt to edit out mistakes is also a courtesy to your reader. It reflects well on your effort to improve your writing and do well in the course.

EDITING

At the beginning of the term, the instructor may mark some of the errors in your paper, probably by underlining the errors. Your task is then to make corrections. The following guidelines can help you in that process.

GUIDELINES

General Guidelines for Editing

1. When you receive a paper marked for error, correct every error you can without asking for help.
2. Take time with the instructor or another student to go over any markings you do not understand.
3. Attempt to understand the causes of your errors.
4. Ask for help if you do not know how to correct an error even after consulting a grammar or usage handbook.

PROOFREADING

In an English class, you have the advantage of readers—your instructors and your classmates—who may proofread your paper for you and point out the errors. But because you will not always have this advantage, you need to develop other ways to find your errors. Only then can you feel confident to edit papers for other courses.

As the semester progresses, you should take increased responsibility for your own proofreading. There are many ways to proofread. You may want to use only one or all of the following suggestions.

GUIDELINES

General Guidelines for Proofreading

1. *Read for error only.*

   Read your paper not to further develop the ideas you have written, but primarily to find your mistakes. Here are two techniques you might find useful:
   a. Read word by word. Put your finger or a pencil under each word and move slowly across the page.
   b. Look for your typical errors. Read just to find the errors you know you tend to make.

2. *Read your paper aloud.*

   Read your paper to someone else or read aloud to yourself as if someone were listening. If you hesitate as you read your own writing, the reason may be that you have come across an error. Mark the spot on the paper and continue reading. Then go back and correct any mistakes.

3. *Learn the rules.*

   Review your previously corrected essays to find commonly made mistakes. Then consult a handbook to find the rules to correct three or four of those mistakes. Then look at your most recent draft, searching for those particular errors, and correct them. You may find it easier to remember the rule once you have applied it to your own writing.

4. *Let someone else proofread your paper.*

   You might find it helpful to have a friend proofread your paper, but *only to point out and discuss the reasons for your mistakes.* Only by going through the process of correction yourself will you learn how to find and correct errors in your writing.

OBSERVING SPECIAL CONVENTIONS FOR WRITING ABOUT LITERATURE

When you write an essay in which you interpret literature, there are specific areas you need to focus on. The following guidelines remind you of what needs to be done when references are made to readings.

GUIDELINES

Guidelines for Proofreading and Editing References to Readings

Quotation
1. Reread the original words of the author.
2. Check to see that you have copied the passage down *exactly* as it was written originally. This means that your essay should contain the exact words, the exact spelling, and the exact punctuation that you find in the original. Careful quotation demonstrates your respect for the author.
3. Make sure that the quotation you have selected is logically integrated into your own writing, that credit is given to the author, and that you have included the correct page number within parentheses.
4. Consult pages 318–27 for instructions on integrating and punctuating quotations.

Citation and Documentation of Sources
Check to see that all references have been properly documented within the paper. (Consult pp. 327–33 for citing and documenting sources.)

Preparation of List of Works Cited
Review the bibliographic forms (consult pp. 333–38 on preparing the list of works cited), and make sure that your sources are listed correctly and alphabetically and are punctuated properly.

One of the conventions that is traditionally observed by writers who interpret literature is to write primarily from the perspective of the present, using the literary present tense.

Guidelines for Using the Appropriate Verb Tense

USE THE PRESENT TENSE

1. When you write about the *fictional events occurring in a story.* This literary present tense conveys the idea that, as a work of art, the story reveals the kind of experience that occurs again and again.

Example

Mrs. Mallard *feels* that something *is* approaching her, and she *is* afraid of it.

2. When you write about your interpretation of an *author's ideas.* This use of tense acknowledges that the author's ideas continue to exist even though the author has finished writing about them.

Example

In "The Story of an Hour," Kate Chopin *seeks* to raise awareness of the role of women.

USE A PAST OR PERFECT TENSE

3. When you write about *fictional events that occurred in the past in relation to other events in the story* (for example, prior to the story's opening or to the narrator's participation in its action). This use of tense allows you to clarify the time when events have occurred. Past and present forms can be included in the same sentence.

Example

In "The Story of an Hour," Mrs. Mallard *remembers* that her husband *had imposed* his will on her.

4. Use the past tense when you provide *historical information or biographical information about an author's past,* since these details actually belong to the past.

Example

In the American society of the nineteenth century, women *had* limited rights.

Consult your instructor when you cannot decide which verb tense to use.

GUIDELINES	*Guidelines for Referring to the Author by Name*

The first time you mention the author's name, include the full name (for example, Kate Chopin or Feng Jicai). After that, refer to the author only by second name given (for example, Chopin); in the case of the writers from China, India, and Japan, refer to the author only by the first name given (Feng, Krishnan, Mishima).

MANUSCRIPT FORM FOR FINAL COPY

After you have revised and edited your paper, you are ready to write or type the final copy for presentation to the instructor. The way your paper looks can have a positive or negative psychological effect on the reader. It is therefore important to make your paper as neat as possible.

Whether a paper is handwritten or typewritten, it will usually mention these features at the top:

- Your name
- The course name and number
- Your instructor's name
- The due date
- The title

The pages should be numbered and stapled together.

The boxes on the next pages provide guidelines for handwritten, type-written, and computer-generated papers.

GUIDELINES	*Guidelines for a Handwritten Paper*

1. Write on white, 8 1/2 by 11 inch lined paper.
2. Use a pen.
3. Write neatly and legibly.
4. Write on every other line.
5. Write on only one side of the paper.
6. Indent each paragraph.
7. If you find errors after the paper is finished, put a line through the error(s) and then neatly handwrite the correction in the space above, or use white correction fluid to cover the error(s) and then neatly handwrite the correction.

Guidelines for a Typewritten Paper

1. Use 8 1/2 by 11 inch unruled paper of good quality. (Avoid onionskin paper and erasable bond.)
2. Use a good ribbon.
3. Double-space.
4. Leave at least one-inch margins all around.
5. Indent each new paragraph five spaces.
6. After you have typed, check for typographical errors.
7. If you find errors after your paper is finished, use white correction fluid to cover the errors and then neatly handwrite or type in the correction.

Guidelines for a Computer-Generated Paper

1. Use white paper.
2. Use a ribbon that produces clear copy.
3. Set the printer to double-space.
4. Set the top and side margins at 1 inch; set the bottom margin at 1 1/4 inches.
5. Use an unjustified right margin.
6. Set the page-length setting at sixty-six lines.
7. Set the default tab stop at five spaces in from the left margin, to indent your paragraphs.
8. Instruct the printer to number the pages.
9. Select the print mode that produces the best copy.
10. Use a style or spellchecker program, if you have one.
11. Proofread carefully to check for errors that may have occurred as a result of deleting or moving text.

Glossary

The following words and expressions are taken from the short stories and poems in this book. You may use the accompanying definitions to interpret them and/or when you need synonyms to write about the stories in your own words. *Note:* each word or expression is followed by one or more definitions. More than one definition may apply, in which case different interpretations of the passage in which the word occurs are possible.

Abbreviations: (adj) = adjective, (adv) = adverb, (n) = noun, (v) = verb

A

abacus: frame with sliding beads for doing arithmetic
abandon (v): give up completely; discontinue; forsake
abandoned (adj): recklessly unrestrained; shameless; deserted
abandonment: complete surrender to emotion; unbounded enthusiasm; giving up of one's inhibitions
abdicate: give up or renounce a throne, power, or rights (term usually associated with a monarch)
abide: tolerate; endure
abounding: overflowing; plentiful
abstractedly: absent-mindedly; without paying close attention
abyss: any area too deep for measurement; a bottomless pit; hell; profound void
acutely: intensely; perceptively; sensitively
adamant: firm in purpose; inflexible
adverse: unfavorable; contrary to one's welfare
afire: burning; intensely engaged
afflicted: suffering mentally or physically
afflicted with: suffering from; predisposed to
aftermath: result or consequence; period of time following a disastrous event
aggressive: bold and active; hostile; assertive
ailment: mental or physical disorder; illness
akin to: similar to
aloof: distant (in one's relation with other people); apart; indifferent
altar: raised platform for sacred purposes in a place of worship
amiable: good-natured; sociable; friendly
ammunition: any means of attack; material fired from weapons
annihilate: destroy entirely; abolish
anonymous: having an unknown or unacknowledged name
antechamber: smaller room leading into a larger room
anteroom: waiting room
anthem: song of praise, usually for one's country
antipathy: intense feeling of dislike or opposition
anxious: eager; earnestly desirous; worried about an uncertain event

appearance: outward aspect; superficial aspect; pretense or show
apprentice: person learning a trade or occupation
aquiver with: shaking in anticipation of; trembling from
ardent: characterized by or displaying strong enthusiasm
askew: turned or twisted to one side; awry
assurances: information designed to inspire confidence or to remove doubt
assure: convince; inform, in order to remove doubt
astray: off the right path; into error
attenuated: slender; weakened; reduced in strength
attribute (v): to think of (something) as connected to or the result of something else
audible: capable of being heard; loud enough to be heard
awe: feeling of wonder; amazement
awful: great; inspiring wonder or fear

B

babble (n): murmuring sounds; confusion of words and sounds
bar (v): keep out; exclude; block
bared: exposed to view; uncovered
baroque: ornate artistic style, named for the Baroque era in the seventeenth century
bastard: child born of parents who are not married; something of irregular, inferior, or questionable origin
bazaar: market consisting of a street lined with shops and stalls; fair at which miscellaneous articles are sold
bearing: transmitting; relating; conveying
beatitude: supreme blessedness or happiness
benumbed: made numb; deprived of the power to feel normally; without sensation; deadened
bespoke: gave a sign of; indicated
bestowed upon: given; presented as a gift or honor
bickering (n): quarrel, usually over a small matter
blasphemy: irreverant or impious act or utterance in regard to something sacred
bleak: gloomy and somber; dreary
blind (n): a window shade; something that shuts out light
blind (adj): See pages 300–01.
bloated: swelled; inflated
blood-shod: with blood as shoes; feet covered in blood
bluff (used in idiom): to "call one's bluff" is to challenge or expose a false display of strength or confidence
bluff (n): cliff; hill
blundering: making a stupid and serious mistake, usually caused by ignorance or confusion
boast: talk about (one's accomplishments or talents) with excessive pride; brag
bonbon: candy, usually chocolate-covered fruit or nuts
boot camp: place where the military are trained
Bosh (informal): Nonsense
botch: ruin through clumsiness or carelessness
boudoir: woman's private room
bourgeois: typical of the middle class; characterized by a preoccupation with respectability

brawl: quarrel; fight

bray: sound loud and harsh (donkey sound)

bread (used in idiom): to "earn one's bread" is to acquire through work the necessities of life; make a living

breeches: pants reaching just to the knee

brittle: likely to break; fragile

bulging: protruding; growing larger or rounder

bulky: extremely large; massive; hard to manage because of large size

bully (v): intimidate; act cruelly toward

burdensome: difficult to bear; oppressive

burglar: one who commits the crime of breaking into a building to steal; thief

C

cabaret: restaurant or nightclub with entertainment

cadaver: dead body

cagy: careful; cautious; tricky

calamity: state of misfortune; extraordinarily serious event marked by terrible loss and lasting distress

callousness: lack of feeling; insensitivity

can (slang) (n): buttocks

candelabra: large branched candlesticks

capital (n): money used to produce more wealth

capricious: unpredictable; impulsive; fickle; characterized by changeableness

caravan: company of travelers journeying together (often in a single file of vehicles and pack animals)

carbine: shoulder rifle

career: speed; rapid course; moment of highest pitch or peak activity; profession or occupation

carry-all: closed automobile with two seats facing each other

cartridge: bullet

cascade (n): small, steep waterfall; a succession of processes

cast (n): tendency; quality

caste: a social class separated from others by heredity, profession, or wealth

cat (used in idiom): "the cat is out of the bag" means the secret is out

catering to: indulging in; satisfying; yielding to

cattle dip: washing preparation for cattle

ceaselessly: without stopping; endlessly

celestial: heavenly; spiritual; divine

chafe against: become annoyed at or irritated by

chagrin: feeling of humiliation caused by failure or disappointment

chalice: cup or goblet; cup for the sacred wine used for communion with God

charity: act or feeling of benevolence, good will, or affection; help given to the needy

chastened (adj): purified; moderate; subdued; having been punished

chastity: state of being pure; virginity; virtuousness

chat: talk in a friendly and informal manner

check (v): restrain; stop

chinks (offensive slang): Chinese

chirp: make short, high-pitched sounds

chitchat: casual conversation; small talk

clad: clothed; covered

clamorous: full of intense sounds; noisy

coax: persuade; urge with soft words

cocktail: mixed alcoholic drink

cognac: a fine brandy (alcoholic liquor)

coherent: orderly or logical

colloquial: informal; conversational

colossal: enormous in size or degree

communal: public; shared by the community

compel: force; pressure

compensation: something given or received as a payment for a loss

complicity: partnership (usually in a crime or wrongdoing)

composedly: calmly; in a self-controlled manner

compromise (n): settlement of differences in which each side gives up something

conceive: develop in the mind; devise

concession: surrender of one's position, often unwillingly; acknowledgment that something is true, just, or proper

conciliate: overcome the distrust or animosity of; placate

concocted: invented; prepared by mixing ingredients

concrete (adj): existing in reality or real experience; having a material existence; actual; physical

condemnation: expression of disapproval; criticism

confectionery: shop selling candy and other sweets

confidential: denoting intimacy; signifying a trusting relationship

confinement: stage of being at rest to prepare for childbirth

confront: face with boldness or defiance

conjugate: give the verb forms in order

conservative: traditional in style; not showy; favoring traditional values; cautious

consideration: thought; concern

consolation: comfort in time of grief or trouble

console (v): comfort in time of grief or trouble

conspicuous: easy to notice; prominent; obvious; attracting attention by being unusual or remarkable

conspire: work or act together secretly toward a specific goal

consternation: great fear or shock

consummate (adj): complete; skilled; perfect

consummate (v): bring to completion; fulfill; fulfill through sexual intercourse

contagious: capable of being transmitted by contact; spreading from one to another; capable of carrying disease

contracted: seemingly reduced in size by being drawn together; shrunk

contrive: manage; plan deviously

convent: building where nuns live; school in which nuns teach

converge: move toward a common point; tend toward a union

convert (n): one who has changed from one way of doing or believing to another

coquettish: attracting attention in a playful or romantic way; flirtatious

corrugated: shaped into ridges and grooves

cosmetician: person whose occupation is applying cosmetics (see definition below)

cosmetics: preparations used to beautify the body

cosmetology: study or art of cosmetics (see definition above) and their use

cotton-wool: cotton in its natural state
coursing: swiftly moving; flowing
cow-turd: piece of cow dung (feces)
cradle (v): hold by enfolding in one's arms; rock, as if in a cradle
cram: squeeze (into a small space); stuff
crane (v): stretch (one's neck)
creaking: making a squeaking sound
crease (n): line made by ironing; wrinkle
crescent: something shaped like the moon in its first quarter
crestfallen: dejected; disheartened; depressed
cross (adj): irritable; showing ill humor
crud: something contemptible or disgusting
crystal (used in idiom): "crystal clear" means completely, unmistakably understood
crystallize: assume a definite and permanent form
cud: regurgitated food (like that chewed by cattle)
culinary: pertaining to a kitchen or to cookery
cultivate: grow and look after; tend, as a plant or crop
curative: having the power to cure
curiosities: rare or interesting objects
curtly: briefly, with rudeness; abruptly

D

dandy (adj): elegant; attentive to clothes and appearance, sometimes excessively so
dapper-looking: stylish; neatly dressed
dart (v): move suddenly and swiftly; shoot out like a dart (pointed missile)
dash: rush; move with haste
dawn (v): begin to be understood; begin to appear; emerge
deceased (n): dead person
deceit: deliberate falsehood or concealment or misrepresentation of truth
deceived: misled; tricked into believing something that is not true
decencies: requirements of respectable behavior; social or moral proprieties
decent: respectable; characterized by conformity to recognized standards of propriety or morality; meeting accepted standards; kind or obliging
decipher: interpret the meaning of; decode
declining: refusing to accept, comply with, or do (something), especially politely
deference: courteous respect; submission or courteous yielding to the opinion, wishes, or judgment of another
deferential: showing deference (see above)
deferred: postponed; put off until a future time; delayed
degenerate (n): morally degraded person; person exhibiting antisocial, especially sexually deviant, behavior
degradation: a process of transition from a higher to a lower quality or level; reduction in worth or value
deluging: flooding; overwhelming
demonstrative: given to showing feelings openly or publicly
denigration: denial of the validity or importance (of something or someone)
derided: ridiculed; laughed at in scorn; treated with contempt
desolate: dismal; without friends or hope
despair: lack of hope; lowness of spirits

despairing: causing loss of hope

desperate: nearly hopeless; extremely intense; violent because of despair; suffering from unbearable need or anxiety

despicable: deserving of contempt or scorn; vile

destiny: fate; the power believed to predetermine events

deteriorating: declining; failing

detour: road used instead of the main route; roundabout way

devil (used in idiom): a "poor devil" is an unfortunate person

devout: deeply religious; earnest

diffidently: timidly; without self-confidence

dignitary: person of high rank; person with a high official position

digress: wander from the main subject

dilapidated: broken-down; in a state of disrepair

dilation: enlargement; expansion; swelling; condition of being stretched out

dim: having a small amount of light; lacking brightness; lacking sharpness of clarity or of understanding

disband: disperse; scatter in different directions

discerning: perceiving differences

discharge: perform the obligations or demands of

discomfiture: frustration; disappointment; defeat; discomfort; embarrassment

disconcerted: upset; frustrated; embarrassed; confused

discord: lack of harmony; inconsistency

discreetly: in a way as to protect modesty; carefully

disdain: an attitude of contempt; scorn

disillusion (n): loss of idealism; loss of a mistaken sense of reality; loss of an erroneous belief or perception; disenchantment

dismay (used in idiom): "in dismay" means filled with apprehension, dread, or discouragement

dispute (n): argument; debate

distort: twist; misshape; give a false or misleading account of

distracted (adj): having conflicting emotions; causing one's attention to turn away

distress: anxiety; suffering; severe strain; condition of being in need of assistance

divan: long backless couch

diverge: go in different directions

diviner: someone who knows by intuition or inspiration; someone who can foretell future events; prophet

divulge: reveal; make known

dodge: move away quickly to avoid something

dog (used in idiom): a "dog-eat-dog world" is a mercilessly competitive society

domesticated: trained to live in a human environment and be of use to human beings (usually refers to plants or animals)

don: put on (a piece of clothing)

downcast: in low spirits; depressed

dowry: money or property brought by a bride to her husband at marriage

draw (n): selection of contest winners

dread (adj): causing terror or fear

dread (v): be in fear of; anticipate with alarm, anxiety, or reluctance

ducking: lowering the head and body; moving swiftly, especially to avoid being seen

dude (Western slang): city fellow

dumbfounded: speechless with astonishment or amazement

dune: hill of wind-blown sand at the beach

duplicity: deliberate deceptiveness; double-dealing; hypocritical deception

E

earnest: deeply serious or sincere; purposeful

earshot (used in idiom): "out of earshot" means out of the range within which sound can be heard

eave: edge of a roof

eavesdrop: listen secretly to a private conversation

echelon: level of command or authority in an organization

economical: not wasteful with money; thrifty in money management; frugal

ecstasy: state of intense joy; a state of emotion so intense that one is carried beyond rational thought and self-control

eerily: in a frightening, mysterious, almost supernatural way

effusive: overflowing with emotion; unrestrained or excessive in emotional expression

elated: joyful; exultant; very happy

elicit: bring out; call forth a reaction; draw out

elixir: medicine sought by ancient scientists to prolong life; a hypothetical substance believed to cure all ills

eluding: avoiding; evading; escaping the mental grasp of

elusive: difficult to define or describe; able to escape the understanding of (someone)

embark: set out on an adventure; engage in a venture

emitting: sending out; uttering

emulation: imitation; effort to equal or excel, especially through imitation; successful competition

enamored of: delighted by; in love with

endeavor: attempt; make the effort

endorse: write one's signature as evidence of legal transfer of ownership; approve

endowed with: provided or equipped with some quality or talent

endure: tolerate; suffer patiently

enterprise: business venture; any projected task or work; boldness, energy, and invention in practical affairs

entourage: group of attendants or associates, usually with a high-ranking person

equanimity: calmness of mind; composure

eradicate: get rid of completely; erase; destroy

ere: before

erect (adj): in a stiff or rigid, upright position

erroneous: mistaken; wrong; incorrect

eschew: avoid; shun

essence: most important ingredient; crucial, fundamental element

evacuate: empty out; send away; withdraw or depart from

eventful: full of happenings; important; significant

evinced: shown; demonstrated

exalted: glorified; honored; heightened; praised; filled with joy

excavating: digging out earth (to make holes for building foundations)

excursion: short journey, usually for pleasure

exhumation: removal from a grave; disinternment

expostulate with: reason with someone earnestly, to object to the person's actions

express (n): train that travels rapidly and makes few or no stops before its destination

extraneous: not essential; irrelevant

exultant: marked by great joy; rejoicing triumphantly

F

facade: front of a building

familiarly: intimately; in a friendly way; in an inappropriately or improperly intimate or friendly way

fancy (v): imagine; suppose; guess

fancy (n): imagination; a fantastic invention created by the mind

fangs: long pointed teeth

fashion (v): shape; form

fate: supposed principle or power that predetermines events; inevitable, predestined events; unfavorable destiny

fawn (adj): pale brown, like a young deer

feeble: weak; without force or effectiveness

feigned (adj): pretended; false

ferret out: uncover; search out by careful investigation

fervent: having or showing great emotion or warmth

fester: become infected; decay; rot; generate pus (fluid formed in infected tissue)

fetch: go after and return with

feudal: like a medieval economic and social system in which serfs worked the lands owned by overlords

feverish: full of emotion; intensely agitated; having a high body temperature

fib (n): lie, usually about something unimportant; untruth

filial: pertaining to a son or daughter; appropriate or suitable for a son or daughter

finger (used in idiom): "put one's finger on" is to discover or understand exactly

fit (adj): proper; right and correct; healthy

flamboyantly: in a showy way; in such a way as to attract attention

flare up: become angry or emotional suddenly

flares (n): brief blazes of light

flaring (adj): bright; lit by a bright flame; angry

flee: run away, as from danger or trouble

flinch: move suddenly and involuntarily, as from surprise, distress, or pain

floundering: making clumsy attempts to move or regain one's balance

foe: enemy; opponent

foible: minor weakness or failure of character

folly: foolish belief or action

fondle: caress or handle affectionately or lovingly

foray: daring adventure; raid in order to seize things

forebodings: sense of impending disaster; premonition

foregone: previously determined; inevitable

forestall: prevent; guard against by taking preventive measures

formaldehyde: gaseous compound used to preserve and disinfect things, such as dead bodies

fowl: various birds, especially chickens

fragile: easily broken or damaged; weak; delicate

frenzy: temporary wild excitement

fret: worry; be irritated, troubled, or angry

fretful: uneasy; agitated

fritter: small cake made of fried batter

front (n): first line of a combat force

froth: salivary foam released as a result of disease or exhaustion

frothing: salivating with foam

frowsy: untidy; unkempt in appearance; having an unpleasant smell

fumble: reach awkwardly and uncertainly to find something; touch or handle clumsily

fume (v): show or feel anger or agitation

furiously: intensely; violently; with anger

furtively: in a secretive or hidden manner

fuss (v): pay attention to unimportant details; act nervously

futility: uselessness; something that has no useful result

G

gabled: sloped; pitched

gallantry: flirtatious remark made to a woman by a fashionable man

gallery: covered walk or roofed promenade; place used for exhibitions

galvanically: like an electric current

gargling: circulating in the mouth; producing a sound like that made by rinsing the throat with mouthwash

garish: loud and flashy; characterized by tasteless and showy features

garret: room directly under a sloping roof; attic room

garrote: collar used for strangling

garrulous: habitually talkative; given to constant trivial talking

gastric: pertaining to the stomach

gauntlet: two lines of people armed with sticks or other weapons with which they beat a person who is forced to run between them

gay: lively; happy; light-hearted; given to social pleasures

genially: with a pleasant or friendly manner

genie: supernatural being who can be called upon to appear quickly to serve humans

gesturing: making motions with one's hands to emphasize speech

gingerly: with great care or delicacy; cautiously

girdled: encircled, as if by a belt or girdle

girth: circumference of a person's waist; distance around something

glare (v): shine intensely or blindingly; stare angrily

glinting: sparkling; flashing with light

glum: gloomy; moody and silent

grandiose: characterized by greatness of intent; large and impressive; characterized by an exaggerated show of dignity or self-importance

grenade: small bomb designed to be thrown by hand

grit (n): rough particles of sand

grit (v): clamp (one's teeth) together

gritty: having a coarse, hard texture

grope: reach about uncertainly; feel one's way

grotesque (n): being characterized by a distorted or bizarre appearance

grudging: resenting; being reluctant to give

guardianship: legal responsibility for the care of a person, especially a child

gulp (v): swallow greedily or rapidly

gum: resin; synthetic substance

guts (slang): courage; daring

guts (n): bowels; essential contents

guttering: burning; melting away

H

hack: cut or chop with repeated blows; mutilate

hags: ugly, frightened old women

hamper (n): large covered basket

hang-over: unpleasant physical effects following excessive consumption of alcohol

harbor (v): hold in the mind; give refuge to

harrowing: extremely distressing; agonizing

hastened: hurried; acted swiftly

haven: place of refuge; sanctuary; shelter from danger

heap: pile; group of things piled haphazardly

heart-rending: evoking anguish or deep distress

heave: raise or lift with great force or effort; utter painfully

hedge (n): row of closely planted bushes

hideous: repulsive; revoltingly ugly

hierarchy: group of people or things ranked according to order of importance

hilarious: noisily merry; full of fun

histrionical: pertaining to acting; excessively dramatic or emotional

hoisted: lifted, as if with the help of a mechanical apparatus

homage: special honor or respect

hoots (n): sounds (like an owl)

hover: remain suspended in the air, usually over one place; linger; remain in an uncertain state

huddled: hunched; crowded together

humble: lowly; of low rank; marked by modesty or submissiveness

husky (adj): hoarse; dry in the throat

hustle (used in idiom): "hustle and bustle" is busy activity

hygiene: cleanliness; system of principles for maintaining health

hypocrisy: a pretending to be what one is not, or to feel or believe what one does not

I

idle (v): pass time without working; move lazily and without purpose

illumination: understanding; intellectual and/or spiritual enlightenment

illusion: erroneous perception of reality; false idea, concept, or belief; condition of being deceived by a false perception; unreal or misleading appearance or image; dream

imbue: inspire; pervade; permeate

immaculately: spotlessly; without a flaw; perfectly

immersed: submerged; completely covered

immoderate: extreme; excessive; exceeding appropriate bounds

imperturbable: unshakably calm; that cannot be disturbed or made uneasy or confused

impinge: hit; strike; intrude

implanted: established permanently

implicit: unquestioning; implied or understood although not directly expressed

imploring: begging; pleading urgently

importunities: repeated and insistent requests; annoyances

impose: force; apply with authority

impoverished: reduced to poverty; deprived of natural richness or strength; lacking resources

improvised: made from whatever materials are available; made without much preparation

inane: empty; lacking sense

inarticulate: incomprehensible; not clearly expressed

inborn: inherited; innate; implanted by nature

incautiously: without exercising sensible judgment

incessant: continuing without interruption; continual

inclination: tendency; preference; frame of mind

inclined (adj): having a tendency; disposed

incongruous: not corresponding to or consistent with what is logical, customary, or correct; inappropriate

incurable: incapable of being restored to health; not capable of recovering from disease

indignant: aroused with anger by something unjust, mean, or unworthy

indiscernible: not clearly recognizable

indolent: habitually lazy; inactive; idle

indomitable: unconquerable; not easily discouraged or defeated; incapable of being overcome

induce: influence; persuade

indulgence: favorable or privileged treatment

inevitable: incapable of being avoided or prevented

inexplicable: incapable of being explained or interpreted

infallible: incapable of making mistakes or failing

inflamed: aroused to strong emotion; excited

inflexibility: rigidness; inability to change one's mind

ingenuity: cleverness; imaginativeness

ingest: take (food, etc.) into the body

initiate: introduce; begin

injured (adj): hurt; wounded; wronged; suffering an injustice

innovation: new and creative production or idea

innumerable: too many to be counted; very numerous; countless

instinct: natural impulse or inborn tendency to behave in a way that is essential to the existence of one's species

insufferable: unbearable; intolerable; unendurable

integrity: uprightness of character; honesty

intensify: become more deeply felt; increase in strength

intercourse: communication; mutual exchange; conversation

interment: placement in a grave; burial

intervening: coming between two things; occurring between two events

intimate (adj): very close or familiar

intolerable: unbearable; too painful to be endured

intonation: distinct pitch; tone

intone: recite in a singing manner; chant

intricate: full of complex detail; complicated
intrusion: inappropriate or unwelcome entrance or addition
intuition: immediate knowing of something without the conscious use of reasoning
iodine: chemical element used in medicine
irreparable: incapable of being repaired, corrected, or set right
irrevocable: irreversible; permanent; incapable of being taken back
itch (n): restless desire; craving

J

jar (n): discord; disturbance
jerk (v): move in a sudden or abrupt motion
jolt (n): sudden shock; sudden jerking movement
jostled: pushed in a crowd; pushed by someone's elbow
judicially: like a judge evaluating a case or determining a person's guilt
judicious: exhibiting sensible judgment; wise
justified: proved to be right; declared free of blame

K

keen (adj): sharp; strong; intellectually acute; acutely sensitive
khaki: color ranging from light olive brown to yellowish brown
knock-kneed: having an abnormal condition in which one knee is turned toward the other

L

laconic: marked by use of few words; concise
laden with: weighed down with; burdened with
lament (n): feeling of grief; expression of sorrow
landmark: identifying feature; significant site; memorable object
latrine: communal toilet
launch: make a beginning; plunge
lavatory: room equipped with washing and toilet facilities
lavish: characterized by extravagance
lethal: capable of causing death; extremely harmful
lilting: rhythmic and lively
linger: continue to stay, as though reluctant to leave
litany: repetitive recitation; prayer
literature: body of writings
litter (n): things lying around in disorder; waste materials
litter (v): make untidy (by scattering things about)
livid: discolored, as from a bruise (black-and-blue); pale; angry
loaf about: pass time; pass time idly
loathing: hating; extreme dislike or disgust
local (n): train that makes many stops on a route
loco weed (slang): marijuana
loin cloth: strip of cloth worn around the hips and pelvis
loom: come into view as a massive image

loot: steal from; rob (a store) of goods
lot (n): one's fortune in life; fate
lottery: game of chance
lucerne: alfalfa plant
lungs (used in idiom): "cry at the top of one's lungs" meaning to cry as loud as one can
lurch: move or roll suddenly to one side; move unsteadily
lurk: hide; lie in wait, as if ready to attack
lustful: having sensual or sexual desire

M

makeshift: used or assembled as a temporary substitute
mango: a sweet, juicy fruit with yellow-orange flesh
mangrove: tropical tree or shrub
maniac: insane person; person who suffers from madness
mantle: loose, sleeveless coat worn over outer garments
martyr: person who makes great sacrifices or suffers much for a cause, belief, or principle
master-race: people who hold themselves to be superior to other races and therefore suited to rule over them
maternity: pertaining to the care of new mothers and newborn babies
matted: tangled; in a disordered condition
meager: inadequate; barely sufficient
mealie-stook: corn stalk
medic: military healthworker; medical aide
medicinal: having the properties of medicine; able to cure or to moderate disease
meditate: reflect upon; ponder; contemplate
meekly: patiently and with humility; submissively
menacing: threatening; dangerous
mercantile: pertaining to merchants or trade
merciful: full of mercy (kind and compassionate treatment of a person under one's power); compassionate
minimize: reduce the degree or importance of
misconception: incorrect understanding or interpretation
misgave: made doubtful, anxious, or uneasy (about the future)
Mission: establishment of persons sent to do religious work in a foreign land
moat: deep, wide ditch, usually filled with water, surrounding a palace as protection against attack
mobility: easy movement from one social class to another
modulate: regulate; adjust
moil: work like a slave; work hard
monologue: long speech made by one person
monstrous: abnormal; frightful; hideously evil; unnatural
mortals: human beings; those who are subject to death
mortuary: place where dead bodies are kept prior to burial
mourning (n): signs of grief for the dead; act of expressing sorrow or grief
moved (adj): aroused or touched emotionally; stirred by emotion; excited; motivated to take action
municipal: belonging to the local government

muster (v): collect; gather
musty: having a stale or moldy odor
muttered (adj): spoken in low or indistinct tones

N

nagging: tormenting; filled with anxiety
naive: lacking sophistication; lacking critical ability or analytical insight; tending to believe too readily; innocent; unconsciously and amusingly simple
nasal: characterized by a sound made through the nose
nestled: settled comfortably; pressed closely in an affectionate manner
noctambulant: moving at night
nonchalantly: casually; indifferently; without concern
nourish: provide the substances necessary for life and growth
nursery: newborn baby's room

O

objective: dealing with outward things, without being influenced by feelings or opinions; unbiased
oblique: having a sloping direction
oblivion: condition of being completely forgotten; condition of lacking conscious awareness or memory
oblivious: lacking conscious awareness; lacking all memory
obscure: vague; not easily understood
obsolete: out-of-date; gone out of use
odious: hateful; offensive; repulsive; disgusting
okra: tropical plant with edible green pods
omen: a sign of the future; foreshadowing
ooze (v): flow or leak out slowly; disappear slowly
oppress: cause to feel troubled or uncomfortable; burden unjustly or cruelly
ordained: prearranged; predestined
ordeal: difficult experience; severe test of character or endurance
outburst: sudden display of emotion; sudden release of energy or feeling
outhouse: outdoor toilet set in a small structure
outrage: any act offensive to decency, morality, or good taste

P

paddock: fenced-in area; enclosure for animals
pagan: having no religion; unconverted; uncivilized; not acknowledging the God of the world's major religions
painstaking: taking great care; very careful
paling: becoming dim, weak or less intense
panting: breathing rapidly in short gasps; gasping for breath
pasties: pies
patriarch: male leader of a family or tribe; any of the biblical fathers of the human race
patron: regular customer; one who supports

pauper's grave: unmarked burial place of an extremely poor person

pawn (v): give (something) as security for the payment of money borrowed

pawnbroker: one who lends money at interest in exchange for personal property left as security

peal: ringing of bells; loud burst of noise

pebble: small, smooth stone

peer (n): person of equal standing; companion

peer (v): look intently or searchingly

penetrate: enter into; permeate

pension: retirement fund; money given to a person who has stopped working (usually because of age)

perceptible: observable; that can be understood; discernible by the senses or mind

perched: sitting on a branch like a bird; resting on an elevated position

persistence: act of holding firmly to an idea or purpose; act of being insistent; refusal to give up or let go

perturbed: greatly disturbed; uneasy; greatly confused

pervade: spread or be present throughout; permeate

petrified: paralyzed with fear; made stiff by terror

petticoat: woman's underskirt; a slip

pettiness: relative unimportance; small-mindedness

petty: small; narrow-minded; spiteful; mean

piccanin (offensive slang): small African child; also spelled **pickaninny**

picturesquely: charmingly; attractively; like a picture

piercing: sharply sounding; deeply moving

pilgrimage: journey to a sacred place; long journey or search, especially one with a moral significance

pillaged: robbed of goods by force, especially in time of war

pillar (used in idiom): a "pillar of society" is one who occupies a responsible or central position

pious: religious; showing religious devotion; devout; high-minded; worthy

piquant: agreeable; pleasantly appealing

pistol: gun designed to be held and fired with one hand

piteous: arousing pity; pathetic

pivotal: able to determine the direction or effect of something

placid: calm; quiet; outwardly composed

platoon: group of people who comprise a unit of a military company

plight: condition of difficulty; distressing situation

plundered: robbed of goods by force, especially in time of war; pillaged

plunge: throw oneself into a place or substance; move forward and downward violently

poignantly: with distress to the mind; with sharp pain to one's feelings; with great emotion

polish off: finish quickly or easily

polluted (adj): impure; unfit; unclean; morally impure; defiled

pore (over): read or study carefully and attentively

portentous: full of unspecifiable significance; foreboding; ominous; hinting at something that is about to occur (such as a misfortune)

possum (used in idiom): to "play possum" is to pretend to be asleep

post (n): military base where troops are stationed; place to which someone is assigned for duty

post-mortem: examination done after death; autopsy

premises: land and the buildings on it; building or part of a building

premonition: warning in advance; dark sense of impending evil; prophetic sense of something to come

priceless: of very high value; of inestimable value; invaluable

prime: age of ideal physical perfection and/or intellectual vigor

primitive: lacking grace; lacking taste; crude; unrefined; plain; not mature; uncultured; unsophisticated; pertaining to an earliest or original state

privation: lack of basic necessities or comforts of life

prize (v): move or force, usually in order to open something

procession: group of persons moving along in an orderly and formal manner, usually in a long line

progressive: advancing socially; favoring progress

promising: hopeful; likely to develop in a desirable manner; suggestive of future success

prop (v): support; keep from falling

prophet: person who speaks by divine inspiration; chief spokesperson of a cause

propitiate: overcome the distrust or anger of an offended power (such as a god); calm or pacify, by giving what is demanded; appease; conciliate

prosper: be successful; flourish

prosperity: condition of having success; wealth

provinces: areas of a country situated away from the capital or population center

provincial: not fashionable or sophisticated; limited in perspective; characteristic of people from the provinces (areas of the country away from the capital city)

provocative: stimulating; stirring desire

pullet: young hen

pup tent: small portable shelter of simple design, made of canvas and stretched over poles

purple heart: U.S. military medal award to soldiers wounded in action

purse-strings (used in idiom): to "hold the purse-strings" is to have control of the money

pyre: heap of flammable materials for burning a dead body

Q

queen (slang): male homosexual

queer: strange; different from the expected

queue (v): form a line

quibbling: evading the truth; avoiding acknowledging the truth (usually by raising trivial objections)

quirk: sudden sharp turn or twist; unpredictable act

quivering: trembling; shaking with a slight motion

R

rack (used in idiom): to "rack one's brain(s)" is to make a great mental effort

rank (n): particular position in a group organized according to position; a position in society

rank (adj): growing excessively; disgusting

rankness: strong and offensive odor or taste

rapped: transported in ecstasy; carried away; deeply engaged (now spelled *rapt)*

rapture: ecstasy; state of being transported

rasping: harsh or grating sound

rattle: talk rapidly, without much thought

realm: field; sphere

rear (v): raise; care for (a child) during the early stages of life; bring up

rebuke: criticize; reprimand

recalcitrant: stubbornly resistant to authority; refusing to obey; hard to handle

reflection: contemplation; thoughtful meditation; serious thought or consideration

rein (used in idiom): to "give rein to" is to release from restraints

relent: soften; become less stern or stubborn

relic: something remaining as a trace of an earlier culture; some remaining portion or fragment of that which has vanished or is destroyed

remedies: medicines that cure diseases; means of removing evil

remote: located far away (from a central place)

render: cause to become; convert or melt down by heating

report (n): noise of an explosion (like the sound of a gun)

repression: unconscious shutting out of painful ideas, impulses, desires, or fears from the conscious mind (psychoanalytical definition)

reproachful: expressing blame or shame

reproof: expression of disapproval; reprimand; rebuke

repulsive: disgusting; grossly offensive

resent: feel bitter toward; feel anger or ill will when one feels wronged or injured by another person

reserve (n): self-restraint; caution

residential: having homes, places where people live

resignedly: submissively; without protest; passively; with unresisting acceptance

resonant: sending back sound; vibrant; mellow

restiveness: uneasiness; nervous resistance

retinue: group of people attending a person of importance

retorted: replied in a quick, direct manner; presented a counterargument

retreat (n): group meeting for prayer, meditation, and study

retreat (v): withdraw in the face of danger or attack; go back

retrospect (used in idiom): "in retrospect" means looking backward or reviewing the past

revelation: disclosure of something not previously revealed or known; demonstration of divine will or truth

reverence: feeling of profound awe and respect; act of showing respect; veneration

riot (used in idiom): "running riot" is moving or acting with wild enthusiasm

rites: prescribed religious or ceremonial acts

ritual (n): ceremony; prescribed form or order of conducting a religious or solemn ceremony

rococo: eighteenth-century ornate artistic style

roguishly: mischievously (in a playful way); dishonestly; in an unprincipled way

row (n): argument; angry dispute

rubble: fragments or debris remaining after severe destruction

ruinous: causing total loss of one's fortune, position, honor and/or health; falling to ruin; dilapidated or decayed

run (n): outdoor enclosure for domestic animals or poultry

rut: fixed and boring routine; habitual and mechanically performed course of action
rutted: with sunken tracks made by vehicles

S

sagging: sinking or settling from pressure or weight
saintly: extremely virtuous; like a holy person
salon: elegant, large room used for receiving and entertaining guests; commercial establishment offering a product or service related to fashion: beauty salon
salver: serving tray
sanctity: holiness of life; saintliness
sanitarium: resort where people go to regain health; institution for the treatment of chronic disease
sash: frame in which the panes of a window or door are set
save: except; but
savvy (slang): understand
scalded: burned, with or as if with hot liquid or steam
scandalized: shocked by what is perceived to be improper or offensive conduct; outraged; morally offended
sceptical: full of doubt (also spelled *skeptical*)
scoundrel: villain; mean, immoral, or wicked person
scour: search over thoroughly; clear (an area) by freeing (it) of weeds or other vegetation
screen (v): conceal; hide
scrutinizing: examining or observing with great care; inspecting critically
searchingly: in such a way as to examine or observe closely
Section Eight: discharge from the U.S. army for military inaptitude or undesirable habits or traits of character
seductive: attracting by arousing desire; leading (someone) away from duty or proper conduct; leading (someone) to have sexual intercourse
seething: agitated; violently excited
select (adj): exclusive; limited to certain people
self-assertion: acknowledgement of one's own personality, wishes, and/or views
serene: tranquil; calm; unperturbed; not agitated
shackled: handcuffed; fastened to a metal restraint
shambles: scene or condition of complete disorder or ruin
shishi: false; shabby
shoots: young leaves or buds
shrewd: clever or sharp in practical matters; skilled in deception or manipulation
shrill (adj): high-pitched and piercing in tone or sound
shrine: holy place; place of worship; receptacle holding sacred relics; tomb of sacred person(s)
shudder (v): slightly shake or tremble, as from fear or horror
shy (v): move back, as from fear or caution
sickle: tool with a semicircular blade
siege (used in idiom): "under siege" means surrounded and blockaded, usually by an army that aims to capture
sinister: suggesting evil or trouble
skeptically: with doubt; in such a way as to question the truth of something
skirting: passing around or along (someplace); avoiding

slaughtered: killed for food; butchered; killed in a violent manner

slickness: condition of being smooth and shiny

slops: waste food; human excrement

sludge: mud or ooze covering the ground; sewage

slum: heavily populated area characterized by poor living conditions

slut: bold, shameless girl; sexually immoral woman; slovenly, dirty woman; prostitute

smug: annoyingly self-satisfied; self-righteous

sneak (n): mean-spirited, cowardly person; deceitful, secretive, or treacherous person

snide: sarcastic; derogatory in a superior way

snivel: cry or weep with sniffling

sodden: thoroughly wet; saturated

sole (adj): only

solemn: serious, characterized by mystery or power; sacred

sombre: dark; gloomy; dismal; sad (also spelled *somber)*

sordid: filthy or dirty; foul; wretched

sore (n): open skin lesion or wound; infected spot on the body

spent itself: lost its energy; exhausted itself

spew up: vomit; force out through the mouth

sphinxlike: mysterious; enigmatic; difficult to know or understand (like the mythical Sphinx whose riddle was difficult to guess)

spirit: soul; ghost

spiritual (adj): concerned with the soul or spirit; not concerned with material things; having higher qualities of mind

spite: ill will; malice for the purpose of humiliating

sponge (used in idiom): "throw up/in the sponge" means to give up; abandon the effort

spur (used in idiom): "on the spur of the moment" means on a sudden impulse

spurt: flow or burst forth suddenly, with force

squadron: unit of military aircraft

squander: spend wastefully or extravagantly

squat: sit on one's heels; put oneself in a crouching position

squeamish: easily offended, disgusted, or sickened

stage fright: fear or nervousness experienced when performing before an audience

stammered: spoke with hesitant and stumbling speech, often from nervousness, excitement, or embarrassment

stance: physical or emotional position or attitude

staple (adj): principal; most important; regularly stocked or used

station: social position; rank

stealthily: with secretive, careful movements; in a concealed manner

steeped: thoroughly involved in; saturated

stern: gloomy or forbidding; firm; inflexible; severe in manner

stifled: smothered; suffocated; suppressed

stimulus: incentive; something that stirs someone to activity or energy

stingy: reluctant or unwilling to spend one's money

stint: deprive (oneself) of; allow (oneself) less of

stoically: in a way seemingly unaffected by or indifferent to pain

stoop (n): forward bending of the head and upper back; self-abasement; condescension

straggling (adj): spread out in a scattered or irregular group

stride (n): long step, usually made in haste or from pride
stride (v): walk with long steps in a hasty or vigorous manner
strident: harsh-sounding; loud and irritating; shrill
strike out: begin a course of action; start out; proceed in a new direction
strive: make a great effort; struggle (to achieve something)
strode: past tense of *stride* (see above)
stroke (n): sudden action or event
stroll (v): walk about leisurely; walk slowly and without haste
strove: past tense of *strive* (see above)
struck out: past tense of *strike out* (see above)
stumble: miss one's step in walking; do wrong
stunned: shocked; amazed; astonished; having one's senses dulled
stunt (n): something done to show one's skill or strength
subdued: brought under control; conquered and calmed; toned down; made less intense
subtle: difficult to detect or analyze; not immediately obvious; operating in a hidden way
successor: one who follows after another; one who replaces another
succinctly: using few words; briefly and clearly; concisely
sulk (n): gloomy mood
sullen: unsociable; stubbornly ill-tempered; gloomy; not responding to friendliness
summons (n): call or order to appear
sundered: broken apart
supine: lying on the back
supperannuated: retired or ineffective because of old age
suppleness: flexibility; adaptability; agility; ability to move in a quick and easy fashion
suppressed (adj): held back; kept from being revealed; kept from consciousness; withheld emotions or ideas regarded as unpleasant or socially unacceptable
surfeited: filled; fed to excess; satiated
surged: increased suddenly, like an electric current; swelled
suspension: temporary stopping; postponement (of judgment, opinion, or decision); interruption
sustenance: support; nourishment
swamp (n): lowland region saturated with water
swathed: enfolded; wrapped as if with bandages
sweat (used in idiom): "the sweat of one's brow" is hard work
swindle (n): act of cheating or defrauding
swoon (v): lose sensation and power of motion, from intense mental emotion

T

taciturn: uncommunicative; habitually untalkative; habitually silent or reserved
tact: perception of the right thing to do without offending; ability to appreciate the delicacy of a situation and do or say the proper thing
tainted: stained; made morally corrupt; spoiled; affected with something unpleasant
tangible: capable of being touched; concrete; actual
tarpaulin: waterproof canvas
tedious: tiresome or uninteresting due to extreme length or slowness

temperament: manner of thinking, behaving, and reacting characteristic of a specific individual

temple: flat region on either side of the forehead

tenacity: tending to hold firmly; persistence; stubbornness

tenant: one who pays rent to use property owned by another; an occupant

tenet: principle; doctrine; opinion

tepid: lukewarm; lacking enthusiasm; indifferent

terminus: final point on a transportation line

thick (used in idiom): "thick with" is to be friendly or intimate with

thoroughfare: place of passage from one location to another; heavily traveled passage

threadbare: old and worn out; frayed or shabby

throng: large group of people gathered closely together; crowd; multitude

timid: hesitant; fearful; having the tendency to shy away from dangerous or difficult circumstances

toil: work continually, with exhausting effort

torrid: passionate; burning

totter: sway as if about to fall; appear about to collapse; walk unsteadily

traitor: person who betrays his or her country or cause

tram: streetcar; public passenger train

tranquil: steady; free from agitation; calm; quiet

transfigured: radically transformed in figure or appearance; transformed so as to be glorified

transom: small window or beam above a door

tread (n): step; walking

trifle: something of little significance or importance; something of very little value

trite: commonplace; worn out by constant use

trivial: unimportant; insignificant

trod: pressed beneath the foot; walked over (past tense of *tread)*

trudge: walk heavily or wearily

tuber: underground stem of a potato, bearing buds from which new plant shoots arise

tumultuously: with confusion; with agitation

turmoil: utter confusion; extreme agitation

twittering: making light chirping sounds (of birds)

U

unalterable: unchangeable; incapable of being modified or adjusted

uncommunicative: habitually untalkative; reserved; self-restrained

underground (n): secret organization planning activities, usually against the government in power

undulant: resembling waves; moving back and forth or up and down

unkempt: lacking neatness; messy

unsettle: disturb; make uneasy; disrupt

unsuitable: unfit; not proper; not having the necessary qualities

unversed in: lacking knowledge of; unfamiliar with

unwittingly: naively; without awareness; unintentionally

unyielding: not giving in to pressure, force, or persuasion; inflexible; unbending
upbraided: scolded; reprimanded
upheaval: sudden disruption or upset
usury: lending of money at an excessive or illegal rate of interest
utilitarian: stressing the value of practical qualities

V

vain (used in idiom): "in vain" means without success
vanity: condition of being vain (excessively proud, worthless, lacking substance, or foolish); futility; quality of being empty
vaudeville: stage show consisting of various acts of songs, dances, and skits
vehemently: with a forceful expression; with intense emotion
veiled: meant to hide or soften the truth
venerable: worthy of respect by virtue of dignity, character, or position; commanding respect by religious association
ventilation: circulating fresh air
venture (v): express at the risk of denial, criticism, or censure
venture (n): undertaking that involves some risk; enterprise
veranda: porch or balcony
vermin: destructive insects, such as cockroaches
vessel: container; hollow receptacle of any form or material
vestibule: small entrance hall or lobby
vicinity: nearby area; adjacent region; nearness in space
vile: unpleasant; tasteless; disgusting; having an abominable taste
virtually all: in fact all; practically all; almost all
vitality: energy; life force
vixenish: ill-tempered; quarrelsome; malicious
voluble: talkative; characterized by a great flow of words; characterized by ready, fluent speech
vowing: promising; pledging

W

wakefulness: alertness; watchfulness
walling: showing the whites of the eyes
wares: things for sale; goods; merchandise
warier: more watchful; more cautious; more wary
wayward: unpredictable; disobedient; wanting one's way in spite of the wishes of another
welfare (used in idiom): "on welfare" is to be receiving assistance from the government because of need or poverty
welling: filling with something rising to the surface, ready to flow; surging from some inner source
whim: sudden notion or fancy
whining: producing a high-pitched nasal sound, usually to beg or complain
whinny: low, gentle sound or cry made by a mule
whither: to whatever place; wheresoever
whooping: sounding like a cough or excited cry

wiles: tricks; seductive ways
wino (slang): one who is habitually drunk on wine
wiry: lean; slender but tough
wistfully: wishfully; with deep tenderness and mournfulness; with sad yearning
wit: power of knowing or perceiving; ability to make clever remarks in a sharp, amusing way; quick perception of unusual relationships between things apparently unrelated
wits (used in idiom): "scared out of one's wits" means to be petrified; very frightened
worm (v): get, through devious means; elicit in a tricky or deceitful way
worm (used in proverb): "the turning of the worm" refers to the retaliation of the meek (if pushed too far)
wrangle (v): argue; dispute noisily or angrily
wrath: violent or resentful anger; rage; fury
wrested: pulled by force or effort
wretched: dismal; miserable; poor or inferior in quality; of a poor or mean character; living in misery and degradation
writhing: twisting or squirming as in pain or struggle

Y

yearn: have a strong desire; be filled with longing
yieldings: products
yonder: at a place far away but within sight

Z

zeal: enthusiastic devotion in pursuit of a cause, ideal, or goal
zest: spirited enjoyment; agreeable excitement
zoot suit: man's suit popular during the 1940s characterized by full trousers and a long coat with wide lapels and padded shoulders

ACKNOWLEDGMENTS (continued from p. iv)

Chekhov, Anton. "A Trifle from Real Life." Reprinted with the permission of Charles Scribner's Sons, an imprint of Macmillan Publishing Company, from *Russian Silhouettes* by Anton Chekhov, translated by Marian Fell. Copyright 1915 Charles Scribner's Sons; copyright renewed 1943 Olivia Fell Vans Agnew.

Farzan, Massud. "The Plane Reservation." Reprinted by permission of Massud Farzan.

Faulkner, William. Excerpt from "Dry September." Copyright 1930 and renewed 1958 by William Faulkner. Reprinted from *Collected Stories of William Faulkner*, by permission of Random House, Inc.

Feng Jicai. "The Street-Sweeping Show," from *Chrysanthemums and Other Stories* by Feng Jicai, copyright © 1985 by Susan W. Chen, reprinted by permission of Harcourt Brace Jovanovich, Inc.

Fitzgerald, F. Scott. "Babylon Revisited." Reprinted with permission of Charles Scribner's Sons, an imprint of Macmillan Publishing Company and Harold Ober Associates Incorporated, from *Taps at Reveille* by F. Scott Fitzgerald. Copyright 1931 by The Curtis Publishing Company; renewal copyright ©1959 by Frances Scott Fitzgerald Lanahan.

Gordimer, Nadine. "Six Feet of the Country," from *Six Feet of the Country* by Nadine Gordimer. Copyright © 1956, 1961, 1964, 1965, 1975, 1977, 1983 by Nadine Gordimer. Used by permission of Viking Penguin, a division of Penguin Books USA Inc. and Jonathan Cape, publisher.

Gutierrez, Rosa. "The Character of Louise Mallard." Reprinted by permission of the author.

Hughes, Langston. "Harlem." From *The Panther and the Lash* by Langston Hughes. Copyright 1951 by Langston Hughes. Reprinted by permission of Alfred A. Knopf, Inc., and Harold Ober Associates Incorporated.

Kincaid, Jamaica. "Girl," from *At the Bottom of the River* by Jamaica Kincaid. Copyright © 1978, 1983 by Jamaica Kincaid. Reprinted by permission of Farrar, Straus & Giroux, Inc., and Pan Macmillan/Picadore (1984).

Koberg, Don, and Jim Bagnall. "How to Criticize Painlessly . . . How to Accept Criticism." Copyright 1991 Don Koberg and Jim Bagnall, Crisp Publications, Inc., 95 First Street, Los Altos, California.

Krishnan Varma "The Grass-Eaters." First published in the *Wascana Review*, vol. 19, no. 2 (Fall, 1984). Copyright © 1985, The University of Regina, Canada.

Maupassant, Guy de. "The Necklace." From *The Necklace and Other Short Stories* by Guy de Maupassant. Reprinted by permission of Dover Publications, Inc.

Mishima Yukio. "Swaddling Clothes." Yukio Mishima: *Death in Midsummer and Other Stories.* Copyright © 1966 by New Directions Publishing Corporation. Reprinted by permission of New Directions Publishing Corporation and Laurence Pollinger Limited.

Oates, Joyce Carol. Excerpt from "Where Are You Going, Where Have You Been?" from *The Wheel of Love* by Joyce Carol Oates. Copyright © 1970 by Joyce Carol Oates. Reprinted by permission of John Hawkins & Associates, Inc.

Ortega, Julio. "Las papas." Copyright © 1988 by Julio Ortega. English language translation by Regina Harrison. Reprinted by permission of author.

Owen, Wilfred. "Dulce et Decorum Est." Wilfred Owen: *Collected Poems of Wilfred Owen.* Copyright © 1963 by Chatto and Windus, Ltd. Reprinted by permission of New Directions Publishing Corporation.

Pirandello, Luigi. "War," from *Better Think Twice about It and Other Stories.* Reprinted by permission of the Pirandello Estate and Toby Cole, Agent. © E.P. Dutton, N.Y. 1932, 1967. © The Luigi Pirandello Estate.

Salih, Tayeb. "A Handful of Dates," from *The Wedding of Zein*, translated by Denys Johnson-Davies. Copyright © 1988 by Denys Johnson-Davies.

Trambley, Estela Portillo. "Village." From *A Rain of Scorpions.* (1993 edition). © 1989 by Estela Portillo Trambley. Reprinted by permission of the author.

Updike, John. Excerpt from "A & P," from *Pigeon Feathers* copyright © 1962. Reprinted by permission of Random House, Inc., Alfred A. Knopf, Inc.

Valenzuela, Luisa. "The Verb *to Kill*" from *Strange Things Happen Here: A Selection of Short Stories* by Luisa Valenzuela, translated by Helen Lane, English translation copyright © 1979 by Harcourt Brace & Company, reprinted by permission of the publisher.

Wright, Richard. "The Man Who Was Almost a Man." From the book *Eight Men* by Richard Wright. Copyright © 1987 by the Estate of Richard Wright. Used by permission of the publisher, Thunder's Mouth Press.

Xi Xi, "A Woman Like Me." Reprinted by permission of the author and the English translator, Howard Goldblatt.

INDEX